CASE STUDIES IN ABNORMAL PSYCHOLOGY

CASE STUDIES IN ABNORMAL PSYCHOLOGY

John M. Neale
State University of N.Y. at Stony Brook

Thomas F. Oltmanns
Indiana University

Gerald C. Davison
University of Southern California

175 YEARS OF PUBLISHING
1807 1982

John Wiley & Sons

New York Chichester Brisbane Toronto Singapore

Library of Congress Cataloging in Publication Data:

Davison, Gerald C.
Case studies in abnormal psychology.

Includes index.
1. Psychology, Pathological——Case studies.
2. Psychiatry——Case studies. I. Oltmanns, Thomas F.
II. Neale, John M., 1943- III. Title.
[DNLM: 1. Psychopathology——Case studies. WM 40 D264c]

RC465.D37 616.89 09 81—15979
ISBN 0-471-08088-8 AACR2

Printed in the United States of America

10 9 8 7 6 5 4

To Gail and Sean

Sara, Mary, and Fran

Warren and Marion

PREFACE

Most textbooks on abnormal psychology include brief descriptions of actual clinical cases. However, these presentations are necessarily brief and too fragmented for students to gain a clear understanding of the idiographic complexities of a person's troubled life. They cannot describe the client's developmental history, the manner in which a therapist might conceptualize the problem, or the formulation and implementation of a treatment plan. In contrast to such brief descriptions, a detailed case study can serve as a mnemonic device that may enhance the students' ability to understand and recall abstract theoretical and research issues.

The purpose of this book is therefore threefold: (1) to provide detailed descriptions of a range of clinical problems, (2) to illustrate some of the ways in which these problems can be viewed and treated, and (3) to discuss some of the evidence that is available concerning the epidemiology and etiology of the disorders in question. The book is appropriate for both undergraduate and graduate courses in abnormal psychology. It may also be useful in courses in psychiatric social work or nursing and could be helpful to students enrolled in various practicum courses that teach how best to conceptualize mental health problems and plan treatment It may be used on its own or as a supplement to a standard textbook in abnormal psychology, such as Davison and Neale's *Abnormal Psychology*, Third Edition (Wiley, 1982).

In selecting cases for inclusion in the book, we have sampled from a variety of problems, ranging from classic psychotic disorders (e.g., schizophrenia and bipolar affective disorder) to personality disorders (e.g., paranoia and sociopathy) to various disorders of childhood and aging (e.g., school phobia and depression in later adult life). We have deliberately focused on cases that illustrate particular problems that are of interest to students of abnormal psychology. We do not mean to imply, however, that all the cases fit neatly into specific diagnostic molds. Some present mixed or complicated diagnostic pictures, such as the case of atypical psychosis with fetishism. Furthermore, in addition to describing "classic" behavioral symptoms (e.g., hallucinations, compulsive rituals, or specific fears), we have emphasized the social context in which these disorders appear as well as attendant problems that are significant in determining the person's overall adjustment, even though they may not be relevant from a diagnostic standpoint. Thus several of the cases include a consideration of marital adjustment, parent-child relationships, and minority issues.

Our social learning/cognitive perspective is clearly evident in these discussions. Nevertheless, we have tried to present alternative conceptual positions. The cases can therefore be used to show students how a given problem can be reasonably viewed from several different perspectives. The treatment implications of nonbehavioral views are also outlined. Although most of the interventions described are behavioral (including rational restructuring and other cognitive techniques), we have also presented nonbehavioral approaches such as Gestalt therapy and biological treatments (e.g., antipsychotic medication, ECT, and psychosurgery) when they are relevant to the case. Whenever possible, we have provided information concerning the long-term results of treatment. In some cases, the outcome was not positive. We have tried to present an honest view of the limitations, as well as the potential benefits, of various treatment programs. Note also that two of the cases were not in treatment; we believe that it is important to point out that many people who have psychological disorders do not see therapists.

Each case study concludes with a discussion of current knowledge about etiology. Some of these discussions are necessarily more brief than others. More research has been done on schizophrenia, for example, than on bulimia or paranoid personality. We had two goals in mind for these discussions. First, we have tried to use the case material to illustrate the application of research to individual clients' problems. Second, we alert readers to important gaps in our knowledge of abnormal psychology, our abiding belief being that realizing what we do not know is as important as appreciating what we do know.

All of the cases in this book are based on actual clinical experience, primarily our own but, in some instances, that of our colleagues and students. Various demographic characteristics (names, locations, and occupations) and some concrete clinical details have been changed to protect the anonymity of clients and their families. In some instances, the cases are composites of clinical problems with which we have dealt. Our intent is not to put forth claims of efficacy and utility for any particular conceptualization or intervention but, instead, to illustrate the ways clinicians think about their work and implement abstractions to help a client cope with life problems. The names used in the case studies are fictitious; any resemblance to actual persons is purely coincidental.

One of the cases was written by Arthur Stone of the Long Island Research Institute; another was written by John Junginger of the Psychology Department at Indiana University. We decided not to identify the authors of specific cases, again for reasons of confidentiality, but we thank these two colleagues for their contributions. We also extend our thanks to the staff at Wiley—especially Jack Burton, Connie Rende, and Cathy Starnella—who provided invaluable assistance throughout this project.

John M. Neale
Thomas F. Oltmanns
Gerald C. Davison

CONTENTS

1. Obsessive-Compulsive Disorder 1
2. Generalized Anxiety Disorder 17
3. Hypertension 36
4. Unipolar Affective Disorder: Major Depressive Episode 54
5. Bipolar Affective Disorder: Manic Episode 73
6. Sociopathy 90
7. Paranoid Personality Disorder 103
8. Alcoholism and Marital Conflict 119
9. Psychosexual Disorder: Exhibitionism 136
10. Psychosexual Disorder: Inhibited Female Orgasm 148
11. Schizophrenia: Paranoid Type 166
12. Schizophrenia: Undifferentiated Type 187
13. Atypical Psychosis and Fetishism 206
14. Infantile Autism 221
15. Attention Deficit Disorder with Hyperactivity 236
16. School Phobia 249
17. Bulimia 267
18. Depression and a Suicidal Attempt in an Older Adult 279

References 297

1

OBSESSIVE-COMPULSIVE DISORDER

Karen Rusa was a 30-year-old married woman and the mother of four children. Although she had been having anxiety-related problems for a number of years, she had never sought professional help prior to this time. During the preceding 3 months, she had become increasingly depressed; her family physician finally suggested that she seek psychological services.

For the past several months Karen had been experiencing intrusive, repetitive thoughts that centered around her children's safety. She frequently found herself imagining that a serious accident had occurred; she was unable to put these thoughts out of her mind. On one such occasion she imagined that her son, Alan, had broken his leg playing football at school. There was no reason to believe that an accident had occurred, but Karen brooded about the possibility until she finally called the school to see if Alan was all right. Even after receiving their reassurance that he had not been hurt, she described herself as being somewhat surprised when he later arrived home unharmed. Karen also noted that her daily routine was seriously hampered by an extensive series of counting rituals that she performed throughout each day. Specific numbers had come to have a special meaning to Karen; she found that her preoccupation with these numbers was interfering with her ability to perform everyday activities. One example was grocery shopping. Karen believed that if she selected the first item (e.g., a box of cereal) on the shelf, something terrible would happen to her oldest child. If she selected the second item, some unknown disaster would befall her second child, and so on for the four children. The children's ages were also important. The sixth item in a row, for example, was associated with her youngest child, who was 6 years old. Thus specific items had to be avoided to ensure the safety of her children. Obviously, the ritual required some concentration because the children's ages changed periodically. Karen's preoccupaton with numbers extended to other activities, most notably the pattern in which she smoked cigarettes and drank coffee. If she had one cigarette, she believed that she had to smoke at least four in a row or one of the children would be harmed in some way. If she drank one cup of coffee, she felt compelled to drink four. Karen acknowledged the irrationality of these rituals but, nevertheless, maintained that she felt much more comfortable when she observed them conscientiously. When she was occasionally in too great a hurry to observe the rituals, she experienced considerable anxiety, in the form of a subjective feeling of dread and apprehension. She described herself as tense, jumpy, and unable to relax during these periods. Her fears were most often confirmed because something unfortunate invariably happened to one of the children within a few days after each such "failure." The fact that minor accidents are likely to occur at a fairly high rate in any family of four children did not diminish Karen's conviction that she had been directly responsible because of her inability to observe the numerical rules.

In addition to her obsessive ideas and compulsive behaviors, Karen reported dissatisfaction with her marriage and problems in managing her children. Her husband, Tony, had been placed on a complete physical disability 11 months prior to her first visit. Although he was only 32 years old, he suffered from a very serious heart condition that made even the most routine physical exertion potentially dangerous. Since leaving his job as a clerk at a plumbing supply store, he had spent most of his time at home. He enjoyed lying on the couch watching television and did so for most of his waking hours. He had convinced Karen that she should be responsible for all of the household chores and family errands. Her days were spent getting the children dressed, fed, and transported to school; cleaning; washing; shopping; and fetching potato chips, dip, and beer whenever Tony needed a snack. He argued, of course, that the stress of walking to the refrigerator would be unhealthy, although the merits of his reasoning—as well as his nutritional judgment—might easily have been questioned. The inequity of this situation was apparent to Karen, and extremely frustrating, yet she found herself unable to handle it effectively. She fantasized about abandoning the family, but she did not feel that she could follow through on this desire.

The children were also clearly out of her control. Robert, age 6, and Alan, age 8, were very active and mischievous. Neither responded well to parental discipline, which was inconsistent at best. Both had been noted to be behavioral problems at school, and Alan was being considered for placement in a special classroom for particularly disruptive children. On one occasion, Karen had been called to take Alan home early after he had kicked the school principal and told him to "go to hell." His teacher described him as always being out of his seat and constantly pestering the other children during study periods. The boys were also prone to minor physical illnesses; it seemed to Karen that at least one of the boys was always sick with a cold or some kind of infection. The girls were also difficult to handle. Denise, age 9, and Jennifer, age 11, spent much of their time at home arguing with each other. Jennifer was moderately obese. Denise teased her mercilessly about her weight. After they had quarreled for some time, Jennifer would appeal tearfully to Karen, who would attempt to intervene on her behalf. Karen was becoming increasingly distressed by her inablility to handle this confusing situation, and she was getting little, if any, help from Tony. During the past several weeks, she had been spending more and more time crying and hiding alone in her bedroom.

SOCIAL HISTORY

Karen was raised in New York City by Italian immigrant parents. She was the first of four children. Her family was deeply religious, and she was raised to be a devout Roman Catholic. She attended parochial schools from the first grade through high school and was a reasonably good student. Her memories of the severe practices of the church and school authorities were vivid. The formal rituals of the church played an important role in her life, as they did for the other members of her family. Beginning at a very early age, Karen was taught that she had to observe many specific guidelines that governed social behavior within the church (not eating meat on Fridays, going to confession regularly, etc.). She was told that her strict adherence to these norms would ensure the safety of her immortal soul and, conversely, that transgressions would be severely punished.

The depth of her belief and the severity of its consequences can be seen in the following story, which Karen recalled during an early session. When she was 8 years old, Karen and her classmates at school were to receive their first communion in the church. This is a particularly important and solemn occasion for Roman Catholics that signifies the child's advancement to adult status in the church community. Before the child is allowed to partake in communion, however, a complete confession must be made of *all* prior sins. Karen was told that she was to confess all of her sins, regardless of their severity or the time of their occurrence, to her priest, who would prescribe an appropriate penance for her sins. She remembered her parents' and teachers' warnings that if she failed to mention any of her sins, her soul would be banished to hell for eternity. This threat was still vivid in Karen's mind many years later. Despite the terror aroused by these circumstances,

Karen intentionally failed to tell the priest about one of her sins; she had stolen a small picture book from her classroom and was now afraid either to return it or to tell anyone about the crime. She lived with intense guilt about this omission for several years and could remember having occasional terrifying nightmares that centered around imagined punishments for not providing a complete confession. In subsequent years, Karen intensified her efforts to abide by even the most minute details of church regulations, but she continued to harbor the conviction that she could never atone for this mortal sin.

Karen remembered her parents as having been very strict disciplinarians. Her mother was apparently a cold, rigid person who had insisted on the maintenance of order and cleanliness in their household. Beyond her unerring adherence to religious rules and regulations, Karen's mother had kept the family on a very tight schedule with regard to meals and other routine activities. When the children deviated from these guidelines, they were severely punished. Karen's most positive recollections of interaction with her mother centered around their mutual participation in prescribed church functions. She did not remember her parents ever demonstrating affection for each other in front of their children.

Shortly after she graduated from high school, Karen married Tony. He was 2 years older than Karen and had been working as a stockboy at a department store. Their courtship was hurried. In retrospect, Karen wondered whether her interest in Tony had been motivated by a desire to escape from the confines of her parents' home.

Karen became pregnant 2 months after their marriage. During this pregnancy, she witnessed an unfortunate accident at her neighbor's apartment. While Karen was chatting with her friend, the woman's 1-year-old daughter crawled off the porch and was run over by another child riding a bicycle. The girl was seriously injured and remained in the hospital for several weeks. Shortly after this accident, Karen began experiencing repetitive, intrusive thoughts about injuring herself. At unpredictable but frequent intervals throughout the day, she would find herself thinking about jumping out of windows, walking in front of cars, and other similar dangerous behaviors. These thoughts were, of course, frightening to her, but she could not prevent their occurrence. When one of the thoughts did come into her mind, she attempted to get rid of it by quickly repeating a short prayer that she had learned as a child and then asking God for forgiveness for having entertained such a sinful impulse. This procedure was moderately successful as a temporary source of distraction, but it did not prevent the reappearance of a similar intrusive thought several hours later. These thoughts of self-injury gradually disappeared after the birth of her first child, Jennifer.

When Jennifer was 9 months old, Karen once again became pregnant. She and Tony decided to move to the suburbs, where they would be able to afford a house with a yard in which the children could play. Tony found a job as a clerk at a plumbing supply store. Karen stayed at home with Jennifer and tended to household responsibilities. Although she was proud of their new home, Karen became somewhat depressed during this period because she missed her old friends.

It was at this time that Karen began to be disillusioned with the church. Her distress centered around a number of reforms that had been introduced by Pope John XXIII and the Ecumenical Council. The Mass, for example, was no longer said in Latin, and nonclerical persons were allowed to administer various rites of the church. Similarly, church members were no longer admonished to give up meat on Fridays and other rituals were modified or completely eliminated. Most people found these changes refreshing, but Karen was horrified. The church's rituals had come to play a central role in her life. In deemphasizing the importance of traditional rituals, the church was depriving Karen of her principal means of controlling her own destiny. She was extremely uncomfortable with these new practices and soon stopped going to church all together.

Karen's situation showed very little change throughout the next few years. By the time she was 25 years old, she had four children. She found this responsibility overwhelming and was generally unhappy most of the time. Her relationship with Tony had essentially reached a stalemate; they were not satisfied with their marriage, but they agreed to stay together for the children. Although they did not fight with each other openly, a sense of covert tension and estrangement pervaded their relationship. Tony refused to participate in what he considered to be unnecessarily rigid and complicated household regulations, particularly those dealing with the children's behavior. Karen had established very specific guidelines for meals, bedtime, and so on, but found that she was unable to enforce these rules by herself. She remained distant from Tony and resisted most of his attempts to display physical affection. They did maintain a sexual relationship, but it lacked spontaneity and genuine warmth. Karen believed that sex was her marital responsibility, so she was willing to perform or acquiesce as necessary. Since the birth of their fourth child, Karen had been particularly anxious about becoming pregnant again. She refused to use any form of artificial birth control, which was, of course, contrary to the teachings of the church. Their sexual encounters were therefore very carefully scheduled to avoid the days surrounding ovulation. This scheduling became increasingly complex until Karen finally settled on two 4-day periods preceding and following menstruation during which she was willing to have intercourse with Tony. When they did engage in sexual activity, it came to follow a careful, routine sequence that was usually limited to the minimum physical stimulation necessary for Tony to achieve orgasm. On most occasions, Karen described herself as being tense and anxious at these times; she did not view herself as an active participant. She was not, however, totally inorgasmic; she did occasionally experience an orgasm during intercourse and was able to reach orgasm through self-stimulation. Masturbation made her feel quite guilty, and she did not discuss this activity with Tony. Thus, overall, Karen was chronically unhappy and generally dissatisfied with her life, but she nevertheless clung to her miserable surroundings and established patterns of behavior out of fear that any change would be for the worse.

This unhappy yet tolerable equilibrium was disturbed by Tony's deteriorating health. One day, while he was working at the store, he experienced sudden chest pains and numbness in his extremities. Recognizing these symptoms as serious in nature (he had had high blood pressure for years and was therefore well informed in this regard), Tony asked a friend to drive him to the hospital. His experience was diagnosed as a mild heart attack. Further testing revealed serious structural abnormalities in his heart. He was eventually discharged from the hospital, given a complete medical disability, and laid off from his job.

Karen became more and more depressed after Tony began staying home during the day. It was during this time that her fears about the children's safety became clearly unreasonable, and she started performing her counting rituals. Karen could not remember when she first began checking the order of items on a shelf or counting the number of cigarettes she smoked in sequence. She did realize that her situation was desperate because she felt that she had lost control of her own behavior and experienced considerable anxiety whenever she attempted to resist performing the rituals. At this point she finally decided to seek professional help.

CONCEPTUALIZATION AND TREATMENT

The ritualistic behavior was seen by the therapist as one part of Karen's overall difficult situation. The counting obsession represented Karen's attempt to reintroduce a sense of personal control over her own life. In this sense, the rituals were being performed instead of either the more socially acceptable religious activities that she had employed as a child or the more effective social skills that she had apparently never developed. For example, she was unassertive in her relationship with Tony and markedly ineffective in her interactions with the children. Treatment was therefore aimed at the development of interpersonal skills that would give Karen more control over her environment. It was hoped that as she was able to effect a more satisfactory relationship with her family, her increased competence would eliminate the necessity of turning to admittedly superstitious, ineffective attempts to achieve self-control.

During the course of their early sessions, it became evident to both Karen and her therapist that Karen was not behaving assertively, particularly with her husband. That is, she was unable to express openly either negative or positive feelings. Instead of standing up for her rights, she would meekly acquiesce to even his most unreasonable demands. At the same time, she would become extremely frustrated and angry with him and would look for subtle ways to "even the score." She was similarly unable to convey her appreciation to him on those (admittedly rare) occasions when he did please her.

Karen quickly recognized her deficiency in this regard but was nevertheless unable to alter her behavior spontaneously. She and the therapist therefore agreed to pursue a systematic program of assertive training. The initial sessions in this sequence were devoted to a careful assessment of the situations in which Karen was unassertive. She was asked to keep a daily notebook of such situations in which she noted the people involved, the nature of their interaction, and her perception of the situation, including what she thought would happen if she did behave assertively. Having identified typical problem situations, Karen and her therapist role-played several incidents as a way of introducing Karen to more appropriate responses. At first, the therapist played Karen's part and modeled appropriate behaviors for her. They then switched roles so that Karen could practice these new responses. After each role-playing sequence, the therapist provided Karen with feedback about the effectiveness of her behavior.

They also discussed some of Karen's irrational fears associated with assertion. These thoughts generally centered around her implicit belief that everyone should love her and that if she stood up for her own rights people would reject her. In many situations, these irrational self-statements were inhibiting the expression of assertive behaviors.

After Karen became proficient with such exercises in the therapy sessions, she was asked to start transferring her skills to life outside the clinic. Beginning with relatively easy assignments to ensure initial successful experiences, she was asked to perform more and more difficult assertion tasks between therapy sessions. These experiences then became the focus of future sessions until she had been successful in even the most difficult situations.

After assertive training had effected some positive results, the therapist began teaching Karen more effective child management skills. These were based primarily on procedures associated with instrumental learning. She was taught, for example, to ignore her daughters when they were quarreling and to reinforce them positively for playing together appropriately. Again, her efforts were initially channelled toward the behaviors that could be changed easily. The most difficult problems, such as getting the children to stop fighting at mealtimes, were left until Karen had mastered some of the general principles of child management.

In addition to these skill-training programs, the therapist also discussed with Karen her concerns about religion. It was clear that the church was still very important to her and that she experienced considerable guilt and anxiety over her failure to attend services regularly. The fact that her children were not involved in church activities was also very troubling to Karen. She worried that if any harm came to one of them, God would not protect them. For these reasons, Karen was encouraged to visit several priests at churches in her area in an effort to find one who was more conservative and thus more compatible with her own views. Although most of the local priests had moved toward contemporary practices in their own churches, they did refer her to an older priest at a church somewhat further from her neighborhood who still adhered to several of the traditional rituals she had learned as a child. She made an appointment to visit this priest and was very pleased and relieved after their initial meeting. He was able to discuss with her some of the changes that had been made in the church. In some cases he was able to explain the rationale behind a particular change in a way that was acceptable to her. This process was, no doubt, facilitated by the fact that he shared many of her concerns about abandoning traditional practices. Karen felt much more comfortable with this priest than she did with the very liberal pastor who was in charge of the church in her immediate neighborhood. Within weeks she was once again attending church regularly with her four children.

The combination of assertive training, parent education, and a renewed interest in church activities did lead to an important improvement in Karen's mood. After 3 months of treatment, she reported an increased sense of self-confidence and an improvement in her family life. There was also some reduction in her anxiety level. She continued to observe her numbers rituals, but they were somewhat less frequent and, when she did fail to perform the counting routines, she was not as panic stricken as she had been at the beginning of treatment.

At this point, the rituals were addressed directly through the combined use of flooding and response prevention. This procedure was instituted as follows. Karen was asked to smoke a single cigarette at the beginning of a session. When she was finished with the cigarette, she would begin to feel anxious and worry about her oldest daughter. She was then instructed to resist the temptation to smoke another cigarette. Thus the respone that she employed to neutralize her anxiety and to control the ruminations was prevented. The therapist believed that this type of prolonged exposure to the anxiety-provoking situation would lead to a reduction in Karen's anxiety. The procedure was carried out during four consecutive 2-hour sessions. Karen was encouraged to practice the same response prevention procedure on her own between sessions. When she had mastered the cigarette-smoking problem, the procedure was extended progressively to other similar situations in which she had been concerned about numbers.

Treatment was terminated after 20 sessions. Karen was no longer depressed and had not engaged in her compulsive counting rituals for 4 weeks.

The children were better behaved at home, and Karen had plans to institute still further changes in this regard. Her relationship with Tony was somewhat improved. Although he had become quite upset initially when Karen began to assert herself, he became more cooperative when he saw an improvement in her adjustment. Karen's reduced anxiety also lead to some initial improvements in their sexual relationship, although this problem was not addressed directly in treatment. These improvements were still evident at a follow-up interview 6 months after termination.

DISCUSSION

Obsessive-compulsive disorder is included in *DSM-III* (p. 235) under the general heading of Anxiety Disorders. It is defined by the following criteria.

A. *Either obsessions or compulsions.*
Obsessions: *recurrent, persistent ideas, thoughts, images, or impulses that are ego-dystonic, i.e., they are not experienced as voluntarily produced, but rather as thoughts that invade consciousness and are experienced as senseless or repugnant. Attempts are made to ignore or supress them.*
Compulsions: *repetitive and seemingly purposeful behaviors that are performed according to certain rules or in a stereotyped fashion. The behavior is not an end in itself, but is designed to produce or prevent some future event or situation. However, either the activity is not connected in a realistic way with what it is designed to produce or prevent, or may be clearly excessive. The act is performed with a sense of subjective compulsion coupled with a desire to resist the compulsion (at least initially). The individual generally recognizes the senselessness of the behavior (this may not be true for young children) and does not derive pleasure from carrying out the activity, although it provides a release of tension.*

B. *The obsessions or compulsions are a significant source of distress to the individual or interfere with social or role functioning.*

C. *Not due to another mental disorder, such as Tourette's Disorder, Schizophrenia, Major Depression, or Organic Mental Disorder.*

Regardless of whether the repetitive element is a thought (obsession) or an overt response (compulsion), the central feature of the disorder is the subjective experience of a loss of *volition*.

Obsessions may be distinguished on the basis of both form and content. Akhtar et al. (1975, pp. 343–344) have outlined five typical forms of obsessional symptoms.

Obsessive doubt: *An inclination not to believe that a completed task has been accomplished satisfactorily.*

Obsessive thinking: *A seemingly endless thought chain, usually one pertaining to future events.*

Obsessive impulse: *A powerful urge to carry out actions which may be trivial or socially disruptive or even assaultive.*

Obsessive fear: *A fear of losing self control and thus inadvertently committing a socially embarrassing act.*

Obsessive image: *The persistence before the mind's eye of something seen, usually recently.*

The content of obsessive thoughts may also vary. Stern and Cobb (1978) analyzed the obsessions of 45 patients and found that the most common theme concerned causing harm to either self or others. Compulsions represent rituals that are performed in accordance with an obsessional thought. For example, a patient experiencing obsessive doubt about locking doors may engage in compulsive checking of the doors in his or her home. The most common compulsive behaviors seem to be cleaning, avoiding, repeating, and checking (Stern and Cobb, 1978). Roughly 75% of patients with obsessive symptoms also exhibit compulsive behaviors (Akhtar et al., 1975).

Obsessive-compulsive disorder should be distinguished from compulsive personality disorder. The latter does not involve specific ritualistic behaviors; it is intended to refer to a general personality style. Individuals with a compulsive personality are preoccupied with rules, organization, and detail; devoted to productivity; indecisive; and restricted in their ability to express positive feelings toward other people (*DSM-III*). Although these two disorders may appear in the same individual, an etiological relationship has not been clearly established, so they should be considered separately.

Obsessive-compulsive disorder is related to phobic disorder in that both involve severe anxiety and both may appear in the same patient. There are, however, some differences between the two disorders that may be important. For example, phobic patients do not show the same tendency toward superstitions or "magical" thinking that is often characteristic of obsessive-compulsive patients, nor do they manifest compulsive symptoms.

Obsessive thoughts or beliefs should also be distinguished from delusions. Two criteria are important in this regard. First, obsessive patients are ambivalent about their thoughts; they recognize their essential absurdity at the same time that they are preoccupied by the ideas. Second, and perhaps most important, is the struggle against the idea. Obsessive patients try, often desperately, to resist their obsessive ideas whereas delusional patients do not.

Depression is a common complication associated with compulsive disorder (see Goodwin, Guze, and Robins, 1969). The relationship between these phenomena is also unclear. Sometimes compulsive symptoms appear before the onset of depression, in other cases this relationship is reversed. Rachman (1976) has suggested that the appearance of a depressed mood may act as a sensitizing event in the precipitation of compulsive symptoms. In other words, a person may initially be prone to ruminative thoughts but not find them particularly disturbing until after the onset of a serious mood disturbance such as agitated depression.

Obsessive-compulsive disorder is a relatively rare phenomenon. It accounts for less than 5% of all psychiatric patients (including inpatients and outpatients). Its prevalence in the general population is estimated at less than 0.05% (Ingram, 1961; Woodruff and Pitts, 1964). The disorder seems to be equally distributed between men and women (Templer, 1972).

Kringlen (1970) has reported the results of a 20-year follow-up of 91 patients who had been hospitalized with obsessive compulsive neuroses.[1] More than 80% of these patients had exhibited nervous symptoms as children. They had typically been raised in strict, puritanical homes. The average age of onset for compulsive symptoms in female patients was between 10 and 20 years, although most of the women did not seek professional help until some years later. Somewhat more than 50% of the patients showed an acute onset of symptoms following a specific stressful event. The clinical literature holds that these patients are usually introverted and of above average intelligence, but Kringlen was unable to confirm this view. Marital problems are common among compulsive patients. The prognosis is mixed. In Kringlen's sample, which included only cases severe enough to be hospitalized, only 25% of the patients were significantly improved 10 to 20 years after admission. The patients who exhibited compulsive personality traits and more severe compulsive symptoms at admission showed the worst outcome.

By these standards, Karen was in many ways a typical case of obsessive-compulsive disorder. She had, in fact, been raised in a strict, puritanical family setting. As a child, she was generally anxious and quite concerned with order and rituals. Since midadolescence, Karen had experienced difficulty with intrusive, repetitive ideas that she found quite distressing. One obvious example was the period shortly after her marriage when she witnessed the little girl's bicycle accident. These problems would come and go without apparent reason. She was also prone to serious depression.

Karen's social history and family background are also consistent with the literature on obsessive-compulsive disorder. There is a relatively high inci-

[1]DSM III has eliminated "neuroses" as a major conceptional category in favor of a more descriptive approach to diagnosis. Compulsive disorders were formerly grouped together with phobias, hysterical disorders, and generalized anxiety disorder because, according to psychoanalytic theory, they shared common etiologic features.

dence of psychiatric anomalies, particularly obsessive-compulsive disorder, among biological relatives of obsessive-compulsive patients (see Templer, 1972). It is not clear, however, whether this relationship reflects the influence of genetic or environmental variables. In Karen's case, her mother's rigid, moralistic behavior may have had an important influence on the development of later symptoms. Karen's mother provided a very salient model for her daughter's subsequent compulsive behavior. She also reinforced early tendencies toward such response patterns.

THEORETICAL PERSPECTIVES AND TREATMENT IMPLICATIONS

According to traditional psychoanalytic theory, compulsive symptoms are the product of the ego's unconscious attempt to fend off anxiety associated with hostile impulses (thus its inclusion with the "defensive neuroses"). Freud (1909/1925) argued that compulsive patients had experienced overly harsh toilet training and were therefore fixated in the anal-sadistic stage of development. Such individuals would presumably suffer serious conflict over the expression of anger. But, since these feelings were dangerous, or unacceptable to the ego, the anticipation of their expression was seen as anxiety provoking. This anxiety was dealt with primarily through the defense mechanism known as "reaction formation," in which the original impulse (anger) is transformed into its antithesis (love or oversolicitude). This conceptual approach is not at all incompatible with Karen's current situation. Her principal symptoms were compulsive rituals that were intended to protect her children from harm. But her feelings about her children were, in fact, ambivalent. It would not be unreasonable to assume that she was most often very angry with them, perhaps to the point that she might have considered doing them physical harm. Of course, this impulse would be very anxiety provoking to the ego, which would convert it to its opposite form. Thus, instead of injuring the children, she spent a good deal of her time every day performing irrational responses aimed at *protecting* them.

Some recognition was given to these considerations in the treatment that was employed. Karen's anger and frustation were identified as central features of her adjustment problems. The therapist did, however, deviate from psychoanalytic tenets in two major regards. First, he did not resort to the use of vaguely defined, inferential constructs (such as defense mechanisms) to explain her behavior. Second, the therapeutic procedures involved went considerably beyond the goal of insight-oriented treatment. Karen's recognition of her anger and hostility was not sufficient to effect change; specific training procedures were used to help her develop a repertoire of more adaptive responses.

The traditional learning, or behavioral, perspective would view Karen's problems in a distinctly different fashion. Within this model, two factors would be given principal consideration. Both involve the notion of *negative reinforcement*;[2] the probability of a response is increased if it leads to the termination of an aversive stimulus. Consider, for example, the net effect of Karen's rituals. Their performance ensured that she would be away from her home for extended periods of time. If she went to her neighbor's house for coffee, she would be gone for at least 2 hours before she could consume enough cups and smoke enough cigarettes to satisfy the rituals. Grocery shopping, which she did by herself, had also turned into a long, complicated process. Given that being at home with her family was mostly an aversive experience for Karen, her rituals might be seen as an operant response that was being maintained by negative reinforcement.[3]

A behavioral clinician might also point to the anxiety reduction associated with the performance of the rituals. Whenever Karen was engaged in an activity that reminded her of numbers and, consequently, her children, she became anxious. She was able to neutralize this anxiety temporarily by counting the appropriate number of boxes, and so on. This ritual was therefore reinforced and maintained by the reduction of anxiety. This notion is similar to the psychoanalytic view in that the symptom is produced as a means of reducing tension. The two views differ in that the behavioral view does not see her anxiety as being directly attributable to the unconscious urge to harm her children, nor does the behavioral view hold that the anxiety reduction is mediated by an unconsciously activated defense mechanism.

Again, some elements of the behavioral view were incorporated into the treatment procedure followed with Karen. In particular, by teaching her to be more assertive and to manage her children more effectively, the therapist was able to make her home life less aversive. In fact, she now experienced pleasurable interactions with her children and her husband. Thus one important source of negative reinforcement for her rituals was removed. Unfortunately, this view of human behavior is fairly limited. In particular, it does not account for the importance of cognitive events. By focusing exclusively on environmental events, behaviorists may ignore important factors associated with the client's perceptions, beliefs, and attitudes. These variables also seemed to play an important role in Karen's problem.

Cognitive theorists (e.g., Mandler, 1966) have argued that the person's perception of control is an important variable in understanding anxiety. People tend to be less anxious when they can control their own environment

[2]Negative reinforcement should be distinguished from punishment, in which the *appearance* of an aversive stimulus is made contingent on the emission of a response, so the probability of the response is therefore *reduced*.

[3]This phenomenon would be labeled "secondary gain" by a psychoanalyst who would give primary emphasis to the ego-defensive nature of the symptom.

and, even if they do not really have control, they will experience situations as less anxiety provoking if they *believe* they have control (see Geer, Davison, and Gatchel, 1970). The extension of this model to compulsive disorders is fairly simple. Carr (1974) has demonstrated that people suffering from compulsive disorders are prone to hold abnormally high subjective estimates of the probability of negative events. Their anticipation of disaster leads to high levels of anxiety. Compulsive rituals are then employed to reduce their anxiety. In this sense, compulsive thoughts and behaviors represent an attempt (albeit an irrational one) to attain control over events.

The relevance of this perspective to Karen's situation is clear. As a child, she had been taught that her strict observation of the rituals of the church would guarantee her salvation. In other words, they were the principal means for controlling her ultimate fate. As an adult, Karen found herself stripped of these control mechanisms. The church now maintained that salvation (or the protection of one's soul) depended more on faith than on the performance of specific overt responses. Thus it may be that Karen's counting rituals represented a substitute for the religious practices she had learned as a child. She admitted that they were irrational and probably unnecessary, but they did make her feel at ease in much the same way that going to church had left her with a comforting feeling as a child.

Treatment was therefore aimed initially at giving Karen alternative means of controlling her environment. These included assertive training and instruction in parenting skills. But these measures could only affect earthly matters. Considering her deeply ingrained religious beliefs, it was also judged necessary to help her reestablish contact with the church. After these procedures had achieved some modest success, it was possible to attack the counting rituals directly through the use of prolonged exposure and response prevention.

This procedure was based on the recommendations made by Hodgson and Rachman (1976). It depends on the assumption that stimuli that precede the performance of a ritual have come to be anxiety provoking. Habituation is presumably prevented by the performance of the compulsive ritual, which can be seen as an avoidance response. It follows, therefore, that if the compulsive response can be prevented for an extended period of time while the person is exposed to the initiating stimuli, the anxiety should extinguish. In Karen's case, this procedure began with a situation in which she had smoked a single cigarette. This event normally evoked increasing anxiety if she did not immediately smoke another cigarette. By encouraging Karen to resist lighting another cigarette, the therapist was able to help her overcome anxiety through an habituation process.

Some empirical data indicate that behavior therapy, including modeling, flooding, and thought stopping, is effective in treating compulsive disorders (Marks, 1973). The most effective procedure seems to be *in vivo*, graduated, prolonged exposure coupled with response prevention. This technique was employed by Marks, Hodgson, and Rachman (1975) with 20 chronic cases of obsessive-compulsive disorder. Two years after the termination of treatment, 15 of the patients were still considered much improved. Although a control group was not included in this study, the poor prognosis generally associated with this kind of patient favors the conclusion that the treatment itself was responsible for the observed change.

In some cases, medication may also be beneficial, particularly in conjunction with behavior therapy. Several recent studies have demonstrated that tricyclic antidepressant medication may be helpful in treating compulsive disorders (Marks, Hodgson, and Rachman, 1975; Yaryura-Tobias and Neziroglu, 1975; Yaryura-Tobias, Neziroglu, and Bergman, 1976). The actual mechanism of action for these drugs is unclear. Their beneficial effect may be in relieving the depression that frequently accompanies compulsive symptoms (instead of affecting the compulsive symptoms directly). In any case, their administration may often be considered, especially when behavior therapy alone is ineffective.

When both psychotherapy and medication fail, one other form of treatment may be considered—psychosurgery. Although psychosurgery was originally intended to be used with psychotic patients, clinical research indicates that it may be most effective with depression and compulsive disorders (see Shevitz, 1976). Tan, Marks, and Marset (1971), for example, compared the long-term outcome of 24 obsessive-compulsive neurotics who received psychosurgery with 13 control patients who did not receive surgery. The two groups were hospitalized and roughly equated with regard to the form, severity, and duration of symptoms. The surgical patients all received a standard, bimedial, frontal leucotomy.[4] In other words, fibers in the center of the frontal lobes were severed in a plane perpendicular to the axis between the eyes and the back of the skull. The leucotomized patients showed greater improvement than the control patients with regard to compulsive symptoms as well as general anxiety and depression. Even better results have been reported by Mitchell-Heggs, Kelly, and Richardson (1976), who used a slightly different surgical technique. These investigators found that 24 out of 27 (89%) obsessive patients were improved 16 months after treatment; 7 of these 24 were considered completely symptom free, and an additional 11 were much improved. Since the mean duration of illness prior to surgery was 13 years for the patients in this study, the reported rates of improvement are probably not due to spontaneous remission.

These results cannot be ignored, but they should also be interpreted with caution. First, it is virtually impossible to conduct a double-blind evaluation

[4]The procedure is known as a lobotomy in the United States and a leucotomy in England.

of psychosurgery. Second, surgical procedures have varied widely across studies, thus making general statements about psychosurgery questionable. Third, and perhaps most important, psychosurgery may produce very general changes in the patient's intellectual and emotional capacities (Valenstein, 1973). These changes are both unpredictable and poorly understood. Thus most investigators agree that such radical procedures should only be considered when the patient's symptoms are chronic and severely disturbing and when other treatment programs have already been unsuccessful.

2

GENERALIZED ANXIETY DISORDER

Dennis Holt was 31 years old, divorced, and a successful insurance salesman. He had experienced panic attacks on several occasions during the past 10 years, but he had not sought psychological treatment until shortly after the last incident. It happened while Dennis and his fiancée, Elaine, were doing their Christmas shopping at a local mall. Their first stop was a large department store where Elaine hoped to find a present for her mother. Dennis was in a good mood when they arrived at the store. Although he was usually uneasy in large crowds of people, he was also caught up in the holiday spirit and looking forward to spending the bonus that he had recently received from his company. Ten minutes after they began shopping, Dennis suddenly felt very sick. His hands began to tremble uncontrollably, his vision became blurred, and his body felt weak all over. He experienced a tremendous pressure on his chest and began to gasp for breath, sensing that he was about to smother. These dramatic physical symptoms were accompanied by an overwhelming sensation of apprehension. He was terrified but did not know why. Without saying anything to Elaine, he whirled and dashed from the store, seeking refuge in their car, which was parked outside. Once there, he rolled down the windows to let in more air, laid down on the back seat, and closed his eyes. He continued to feel dizzy and short of breath for about 10 minutes more. Elaine did not find him for more than an hour because she had been browsing in an adjacent aisle and had not seen him flee from the store. When she realized that he was gone, she had looked for him in other stores before she realized that something was wrong and finally decided to check the car. This was the first panic attack that Dennis had experienced since he and Elaine had begun dating several months previously. After they returned to his apartment, he explained what had happened and his past history of attacks in somewhat greater detail; she persuaded him to seek professional help.

When Dennis arrived at the psychological clinic for his first appointment, he was neatly dressed in an expensive three-piece suit. He was 5 minutes early, so the receptionist asked him if he would like to take a seat in the large, comfortably furnished waiting room where several other clients were sitting. Politely indicating that he would prefer to stand, Dennis lit a cigarette and leaned casually against the corridor wall. Everything about his physical appearance—his posture, his neatly trimmed hair, his friendly smile—conveyed a sense of confidence and success. Nothing betrayed the real sense of dread with which he had struggled since he had promised Elaine that he would consult a psychologist. Was he, in fact, crazy? He wanted help, but he did not want anyone to think that he was emotionally unstable.

The first interview was not very productive. Dennis began by cracking jokes with the psychologist and attempted to engage in an endless sequence of witty small talk and verbal banter. In response to the psychologist's persistent but gentle queries, Dennis explained that he had promised his fiancée that he would seek some advice about his intermittent panic attacks. Nevertheless, he was reluctant to admit that he had any really serious problems, and he evaded many questions pertaining to his current adjustment. Dennis seemed intent on convincing the psychologist that he was not "just another nut." He continued to chat on a superficial level and, at one point, even began asking the psychologist whether he had adequate life insurance coverage.

In subsequent sessions it became clear that the panic attacks, which never occurred more than two or three times per year, were simply the most dramatic of Dennis' problems. He was also an extremely tense and anxious person between attacks. He frequently experienced severe headaches that sometimes lasted for several hours. These generally took the form of a steady, diffuse pain across his forehead; Dennis sometimes felt as if a very tight band were stretched around the top of his head. The headaches were accompanied by an aching sensation in his neck and shoulders. Dennis also complained that he could not relax, noting that he suffered from chronic muscle tension and occasional insomnia. His job often required that he work late in the evening, visiting people at their homes after dinner. When he returned to his apartment, he was always "wound up" and on edge, unable to sleep. He had tried various distractions and popular remedies, but nothing worked. His attempt at transcendental meditation had failed, and the expensive reclining chair with an electric vibrator seemed to add to his discomfort.

Dennis was very self-conscious. Although he was an attractive man and one of the most successful salespersons in his firm, he worried constantly about what others thought of him. This concern was obvious in his behavior both before and after sessions at the clinic. At the end of every session, he seemed to make a point of joking loudly so that anyone outside the psychologist's office would hear the laughter. He would then open the door, as he continued to chuckle, and say something like, "Well, Bill (the therapist's first name) that was a lot of fun. Let's get together again soon!" as he left the office. The most peculiar incident of this sort occurred prior to the fourth treatment session. Dennis had continued to avoid the clinic waiting room on past visits, but this time it happened that he and his therapist met at a location that required them to walk through the waiting room together in order to reach the therapist's office. Thinking nothing of it, the therapist set off across the room in which several other clients were waiting, and Dennis quickly followed. When they reached the middle of the long room, Dennis suddenly clasped his right arm around the therapist's shoulders, smiled, and in a voice that was slightly too loud said, "Well, Bill, what's up? How can I help you today?" The therapist was taken completely by surprise but said nothing until they reached his office. Dennis quickly closed the door and leaned against the wall, holding his hand over his heart as he gulped for air. He was visibly shaken. Once he had caught his breath, he apologized profusely and explained that he did not know what had come over him. He said that he had always been afraid that the other people in the clinic, particularly the other clients, would realize that he was a client and therefore think that he was crazy. He had panicked as they walked across the waiting room and had been unable to resist the urge to divert attention from himself by seeming to be a therapist.

This preoccupation with social evaluation was also evident in Dennis' work. He became extremely tense whenever he was about to call on a prospective client. Between the point at which an appointment was arranged and his arrival at the person's home, Dennis worried constantly. Would they like him? Could he make the sale? His anxiety became most exaggerated as he drove his car to the person's home. In an effort to cope with this anxiety, Dennis had constructed a 45-minute recording that he played for himself on the cassette deck in his car. The tape contained a long pep talk, recorded in his own voice, in which he continually reassured and encouraged himself: "Go out there and charm 'em, Dennis. You're the best damn salesman this company's ever had! They're gonna be putty in your hands, big fella. Flash that smile and give 'em the old Holt handshake. They'll love you!" and on and on. Unfortunately, the net effect of the recording was probably to increase his tension. Despite this anxiety, he managed to perform very effectively in the selling role, just as he was able to project an air of confidence in the clinic. But, on the inside, he was miserable. He worried constantly about his performance and what others thought of him. Every 2 or 3 months he would become convinced that he could no longer stand the tension and decide to quit his job. Then he would make a big sale or receive a bonus for exceeding his quota for that period and change his mind.

SOCIAL HISTORY

Dennis was an only child. His father was an accountant and his mother was an elementary-school teacher. No one else in his family had been treated for serious adjustment problems.

Dennis and his mother got along well, but his relationship with his father had always been difficult. His father was a demanding perfectionist who held very high, probably unrealistic, expectations for Dennis. When Dennis was in elementary school, his father always wanted him to be the best athlete and the best student in his class. Although Dennis was adequate in both of these areas, he did not excell in either. His father frequently expressed the hope that Dennis would become an aeronautical engineer when he grew up. Now that Dennis was working as an insurance salesman, his father never missed an opportunity to express his disapproval and disappointment. He was also unhappy about Dennis' divorce. Most times his parents came to visit, Dennis and his father ended up in an argument.

Dennis remembered being shy as a child. Nevertheless, he enjoyed the company of other children and always had a number of friends. When he reached adolescence, he was particularly timid around girls. In an effort to overcome his shyness, he joined the high-school drama club and played bit parts in several of their productions. This experience provided an easy avenue for meeting other students with whom he became friends. He also learned that he could speak in front of a group of people without making a fool of himself, but he continued to feel uncomfortable in public speaking and social situations.

After graduating from high school, Dennis attended a private liberal arts college for 2 years. Although he had been a reasonably good student in high school, he began to experience academic problems in college. He attributed his sporadic performance to test anxiety. In his own words, he "choked" on examinations. Shortly after he entered the classroom, the palms of his hands would begin to perspire profusely. As the time period slowly elapsed, his breathing would become more rapid and shallow and his mouth would become very dry. He sometimes found himself glancing back and forth from his watch to the clock on the wall, worrying about the grade he would get and unable to concentrate on the test questions. On the worst occasions, his mind would go blank. Some of his instructors were sympathetic to the problem and allowed him to take extra time to finish examinations; others permitted him to turn in supplementary papers that were written out of class. Nevertheless, his grades began to suffer and by the end of his first year he was placed on academic probation.

During his second year in college, Dennis began to experience gastrointestinal problems. He had always seemed to have a sensitive stomach and avoided rich or fried foods that often led to excessive flatus or nausea. Now the symptoms were getting worse. He suffered intermittently from constipation, cramping, and diarrhea. He would frequently go for 3 or 4 days without having a bowel movement. During these periods, he experienced considerable discomfort and occasional severe cramps in his lower abdominal tract. These problems persisted for several months until, at the urging of his roommate, Dennis finally made an appointment for a complete gastrointestinal examination at the local hospital. The physicians were unable to find any evidence of structural pathology and diagnosed Dennis' problem as "irritable colon." They gave him prescriptions for a laxative and tincture of belladonna, which suppresses motor and secretory activity in the gastrointestinal tract. These medications provided some relief, but Dennis continued to suffer from intermittent bowel problems.

Dennis had several girlfriends and dated regularly throughout high school and college. During his sophomore year in college, he developed a serious relationship with the younger sister of one of his closest friends. Mary was a freshman at the same school. She and Dennis shared some interests and enjoyed each other's company, so they spent a great deal of time together. At the end of the academic year, Dennis decided that he had had enough of college. He was bored with his classes and tired of the continual pressure from his parents to get better grades. An older friend of his had recently landed a well-paying job with an insurance firm, so Dennis decided that he would complete applications with a number of companies. Two of them invited him to interviews, and one eventually offered him a position in sales. The new job required that he relocate in a nearby state. For the first several months, he and Mary drove back and forth to visit each other on weekends. At the end of the fall semester, Mary decided that she would also drop out of school. She and Dennis began living together; they were married 2 years later.

Dennis and Mary were reasonably happy for the first 3 years. He was successful at his job, and she eventually became a certified realtor. As they were both promoted by their respective firms, they found themselves spending more and more time working and less and less time with each other. Their interests also began to diverge. When Mary had some time off or an evening free, she liked to go out to restaurants and parties. Dennis liked to stay home and watch television.

Dennis' first real panic attack occurred when he was 24 years old. He and Mary were at a dinner theater with three other couples, including Mary's boss and his wife. The evening had been planned for several weeks, in spite of Dennis' repeated objections. He was self-conscious about eating in public and did not care for Mary's colleagues; he had finally agreed to accompany her because it seemed that it would be important for her advancement in the firm. He was also looking forward to seeing the play *Chorus Line*, which would be performed after the meal was served. As the meal progressed, Dennis began to feel increasingly uncomfortable. He was particularly concerned that he might experience one of his gastrointestinal attacks during dinner and be forced to spend the rest of the evening in the men's restroom. He did not want to have to explain the problem to all of Mary's friends. In an attempt to prevent such an attack, he had taken antispasmodic medication for his stomach and was eating sparingly. Just as everyone else had finished eating their dessert, Dennis began to experience a choking sensation in his throat and chest. He could not get his breath, and it seemed certain to him that he was going to faint on the spot. Unable to speak or move, he remained frozen in his seat in utter terror. The others quickly realized that something was wrong and, assuming that he had choked on some food, Mary began to pound on his back between the shoulder blades. There was now a sharp pain in his chest, and he began to experience heart palpitations. Dennis was finally able to wheeze that he thought he was having a heart attack. Two of the other men helped him up, and a waiter directed them to a lounge in the building where he was able to lie down. In less than 30 minutes, all of the symptoms had passed; Dennis and Mary were able to excuse themselves from the others and drive home.

Dennis was frightened by this experience, but he did not seek medical advice. He was convinced that he was in good physical condition and attributed the attack to something he had eaten or perhaps to an interaction between the food and medication. He did, however, become even more reluctant to go to restaurants with Mary and her friends. Interestingly, he continued to eat business lunches with his own colleagues without apparent discomfort.

The second panic attack occurred about 6 months later, while Dennis was driving alone in rush hour traffic. The symptoms were essentially the same: the sudden sensation of smothering, accompanied by an inexplicable, intense fear. Fortunately, Dennis was in the right lane of traffic when the sensation began. He was able to pull his car off the road and lie on the seat until the experience was over.

By this point, Dennis was convinced that he needed medical help. He made an appointment with a specialist in internal medicine who gave him a complete physical examination. There was no evidence of cardiovascular or gastrointestinal pathology. The physician told Dennis that the problem seemed to be with his nerves and gave him a prescription for Valium, a minor tranquilizer often used in treating anxiety states. Dennis took 5 milligrams of Valium three times per day for 4 months. It did help him relax and, in combination with his other medication, seemed to improve his gastrointestinal distress. However, he did not like the feeling of being dependent on medication to control his anxiety. He saw it as a sign of weakness and eventually discontinued taking the Valium.

Mary asked Dennis for a divorce 3 years after they were married (2 years after his first panic attack). It came as no surprise to Dennis; their relationship had deteriorated considerably. He had become even more reluctant to go out with her in the evening and on weekends, insisting that he needed to stay home and rest his nerves. He was very apprehensive in crowded public places and also careful about where and when he drove his car. He tried to avoid rush hour traffic. When he did drive in heavy traffic, he always stayed in the right lane, even if it was much slower, so that he could pull off the road if he had an attack. Long bridges also made him extremely uncomfortable because they did not afford an opportunity to pull over; he dreaded the possibility of being trapped on a bridge during one of his "spells." These fears did not prevent him from doing his work. He continued to force himself to meet new people, and he drove long distances every day. The most drastic impact was on his social life. These increased restrictions led to greater tension between Dennis and Mary. They had both become more and more irritable and seldom enjoyed being with each other. When she decided that she could no longer stand to live with him, he agreed to the divorce.

After Mary left, Dennis moved to an apartment in which he was still living when he entered treatment 5 years later. His chronic anxiety, occasional panic attacks, headaches, and gastrointestinal problems persisted relatively unchanged, although they varied in severity. He had a number of friends and managed to see them fairly frequently. He did, however, avoid situations that involved large crowds. He would not, for example, accompany his friends to a professional football game, but he did like to play golf, where he could be out in the fresh air with very few people and lots of open space around him. He met Elaine 4 years after the divorce. She was slightly older than he and much less active socially than Mary had been. They enjoyed spending quiet evenings watching television and occasionally got together with one or two other couples to play bridge. Although they planned to get married, neither Dennis nor Elaine wanted to rush into anything.

CONCEPTUALIZATION AND TREATMENT

When Dennis entered treatment, he expressed a desire to learn how to control his anxiety, particularly when it reached its most excessive proportions in the form of panic attacks. He did not feel comfortable taking medication because he considered it to be an artificial "crutch." On the other hand, he was also opposed to the idea of long-term psychotherapy aimed at uncovering deeply ingrained psychic conflict. He had read about behavioral approaches to the treatment of anxiety and was looking for a psychologist with whom he could follow such an approach and had, in fact, found such a person. His therapist viewed Dennis' problem as being largely attributable to a deficiency in particular behavioral and cognitive skills. They discussed this conceptual approach to anxiety. The therapist agreed to help Dennis identify problem areas and teach him more appropriate responses that might substitute for his current, maladaptive efforts to cope with his environment. The process of arriving at this agreement was accompanied by an obvious change in Dennis' behavior toward the therapist. He became much less defensive and dropped his annoying, superficial displays of bravado when he realized that the psychologist intended to function as a teacher, not a judge who would rule on his sanity, or a detective who might probe for long-lost secrets.

After establishing a working relationship, the first major task was to determine the situations in which Dennis was most likely to become anxious. These fell into two general classes: situations in which he had experienced panic attacks and situations in which he became tense and anxious but did not progress to a full attack. The most frequent anxiety-provoking situations were his visits to prospective clients' homes. It was interesting that he had never experienced a panic attack while in the presence of a client. One possible explanation for this phenomenon, and the one adopted by the therapist, was that Dennis was at least nominally in control of these situations and he had very well-rehearsed responses that might be used in almost any circumstance that might arise. Nevertheless, he was almost always uncomfortable during these presentations. The panic attacks had always occurred in crowded public places such as department stores and theaters and in traffic jams. These situations shared two common features. First, they were usually places that he had tried to avoid, such as the dinner theater in which his first attack occurred. Second, they were situations that he could not control; he could not make the traffic start moving, for example, and he could not make Elaine shop more quickly.

The therapist hypothesized that Dennis contributed to the onset of his own panic attacks. Presumably without awareness, he would maintain excessive muscle tension in his neck, shoulders, arms, and legs for extended periods of time while breathing in a shallow, rapid manner, thus leading to the experience of dizziness and exhaustion. Of course, when these physical sensations suddenly became apparent, Dennis did not have a ready explanation for their appearance. The emotional response of fear could therefore be seen as the inevitable product of a dramatic change in arousal that Dennis could not attribute to external stimuli. Given this hypothesis, it seemed that future panic attacks might be avoided by teaching Dennis to control, and be aware of, the muscle tension in various parts of his body and by helping him realize that he could precipitate the physical phenomena associated with a panic attack through his own muscular responses. These goals could be accomplished through a procedure known as systematic relaxation, originally developed by Jacobson (1938), in which he would be taught to relax specific muscle groups throughout his body.

Dennis' anxiety in work-related situations, on the other hand, did not seem to be the product of a deficiency in his overt response repertoire; he knew what to say and was obviously very successful at it, as judged by his outstanding sales record. The therapist's hypothesis was that Dennis' perceptions and expectations—the things that he said to himself and other people—were at the root of this area of his problem. It became clear, for example, that Dennis believed that it would be a catastrophe if someone did not like him. He also insisted to himself that he had to be the *best* salesperson in his firm. These were most likely attitudes that had been instilled in Dennis by his father, who had continually emphasized his demand for perfection and whose affection seemed to hinge on its attainment. More adaptive self-statements would have to be substituted for these irrational demands before Dennis would feel more comfortable in social situations, particularly those that involved his work.

The therapist had agreed to help Dennis learn new, adaptive responses; he decided to begin with systematic relaxation. His purpose at the outset was not to eliminate the occurrence of any more panic attacks. They were, of course, the most dramatic and perhaps the most difficult of Dennis' problems. But their infrequency also meant that even if Dennis learned to control them, he would not be able to notice any improvement in his adjustment for a very long period of time. Therefore the therapist's first goal was to select a simpler problem and an area in which Dennis could see rapid improvement, thus enhancing his motivation for further change efforts. The most suitable place to begin, therefore, was his inability to relax when he returned to his apartment after work.

Systematic relaxation was introduced to Dennis as an active coping skill that he could use to control muscular tension. Just as he had learned to be tense and anxious, he could now learn to relax. The therapist explained that he would begin by teaching Dennis how to use the procedure in the clinic setting. Dennis would then be expected to practice systematic relaxation at home on a daily basis for a period of several weeks. He was cautioned against expecting a sudden change in his anxiety level and told that, for most people, the development of relaxation skills takes considerable effort. He was also asked to purchase a small, cassette tape recorder to record the therapist's relaxation instructions. The tape would be used to guide his practice sessions at home.

Relaxation training was begun during the sixth treatment session. The lights in the room were dimmed and a small, white-noise generator was turned on to minimize the distraction from noise in the hall and waiting room. A large, comfortable reclining chair had been moved into the office for use in this exercise. The therapist began by asking Dennis to watch as he stretched out in the recliner and demonstrated the procedure, which involved the alternate tensing and relaxing of a sequence of major muscle groups. Then they exchanged places. Speaking in a low, soft voice, the therapist asked Dennis to close his eyes and move around in the chair until he could settle into a comfortable reclining position. He drew Dennis' attention to his pattern of breathing and asked him to take deep, slow breaths while imagining that he was inhaling feelings of relaxation and exhaling tension. When Dennis seemed to be comfortable, the therapist asked him to lift his forearms off the arms of the chair and tighten his hands into fists. He was instructed to hold that position for 5 seconds, noting the muscular tension, and then let go, releasing the tension and allowing his hands to slip back onto the arms of the chair. The therapist asked Dennis to study the difference between the feeling of tension that he had just experienced and the relaxation that he now enjoyed. After a 10-second pause, the therapist asked Dennis to clench his fists again, hold that position for another 5 seconds while concentrating on the sensation of muscular tension, and then relax. This cycle was then repeated through a sequence of several other groups of muscles, including his upper arms, shoulders, neck, face, back, abdomen, legs, and feet. Throughout this process, the therapist continued to remind Dennis to breath slowly and deeply. When all of the muscle groups had been completed, the therapist conducted a leisurely review, beginning with the hands and arms. Instead of tensing his muscles again, Dennis was simply asked to concentrate on each area of his body in sequence and relax away any tension that remained. This review was followed by a 30-second period in which Dennis was instructed simply to rest and enjoy the sensation of total relaxation that he had now accomplished. The therapist told Dennis that he would count backward slowly from 5 to 1 and that when he reached 1 Dennis should open his eyes and stretch, thus ending the exercise.

Dennis responded positively to relaxation training from the very beginning. He noted that he had felt awkward and self-conscious at the beginning of the procedure but had quickly overcome his apprehension. Although he did not feel that he had reached a state of complete relaxation, he did feel much more relaxed than he had when he arrived for the session; he indicated that he was looking forward to practicing the procedure during the coming week. He and the therapist then discussed the manner in which this practice would take place. The therapist asked Dennis to pick a regular time that he could set aside for the exercise, preferably the same time every day, and also a time in which he would not be so tired that he would fall asleep. Dennis decided on midmorning. He usually stayed at home to finish paperwork in the morning before going out to call on clients. His home office had a reclining chair that would be ideal for this purpose, and no one was likely to call or disturb him at that time of day. The therapist then explained a subjective rating scale that he could use to keep track of his progress. Using a 10-point scale, with 0 being complete relaxation ("similar to the quiet, drifting feeling that you have before you go to sleep") and 10 being maximum tension ("like you feel when you've already had a tough day and a potential client has just decided against buying a policy"), Dennis was asked to keep a written record of his subjective level of tension both before and after each practice session.

Dennis was very faithful in fulfilling his homework assignment. He practiced relaxation every morning except Sunday, when he had overslept and delayed the exercise until early evening. His average self-rating of tension was about 6 or 7 before practice and 3 or 4 at the end of each session. He said that he enjoyed the exercise and stated that he was pleased finally to be learning a skill with which he could cope with his tension. His outlook was clearly hopeful but not overly optimistic. The therapist expressed confidence in Dennis' ability to overcome his anxiety, noting once again that relaxation had been demonstrated to be a very effective procedure for this kind of problem and adding that Dennis' willingness to practice regularly outside of their weekly sessions was a very good prognostic sign.

The next three sessions were mostly spent discussing Dennis' progress with his relaxation training. In order to provide additional practice and iron out any small difficulties in his technique, they still took time to practice relaxation during each session. By the end of the first month of training, Dennis was consistently able to reduce his subjective tension to a level of 1 or 2 at the end of each practice session. His only problem arose in trying to use the procedure during periods of very high tension. For example, during the second week of practice, he had tried unsuccessfully to use the exercise to eliminate a severe headache that had developed in the afternoon and persisted throughout the evening. The therapist pointed out that Dennis should not be discouraged because he had not reached a stage of proficiency that would allow him to deal with the most serious levels of stress. He also noted that the object of relaxation was primarily to teach Dennis to be aware of muscular tension before it had progressed to such an advanced level. Relaxation could therefore be seen as a kind of preventive procedure, not a way of coping with problems like headaches after they became severe.

After 4 weeks, the therapist asked Dennis to try practicing relaxation without the taped instructions and without following the tension-relaxation procedure. He was asked to find a comfortable reclining position and spend 15 to 20 minutes in relaxation. Instead of alternately tensing and relaxing specific muscle groups, he was instructed simply to concentrate on breathing slowly and "letting go." His daily records showed that he was soon able to achieve a comparable level of relaxation using this simplified procedure. He also noted that he had gradually become more aware of muscle tension, particularly in the muscles of his face, neck, and shoulders, as it developed throughout the day. When he became aware of these sensations, he tried to shrug his shoulders or roll his head back and forth on his shoulders and think about relaxing the muscles that were becoming uncomfortable. It was not surprising that he also found that he was experiencing fewer and less severe headaches than he had prior to treatment.

After Dennis was making satisfactory progress with relaxation, the therapist shifted the focus of their discussions to introduce a process known as rational restructuring.[1] He began with the observation that emotions, or feelings, are influenced by what people say to themselves. In other words, it is not necessarily the objective situation with which we are confronted, but rather what we tell ourselves about that situation, that determines our emotional response. For example, a woman who is fearful when speaking in front of a large group of people is not in physical danger. It is probably what that woman is telling herself about the audience ("They'll all think that I'm stupid," or "I'm sure none of them will like me") that leads to undue levels of anxiety. The therapist provided several similar examples and explained the general principles behind rational restructuring while carefully avoiding specific reference to Dennis' own experience. By following this gradual introduction, he was able to help Dennis understand the rationale for their future discussions and get him to agree that cognitive processes may mediate inappropriate emotional responses without triggering unnecessary defensive arguments (e.g., "I don't say those things to myself!").

Once Dennis agreed to the general assumptions behind rational restructuring, the therapist outlined a number of the common irrational beliefs that have been identified by Ellis (1962). These include the notions that people have to be *perfect* in *everything* they do and that people should be *loved* by *everyone* they know. As Ellis points out, these demands are impossible. If you make your happiness contingent on their fulfillment, you will inevitably make yourself miserable. It would be nice if everyone loved us. We might feel better if they did, but it is not a *disaster* if they do not. Dennis

[1]This procedure is also referred to as rational emotive therapy by one of its principal proponents, Albert Ellis.

was intrigued by these notions and, throughout the discussion, often thought of examples of situations in which other people (such as his former wife, Mary) seemed to be making themselves unhappy by harboring such irrational beliefs. As they talked further, the therapist asked Dennis if he could think of examples in which he engaged in this kind of thinking. Initially, this was difficult. The therapist noted that we are often unaware of the irrational statements that we make to ourselves; they have been so deeply instilled and overlearned that they become essentially automatic responses. Confronted with an audience, the person with public speaking anxiety does not literally whisper, "I have to be perfect in everything I do, including public speaking, and it is imperative that they all think that I am witty and clever. If they do not, I am a miserable failure." The only subjective experience may be an immediate sensation of overwhelming fear. Nevertheless, that emotional response may be mediated by these beliefs. Furthermore, if that person could learn to make more rational statements (e.g., "I hope that I will do well and that many of the people will enjoy my talk, but if they do not, it's not the end of the world"), anxiety could be controlled.

These discussions filled the next several sessions. Much of the time was spent taking specific experiences that had been anxiety provoking for Dennis and analyzing the self-statements that might have accompanied his response. Many of these centered around contacts with clients. The applicability of the rational restructuring approach to these situations was particularly evident given the tape recording that he had made to coach himself before appointments. The therapist pointed out that Dennis had been on the right track in this attempt to cope with his anxiety but many of the statements in the tape created unrealistic, or irrational, expectations that probably exacerbated his problem. Instead of assuring himself that the client would like him because he was the best salesman in the company, Dennis would have been better able to control his anxiety if he had been able to reduce the demands that he placed on himself and recognize that the success or failure of his career did not depend on the outcome of a single client contact.

Dennis gradually became proficient in recognizing the irrational beliefs that led to his anxiety in various situations. At first, he could only dissect these situations in discussions with his therapist. The goal, of course, was to help him practice this skill until he could employ rational self-statements as a coping response before and during stressful experiences. In order to facilitate this process and provide for generalization of these new cognitive responses outside of the therapy sessions, the therapist asked Dennis to begin a kind of diary. Each night, he was to take a few minutes to write down a description of any situation in which he had become particularly anxious during the day. He was instructed to note the irrational statements that he must have been making in order to become anxious as well as complementary rational statements that would have been more appropriate. After keeping this record for 4 weeks, Dennis noted that he was beginning to be able to feel less anxious in social situations and during sales visits.

The final step in treatment was concerned with Dennis' avoidance of situations that had previously been associated with panic attacks. He had not experienced an attack in the 3 months since his first visit to the psychologist, probably because he had refused to accompany Elaine to any movies, restaurants, or department stores. He was now able to achieve a state of complete relaxation quickly and without the aid of the formal tension-relaxation procedure. The therapist therefore decided to begin a program of graduated, prolonged exposure. This would be accomplished *in vivo* (i.e., in the natural environment), by having Dennis purposefully enter situations that had previously led to feelings of apprehension and dread and then remain there until he had successfully demonstrated to himself that he would not have a panic attack. At the beginning of treatment, this procedure would have been likely to fail because Dennis did not believe that he could handle such situations. The therapist noted that he had now acquired new skills with which he would be able to cope with whatever anxiety if any, he might experience. They intentionally began with a fairly easy situation and arranged for Elaine to accompany Dennis. He indicated that her presence would make him feel less vulnerable. His assignment for the week was to go to a specific department store, during the morning on a weekday when there would not be a large crowd present, and spend 15 minutes browsing in the men's department, which was located just inside the front entrance. When this task had been successfully accomplished, Dennis and the therapist designed a hierarchy of stressful situations to which he would expose himself in sequence and for increasing amounts of time. These began with more simple situations, such as the first one at the men's department, and continued on to those that had previously been most difficult for him. The latter included activities such as attending a play for which all of the tickets had been sold and Dennis and Elaine sat in the middle of a center row (where he did not have easy access to an aisle or exit).

The treatment sessions were terminated after 6 months. Dennis had made considerable progress during that time. He had successfully mastered all of the situations in the prolonged exposure hierarchy and had not experienced a panic attack since the one that provoked his entry into treatment. His general anxiety level was also considerably reduced. He continued to experience occasional tension headaches, particularly after very busy days, but they were less frequent (perhaps two or three each month) and less severe than they had been in the past. His insomnia had disappeared completely. Whenever he did have trouble sleeping, he would utilize the formal tension-relaxation procedure. In this way he was able to eliminate muscular tension and simultaneously distract himself from whatever problems he was worrying about. Of course, he and Elaine were also getting along much better because he seldom refused to join her in social activities that he had previously avoided. Unfortunately, his gastrointestinal problems remained. He still suffered from intermittent constipation and diarrhea and continued to use medication to relieve these discomforts on an *ad hoc* basis.

DISCUSSION

DSM-III divides anxiety disorders into four major groups: phobic disorders, panic disorders, generalized anxiety disorders, and obsessive-compulsive disorders.[2] In phobic disorders, the most important element is a persistent, irrational fear of a specific object or situation that the person goes out of his or her way to avoid. Common examples are fears of small animals such as rodents, insects, and snakes, fear of social situations such as public speaking and the use of public rest rooms, and fear of small enclosed spaces such as elevators.

Agoraphobia is a special category that is defined as an exaggerated fear of being alone or in public places from which escape might be difficult. In severe cases of agoraphobia, the person becomes entirely housebound, unable to venture outside for fear of experiencing intense anxiety. Some clinicians (e.g., Hallam, 1978) have questioned the inclusion of this syndrome under the general heading of phobic disorders because it fails to meet the most specific criteria for that category. First, the stimuli that elicit fear are diffuse, not specific (i.e., *any* stimuli other than those in the person's home). Second, the criterion of avoidance may also be questionable, since many agoraphobics continue to experience panic attacks even when they remain at home. In any case, it is useful to note that there are important differences between agoraphobia and other categories of phobic disorder. In addition to being the most common form of phobia, it is the most severely debilitating because of the diffuse nature of the stimuli involved and the difficulty these patients have in avoiding the experience of very high levels of anxiety.

In *DSM-III* the criteria for panic disorders require that the patient experience "at least 3 panic attacks within a 3-week period in circumstances other than during marked physical exertion or in a life-threatening situation" (p. 231). Panic attacks are described as discrete periods of apprehen-

[2]The latter category has been defined and discussed in Chapter 1. Phobic disorders are also discussed in Chapter 16.

sion or fear, accompanied by sensations such as shortness of breath, palpitations, chest pain, choking or smothering sensations, dizziness, perspiring, and trembling or shaking. These attacks seldom last more than a few minutes.

Generalized anxiety disorders are characterized by generalized, persistent anxiety as manifested by motor tension, autonomic hyperactivity, apprehensive expectations, and an uncomfortable state of vigilance that interferes with the ability to concentrate and may lead to insomnia. *DSM-III* also requires a duration of at least 1 month for the patient to be diagnosed in this category.

Dennis exhibited aspects of several of these categories. His behavior was similar to that described in the criteria for agoraphobia in that he was apprehensive about being in public places from which escape might be difficult. On the other hand, prior to entering treatment, he had occasionally continued to force himself to enter such situatons and his fear had not actually come to dominate his life. Thus he did not specifically meet the *DSM-III* criteria for agoraphobia. Panic disorder was another possible diagnosis, but he had never experienced three attacks within a 3-week period. The most appropriate diagnosis was therefore generalized anxiety disorder. His motor tension was clearly evidenced by his inability to relax, his frequent tension headaches, and the constant fatigue from which he suffered. Autonomic hyperactivity was obvious during his panic attacks, when he broke out into a cold sweat and experienced palpitations, dry mouth, and dizziness. His irregular bowel movements and diarrhea were further signs of autonomic difficulties. He experienced continual apprehension and frequently had difficulty sleeping.

Generalized anxiety disorder, which was formerly know as anxiety neurosis in *DSM-II*, is a relatively common problem. The most commonly cited estimate of the prevalence of anxiety neurosis is 5% of the population (e.g. Greer, 1969), but some recent data suggest that the actual figure may be higher (Noyes et al., 1980). The generally accepted age of risk for the onset of anxiety disorders ranges from the midteens to the early thirties, with the average patient experiencing symptoms for about 5 years before entering treatment (Marks and Lader, 1973). Panic attacks may vary in frequency. Some patients, like Dennis, experience only one or two attacks a year, while others may have them on a daily basis. Because of the dramatic physiological symptoms that may accompany these attacks, many patients seek medical attention from cardiovascular and gastrointestinal specialists before being referred to a psychologist or a psychiatrist. Irritable colon is frequently associated with anxiety disorders (Liss et al., 1973), but the relation to other psychosomatic disorders is unclear. One study has reported an increased prevalence of hypertension and peptic ulcer among anxiety neurotics (Noyes et al., 1980), while another study failed to find a relationship (Wheeler et al., 1950). Although these patients experience considerable subjective distress, their anxiety is seldom associated with serious occupational or social impairment. The prognostic picture is generally favorable. One study, for example, conducted 6-year follow-up interviews with 112 patients, most of whom had been treated with either medication or a combination of medication and psychotherapy. Sixty-eight percent were completely recovered or only mildly impaired (Noyes et al., 1980).

Depression and drug abuse are frequently associated with chronic anxiety disorders. In the study reported by Noyes and his colleagues (1980), 44% of the patients reported episodes of secondary depression.[3] Alcoholism and barbiturate abuse are common results of attempts to use drugs to cope with chronic tension. In fact, some patients become addicted to minor tranquilizers such as Valium that have been prescribed by well-intentioned physicians. Fortunately, Dennis did not become dependent on the use of medication. Although Valium did make him feel more relaxed, he resisted its use because it made him feel even less in control of his own emotions.

THEORETICAL PERSPECTIVES AND TREATMENT IMPLICATIONS

A psychoanalytically oriented therapist would have viewed Dennis' chronic anxiety as a symptom of unconscious conflict between the ego and previously punished id impulses. These impulses are usually presumed to be sexual or aggressive in nature and traceable to early childhood experiences. In an effort to avoid their imminent expression, which is signaled by the subjective experience of anxiety, the ego employs the defense mechanism know as repression. This theoretical position is so general that it could be applied to almost any case. It might have been argued, for example, that Dennis secretly harbored violent impulses toward his father, who criticized and belittled him. Since he was also afraid of his father (a classic assumption of psychoanalytic theory) and since he would be punished if he harmed his father, these impulses were anxiety provoking and therefore repressed. But when he entered situations in which he might be evaluated by other people, he was reminded of his father's criticism. The hostile impulses then became more intense, and his anxiety would increase proportionately. Alternatively, one might have argued that Dennis had not gotten over his sexual desire for his mother (another classic assumption) and that he was currently troubled by unconscious impulses to perform incestuous sexual acts. There was, however, no clear evidence to support either of these notions. Dennis

[3]Affective disorders are considered *secondary* when they appear in individuals who have previously experienced other forms of abnormal behavior.

did not hide his resentment of his father. They argued openly and frequently about every imaginable topic. Nor was there any evidence of sexual problems. Dennis and Elaine had intercourse regularly, and both were satisfied with this aspect of their relationship.

The conditioning model (e.g., Miller, 1948; Mowrer, 1947) would view Dennis' problem as a fear response that had been learned through the association of previously neutral stimuli (e.g., a crowded theater) with a painful or frightening stimulus. Once Dennis had learned to fear particular situations, his avoidance of them would presumably be reinforced by the reduction in anxiety that he experienced after he fled. There are a number of problems with this model (e.g., Costello, 1970; Seligman, 1971). One is that very few patients with anxiety disorders can remember having experienced a traumatic event (Solyom et al., 1974). In Dennis' case, his first panic attack was certainly a terrifying experience, and the fear that he experienced may have become paired with the stimuli that were present when it occurred. This process might account for the maintenance of his tendency to avoid crowded public places, but it does not explain the original onset of his intense fear.

Another problem with the conditioning model is that it has trouble accounting for diffuse or global anxiety. It has more intuitive appeal in the case of very specific phobias, such as fear of spiders. Although Dennis' anxiety was worse in some situations than in others, it would be difficult to argue that his fears were associated with a particular set of stimuli in the sense that the latter term is used in laboratory experiments. If the fear that he experienced in panic attacks became associated with whatever stimuli were present when they occurred, why did he not learn to fear automobiles after the attack that he experienced in a traffic jam? What were the critical stimuli that prompted his strange behavior in the clinic waiting room (it was not particularly crowded when he suddenly put his arm around the therapist)? The conditioning principle of stimulus generalization might be invoked to explain the extension of his fears to a broad range of stimuli, but the analogy between the natural environment and laboratory experiments seems strained in this regard.

The therapist who treated Dennis adopted a cognitive approach to the problem. He hypothesized that Dennis' perceptions of social events and the things that he said to himself about these events played an important role in the maintenance of his anxiety. This cognitive view of maladaptive emotional responses can be traced to the views of ego analysts, such as Horney (1950), whose modified psychoanalytic perspective emphasized the conscious mental processes of the ego and the importance of the person's current environment. Following the approach developed by Ellis (1962) and subsequently modified by Goldfried (Goldfried, Decenteceo, and Weinberg, 1974), the therapist helped Dennis recognize the general kinds of self-statements that were associated with his anxiety and then modeled more appropriate statements that he would be able to use to cope more effectively with stressful situations. The latter component of the process is particularly important. In addition to helping Dennis gain "insight" into his problem, the therapist taught him specific cognitive skills (adaptive self-statements) that had previously been absent from his repertoire of coping responses. If insight had been sufficient, Dennis would have experienced a decline in his anxiety level as soon as he recognized that he clung to several of Ellis' irrational beliefs, but he did not. Positive change was only evident after a prolonged period of practice in employing rational self-statements, both in and out of therapy sessions.

It should also be noted that the therapist did not rely solely on the cognitive form of intervention. In addition to talking with Dennis about his problem, the therapist helped him learn specific behavioral responses (e.g., systematic relaxation) and insisted that he confront various situations in the natural environment. This approach was founded on the realization that although cognitive variables may play an important role in the change process, the most effective treatment programs are performance based. Bandura (1977) has proposed a theory of behavioral change that accounts for this phenomenon. According to this theory, behavioral change is mediated by changes in a hypothetical construct that Bandura calls *self-efficacy*—the conviction that one is capable of successfully performing whatever responses are necessary to accomplish a designated goal. Perceived self-efficacy presumably reduces anticipatory fears of the kind that Dennis experienced in social situations and also influences the amount of effort that will be expended in attempts to cope with stressful events. High self-efficacy is associated with increased activity and persistence. Bandura argues that efficacy expectations can be affected by a variety of factors, including performance accomplishments, vicarious experience, and verbal persuasion and that the most effective process is performance accomplishment. This was clear in Dennis' case. His apprehension in crowded public places was not significantly reduced until he had actually mastered a series of such situations in the prolonged exposure procedure.

3

HYPERTENSION

John Williams had been complaining to his wife of dizziness, fatigue, and occasional light-headedness that almost caused him to faint one day at the water-cooler in the law office he worked in downtown. His boss had been after him for weeks to see a doctor, but John had stubbornly refused. He felt angry and frightened when suggestions were made that he see a physician—angry because he interpreted the suggestion as condescending on his boss's part, and frightened because he had an ineffable feeling that all was not right with him physically.

He was correct about the latter. His first clear knowledge of having hypertension, or high blood pressure, came during a visit to his dentist. Before taking x-rays of his mouth, the dental assistant, as had become routine in the office, wound the black blood pressure cuff around John's right arm, pumped it full of air until the blood stopped flowing, and then slowly released the valve, noting when the first sounds of the pulse could be heard through the stethoscope pressed to the vein in his arm below the cuff. Alarmed at the reading—145/94—she took the pressure reading again after doing the x-rays and found it to be almost exactly the same. She tried to smile pleasantly and reassuringly to the powerfully built patient waiting for his teeth to be cleaned, but she found it hard to do, especially when she noticed a worried expression on his face.

He did not ask about the blood pressure reading until he was sitting across from the dentist's desk in the consulting room to discuss treatment plans. How have you been feeling lately, John was asked by the dentist he had known for the past 10 years. Have you been feeling tired, irritable? Any headaches? How has the work been going? John searched the man's face for some hint of what was going on, but he already sensed that he had high blood pressure. Finally, he just asked for the numbers and what they meant, thanked the dentist, and went home.

It took him 30 minutes to reach his condominium in the suburbs. As he turned the key, he wondered how, or whether, he would raise the issue with his wife. Although not a physician himself, he knew what the kind of high blood pressure he seemed to have might mean to a 40-year-old like himself, especially someone who was so driven to succeed professionally and financially. Certainly he would have to slow down, and perhaps also take some medication. But what else, he wondered.

SOCIAL HISTORY

John Williams was the only child of a well-to-do black family in Atlanta. Born in 1939, he grew up in an upper-middle-class environment. His father was a successful attorney, and his mother was a music teacher in one of the local high schools. Life was sweet in his childhood, as John recalled during one of his therapy sessions with a clinical psychologist. There were many friends in the neighborhood; even though they were all black in the segregated part of the city that was his home, he seldom had the feeling of being excluded from anything important. More fortunate than most blacks, whether in the South or the North, John knew no material wants and was taught during countless dinnertime conversations that there was plenty of success available to a black youngster like him; he had superior intelligence, an engaging wit, and a degree of ambitiousness that matched that of his hard-working father.

In high school John excelled at everything he attempted. A straight "A" student, he was also a varsity athlete in three sports, dated the young women generally regarded to be the most desirable by his chums and, in his senior year, was elected president of his class. This was the middle 1950s, well before the civil rights struggles and other social activist movements that led to some major legal and social changes in the country, especially in the South. The idea of leaving Georgia for college was tempting, but it created as much anxiety in John's mother as it occasioned anticipatory pride in his father. Mr. Williams wanted his son to have a college education with "class," as he put it. To be sure, there were first-rate black colleges that he would apply to, such as Howard University in Washington, D.C.; however, with the encouragement of his guidance counselor and the urging of his father, John also applied to several Ivy League schools. The excitement was considerable in April when the acceptance from Harvard arrived in the mail.

Even though Harvard was located in the "liberal" Northeast, racial discrimination had to be considered. Years later, John told the therapist, a white man with whom he had roomed confided to John that 1 month before school was to begin their freshman year, he had received a letter from the housing office indicating that they would like to have him room with a black student, but that this assignment would be made only if the student had no objection. The student, a Jew from Brooklyn, New York, was outraged because he immediately and automatically empathized with the discrimination and prejudice that lay behind a seemingly genteel and considerate inquiry. This incident, and others throughout the 4 years of friendship between the two young men, was a prototype for many discussions they would have about the pressures on members of minority groups who elected to try "to make it" in society, especially in the elite circles of a private, selective college.

John knew what a "house nigger" was, but it took the handwritten invitation slipped under his door one night to teach him about what he and Matt, his roommate, would call a "club nigger." Fraternities existed at Harvard, but they differed from their Greek-letter counterparts on other campuses in that they were not residential. All undergraduates were affiliated with a house, modeled after the "colleges" of Oxford and Cambridge, in which they lived and took all their meals. The clubs operated outside the house system and were very much by invitation only; some of them bore names of winged and sharp-toothed animals such as bats and wolves, others the more familiar-sounding Greek initials. It seemed to John that his being black, or Negro, as he called himself then, would exclude him from these clubs, although he hated himself for even thinking about it. Thinking, he would tell himself, implied that he cared, and to care about the clubs was to accord them a legitimacy and importance he desperately resisted giving them. As he stopped to pick up the engraved envelope, he could feel the blood pound in his ears, his heart beat irregularly, and his breath come in short gasps.

When he looked back on things, this single moment crystallized much of the conflict John felt about his blackness in a white world. He and his race had come far from the days a fair-skinned youngster might hope to "pass" for white. As light as John's complexion was, and as little curliness was to be found in his hair—there was more than one white slave owner in his ancestry—he had grown up proud of the fact that he was black and feeling that whatever barriers there might be in "making it" were of lesser import than his self-respect and pride. But still, as he lingered over breakfast coffee with Matt the morning of the invitation, wasn't it "a gas" that one of the more prestigious clubs wanted him as a member?

Not that he got any encouragement from Matt, who viewed his own candidacy for this sort of thing as unlikely an event as John had considered his own. Matt had an uneasy feeling about it all, but he kept it to himself, wondering, for one thing, whether it was just not sour grapes on his own part that this black man was sought after when he, a Caucasian, was not.

John agonized all day over whether to attend the punch for newly solicited members. He was tempted to phone his parents, but what would he tell them, and how? Was there something to celebrate? Would his father smile quietly to himself as he heard the news, confirming his own good judgment in sending his son to one of the bastions of Eastern elitism? Surely John was going to succeed—and in the white world, no less. In the end, John did not phone; he feared at one and the same time that his father would either congratulate him on the invitation or chide him for even considering it. No way to win on that score, he told himself. At some level he knew that it was his own conflict he was wrestling with, not his father's reaction.

The day of his initiation, John awoke with a screaming headache, felt dizzy, and was aware of a tension building inside his skull, almost as if his brain were about to burst from his cranium. He took three aspirin—a habit he had gotten into since coming to college—and told himself to stop worrying about the party that evening. Perhaps he need not have worried. The welcome he received seemed genuine. And yet he could not shake the feeling that his new "brothers" were being nicer to him than they were to the other initiates, too nice somehow. His wine glass was never empty, always kept filled by a brother who, it struck John, smiled a bit too ingratiatingly. In fact, it seemed to him that his new friends must have suffered from aching mouths, so broadly did they smile whenever they talked to him. He tried to reassure himself that the cordiality was real, and maybe it was. The problem, he knew, was that he did not really know, nor could he devise a practical way to find out.

His membership in the club turned out to be a boon to his social standing but an emotional disaster. His headaches and feelings of pressure in the brain were more regularly part of his existence than ever before. He hated himself for even being in the club, yet he prided himself on being the only black member. He was furious at the fact that so few Jews were in the club and was also suspicious that there were no other Blacks, but he found these young men congenial and enjoyable to spend time with and he did experience a thrill whenever he donned the club necktie. His friends were certainly no less bright than his other classmates, no less interested in abstract ideas and "deep" conversations over sherry after dinner. But the clubs were by nature exclusionary, and John was coming to realize that his race was excluded from the white power structure and that he might be seen as the quintessential Uncle Tom for being a member.

His anger at himself and at his brothers grew to an intensity that was frightening. To Matt, in whom he confided his doubts, fears, guilt, and rage, John seemed a tragic figure. There was no way for him to win. To express his concerns to his club brothers seemed out of the question. But not to do so, at least to one of them, had begun to make the thought of going to the handsome Georgian building for the evening a challenge, almost a dare. He dreaded the possibility of someone making a racist remark. How should he react? He had learned, since coming North, to let it pass, but the muscle tension that mounted in his body told him this was not the best thing for him to do. Once a club member used the word "niggardly," and he felt himself blush. How infantile to react that way, he told himself. And yet, maybe the word was used to taunt him. But how inane to think that. Sure, Uncle Tom, he concluded.

The 4 years of college passed quickly. As his family and friends expected, John did very well academically and also managed to earn a varsity letter in baseball. His admission to a first-rate law school was a foregone conclusion, although John's problem by this time was his uncertainty as to whether he had been admitted solely on his academic merits or whether the several prestigious schools, like the club, wanted him primarily for his color. And so the conflicts continued through law school. By this time they took the form of John having to excel to what even his ambitious father regarded to be an unreasonable degree. John just had to prove he was good, indeed, that he was the best.

John became engaged to a lovely young woman from a prominent black family, but the joys of the relationship were dulled by his constant driving for excellence and perfection. One major change was that his problems with hypertension were now impossible to hide; she insisted that he have a complete physical examination, something he had consciously avoided since entering college. The reading was 130/85, something the doctor called "high normal," sufficient in magnitude to be worrisome in a young man. His fiancée was convinced that John's unrelenting pursuit of straight "A's," law review, and all the rest were at fault. But she knew little as yet about the reasons that lay behind this near-obsessive push.

John graduated at the top of his class. It was now the middle 1960s, and the developing social turmoil surrounding Vietnam and the civil rights movement seemed to affect him deeply. On the one hand, he felt that he should be out on the barricades, but his studies and his new job at a top law firm took precedence. He tried to assuage his guilt by donations to some of the black civil rights groups, but it did not seem to help. He had cast his lot with the white world, he told himself, and his wife and his own family back in Atlanta supported that decision. Middle-and upper-middle-class professional Blacks had their role to play, his father continually reminded him, and who was better to play that role than John Williams? The sense he had that it was, indeed, a *role*, turned out to be important in the psychotherapy he began some weeks after the alarmingly high blood pressure reading in the dentist's office.

CONCEPTUALIZATION AND TREATMENT

The choice of a therapist is never an easy matter. For John it presented special difficulties. He lived near a metropolitan area, but there were few black psychiatrists or psychologists. As he had grown accustomed to doing in most other areas of his life, John decided to work with a white person, in this instance in a very special relationship. He was uncertain whether he could relate openly to a white. His only really close white friend was his old college roommate, Matt, and even then he recalled holding back on the expression of thoughts and emotions having to do with race. Would this same problem arise in a therapeutic relationship? In fact, was race even an issue?

"Well, what do you really want out of life?" asked Dr. Shaw, a distinguished and experienced clinical psychologist. "The same thing everyone else is after," was his reply. "But what is that?" queried the psychologist.

The first couple of sessions were like this: Dr. Shaw trying to get John to examine what he really wanted, and John sparring with him, fending off the probes with generalities about "all other people." In Shaw's mind, John Williams did not want to confront the conflicts of playing a role in the white professional world. He identified with being black, Shaw believed, but he sensed a falseness about his life. Racial slurs went uncommented on. He took pride in the fact that his wife wore her hair straight but, at the same time, castigated himself for feeling this way. He hid from his law office colleagues the fact that he was a member of several civil rights groups and that he considered Martin Luther King somewhat too moderate. But what was *he* doing about it? King and others risked personal safety in freedom marches, but John was terrified of being seen in one. What would the people in the firm think of him? Would they want a "radical" in the office?

Dr. Shaw thought to himself during these early sessions that he should pressure his client more, but he realized he was holding back in a way he would not do with a white client. Was it his right to suggest to John that he was at the same time proud and ashamed of his blackness, that he despised himself for hiding his feelings? Indeed, was it his duty? But how could Shaw be certain, and wouldn't it be terrible if he intimated something to John that was off base? But that, too, was something he worried far less about with his white clients. No therapist is infallible. Yet somehow he felt that with John he had to be more certain about his interpretations.

Dr. Shaw routinely referred clients with medical or psychophysiological problems to an internist. This doctor prescribed some antihypertensive medication for John, to be taken daily. But the physician's hope was that this relatively young patient not come to rely on the drug. In an extended consultation, Shaw and his medical colleague agreed that John's high-pressure life-style was a major factor. What they could not agree on was what role the man's race played. Absence of similar problems in John's family going back three generations did not support the assumption that the patient had inherited a predisposition for hypertension, although the two men agreed at the same time that, for whatever reason, John's particular response to stress was hypertension, more specifically essential hypertension, since physical causes had been ruled out through a complete medical workup.

A crisis took place in the fifth and final session. For months afterward Dr. Shaw wondered whether he had blundered so badly that his client was driven from therapy.

Dr. Shaw: John, I've been wondering about what you've told me about your college days.

John (a bit suspiciously): What aspect of them?

Dr. Shaw: Well, I guess I was thinking about the club. (Shaw noted to himself that he seldom said "I guess" in such circumstances. Stop pussyfooting, he told himself.)

John (feeling his ears becoming warm): Well, what about the club?

Dr. Shaw: Your feelings of being the only Black.

John: Well, I felt really good about it. I used to daydream about what my high school chums would think.

Dr. Shaw: And what would they have thought?

John: They'd have envied me to the utmost. I mean, I must be doing something right to get into one of the Greeks.

Dr. Shaw: Yes, I know you were quite proud about it. . . . But I wonder if you had any other feelings about it.

John (definitely on edge, wary): What do you mean?

Dr. Shaw: Well, lots of times people are conflicted about things that are important to them. Like the nervous bridegroom on the wedding day. He's eager for the honeymoon, but he knows he's giving up something.

John: What do you think I was giving up?

Dr. Shaw: You feel you were giving up something by being in the club?

John: Come on, Doc, don't play games. You know damn well that *you* think I gave up something. What did I give up?

Dr. Shaw: John, if anything was given up, it was you who gave it up, not I. (That sounded too harsh, he told himself immediately, but maybe it was time to get a little rough with him. Otherwise he may never move.)

John: I resent what you're implying.

Dr. Shaw: Okay, but can you explore it, just hypothetically?

John (suspicion mounting, almost a feeling of panic setting in): Okay Shaw, let me think of what I gave up.

(At this point there was a lengthy silence. John stared at his feet, Dr. Shaw at his notes, occasionally glancing up at John but not wanting to look at him too much. John began to dwell on the thoughts he had never shared with anyone, not even with his roommate, Matt. Oreo cookie, he called himself, black on the outside and white on the inside. Who needs the damned club? If they were serious about being democratic, I would not be the only Black. Just me, and oh, that Chinese kid, whose family just happened to own half of Hong Kong. Yuh, David and me, the two typical minority members. And they can congratulate themselves for being so damned liberal. And I can congratulate myself for making it in the door. But how would they have reacted if I had dated a white girl? Or worn my hair in an Afro? And put on a dashiki? Ha! How do you wear a club tie with a dashiki? Even the one overt sign of club membership conflicts with a dashiki! What am I doing with these mothers? How hypocritical can I be?)

Dr. Shaw: John, can you share some of your thoughts with me?

John: Doc, I can't do it. You're one of them.

Dr. Shaw: One of whom?

John: Doc, I can't talk to a white man about this. I can't talk to a black man about this. I'm too ashamed, too mixed up. (Beginning to sob.) I can't handle this.

Dr. Shaw: This is hard for you, I know, John. But this is a place you can use to look at those feelings. Try to sort them out. Try to figure out what you really want. . . .

John (interrupting the psychologist): No! It's not for you to tell me what I should be doing. *I'm* the one who has to decide.

(Long silence again.)

Dr. Shaw: John?

(John just stares at his feet, jaws clenched, that familiar tightness in his head. My blood pressure must be soaring, he told himself. I can't handle this. If I'm not careful I'll be a psychological success, but I'll die from a stroke. No, that's an exaggeration. Or is it? I'm bullshitting myself so much that I don't even know what I want, or think, or feel. . . .)

Dr. Shaw: John, perhaps that's enough for today.

John (relieved): Yes, that's right. That's enough . . . for today.

Dr. Shaw: See you next week, same time.

John (knowing he would break the appointment and never return): Yuh. Thanks. I'll see you next week.

DISCUSSION

It has been know for thousands of years that mental and emotional states can affect the functioning of the body. Anxiety in particular is of interest to psychopathologists in their study of psychophysiological disorders because the autonomic nervous system is markedly affected by stress. When a person is under strain, there are numerous autonomic changes, such as increases in heart rate and in blood pressure; these changes are usually temporary, diminishing when the stressor is removed. But in some individuals the changes persist; when this happens over a long period of time, a psychophysiological disorder can result.

Perhaps you have heard the expression "Oh, don't worry about that. It's only in your mind." A person suffering from asthma that has some psychogenic components is often seen as someone of weak will or someone with a physical malady that is somehow not genuine. To believe this is to overlook the simple and important fact that many medical illnesses are caused in part by psychological factors. A disease such as hypertension can be life-threatening even when a person's emotions seem to be playing a major role in causing the sustained high blood pressure.

The classic psychophysiological disorders are grouped in terms of the organ system affected. Some of the major ones follow (Davison and Neale, 1982).

1. *Skin Disorders.* Neurodermatitis and hyperhydrosis (dry skin).
2. *Respiratory Disorders.* Bronchial asthma, hyperventilation (breathing very rapidly, often leading to fainting).
3. *Cardiovascular Disorders.* Migraine headache and high blood pressure (hypertension).
4. *Gastrointestinal Disorders.* Peptic ulcers, ulcerative colitis, heartburn.

Psychophysiological disorders are common in highly industrialized societies. One survey (Schwab, Fennel, and Warheit, 1974) found that over 40% of Americans had headaches during the previous year and over 50% had gastrointestinal symptoms such as constipation and diarrhea. More and more the contributions of psychological factors are being recognized in bodily illnesses, to the extent that in *DSM-III* a judgment about them is made on Axis I with the diagnosis, Psychological Factors Influencing Physical Condition. If, for example, a person is suffering from profound depression, the diagnostician must also decide whether psychological factors are affecting the person's health. If so, the judgment is recorded on Axis I and the physical condition itself on Axis III.

Before we turn to hypertension, let us review briefly the major types of theories that have been advanced about psychophysiological disorders in general. Three basic questions must be addressed in any attempt to understand these problems: (1) Why do only some people exposed to stress develop psychophysiological disorders? (2) Why does stress not always produce a psychophysiological disorder? (3) Given that stress does produce such a disorder, what determines which of them will arise? As with other psychopathologies, both physiological and psychological theories have been proposed.

PHYSIOLOGICAL THEORIES

The somatic weakness theory states that a particular organ—for genetic reasons or because of poor diet or earlier illnesses—can be weak and thus vulnerable to stress. For example, a congenitally weak respiratory system might predispose a person to developing asthma under stress.

According to the specific-reaction theory, people are genetically predisposed to react to stress with overreactions in particular autonomic systems. Thus one person has elevated blood pressure when stressed and another secretes an excess of stomach acid under similar circumstances. The first individual would be a candidate for hypertension, the second person for ulcers.

A third kind of physiological theory is couched in terms of evolution. Over millions of years, we have developed autonomic nervous systems that equip us to respond to danger with either fight or flight. In either event, the healthy body prepares itself by increasing the rate of breathing, diverting blood into the muscles, releasing sugar into the bloodstream, and the like. When the danger has passed, this burst of sympathetic nervous system activity subsides. Humankind has developed the dubious distinction, however, of being able to respond in this way to *psychological* dangers, not just to the life-threatening challenges that beset other animals. Indeed, we are able to stir up our autonomic nervous systems by our very thoughts and imaginings, thereby maintaining our bodies in a state of hyperarousal. It is as if we are runners for a 100-yard dash, crouched at the starting line, and tensely ready for the signal to "go!" Only no signal comes, and we just stay there, expectant and highly aroused.

PSYCHOLOGICAL THEORIES

Psychoanalysts have for many years viewed psychophysiological disorders as symbolic manifestations of unresolved repressed conflicts. Franz Alexander (1950), for example, proposed that an ulcer can be formed if a person has repressed a childhood longing for unfulfilled parental love; the stomach, as it were, is continually preparing itself for food, equated symbolically with love. Analytic interpretations of hypertension implicate undischarged hostile impulses. Controlled research fails to support this notion (Mann, 1977), although John Williams seemed to fit the pattern.

The specific-attitudes theory proposes that particular attitudes cause one or another psychophysiological disorder. For example, asthma sufferers are believed to prefer ignoring difficult situations instead of dealing with them directly. Hypertensives are said to be constantly vigilant to danger, again reminding us of John (Grace and Graham, 1952).

There are also hypotheses that implicate classical and operant conditioning. A person who is allergic to pollen may associate the reaction to a neutral stimulus, such as another individual, and subsequently react to that person with the same wheezing and breathing difficulty that occurs to pollen.

None of these theories enjoys unequivocal support; some views, such as the psychoanalytic one, are difficult to test at all. It would seem that a multifactorial point of view should be adopted in attempting to understand these puzzling disorders. Investigators will have to consider both physical diatheses, or predispositions, and highly specific psychological ways of reacting to stress. Thus Jane Doe might have a genetically determined tendency to react to emotional situations with elevated blood pressure and thus be at risk for hypertension; however, she will not develop this disorder if her life does not contain a certain amount of stress. Furthermore, the way she construes an event as stressful will be a function of her psychology; failing a test, for instance, might be something she has learned to disregard as threatening, while a cross look from her boyfriend is a catastrophe. John Doe, on the other hand, might have a constitution that is fortunately not disposed to react in any abnormal way to stress; that is, his blood pressure declines rapidly once a stressor is removed. But his psychology might have him construe as very threatening an event such as failing an examination. He will therefore end up with some sort of emotional disorder, such as an anxiety disorder, *but* his organ systems will not be affected as seriously as they might be if he were predisposed as Jane is. The outcome will be that John will not develop a psychophysiological disorder but, instead, another kind of emotional problem.

ESSENTIAL HYPERTENSION

We are now ready to consider what is known or hypothesized about the problem from which John Williams suffers. High blood pressure is estimated to be involved in a great many deaths in the United States each year, and the problem is showing up in younger and younger age groups. Everyone has blood pressure, of course, because the heart pumps the blood throughout the body under pressure. If it remains at an elevated level—readings of 140/90 and above are regarded as abnormally high—a strain is placed on the cardiovascular system and, over a period of years, there is an increased risk of stroke or heart attack.

It is believed that as much as 33% of the adult population of this country has high blood pressure; of these, as few as 10 percent have the problem because of a physical cause, such as kidney dysfunction (Benson, 1975). Thus millions of people go about their daily lives with chronically elevated blood pressure that is attributable to causes other than bodily defects. It is widely assumed that the nonorganic causes of what is termed essential hypertension are to be understood in psychological terms.

High blood pressure is known as "the silent killer" because (1) it is very dangerous to one's physical health, and (2) it can be present for years without the person knowing it unless a blood pressure reading is taken. Symptoms do develop, however, as we saw in John Williams' case: fatigue, nervousness, dizziness, heart palpitations, headaches and, for some people, even a feeling of pressure in the head.

We know from various research studies that stress increases blood pressure in the short term. Kasl and Cobb (1970), for example, found that people who knew that their jobs were to be terminated in 2 months had higher blood pressure during that period as well as 2 years following the loss of the job than control subjects whose employment remained constant. More directly relevant to John Williams is research by Hokanson and his colleagues (Hokanson and Burgess, 1962; Stone and Hokanson, 1969). In a laboratory setting subjects were given a task but were then made angry by a confederate of the experimenter. Fifty percent of the subjects were given the opportunity to retaliate against their harasser, but the others were not. Results showed that being harrassed in this way raised blood pressure, which is not surprising. Of greater interest was the fact that subjects who could take retaliatory action against the source of their frustration showed larger decreases in their elevated blood pressure than did control subjects who were denied that opportunity. Applying these analogue findings to John Williams, we can hypothesize that his habit of inhibiting anger and resentment at white people played a role in the development of his high blood pressure. An additional finding of Hokanson, however, provides an even more important possibility. Considering only the subjects who retaliated, blood pressure decreases were found only when they aggressed against a fellow college student, not when their harrasser was presented to them as a visiting professor. Expressing resentment and anger to a high-status source of frustration, then, did not reduce blood pressure. In John's case, if he *had* asserted himself more, this might not have helped him *if* he perceived the people angering him as higher in status than himself. This is where issues of black versus white enter, since the therapist would have had to discuss with John his underlying feelings about white people: whether he regarded them as superior and so forth. One can appreciate how much more subtle and complex things become when moving from the laboratory study to a real-life case.

Any consideration of autonomic arousal and stress should include the concept of learned helplessness. It has been recognized for some time that lack of control over unpleasant events can cause stress for both humans and nonhuman animals. Psychoanalytic theory holds that the core of psychopathology is the ego's terrible fear of being overwhelmed by id impulses. This theme is also to be found in behavioral theory and research. One of the earliest, and classic, experiments was done by Mowrer and Viek (1948), who trained rats to obtain food by performing an operant response. The rats were then shocked while being fed. Fifty percent of them were able to learn a response such as jumping that would terminate the shock; the other 50% gained no control over the aversive stimulation. Both groups of rats received the same amount of shock, but the rats who had acquired control over the unpleasant stimuli exhibited less fear. Since that first study, hundreds of similar experiments with both animals and humans have confirmed that control over events, especially negative ones, reduces anxiety and, conversely, that lack of control increases anxiety. For humans, that lack of control need not even be real; that is, it seems sufficient that the person only *believe* he or she lacks control (Geer, Davison, and Gatchel, 1970).

Some confirmatory data are closer to actual life circumstances. It is widely known that black Americans as a group have an especially high incidence of hypertension. Is there a racial basis to this? Probably not. The causes are to be found in social factors. Harburg et al. (1973) studied two areas of Detroit; one was a poor neighborhood with high crime rates, much crowding, and many marital breakups; the other was a middle-class neighborhood. In both, black and white married men had their blood pressure taken several times in their homes, and they were also given a test that posed stressful situations to them and asked how they would respond. One test item, for example, had them imagine that they were seeking a place to rent and that the landlord refused them because of their race or religion. The response categories were: "(1) I'd get angry or mad and show it, (2) I'd get annoyed and show it, (3) I'd get annoyed, but would keep it in, (4) I'd get angry or mad but would keep it in, (5) I wouldn't feel angry or annoyed" (p. 280).

Results showed that blood pressure was higher among Blacks than among whites. But Blacks living in the poor neighborhood had higher blood pressure than Blacks living in the middle-class area. Thus, while race was one factor, of equal importance was social class and the accompanying stress that comes with living in marginal circumstances. It would seem that the high blood pressure among Blacks has a great deal to do with the socially created stress under which they live. In the case of John Williams, stress was not socioeconomic but, like many people, he "succeeded" in increasing his life pressures by his constant striving for perfection, over and above the pressure probably created by the prejudice encountered in his frequent contacts with whites. His blood pressure was apparently increased as well by the tremendous conflicts he experienced as a black man who was false to himself, who compromised his beliefs and his ideals in order to succeed in white society.

Remember that the studies discussed so far have at least two major limitations. First, in no instance was true high blood pressure created, only temporary increases in blood pressure. Second, most of the research was analogue in nature; that is, the situations studied were different from real life. We must always be mindful when we are extrapolating from "make-believe" to the real world. What we learn from laboratory studies provides fruitful leads and a way of thinking about problems, but things are still far from proven.

Going back to our general discussion of theories of psychophysiological disorders, we suggested that a diathesis-stress view was the best one to employ. John Williams' life was full of emotionally stressful events. But it was a psychophysiological disorder that he developed, not any of the many other problems that people under duress are subject to, such as schizophrenia, affective disorders, or anxiety disorders. Furthermore, given that it was a psychophysiological problem, he had essential hypertension, not asthma, hives, or any of the other such disorders. Did he have a somatic weakness in his cardiovascular system, or was his system somehow predisposed to overreact to stress, as in the specific-reaction theory? We do not know in John's case. Evidence that should lead us to consider the possibility—although it is unclear what the treatment implications would be—is in research such as a study by Hodapp, Weyer, and Becker (1975). The blood pressure of hypertensives and normals was measured while resting, while viewing slides of landscapes, and while performing a demanding intellectual task (the stressor). All subjects showed blood pressure increases during the stress, but hypertensives maintained that increase even when the stressor was removed. It is as though some people's cardiovascular system is preset to be elevated and to maintain that elevation once it is stressed. Of course, this study and others like it cannot demonstrate a cause-effect relationship because the hypertensive patients were, in fact, already hypertensive! Hence, their particular way of responding might have been a consequence rather than a cause of the hypertension.

ISSUES OF RACE AND PSYCHOTHERAPY

Mention has already been made of how being black might contribute to high blood pressure. John Williams' race also played a role in the therapy he terminated prematurely. Recent reviews of the psychotherapy literature involving Blacks (e.g., Gardner, 1971; Jackson, 1973) reveal scant attention to the issues of Blacks and other minorities who seek help from mental health professionals. Regrettably, stereotyped thinking abounds, linking racial membership per se with negative traits such as superficiality, magical thinking, apathy, rejection of education, and undue hedonism (Kardiner and Ovesey, 1951). Not adequately appreciated are the social conditions under which Blacks have been living in this country as well as the sometimes subtle, unconscious biases existing in the primarily white investigators who offer the generalizations (Gardner, 1971).

Complicating the matter still further is the difficulty a white therapist can experience with a Black client. It is said that racism entails not only negative stereotypes (e.g., all Blacks are sexually promiscuous) but also positive ones (e.g., that Joe Louis was certainly a great fighter; Blacks have a natural talent for athletics that I envy). The therapist has no easy task to get past these prejudgments, or prejudices, to look at the Black client as he or she would regard a white client, to consider the person's psychological difficulties in useful ways, placing race in a context that will promote a fruitful assessment and intervention instead of impeding one.

These issues are to be seen in the case of John Williams. Should the therapist have encouraged a more assertive (would we call it "militant" because he is black?) stance towards the prejudices that seemed to be oppressing him? Or should the therapist have promoted an adjustment to the situation, an attitude that he really had things good, that life is imperfect, and perhaps he should just find a way to make the best of it? Did John Williams really wish that he were white—a conclusion some whites come to when blacks complain of the obstacles in their paths to general social acceptance? Should John have declined that seductive invitation to the club at Harvard on the basis that a token Black was worse than no black at all? Was his wish to be accepted by his white classmates an unhealthy one, or could it be seen as no less healthy than the wish a white initiate would have? Was John really "Uncle-Tomming" by joining the exclusive group while knowing that true acceptance would ultimately be denied him? Indeed, what evidence did he have that he was not "truly" accepted by his club members? If someone was being nice to him, was it because he was black and because they were trying to demonstrate their liberalism and open-mindedness? How was he to know if a display of affection or approval arose from such motivations?

Dr. Shaw was more reluctant to push John than he would have been a white client. It has been suggested that some white therapists are oversympathetic towards their black clients lest they seem to be expressing racial prejudice (Adams, 1950). There is a general issue in psychotherapy about how much pressure a therapist should place on a client. In one well-known study of group therapy (Yalom and Lieberman, 1971), casualties occurred most often when the group leader was confrontative and authoritative. Clearly clients can be hurt if their therapists demand more of them than they are capable. On the other hand, the art of therapy requires that therapists encourage movement on the part of their clients that might not occur otherwise. After some hesitation, Dr. Shaw did apply such pressure, but he seemed to misread his client's readiness to explore his conflicts and lost the opportunity to work further with him. By most standards, Dr. Shaw failed with John Williams, even though he saw him for only five sessions.

The difficulties in establishing rapport should have been anticipated by Dr. Shaw. Clients in general may need time to feel comfortable with a therapist, to come to trust that this stranger has their best interests at heart and will be able to relate in a nonjudgmental way so that secrets of the heart can be shared. But John, like many Black clients, was suspicious and hostile because of the racial difference itself, as earlier workers observed (Kennedy, 1952; St. Clair, 1951). Will this white person be able truly to empathize with my suffering? Will he or she translate whatever personal prejudices exist into a lack of sympathy, or too much sympathy? Will he or she be able truly to appreciate the tensions I am under? How will he or she judge my desires to be accepted by whites for what I am, my fierce pride in being black, especially as I succeed in a white world? Will he or she see me as copping out, or decide that my inhibition of resentment is adaptive and healthy? Indeed, will and can the therapist help me explore within myself what *I* really want? Must I want only what other Blacks want in order to be a whole person?

THE PSYCHOLOGICAL TREATMENT OF HYPERTENSION

What kinds of treatment show promise in dealing with essential hypertension? In the most general terms, therapists of various persuasions agree that anxiety must be reduced to lessen the sympathetic nervous system arousal that maintains the blood pressure at abnormally high levels. Although there are probably limits to how normal the client can become—over time structural changes occur in the cardiovascular system that render it chronically hyperaroused to some extent—therapy can justifiably be attempted to help the client cope better with pressures and anxiety and thereby reduce blood pressure to a degree.

A psychoanalytic worker employs techniques such as free association and interpretation in efforts to lift repressions so that the person can examine hitherto repressed conflicts. John might have learned as a young child that to be loved one had to achieve, even if that meant denying oneself what one really wanted. Operating with the hypothesis that hypertension arises from hostile impulses pressing for discharge, an analyst might encourage the client to recognize and express anger. Hypertension as an illness lends itself well to the hydraulic metaphor of psychoanalysis; siphoning off undischarged energy is expected to reduce the pressure in the psychic apparatus.

Client-centered therapists would focus on John's denial of his inner self, his not marching to the beat of his own drum, his compromising his ideals and deeply felt beliefs in order to meet with favor and acceptance from others. Dr. Shaw was operating in this framework, but we have seen that he did not get further than suggesting to John how he might be acting against his own self. The preceding transcript shows the kind of empathic listening and reflection common in client-centered therapy. Note, however, that Dr. Shaw did not merely reflect back to John what he had just said. A useful distinction should be drawn between what one writer has termed primary accurate empathy and advanced empathy (Egan, 1975) or what we have elsewhere likened to interpretation (Davison and Neale, 1982). Primary empathy is seen in the following exchange in the transcript.

John: Doc, I can't talk to a white man about this. I can't talk to a Black man about this. I'm too ashamed, too mixed up. (Beginning to sob.) I can't handle this.

Dr. Shaw: This is hard for you, I know, John. . . .

Dr. Shaw acknowledges that he appreciates how difficult it is for John to be talking about his private thoughts. The hope is that the relationship will be strengthened and that John will be encouraged to continue exploring his feelings. In another part of the session, however, Dr. Shaw goes beyond what John has expressed, restating to John what is implied, what he, Dr. Shaw, believes is going on with John. He makes an *inference* about what is troubling the client in the hope of helping John view himself in a new, better perspective, one that will generate movement, greater honesty with the self. (Dr. Shaw has asked John how he felt about being the only Black in his club at college.)

Dr. Shaw: [I'd like to know about] Your feelings of being the only Black.

John: Well, I felt really good about it. . . . [My high school friends] would've envied me to the utmost. . . .

Dr. Shaw: Yes, I know you were quite proud about it. . . . But I wonder if you had other feelings about it.

Advanced empathy can be confrontative, as it certainly was in this instance. Too confrontative, it turned out. From our perspective, Dr. Shaw was on target, but John was too frightened, too angry to consider the interpretation. Therapists, beginning with Freud, have been mindful of the importance of timing. Shaw erred, perhaps due to the impatience he felt with himself for dancing too gingerly around John's problems for fear of sounding like a bigoted white person, an insensitive therapist who does not truly understand the client's torment.

If John had consulted a behavior therapist, some of the things already mentioned might have happened because contemporary behavior therapists also believe that many clients can benefit from expression of feelings (they call it assertion training, not the discharge of repressed hostility) and from a clearer idea of what is motivating them (they call it behavioral assessment.) However, behavior therapists tend to be more concrete and active in prescribing techniques for their clients. For John, there might have been role-playing in the consulting room to help him rehearse with the therapist ways of expressing resentment and disagreement with people. The therapist, however, would have had to make the ethical judgment of how "activist" John should be: would an assertive response be called for at the very hint of a racial slur, even at the risk of alienating, say, one of the partners in John's law office? Or would the therapist suggest systematic desensitization to harden John to these racist comments so that they would bother him less and presumably elicit little if any overt response. These are weighty moral questions.

There is great interest nowadays in biofeedback, a technique that uses a highly sensitive electronic apparatus to inform a person of bodily changes that are usually too subtle to be aware of normally. John might have learned when his blood pressure had passed a certain level and then been reinforced for bringing it down below that level. Statistically significant changes have been achieved with both normals and hypertensives in laboratory settings, but little clincial success has been achieved in generalizing these findings to real life (Shapiro and Surwit, 1979). Attention to the person's driven life-style seems to be essential if anything like biofeedback is going to play a significant role in lowering blood pressure.

4

UNIPOLAR AFFECTIVE DISORDER: MAJOR DEPRESSIVE EPISODE

Janet called the mental health center to ask if someone could help her 5-year-old son, Adam. He had been having trouble sleeping for the past several weeks, and Janet was becoming concerned about his health. Adam refused to go to sleep at his regular bedtime and also woke up at irregular intervals throughout the night. Whenever he woke up, Adam would come downstairs to be with Janet. Her initial reaction had been sympathetic; she would give him some water, talk to him, and rock him back to sleep. As the cycle came to repeat itself night after night, Janet's tolerance grew thin and she became more belligerent. She found herself engaged in repeated battles that usually ended when she agreed to let him sleep in her room. Janet felt guilty about giving in to a 5-year-old's demands, but it seemed like the only way they would ever get any sleep. The family physician was unable to identify a physical explanation for Adam's problem; he suggested that Janet contact a psychologist. This advice led Janet to inquire about the mental health center's series of parent training groups.

Applicants for the groups were routinely screened during an individual intake interview. The therapist began by asking several questions about Janet and her family. Janet was 30 years old and had been divorced from her husband, David, for a little more than 1 year. Adam was the youngest of Janet's three children: Jennifer was 10 and Claire was 8. Janet had resumed her college education on a part-time basis when Adam was 2 years old. She had hoped to finish her bachelor's degree at the end of the next semester and enter law school in the fall. Unfortunately, she had withdrawn from classes 1 month prior to her appointment at the mental health center. Her current plans were indefinite. She spent almost all of her time at home with Adam.

Janet and the children lived in a large, comfortable house that she had received as part of the divorce settlement. Finances were a major concern to Janet, but she managed to make ends meet through the combination of student loans, a grant-in-aid from the university, and child-support payments from David. David lived in a nearby town with a younger woman whom he had married shortly after the divorce. He visited Janet and the children once or twice every month and took the children to spend weekends with him once a month.

Having collected the necessary background information, the therapist asked for a description of the circumstances surrounding the development of Adam's sleep difficulties and the factors that currently affected the problem. This discussion covered the sequence of a typical evening's events, beginning with dinner and progressing through the following morning. It was clear during this discussion that Janet felt completely overwhelmed by the situation. She was exasperated and felt that she was completely unable to control her son. At several points during the interview, Janet seemed to be on the verge of tears. Her eyes were watery, and her voice broke as they discussed her response to David's occasional visits. The therapist, therefore, suggested that they put off a further analysis of Adam's problem and spend some time discussing Janet's situation in a broader perspective.

In the subsequent conversation it became clear that Janet's mood had been depressed since her husband had asked for a divorce. She felt sad, discouraged, and lonely. This feeling seemed to become even more severe just prior to her withdrawal from classes at the university (1 year after David's departure and 2 months before her first clinic appointment). When David left, she remembered feeling "down in the dumps," but she could usually cheer herself up by playing with the children or going for a walk. Now she was nearing desperation. She cried frequently and for long periods of time. Nothing seemed to cheer her up. She had lost interest in her friends, and the children seemed to be more of a burden than ever. Her depression was somewhat worse in the morning, when it seemed that she would never be able to make it through the day.

Janet was preoccupied by her divorce from David and admitted that she spent hours each day brooding about the events that led to their separation. These worries interfered considerably with her ability to concentrate and seemed directly related to her withdrawal from the univeristy. She had found that she was totally unable to study the assigned reading or concentrate on a 45-minute lecture. Withdrawing from school had precipitated further problems. She was no longer eligible for student aid and would have to begin paying back her loans within a few months. In short, one worry led to another, and her attitude became increasingly pessimistic. Janet harbored considerable resentment toward David and his new wife, although she blamed herself for the divorce. Among other things, she believed that her return to school had placed additional strain on an already difficult situation, and she wondered whether she had acted selfishly. The therapist noted that Janet's reasoning often seemed somewhat vague and illogical. She argued that she had been a poor marital partner and cited several examples of her own misconduct. These included events that struck the therapist as being very common, if not entirely reasonable. She sometimes spent too much money on her clothes, complained too openly and too often about many of David's faults, failed to show interest in sports, and so on. Janet seemed to blow these events totally out of proportion until they appeared to her to be terrible sins. She also generalized from her marriage to other relationships in her life. If her first marriage had failed, how could she ever expect to develop a satisfactory relationship with another man? Furthermore, Janet had begun to question her value as a friend and parent. The collapse of her marriage seemed to affect the manner in which she viewed all of her social relationships.

The future looked bleak from her current perspective, but she had not given up all hope. Her interest in solving Adam's problem, for example, was an encouraging sign. Although she was not optimistic about the chances of success, she was willing to try to develop new skills that would help her become a more effective parent.

SOCIAL HISTORY

Janet's early childhood had been uneventful. Not having any siblings, she spent most of her time with adults, particularly her mother. She remembered her parents' relationship as being warm and pleasant. The family took frequent outings together and, despite the usual number of quarrels and disagreements, everyone seemed to enjoy being together.

When Janet was 10 years old, her mother died in an automobile accident. Janet could remember the events of that day with terrible clarity. When she arrived home from school, her mother's best friend was there to meet her. She explained that Janet's mother had been in an accident and that her father had gone to the hospital. He arrived home several hours later and told Janet that her mother had died. The following months were very difficult for Janet and her father. Janet's father was overcome with grief, but he managed to continue working and arranged for neighborhood friends to care for Janet when he was not home. Janet also managed to struggle through her normal schedule of activities. Her performance at school was not markedly affected, and she continued to play with her small circle of friends. She did remember, however, that she often spent long hours sitting in her mother's room gazing at old photographs and crying softly to herself. On one occasion, her father found her wearing some of her mother's clothes and makeup. His response seemed to be appropriate and sympathetic. They had a long talk about how much they both missed Janet's mother and how they could help each other through this difficult time. Shortly after this incident, Janet's father donated her mother's clothes to the Salvation Army.

Even prior to her mother's death, Janet had been reserved socially. She tended to have one or two special friends with whom she spent much of her time outside of school, but she felt awkward and self-conscious in larger groups of children. Although her friends were important to her and she enjoyed spending time with them, Janet usually waited for them to contact her. She did not initiate activities and hesitated to express her own preferences when they were trying to decide what to do. In retrospect, Janet attributed this lack of assertion to her fear that her friends would abandon her or ridicule her interests. She was also self-conscious about her weight. She was not really fat, but she tended to be a bit plump and was therefore afraid that the others would tease her if she drew attention to herself.

This friendship pattern persisted throughout high school and into her college years. She was interested in boys and dated intermittently until her junior year in high school, when she began to date one boy on a regular basis. Janet was certain that she was in love with him and soon lost all contact with the few girlfriends with whom she had been close. She and her boyfriend, John, spent all of their time together, both after school and on the weekends. Janet remembered that the other kids seemed to make fun of her relationship with John and admitted that it did seem silly from her current perspective. Whether they were alone or in a group, Janet always sat next to John, holding his hand and giggling at his dreary jokes. The others teased Janet and John about acting as if they were married. This criticism troubled Janet, even though she fully expected that she and John would be married shortly after they graduated from high school.

Unfortunately, her nuptial plans did not work out. She and John broke up during Janet's first year in college. He announced suddenly that he wanted to date other women and that their relationship was over. Fortunately, she met David a few weeks afterward, and they were married the following summer. Janet later wondered whether she had rushed into her relationship with David primarily to avoid the vacuum created by John's suddent exit. Whatever her motivation might have been, her marriage was followed shortly by her first pregnancy, which precipitated her withdrawal from the university during her sophomore year. For the next 7 years, Janet was occupied as a full-time mother and housekeeper.

When Adam was 2 years old and able to attend a day-care center, Janet decided to resume her college education. She and David had discussed her desire to complete her degree and pursue a profession on several occasions. He was less than excited about this prospect and preferred that Janet continue in her present role. She disagreed, but admitted that the children were too young and they could not afford both tuition and day care. When Adam was 2 years old, the circumstances were finally in Janet's favor, and David agreed to take a more active role in various responsibilities that had previously been assumed by Janet alone. Adam was enrolled at a day-care center on a half-time basis, and Janet began taking two courses each semester.

Following Janet's return to school, her relationship with David became increasingly strained. They had even less time than usual to spend with each other. David found it difficult to adjust to his increased household responsibilities. Janet was no longer able to prepare meals for the family every night of the week, so David had to learn to cook. He also had to share the cleaning and drive the children to many of their lessons and social activities. A more balanced and stable relationship would have been able to withstand the stress associated with these changes. Unfortunately, Janet and David were unable to adjust. Instead of working to improve their communications, they bickered continuously. They found it impossible to negotiate a mutually acceptable exchange of responsibilities. The final blow came when David met another woman to whom he was attracted and who offered him an alternative to the escalating hostility with Janet. He asked for a divorce and moved to an apartment.

Janet was shaken by David's departure, in spite of the fact that they had not been happy together. Fortunately, she did have a few friends to whom she could turn for support. The most important one was a neighbor who had children of approximately the same ages as Janet's daughters. There were also two couples with whom she and David had socialized. They were all very helpful for the first few weeks, but she quickly lost contact with the couples. It was awkward to get together as a threesome, and Janet had never been close enough with the women to preserve their relationships on an individual basis. That left the neighbor, Susan, as her sole advisor and confidante. Susan was the only person with whom Janet felt she could discuss her feelings openly. They spent hours talking about the recent events in Janet's life and her plans for the coming months.

For the next few months, Janet was able to continue her studies. With the children's help, she managed the household chores and kept up with her work. She even found time for some brief social activities. She agreed to go out on two blind dates arranged by people with whom she and David had been friends. These were generally unpleasant encounters; one of her dates was boring and unattractive, and the other was obnoxiously aggressive. After the latter experience, she discontinued the minimal efforts she had made to develop new friendships. The process seemed too difficult and threatening. Janet referred to single-parent clubs as "meat markets" where people paired off for casual sexual encounters. She might have gotten acquainted with other people in her classes at the university, but she did not know how to initiate or maintain a conversation with her classmates.

As time wore on, Janet found herself brooding more and more about the divorce. She was gaining weight at the rate of 3 or 4 pounds a month. The first few pounds had been easy to ignore and were more of a nuisance than anything else. But soon her clothes no longer fit, and the children began to comment on her appearance. To make matters worse, Claire developed a serious ear infection just prior to Janet's midterm exams. The added worry of Claire's health and her concern about missed classes and lost studying time contributed substantially to a decline in Janet's mood. She finally realized that she would have to withdraw from her classes to avoid receiving failing grades.

By this point, 1 month prior to her appointment at the mental health center, she had lost interest in most of her previous activities. Even casual reading had come to be a tedious chore. She did not have any hobbies because she never had enough time. She also found that her friend Susan was becoming markedly aloof. When Janet called, Susan seldom talked for more than a few minutes before finding an excuse to hang up. Their contacts gradually diminished to an occasional wave across the street or a quick, polite conversation when they picked up their children from school. It seemed that Susan had grown tired of Janet's company.

This was Janet's situation when she contacted the mental health center. Her mood was depressed and anxious. She was preoccupied with financial concerns and her lack of social relationships. Adam's sleeping problem, which had begun about 1 week after she withdrew from her classes, was the last straw. She felt that she could no longer control her difficult situation and recognized that she needed help.

CONCEPTUALIZATION AND TREATMENT

The therapist and Janet discussed her overall situation and agreed that Adam was only a small part of the problem. They decided to work together on an individual basis instead of having Janet join the parent training group.

Janet's depression was viewed as being directly related to important gaps in her repertoire of social behaviors. The two most important examples involved her inability to establish and maintain new friendships and her lack of appropriate responses to the children's behavior. The therapist pointed out that her depressed mood would be very likely to improve if she felt that she was able to control a greater percentage of events in her life and engage in more pleasant activities. In other words, instead of concentrating on her patterns of thinking about the world or her perception of recent events, the therapist decided to help her learn to perform specific behaviors more effectively. His assumption was that new behaviors would be maintained by their own natural consequences.

As an initial step, the therapist asked Janet to list all of the activities that she enjoyed. This procedure was used both as a way of identifying pleasurable events that could be increased in frequency and a way of shifting the focus of attention away from the unpleasant factors with which Janet was currently preoccupied. Most of the activities Janet mentioned were things that she had not done for several months or years. For example, prior to her return to school, her favorite pastime had been riding horses. She said that she would like to begin riding again, but she felt that it was prohibitively expensive and time consuming. Sex also occupied an important position on Janet's list. Even prior to her divorce, she and David had not been active sexually. She was currently somewhat ambivalent about beginning another sexual relationship because her experience with David had not been entirely positive. Nevertheless, she included it as an important pleasant event. With considerable prodding from the therapist, Janet also listed a few other less important activities. These included talking with a friend over a cup of coffee, listening to music late at night after the children were asleep, and going for walks in the woods behind her home. In some cases, Janet indicated that these activities used to be pleasant, but she did not think that they would be enjoyable at the present time.

Despite Janet's ambivalence, the therapist encouraged her to pick one activity that she would try at least twice before their next meeting. A short walk in the woods seemed like the most practical alternative, considering that Adam might interrupt listening to music and she did not want to call Susan. The therapist also asked Janet to call the campus riding club to inquire about their activities.

At the same time that the therapist encouraged Janet to increase her activity level, he also began to concentrate on an assessment of her skills in social interactions. For several sessions, they covered topics such as selecting situations in which Janet might be likely to meet people with whom she would be interested in developing a friendship, initiating a conversation, maintaining a conversation by asking the other person a series of consecutive questions, and other elementary issues. Having identified areas that were problematic for Janet, they discussed solutions and actually practiced, or role-played, various social interactions.

During the first few weeks of treatment, Janet's mood seemed to be improving. Perhaps most important was her luck in finding a part-time job at a local riding stable. She learned of the opening when she called to ask about the campus riding club. They were looking for someone who would feed and exercise the horses every morning. The wages were very small, but she was allowed to ride as long as she wanted each day without charge. Furthermore, the schedule allowed her to finish before the girls returned from school. The wages were also sufficient to allow her to return Adam to the day-care center on a part-time basis. Janet reported that she still felt depressed when she was at home, but she loved to ride and it helped to know that she could go to work in the morning.

An unfortunate sequence of events led to a serious setback shortly after it seemed that Janet's mood was beginning to improve. Her financial aid had been discontinued, and she could no longer cover her monthly mortgage payments. Within several weeks, she received a notice from the bank threatening to foreclose her mortgage and sell her house. Her appearance was noticeably changed when she arrived for her next appointment. She was apathetic and lethargic. She cried through most of the session, and her outlook had grown distinctly more pessimistic. The therapist was particularly alarmed by an incident that Janet described as happening the previous day. She had been filling her car with gas when a mechanic at the service station mentioned that her muffler sounded like it was cracked. He told her that she should get it fixed right away because of the dangerous exhaust fumes. In his words, "that's a good way to kill yourself." The thought of suicide had not occurred to Janet prior to this comment, but she found that she could not get it out of her mind. She was frightened by the idea and tried to distract herself by watching television. The thoughts continued to intrude despite these efforts.

The therapist immediately discussed several changes in the treatment plan with Janet. He arranged for her to consult a psychiatrist who prescribed Tofranil, a tricyclic, antidepressant drug. She also agreed to increase the frequency of her appointments at the clinic to three times each week. These changes were primarily motivated by the onset of suicidal ideation. More drastic action, such as hospitalization or calling relatives for additional support, did not seem to be necessary because her thoughts were not particularly lethal. For example, she said that she did not want to die, even though she was thinking quite a lot about death. The idea frightened her, and she did not have a specific plan arranged by which she would accomplish her own death. Nevertheless, the obvious deterioration in her condition warranted a more intense treatment program.

The next month proved to be a difficult one for Janet, but she was able to persevere. Two or three weeks after she began taking the medication, her mood seemed to brighten. The suicidal ideation disappeared, she became more talkative, and she resumed most of her normal activities. Fortunately, the people who owned the riding stable were very understanding and held Janet's new job for her until she was able to return. The financial crisis was solved, at least temporarily, when her father agreed to provide her with substantial assistance. In fact, he expressed surprise and some dismay that she had never asked him for help in the past or even told him that she was in financial trouble. The social skills program progressed very well after Janet began taking medication. Within several weeks, she was able to reestablish her friendship with Susan. She was also able to meet a few people at the riding stable, and her social network seemed to be widening.

After Janet's mood had improved, the issue of Adam's sleeping problem was addressed. The therapist explained that Janet needed to set firm limits on Adam's manipulative behavior. Her inconsistency in dealing with his demands, coupled with the attention that he received during the bedtime scenes, could be thought of as leading to intermittent reinforcement of his inappropriate behavior. Janet and the therapist worked out a simple set of responses that she would follow whenever he got up and came downstairs. She would offer him a drink, take him back to his room, tuck him in bed, and leave immediately. Three days after the procedure was implemented, Adam began sleeping through the night without interruption. This rapid success enhanced Janet's sense of control over her situation. Her enthusiasm led her to enroll in the parent training program for which she had originally applied. She continued to improve her relationship with her children.

Janet's individual therapy sessions were discontinued 9 months after her first appointment. At that point, she was planning to return to school, was still working part-time at the riding stable, and had started to date one of the men she met at work. Her children were all healthy, and she had managed to keep their house. The antidepressant medication had been decreased to a small dosage for 6 months and was discontinued 8 months after it was initiated.

DISCUSSION

A sad or dysphoric mood is obviously the most prominent feature of clinical depression. Depressed patients describe themselves as feeling discouraged, hopeless, and apathetic. This dejected emotional state is usually accompanied by a variety of unpleasant thoughts that often include suicidal ideation. Beck (1967) has described these cognitive features of depression as the *depressive triad*: a negative view of the self, the world, and the future. Depressed people see themselves as inadequate and unworthy. They are often filled with guilt and remorse over apparently ordinary and trivial events. These patients hold a similarly dim view of their environment. Everyday experiences and social interactions are interpreted in the most critical fashion. The future seems bleak and empty. In fact, some extremely depressed patients find it impossible to imagine any future at all.

Clinical depression is identified by changes in several important areas in the person's life. In addition to a prominent and relatively persistent dysphoric mood, *DSM-III* (p. 214) lists several features for major depressive episodes. Specifically, at least four of the following symptoms must have been present on a daily basis for at least 2 weeks if the patient is to meet the criteria for this diagnostic category.

1. *poor appetite or significant weight loss (when not dieting) or increased appetite or significant weight gain.*
2. *insomnia (inability to fall asleep, difficulty staying asleep, and/or early morning awakening) or hypersomnia (excessive amount of sleep, with confusion on wakening).*
3. *psychomotor agitation or retardation (but not merely subjective feelings of restlessness or being slowed down).*
4. *loss of interest or pleasure in usual activities, or decrease in sexual drive not limited to a period when delusional or hallucinating.*
5. *loss of energy; fatigue.*
6. *feelings of worthlessness, self-reproach, or excessive or inappropriate guilt (either may be delusional).*
7. *complaints or evidence of diminished ability to think or concentrate, such as slowed thinking, or indecisiveness not associated with marked loosening of associations or incoherence.*
8. *recurrent thoughts of death, suicidal ideation, wishes to be dead, or suicidal attempt.*

Janet clearly fit these criteria. Her mood had been markedly depressed since her separation from David. She had gained considerable weight—25 pounds in 9 months. Her concentration was severely impaired, as evidenced by her inability to study, and she had lost interest in almost everything. Excessive and inappropriate guilt was clearly a prominent feature of her constant brooding about the divorce. Although she did not actually attempt to harm herself, she experienced a distressing period of ruminative suicidal ideation. Sleep impairment may also have been a problem, but it was difficult to evaluate in the context of Adam's behavior. Prior to her first visit at the clinic, Janet had been sleeping less than her usual number of hours per night, and she reported considerable fatigue. It was difficult to know whether she would have been able to sleep if Adam had not been so demanding of her attention throughout the night.

Most therapists agree that it is important to recognize the difference between clinical depression and other states of unhappiness and disappointment. Consider, for example, people who are mourning the loss of a friend or relative. *DSM-III* suggests that if bereavement is either too severe or prolonged, the diagnosis of major depression should be considered. But is this a qualitative or a quantitative distinction? Are patients who might be considered clinically depressed simply more unhappy than their peers, or are these phenomena completely distinct? This is one of the most interesting and difficult questions facing investigators in the field of affective disorders. The present diagnostic system handles the problem by including an intermediate category, dysthymic disorder, that lies between major depressive disorder and normal mood. This category includes patients who exhibit depressed symptoms that are not of sufficient severity or duration to meet the criteria for major affective disorder.

Depression may also be difficult to distinguish from certain other forms of psychopathology. The presence of psychotic symptoms, such as hallucinations and delusions, are often taken to suggest schizophrenia, but they may be found in association with major depression (Akiskal and Puzantian, 1979). Depressed patients may report hallucinations and delusions that are congruent with their emotional state. These include the experience of voices instructing the patient to commit suicide or chastising the patient for past transgressions. Affectively toned delusions range from hypochondriacal complaints (e.g., "My insides have rotted") and imagined guilt to expressions that "I am dead" or "The world is coming to an end." The distinction between severe depression and emotional blunting, as seen in schizophrenia, is also subtle but clearly important. Observations regarding the course of the patient's disturbance may help separate these two phenomena, since patients with affective disorders are more likely to achieve complete remission.

PSYCHOLOGICAL MODELS

Freud's explanation for the development of depression began with a comparison between depression and bereavement (Freud, 1917).[1] The two conditions are very similar. Both involve a dejected mood, a loss of interest in the outside world, and an inhibition of activity. One principal feature distinguishes between the person who is depressed and the person who is mourning: a disturbance of self-regard. Depressed people chastise themselves, saying that they are worthless, morally depraved, and worthy of punishment. Freud noted the disparity between such extreme negative views and the more benign opinions of other people who do not hold the depressed person in such contempt. In other words, the depressed person's view does not seem to be an accurate self-perception. Freud went on to argue that the depressed people are not *really* complaining about themselves but are, in fact, expressing hostile feelings that pertain to someone else. Depression is therefore the manifestation of a process in which anger is

[1]Freud pointed out that his account was only intended to apply to a subset of depressed patients and that biological factors were probably more important in other cases.

turned inward and directed against the self instead of against its original object.

Why would some people direct hostility against themselves? Freud argued that the foundation for this problem is laid in early childhood. For various reasons, people who are prone to depression have formed *narcissistic* interpersonal relationships. In such relationships the predepressive is highly dependent on the other person. This dependency fosters frustration and hostility. Because these negative feelings might threaten the relationship if they are expressed openly, they are denied awareness. Problems then arise when the relationship is ended, for whatever reason. The depressed person's ego presumably identifies with the lost loved one. The intense hostility that had been felt for that person is now turned against the self, or *introjected*. Following this model, treatment would consist of an attempt to make the client aware of these unconscious, hostile impulses. Their more direct expression would presumably eliminate the depression.

At least one aspect of this model seems consistent with Janet's situation. She had, in fact, formed a series of intense, dependent relationships with men, beginning in high school. One might argue that her depression was precipitated by the loss incurred during her separation and divorce from David. She resented the separation deeply. Her guilt might be seen as a criticism of David's behavior. Other aspects of Janet's behavior, however, are inconsistent with Freud's model. Although Janet was critical of herself, she was also very vocal in David's presence. They fought openly several times, both before and after the divorce, and he was fully aware of Janet's feelings. On one occasion about 4 months after their separation, things had gotten particularly out of hand. David arrived on a Friday evening to pick up the children for the weekend. Janet had had a bad week. Claire had a serious cold and had stayed home from school for 3 days. It was the end of the month, money was tight, and Janet did not know how she would pay the doctor's bill. Furthermore, because she had to stay home with Claire, she had missed two lectures and subsequently received a C− on a statistics exam. When David walked into the house, he casually mentioned that the place looked like a mess and asked Janet why she never cleaned or straightened up. Janet instantly flew into a rage. She screamed and shouted, told David what she thought of him and his new girl friend, and ended her tirade by throwing half a set of china across the living room. Both Janet and David were keenly aware of her anger and resentment. It therefore seems unlikely that Janet's depression was a simple manifestation of misdirected hostility. It is also unlikely that her depression would be relieved by simply encouraging her to express her feelings more openly.

The research literature is also inconsistent with the psychoanalytic position. Weissman and Paykel (1974) studied a group of depressed women for several months. Contrary to Freud's hypothesis, the depressed women were rated as being more hostile and critical than a group of control women from similar neighborhoods. These investigators also found that the depressed women became less hostile as they became less depressed. Thus there appears to be a direct and not an inverse relationship between depression and anger. Although Weissman and Paykel noted that the depressed women were frequently hostile and combative, they also found that these women were less able to express their needs appropriately. They were relatively ineffective at routine interpersonal communication. This impairment was still evident after the women's symptoms had improved. For example, a depressed woman who is angry with her husband might be able to express her dissatisfaction by shouting or throwing things but might not be able to initiate or carry out a meaningful negotiation that might effect a change in his behavior. These data fit nicely with another psychological model of depression proposed by Lewinsohn (1974).

According to Lewinsohn's model, depression is the product of reduction in the rate of response-contingent, positive reinforcement. Reduced activity, not self-criticism, is seen as the central feature of depression. The depressed person is considered to be on a prolonged extinction schedule. The model posits a reciprocal relationship among mood, activity, and pleasant events. As the person becomes more depressed, he or she becomes less active and therefore experiences fewer pleasant events. He or she then becomes more depressed, even less active, and so on. Lewinsohn also places considerable importance on interpersonal relationships. He notes that the depressed person is initially reinforced for behaving in a depressed manner. Others respond empathically and are initially very attentive whenever the depressed person cries or talks about depressing ideas or events. Unfortunately, the long-range result of this process is usually negative: the depressed person's few remaining friends eventually become tired of this behavior and begin to avoid further interactions. Thus whatever sources of social reinforcement may have been available are eventually driven away. The model allows for several factors that might lead to a low rate of response-contingent, positive reinforcement. One important factor in this regard is a lack of social skills. Depressed people may be ineffective in their interactions with other people. An important aspect of treatment would therefore be to identify specific skills in which the person is deficient and to teach the person more effective ways of interacting with others.

Several aspects of this model are consistent with the present case. First, Janet had experienced a marked decline in pleasant social activities. After her separation from David, she had become isolated. Furthermore, her long discussions with Susan had eventually soured their relationship and eliminated one of her last sources of social support. When Janet and her therapist discussed things that she might do to meet new friends, she seemed lost. The few attempts that she had made, such as her blind date, had gone badly, and she did not know where else to begin.

Despite these positive features, the Lewinsohn model leaves some important questions unanswered. Perhaps most important is the issue of causality. Lack of activity and depression are certainly correlated; depressed people tend to stay at home, avoid other people, and lose interest in activities. But which comes first? Lewinsohn recognizes that the process is reciprocal; however, he clearly implies that the reduction in pleasant events precedes and triggers the change in mood. As in Janet's case, it may be reasonable to suggest that loss of interest and reduced activity are consequences of a depressed mood rather than antecedents. This issue is critical to an evaluation of the model and has plagued several efforts to evaluate it empirically. For example, Lewinsohn and Libet (1972) found that depressed people reported experiencing fewer pleasant events than a group of nondepressed subjects. Critics have argued that the demonstration of such a correlation does not support the notion that the reduction in pleasant events *caused* the change in mood. One might also wonder whether the depressives' self-reports were accurate. Considering the pessimistic outlook of depressed patients, it would not be surprising if they underestimated the frequency of pleasant events, even if the actual rate was the same as that experienced by control subjects. In fact, Buchwald (1977) has demonstrated a significant relationship between scores on a depression inventory and estimates of the frequency of positive feedback on a verbal learning task; students with higher depression scores tended to underestimate the number of times that they had been told their responses were correct. It is therefore still an open question whether depressed people do, in fact, experience fewer pleasant events and, if they do, whether this phenomenon plays a causal role in the development of depression.

The social skills aspect of Lewinsohn's model has received more clear-cut support. Weissman and Paykel (1974), for example, noted that depressed women exhibited communication problems that persisted after their mood had improved. A study by Coyne (1976) offers further support for this idea. Coyne arranged for female college students to hold 20-minute telephone conversations with depressed and nondepressed women who were being treated on an outpatient basis at a mental health center. The students completed various self-report measures before and after these verbal interactions. Two results were particularly striking. First, the students who spoke with the depressed women showed a significant decline in their own mood at the end of the conversation. Second, the students who spoke with the depressed women were much more likely to indicate that they did not want to have any further contact with their conversational partners and, if they participated in the study again, they did not want to have the same partner. In short, the depressed women clearly had a very negative impact on the students in the study. This effect could not be traced to any obvious differences between the speech of the depressed and nondepressed women subjects. The depressed women did *not* differ from the nondepressed patients with regard to total amount of speech, number of approval responses ("yeah," "hm-hmm"), or ratings of hope statements and genuineness. It is therefore unclear why the students found their interactions with the depressed women to be so aversive. Nevertheless, the depressed women were doing *something* that caused the students to reject them. In the natural environment this effect could cut off sources of social support and lead to further depression. This kind of phenomenon seemed to be operating in Janet's relationship with Susan.

STRESSFUL LIFE EVENTS

The psychoanalytic and social skills models are concerned with the characteristics of the depressed individual. They assume that the personality traits or behavioral repertoires of some people make them more vulnerable to depression. These views are complemented by another large body of research that is concerned with the role of environmental events that may be outside of the person's control. Once again, consider Janet's experience. Several specific incidents may have been causally related to the development of her depression. These may be roughly divided into *predisposing* and *precipitating* events. The death of Janet's mother when Janet was 10 years old may have been an important predisposing factor. In other words, this incident did not lead to an immediate, lasting change in Janet's mood, but it may have increased the probability that Janet would become depressed at a later time. Her separation and divorce may have been an important precipitating factor; given that she was vulnerable to depression, this event may have triggered the specific episode.

Despite some inconsistencies, the research literature indicates that stressful life events probably play a causal role in the etiology of depression. One major study by Brown and Harris (1978) has received considerable attention. These investigators interviewed 114 women who were being treated for depression and a random sample of 458 women who were living in the community. The latter group was subsequently divided into those who exhibited clear symptoms of depression during the interview (76, or 17% of the sample) and those who did not. All of the women were asked about the occurrence of stressful events, particularly during the past year. Several interesting patterns emerged in the subsequent data analyses. First, Brown and Harris did find an increased incidence of stressful events among the depressed patients, but only with regard to a particular subset of such events—those that were severe and that involved long-term consequences for the woman's well-being. Divorce and marital separation were prominent among these events. Sixty-one percent of the depressed patients had experienced such an event in the 9 months preceding the onset of their symptoms; only 25% of the women in the community sample had experienced an event of this nature in the 9 months prior to their interview. Thus the experience of a severe event with long-term consequences led to a pronounced increase in the probability of depression.

Brown and Harris referred to these events as "provoking agents." They also found other events or social circumstances that they called "vulnerability factors." These were not capable of precipitating depression on their own, but they did lead to a substantial increase in risk *given the experience of a stressful life event*. The vulnerability factors were: (1) lack of an intimate, confiding relationship (generally with a spouse or boyfriend); (2) presence in the home of three or more children under the age of 14; (3) lack of full- or part-time employment; and (4) loss of the woman's mother before the age of 11. Consider, for example, the intimacy factor. Among the women who did experience a severe event and who also were involved in an intimate relationship, only 1 in 10 became depressed. The comparable figure among women who experienced a severe event in the absence of such a relationship was 1 in 3. The social support afforded by such a relationship is thus a powerful mediator between stress and the onset of depression, even if the absence of intimacy does not provoke depression by itself.

These data should not be accepted uncritically. There are some very difficult problems associated with this line of research, including the fact that the data were collected retrospectively. The subjects were asked to recall events that had happened some time in the past, often several months prior to the interview. It is therefore possible that biased reporting may account for some of the differences between depressed and nondepressed women. There are other problems with the manner in which depressed women were identified, particularly among the community sample. What should we make of a person who admits certain symptoms of depression but does not consider her problem serious enough to seek treatment? Is she comparable to hospitalized patients? What do we make of differences between results for depressed patients and depressed women in the community who are not being treated? These are difficult issues that must be addressed by further research (Tennant and Bebbington, 1978). Nevertheless, Brown and Harris have raised interesting issues, proposed a multifaceted model for the development of depression, and stimulated considerable interest in the area of life events and affective disorder.

Several of the findings from the Brown and Harris study are consistent with Janet's situation. She had clearly experienced a high level of stress in the months preceding her first treatment. The divorce from David is one obvious example. Her difficulties with the children may be another instance. When Claire's illness eventually forced her to withdraw from the university, there were important long-term consequences for her graduation and subsequent plans to enter law school. It is also interesting that each of the vulnerability factors outlined by Brown and Harris were present in this case. Janet had, in fact, lost her mother at the age of 10. She was not involved in an intimate, confiding relationship, although her friendship with Susan may have been an important substitute until it dissolved. Her three children were all young and living at home. Following her withdrawal from classes, she was not involved in occupational activities outside of her home. These were probably important factors affecting the development of her depression. The manner in which they combine to take their effect is currently a matter of speculation. One possibility has been suggested by Brown and Harris. They argue that their vulnerability factors operate by affecting the person's self-esteem. In other words, separately and in combination, they are all likely to lead to a general sense of hopelessness and despair. Given this general cognitive set, it will be difficult, if not impossible, for a person to remain optimistic in the face of severely stressful experiences. The result is depression.

TREATMENT

Janet's treatment involved a combination of behavior therapy and antidepressant medication. Following Lewinsohn's model, the therapist focused on increasing Janet's level of participation in pleasant events and helped her learn new social skills. By encouraging activities such as riding, the therapist hoped to interrupt and reverse the ongoing, interactive process in which social isolation and inactivity lead to increased depression, depression leads to further withdrawal, and so on. Through the development of new response patterns, particularly those involving interpersonal communication and parenting skills, he hoped to enable Janet to deal more effectively with future stressful events. Increased social activity and more effective communication would also lead to a more supportive social network that might help reduce the impact of stressful events.

Antidepressant medication was introduced when the risk of suicide became apparent. Janet's suicidal ideation was not extremely lethal. She had not planned a particular method by which she planned to end her life, and she reported that the idea of harming herself was very frightening. The risk would have been much greater if she did have more specific plans and if she had really wanted to die. Nevertheless, her morbid ruminations marked a clear deterioration in her condition that called for more intensive treatment.

Two general classes of drugs are useful in the treatment of depression: tricyclics and monoamine oxidase (MAO) inhibitors. Tricyclics are used more frequently than MAO inhibitors, particularly in the United States, because the latter are sometimes associated with more troublesome side effects, most notably cardiovascular problems. Both forms of medication have been shown to be effective antidepressants in double-blind, placebo-controlled studies (Morris and Beck, 1974). Improvements in the patient's mood and other specific affective symptoms are typically evident after 2 to 4 weeks of drug treatment. Their continued administration also seems to reduce the probability of symptomatic relapse (Davis, 1976).

Although medication does have positive effects on symptoms of depression, such as dejected mood, sleep disturbance, and disturbed concentration, it does not have a specific effect on the social maladjustment that is often associated with affective disorders. This limitaton of drug treatment was illustrated in a longitudinal study conducted by Weissman and her colleagues (Weissman et al., 1974). Patients who showed an initial positive response to tricyclic medication were randomly assigned to further treatment conditions. Fifty percent of the patients were involved in individual psychotherapy and 50% were not. Within each of these groups, 33% of the patients continued to receive trycyclic medication, 33% were switched to placebos, and the remaining patients received no medication. The psychotherapy was supportive, not insight oriented, and it focused on the patient's current problems. Outcome was compared for those patients who completed 8 months of follow-up care without relapse. The effects of psychotherapy and medication were both positive and apparently independent; patients who continued to receive tricyclics were less likely to exhibit affective symptoms, and those who received psychotherapy were less impaired in terms of social adjustment. These data indicate that the use of antidepressant medication should be supplemented by psychosocial treatment aimed at the solution of the patient's current interpersonal problems. The sort of directive, learning-based program employed with Janet provides one promising approach in this regard, but other forms of psychotherapy may also be effective.

One obvious disadvantage associated with both medication and behavior therapy is the extended delay involved in achieving therapeutic effects. In the face of a serious suicidal threat, for example, the therapist may not be able to wait several weeks for a change in the patient's adjustment. There are also many patients who do not respond positively to medication or psychosocial treatment approaches. Another form of intervention that may be tried with depressed patients, particularly if they exhibit profound motor retardation and have failed to respond positively to antidepressant medication, is electroconvulsive therapy (ECT). In the standard ECT procedure, a brief seizure is induced by passing an electrical current between two electrodes that have been placed over the patient's temples. A full course of treatment generally involves the induction of six to eight seizures spaced at 48-hour intervals. The procedure was first introduced as a treatment for schizophrenia, but it soon became apparent that it was most effective with depressed patients (Group for the Advancement of Psychiatry, 1947). More recent studies have supported this conclusion (Royal College of Psychiatrists, 1977).

Much of the controversy surrounding ECT is based on misconceptions concerning the procedure and its effects (Fink, 1977). Although it is often referred to as "shock therapy," ECT does *not* involve the perception of an electrical current. In fact, a short-acting anesthetic is administered prior to the seizure so that the patient is not conscious when the current is applied. Many of the deleterious side effects of ECT have been eliminated by modifications in the treatment procedure, such as the use of muscle relaxants to avoid bone fractures during the seizure. The extent and severity of memory loss can be greatly reduced by the use of unilateral electrode placement. If both electrodes are placed over the nondominant hemisphere of the patient's brain, the patient can avoid verbal memory impairment with little, if any, loss in clinical effectiveness (D'Elia, et al., 1976; Squire and Slater, 1978). Although the mechanism by which ECT produces its effect has not been established, this criticism could also be leveled against most forms of psychiatric medication. There is, of course, the very important question of permanent changes in brain structure and function. Some critics of ECT have argued that it produces irreversible neurological impairment (Friedberg, 1977). Proponents of ECT maintain that the evidence for this conclusion is inadequate (Fink, 1977), but the possibility has not been ruled out. Nevertheless, most of the objections to the use of ECT are based on misconceptions. The evidence supporting its therapeutic efficacy seems to justify the continued use of ECT with some severely depressed patients who have not responded to less intrusive forms of treatment.

5

BIPOLAR AFFECTIVE DISORDER: MANIC EPISODE

By the time he was admitted to the hospital, George Lawler was talking a mile a minute. He harangued the other patients and ward staff, declaring that he was the coach of the U.S. Olympic track team and offering to hold tryouts for the other patients in the hospital. His movements were rapid and somewhat erratic as he paced the halls of the ward and explored every room. At the slightest provocation, he flew into a rage. When an attendent blocked his entrance to the nursing station, he threatened to report her to the president of the Olympic committee. He had not slept for 3 nights. His face was covered with a stubbly growth of beard, and his hair was scattered in various directions. His eyes were sunken and bloodshot, but they still gleamed with an intense excitement.

His life had taken a drastic change over the past 2 weeks. George was 35 years old, married, and the father of two young children. He worked at a small junior college where he taught physical education and coached both the men's and women's track teams. Until his breakdown, the teams had been having an outstanding season. They were undefeated in dual competition and very heavy favorites to win the conference championship. The campus was following their accomplishments closely because it had been 12 years since one of the school teams had won a championship. In fact, track was the only sport in which the school had a winning record that season.

This was not the first time that George had experienced psychological problems. His first serious episode had occurred during his junior year in college. It did not seem to be triggered by any particular incident; in fact, things had been going well. George was majoring in physical education and playing defensive back on the university football team. He was in good academic standing and fairly popular with the other students; his scholarship removed many of the financial concerns that plagued other students. Nevertheless, during the spring semester, George found that he was losing interest in everything. It was not surprising that he did not look forward to classes or studying. He had never been an outstanding student. But he noticed that he no longer enjoyed going out with his friends. They said he seemed depressed all the time. George said he just did not care anymore. He began avoiding his girl friend and, when they were together, he found fault with almost everything she did. Most of his time was spent in his apartment in front of the television. It did not seem to matter what program he watched because his concentration was seriously impaired. He kept the set on as a kind of distraction, not as entertainment. When he did not show up for spring football practice, the coach called him to his office for a long talk. George told his coach that he did not have the energy to play football. In fact, he did not feel he could make it through the easiest set of calisthenic exercises. He did not care about the team or about his future in sports. Recognizing that George's problem was more than a simple lack of motivation, the coach persuaded him to visit a friend of his—a psychiatrist at the student health clinic. George began taking antidepressant medication and attending individual counseling sessions. Within several weeks he was back to his normal level of functioning, and treatment was discontinued.

George had also experienced intervals of unusual ambition and energy. As a student, George had frequently spent several days cramming for exams at the end of a semester. Many of his friends took amphetamines to stay awake, but George seemed able to summon endless, internal reserves of energy. In retrospect, these periods seemed to be clear-cut hypomanic episodes but, at the time, they went relatively unnoticed. George's temporary tendency toward excess verbosity, his lack of need for sleep, and his ambitious goals did not seem pathological. In fact, these energetic intervals were quite productive, and his behavioral excesses were probably adaptive in the competitive university environment.

There had been two subsequent episodes of depression whose symptoms were similar to those of the first episode. Both were over quickly. The most recent incident had occurred 8 months prior to the current hospitalization. It was September, 2 weeks after the start of the fall semester. George had been worried about his job and the team all summer. Who would replace his star sprinter, who had transferred to the state university? Would his high jumper get hurt during the football season? Could they improve on last year's winning record? Over the past month, these concerns had become obsessions. George was having trouble getting to sleep; he was also waking up in the middle of the night for no apparent reason. He felt tired all the time. His wife and children noticed that he was always brooding and seemed preoccupied. Then came the bad news. First, he was told by the athletic department that he would not get the increase in travel funds that he had expected. Then he learned that one of his assistant coaches was taking a leave of absence to finish working on her degree. Neither of these events would have a drastic effect on the upcoming season, but George took them to be disasters. His mood changed from one of tension and anxiety to severe depression. Over several days, George became more and more lethargic until he was almost completely unresponsive. His speech was slow and, when he did say more than a word or two, he spoke in a dull monotone. Refusing to get out of bed, he alternated between long hours of sleep and staring vacuously at the ceiling. He called the athletic director and quit his job, pointing to minor incidents as evidence of is own incompetence. He believed, for example, that the assistant coach had quit because of a brief argument he had with her 6 months earlier. In fact, they had a very positive relationship, and she had always planned to return to school at one time or another. She was leaving earlier than she had expected for personal reasons. George seemed to blame himself for everything. He apologized profusely to his wife and children for failing them as a husband and father. His despair seemed genuine. Suicide seemed like the only reasonable solution. He threatened to end it all if his family would only leave him alone.

George's wife, Cheryl, called the psychiatrist who had treated him during his last episode (2 years earlier) and arranged a special appointment. The psychiatrist decided to prescribe lithium carbonate, a drug that is used to treat manic episodes but that is also an effective antidepressant with bipolar patients (those who show both manic and depressed phases of disturbance). Although George had never been hospitalized for a manic episode, the psychiatrist suggested that his past history of "maniclike" behavior (increased energy, sleeplessness, inflated self-esteem, etc.) and his positive family history for bipolar affective disorder (his uncle Ralph) were both consistent with the diagnosis of bipolar disorder. The lithium seemed to be effective. Three weeks later, George was back at work. Maintenance doses of lithium were prescribed in an attempt to prevent future mood swings.

His first fully developed manic period began suddenly near the end of the next spring track season. The team was having a very good year, and a few team members had turned in remarkable individual performances. Two days before the conference meet, Cheryl noticed that George was behaving strangely. There was a driven quality about his preparation for the meet. He was working much longer hours and demanding more from the athletes. When he was home, he talked endlessly about the team, bragging about their chances for national recognition, and planning intricate strategies for particularly important events. Cheryl was clearly worried about this change in George's behavior, but she attributed it to the pressures of his job and assured herself that he would return to normal when the season was over.

George was clearly losing control over his own behavior. The following incident, which occurred on the day of the conference meet, illustrates the dramatic quality of his disturbance. While the men's team was dressing in the locker room prior to taking the field, George paced rapidly up and down the aisles, gesturing emphatically and talking at length about specific events and the virtues of winning. When the men were all in uniform, George gathered them around his own locker. Without Cheryl's knowledge, he had removed a ceremonial sword from their fireplace mantel and brought it with him that morning. He drew the sword from his locker and leaped up on a bench in the midst of the men. Swinging the sword above his head, he began chanting the school fight song. The athletes joined in, and he lead them out onto the field screaming and shaking their fists in the air. A reporter for the school newspaper later described the incident as the most inspirational pregame performance he had ever seen in a locker room. Without question, the team was driven to an exceptional emotional peak, and they did go on to win the meet by an embarrassing margin. In fact, George was later given the school's annual coaching award. His behavior prior to this meet was specifically cited as an example of his outstanding leadership qualities. Unfortunately, the action was also another manifestation of psychopathology and a signal of further problems that would soon follow.

George did not return home after the meet. He stayed at his office, working straight through the night in preparation for the regional meet. Cheryl was finally able to locate him by phoning his friend who worked in the office next door. She and his colleagues tried to persuade him to slow down, but he would not listen. The next morning George was approached by a reporter from the school newspaper. Here, George thought, was the perfect opportunity to expound on his ability as a coach and to publicize his exciting plans for future competition. The interview turned into a grandiose tirade, with George rambling uninterrupted for 3 hours. The reporter could neither interrupt nor extract himself from this unexpected and embarrassing situation.

The interview turned into a professional disaster for George. Among other things, George boasted that he was going to send the star high jumper from the women's team to the NCAA national meet in Oregon. He planned to go along as her chaparone and said that he would pay for their trip out of the proceeds of a recent community fund-raising drive. This announcement was startling in two regards. First, the money in question had been raised with the athletic department's assurance that it would be used to improve the college's track facilities and to sponsor running clinics for local youngsters. George did not have the authority to reroute the funds. His announcement was certain to anger the business leaders who had organized the drive. Second, the prospect of a married male coach chaperoning a female athlete, who also happened to be quite attractive, promised to raise a minor scandal. Recognizing the sensitive nature of these plans, the reporter asked George if he might want to reconsider his brash announcement. George replied—asking the reporter to quote him—that it was not every year that he had the opportunity to take a free trip with a pretty girl and he was not about to pass it up. He added that this might blossom into a genuine romance.

The article appeared, along with a picture of George, on the front page of the school paper the next morning. His disheveled appearance and outrageous remarks raised an instant furor in the athletic department and the school administration. The head of the department finally located George in his office making a series of long-distance calls. The director demanded an explanation and immediately found himself in the midst of an ear-shattering shouting match. George claimed that he had just been named head coach of the Olympic track team. He was now calling potential assistant coaches and athletes around the country to organize tryouts for the following month. Any interference, he claimed, would be attributed to the communist countries that were reluctant to compete against a team led by a coach with such a distinguished record. The department head realized that George was not kidding and that he could not reason with him. He returned to his own office and phoned Cheryl. When she arrived, they were unable to convince George that he needed help. They eventually realized that their only option was to call the police, who then took George to a psychiatric hospital. Following an intake evaluation, George was committed for 3 days of observation. Because he did not recognize the severity of his problems and refused to cooperate with his family and the hospital staff, it was necessary to follow an involuntary commitment procedure. The commitment order was signed by a judge on the following day, after a hospital psychiatrist testified in court that George might be dangerous to himself or others.

SOCIAL HISTORY

In most respects George's childhood was unremarkable. He grew up in a small, Midwestern town where his father taught history and coached the high-school football team. He had one older brother and two younger sisters. All of the children were fair to average students and very athletic. George loved all sports and excelled at most; he was the quarterback of the high-school football team and a starting forward in basketball; in the spring he doubled as the first baseman on the baseball team and quarter-mile specialist in track. When he accepted a football scholarship to the state university, everyone expected him to go on to play professional ball.

He was always very popular with other children. They looked to him for leadership, and he seemed to enjoy the role. He and his friends were mischievous but were never serious discipline problems. Although some of his friends began drinking alcohol quite a bit during high school, George always refused to join them. He had seen the problems created by his father's drinking and did not want to follow the same path.

George's father was an alcoholic. He had been abstinent for 10 years, but the family could remember vividly how difficult the problem had been. When George was 5 years old, he began to notice that his parents argued quite a lot—when his father was home, that is. His mother was distraught over her husband's drinking. She pleaded with him, screamed, and frequently threatened to take the children and leave if he touched another drop. He would agree, then disappear over night or lock himself in the bathroom to drink liquor he had hidden there. The principal of the high school and the school board finally became involved after receiving complaints about George's father being drunk in the classroom. Instead of losing his job, George's father agreed to a period of hospitalization at a nearby drug treatment center. He joined Alcoholics Anonymous and managed to recover completely. Everyone agreed that the change in his behavior was remarkable.

George's uncle Ralph, his mother's brother, had also experienced serious adjustment problems. Ralph was several years older than George's mother, and the principal incidents occurred before George was born. George was therefore uncertain of the details, but he had been told that Ralph had been hospitalized twice following periods of rather wild behavior. A later search of hospital records confirmed that these had, in fact, been maniclike episodes. Although Ralph had been assigned a diagnosis of acute schizophrenic reaction, contemporary criteria would certainly have required a diagnosis of manic disorder.

CONCEPTUALIZATION AND TREATMENT

When George was admitted to the hospital, he was clearly out of control. He was racing in high gear despite the fact that he had not slept for several days. He was nearing a state of physical exhaustion. The psychiatrist immediately prescribed a moderate dosage of Haloperidol (Haldol), an antipsychotic drug that is also used to treat schizophrenic patients. George was supposed to have been taking lithium carbonate prior to the onset of the episode, but a check of his blood lithium level indicated that he had not been following the prescribed procedure. He was therefore started on a dose of 900 milligrams of lithium on the first day. This was increased to 1800 milligrams per day over the next 2 weeks. The hospital nursing staff took blood tests every third day to ensure that the blood lithium level did not exceed 1.4 milliequivalents per liter—the point at which toxic effects might be expected. After 3 weeks, the Haldol was discontinued and George continued to receive maintenance doses of lithium (2100 milligrams per day).

George and Cheryl were, once again, given very specific instructions pertaining to the potential hazards of taking lithium. The importance of a proper diet, and particularly a normal level of salt intake, was stressed. They were also told about the early warning signs of lithium intoxication (e.g., nausea, gastrointestinal distress, muscular weakness) so that they could warn George's psychiatrist if the dosage needed to be reduced.

In addition, George was involved in a number of other therapeutic activities. He and the other patients on the ward met daily for sessions of group psychotherapy. There were also several recreational and occupational activities that could be chosen by the patients according to their own interests. Visits by family members and close friends were encouraged during the evening hours. When George's behavior had improved, he was taken off restricted status and allowed to leave the ward for short periods of time.

George was discharged from the hospital after 27 days. His behavior had improved dramatically. The first few days in the hospital had been very difficult for everyone concerned. He had been so excited that the entire ward routine had been disrupted. Mealtimes were utterly chaotic and, when the patients were supposed to go to sleep for the night, George shouted and ran around like a child going to his first slumber party. The physical exertion finally took its toll. He fell into a state of nearly complete exhaustion. After sleeping for the better part of 3 days, George's demeanor was somewhat more subdued. He had given up the grandiose notion about Olympic fame and seemed to be in better control of his speech and motor behavior. But he had not returned to normal. He was still given to rambling speeches and continued to flirt with the female staff members. His mood was unstable, fluctuating between comical amusement and quick irritation. In contrast to most of the other patients, George was gregarious and energetic. He organized group activities and saw himself as an involuntary hospital aide, not as a patient.

These residual symptoms dissipated gradually over the next 2 weeks. He was switched to voluntary status and now recognized the severity of his previous condition. In retrospect, the events that had struck him as exhilarating and amusing seemed like a nightmare. He said that his thoughts had been racing a mile a minute. He had been totally obsessed with the conference meet and upcoming events. The locker room incident caused him considerable concern as he admitted the possibility that he could have seriously injured someone with the sword.

Following discharge, George was kept on a maintenance dosage of lithium. He attended the hospital's outpatient clinic regularly for individual psychotherapy, and his blood levels of lithium were carefully monitored. George and Cheryl also began conjoint therapy sessions with a dual purpose in mind. They needed to work on improving their own relationship, and they also wanted to acquire more effective means of interacting with and controlling their children.

Unfortunately, this aspect of the treatment program was unsuccessful. Cheryl had been seriously embarrassed by George's behavior during the manic episode. The cruelest blow came with the newspaper article in which George had announced his affection for another woman. This incident seemed to leave an insurmountable wall of tension between George and Cheryl. They both made a serious effort to improve their relationship. Their therapist designed a contractual program in which they agreed to change specific behaviors identified by their partner as particularly problematic. For example, Cheryl had always been annoyed by George's absence from their evening meal. His track season was over, and she argued that he could easily arrange to be home by 6 P.M. for dinner if he cared for her and the children. George, on the other hand, complained that Cheryl never showed any interest in sports. They agreed to an exchange of the following format: George would be home from work by 6 P.M. every day during the week, and Cheryl would go to a baseball game with him once a month. Other agreements were reached involving things such as Cheryl's long-distance telephone calls, George leaving his clothes all over the house, and so on. A concurrent program of communication training was begun to improve their ability to listen, make requests, provide positive feedback, and a variety of other important skills. The therapist noticed an improvement in their interactions during therapy sessions, but they continued to have periodic, heated fights at home. Cheryl finally decided that the situation was hopeless and, 6 months after George was discharged from the hospital, she filed for a divorce.

George was, of course, shaken by this development, but managed to avoid becoming seriously depressed. His friends from work were an important source of social support, particularly during the first few weeks after Cheryl and the children moved to another apartment. He also met more frequently with his therapist during this period and continued to take lithium carbonate.

DISCUSSION

Affective disorders are characterized by a serious, prolonged disturbance of mood. These disturbances may take the form of depression or elation. They are accompanied by a host of other problems, including changes in sleep patterns, appetite, and activity level. Several classification systems have been used to subdivide this broad category into more homogeneous groups. For example, a distinction has been drawn between psychotic and neurotic depression on the basis of the severity of the symptoms. Another system, known as the exogenous/endogenous distinction, relies on the presence or absence of an external event that may have triggered the change in the patient's mood. Most of these systems have now been abandoned. Some were difficult to use reliably. In other cases the distinction being drawn did not lead to meaningful treatment considerations. Consider, for example, the exogenous/endogenous distinction. It is often difficult to determine whether or not an event had occurred at the time that the patient began to feel depressed. The patient's memory may be blurred by subsequent emotional experiences, and friends may provide conflicting reports. Furthermore, even if everyone agrees that a particular event did occur, how can we determine whether it actually led to a change in the patient's mood? The loss of a job, for example, might be a *consequence* of the early signs of depression (e.g., loss of concentration, erratic sleeping patterns) and not a precipitant of the disorder.

The classification system that currently seems most useful and that is represented in *DSM-III* draws a distinction between bipolar and unipolar affective disorders. In bipolar disorders the patient experiences periods of extreme elation known as manic episodes. These periods usually alternate with periods of normal mood and periods of severe depression to form a kind of unpredictable emotional cycle that some patients liken to a roller coaster ride. Unipolar patients, on the other hand, experience serious depression without ever swinging to the opposite extreme. George had exhibited manic as well as depressive symptoms, so his problem would be diagnosed as a bipolar affective disorder.

DSM-III (pp. 208–209) lists the following criteria for manic episode.

A. *One or more distinct periods with a predominantly elevated, expansive, or irritable mood. The elevated or irritable mood must be a prominent part of the illness and relatively persistent, although it may alternate or intermingle with depressive mood.*

B. *Duration of at least one week (or any duration if hospitalization is necessary), during which, for most of the time, at least three of the following symptoms have persisted (four if the mood is only irritable) and have been present to a significant degree:*

- *(1) increase in activity (either socially, at work, or sexually) or physical restlessness*
- *(2) more talkative than usual or pressure to keep talking*
- *(3) flight of ideas or subjective experience that thoughts are racing*
- *(4) inflated self-esteem (grandiosity, which may be delusional)*

(5) decreased need for sleep

(6) distractibility, i.e., attention is too easily drawn to unimportant or irrelevant external stimuli

(7) excessive involvement in activities that have a high potential for painful consequences, which is not recognized, e.g., buying sprees, sexual indiscretions, foolish business investments, reckless driving

C. Neither of the following dominates the clinical picture when an affective syndrome is absent (i.e., symptoms in criteria A and B above):

(1) preoccupation with a mood-incongruent delusion or hallucination

(2) bizarre behavior

D. Not superimposed on either Schizophrenia, Schizophreniform Disorder, or a Paranoid Disorder.

E. Not due to any Organic Mental Disorder, such as Substance Intoxication.

Bipolar affective disorders should be distinguished from schizophrenia as well as from unipolar affective disorders. Kraepelin (1917) recognized that manic and schizophrenic (dementia praecox) patients often exhibit similar symptoms. These include disorganized speech, flight of ideas, and delusional thinking. He argued that the difference between the two disorders became apparent on examination of their long-term course. Most patients who fit Kraepelin's definition of schizophrenia showed a progressive deterioration without periods of recovery. Manic-depressive patients, on the other hand, frequently followed a remitting course. Although they might have repeated episodes of psychotic behavior, their adjustment between episodes was relatively unimpaired. This distinction has continued to be one of the most important considerations in the classification of psychotic disorders.

Until recently, the diagnostic practices of many American psychiatrists had drifted away from the tradition established by Kraepelin. Between the 1930s and the 1970s, mental health professionals in the United States considered the vast majority of psychotic patients to be schizophrenic, regardless of the presence of affective symptoms. This trend was clearly illustrated in the United States-United Kingdom Cross-National Study (Cooper et al., 1972). Patients in New York and London were diagnosed by local hospital staff and by British investigators from the project. Over 90% of the patients who were diagnosed as being manic by the British research team were considered schizophrenic by the American psychiatrists. This tendency toward overdiagnosing schizophrenia and underdiagnosing manic-depressive disorder has been reversed with the introduction of *DSM-III*.

The distinction between bipolar and unipolar affective disorders has generally been based on the presence or absence of manic episodes. Patients who exhibit manic episodes will be considered bipolar. If a patient has never been hospitalized or treated during a manic phase, he or she will usually be considered to be suffering from a unipolar disorder. Recent evidence suggests that the picture may not be this simple (Depue and Monroe, 1978). Several investigators have suggested that some patients who seem to be unipolar may, in fact, be more closely related to bipolar disorders. For example, what about the patient who has never had a full-blown manic episode but nevertheless experiences periodic bouts of sleeplessness, irritability, and dramatically increased energy? This kind of subclinical manic phase is known as *hypomania*. In terms of response to medication and family history, many patients of this type share more in common with bipolar than with unipolar patients. For this reason, they have come to be known, at least among researchers, as bipolar II patients. A third category, bipolar III patients, includes depressed patients who have not experienced manic or hypomanic phases themselves but who have a close relative who has a bipolar affective disorder. Future research will clarify the relationship among these various categories. For the present, it is useful to recognize the variety of problems represented within affective disorders and to distinguish among the various forms of bipolar and unipolar disorders.

The incidence of affective disorders has not been clearly established. The failure to agree on a specific set of diagnostic criteria probably accounts for most of the variability among studies. Some investigators have reported the incidence of affective disorders to be less than 2% of the population; others cite figures as high as 7% (Rosenthal, 1970). All of the studies agree that unipolar disorders are more common than are bipolar disorders. The most typical estimates indicate that 10 to 20% of affective patients have bipolar disorders (Bratfos and Haug, 1968; Clayton, Pitts, and Winokur, 1965). Both unipolar and bipolar disorders are more common in women than in men, but the sex ratio is smaller in bipolar disorders. In contrast to schizophrenia, bipolar affective disorders are not more common in lower social strata (Dohrenwend and Dohrenwend, 1974).

There are important differences between unipolar and bipolar disorders in terms of both the age of onset and the course of the disorder (Depue and Monroe, 1978). Bipolar patients tend to be younger at the time of their first episode of disturbance than unipolar patients, usually between the ages of 20 and 30. A follow-up study reported by Angst and his colleagues indicated that bipolar patients also tend to experience a greater number of psychotic episodes during subsequent years and are more likely to experience impairment between episodes (Angst et al., 1978). These data have been supported by a more recent American study. Welner and his colleagues found that approximately 30% of the bipolar patients studied showed a long-term impairment either in terms of continued expression of symptoms or chronic social impairment. Furthermore, another group of patients, who did not follow a chronic course, experienced a permanent decline in their social and occupational status as a consequence of their behavior during periods of acute psychosis (Welner, Welner, and Leonard, 1977).

George's case was typical of the classic picture of manic-depressive illness. He showed an early onset of symptoms and a relatively complete remission between episodes. On the other hand, his experience was also consistent with that of many patients in Welner's study. Although he did not exhibit symptoms of social impairment following a period of disturbance, his behavior was so disruptive during each manic episode that it had serious long-term consequences. He was eventually fired from his job, and his marriage had been pushed to the edge of divorce.

ETIOLOGY

The fact that George's maternal uncle had also experienced manic episodes is consistent with the literature concerning genetic factors in affective disorders. Several family studies have found that the biological relatives of affective patients are more likely to develop affective disorders than are people in the general population. These data are usually reported in terms of "morbid risk," or the probability that given individuals will develop the disorder during their lifetimes. Several studies have now reported that the relatives of unipolar depressives are at increased risk for unipolar depression, but that they are unlikely to exhibit bipolar affective disorder (e.g., Angst, 1966; Perris, 1966). The relatives of bipolar patients, on the other hand, typically demonstrate an increased risk for both unipolar and bipolar disorders (see Gershon et al., 1977). These data have generally been taken to indicate that the bipolar and unipolar subgroups are genetically distinct. George's positive family history for bipolar disorder thus may be taken as further validation of his bipolar diagnosis and was, in fact, helpful in the decision to try lithium carbonate prior to his first full manic episode.

The role of genetic factors in the etiology of affective disorders would be much clearer if a specific model of genetic action could be identified. As in the case of schizophrenia, numerous investigators have compared the relative merits of polygenic models versus single-locus models, dominant versus recessive models, and so on. Among the most interesting and persuasive arguments has been the suggestion that bipolar affective disorders follow an X-linked, dominant pattern of transmission. Winokur and his colleagues noticed two important patterns in a family history study of bipolar affective disorder. First, the patients' female relatives were at greater risk than the patients' male relatives. The ratio of females to males was approximately 2:1. Second, the investigators noticed a complete absence of father-to-son transmission. Depressed mothers produced an equivalent number of depressed sons and daughters; depressed fathers produced only depressed daughters. These facts are consistent with the notion that bipolar affective disorder is controlled by a dominant gene that is located on the X chromosome. The logic is as follows. Women possess two X chromosomes; one is inherited from their mothers and one from their fathers. Men, on the other hand, possess one X chromosome that is inherited from their mothers and one Y chromosome that is inherited from their fathers. If bipolar affective disorder is controlled by a dominant gene on the X chromosome, women should be twice as likely to develop bipolar disorders; men with bipolar disorders should not transmit the disorder to their sons (Winokur, Clayton, and Reich, 1969).

Further support for this theory has come from studies concerned with genetic linkage. Geneticists have already identified some characteristics that are clearly expressions of genes located on the X chromosome, such as color blindness and some blood groups. If bipolar depression is related to a dominant gene that is also located on the X chromosome,[1] we would expect the two characteristics to appear together within a particular family tree, or pedigree. Mendlewicz and Fleiss (1974) have reported on a series of 21 pedigrees in which there seems to be a strong relationship between bipolar affective disorder and the Xg blood group. They have also found a relationship betwen bipolar disorders and color blindness. Taken together with the data regarding sex ratios and parent-child transmission pattern, these results provide convincing evidence for the dominant, X-linked hypothesis. There are, of course, conflicting bits of evidence and problems with the methods employed in the linkage studies (Gershon et al., 1977). In contrast to Winokur's data, several cases have now been reported in which father-son pairs have both exhibited bipolar affective disorders. According to the X-linkage hypothesis, this pattern should never appear. Proponents of the hypothesis now argue that it does not apply to all cases of bipolar disorder, but that it may account for a substantial subset of these cases (e.g., Mendlewicz, 1980).

Perhaps the most prominent biochemical theory of bipolar affective disorder is concerned with norepinephrine, one of the major neurotransmitters. Neurotransmitters are chemicals that facilitate the transmission of nerve impulses by bridging the synaptic cleft between individual neurons. Several investigators have proposed that depression is the result of *decreased* levels of norepinephrine and that mania is the product of an *excess* amount of this same substance (e.g., Schildkraut, 1965). In lieu of a

[1]The demonstration of linkage assumes that the two loci are not only on the same chromosome but are also sufficiently close together to detect the relationship.

technology to measure chemical substances in live human brains, two indirect methods have been used to test this hypothesis. One method involves measuring the metabolites, or by-products, of norepinephrine in patients' blood, urine, and cerebrospinal fluid. Several studies have reported lower levels of MHPG in depressed patients (e.g., Greenspan et al., 1970). One longitudinal study of bipolar patients indicated that norepinephrine levels decreased when the patients became depressed and increased when they became manic (Bunney, Goodwin, and Murphy, 1972). The second method involves injecting drugs that should change the level of norepinephrine in the brain and then examining its effect on the patients' mood. In at least one case, a drug that increases norepinephrine levels precipitated a manic episode in a bipolar patient (Bunney et al., 1970). Thus there is some support for the norepinephrine theory.

Despite these encouraging findings, the biochemical data must be interpreted with caution. They are mostly correlational in nature and therefore subject to the problems of directionality and third variables. For example, depression has been shown to be correlated with low levels of MHPG. Inactivity can also lead to low levels of MHPG (Post et al., 1973). It may be, therefore, that low MHPG is a by-product of depressives' low activity level and not of a preexisting biochemical deficiency that is causally related to the disorder.

Although genetic factors play some role in the development of bipolar affective disorder, they cannot account for it completely. Various experiences throughout the person's life must also influence the onset or expression of psychotic symptoms. The generally accepted diathesis-stress model would suggest that bipolar patients inherited some unidentified form of predisposition to the disorder and that the expression of this predisposition then depends on subsequent environmental events. In George's case it would be reasonable to wonder whether the highly competitive atmosphere associated with college coaching might have triggered the onset of his manic symptoms or his depressive episodes. The weeks preceding his manic episode were busier than usual. His teams had been winning, and the athletic department's administration seemed to be putting considerable emphasis on the final meets of the season. Viewed from George's perspective, this amounted to enormous pressure. The job situation was also compounded by his family responsibilities. As he began to spend more and more time with his team, his wife became increasingly discontent and irritable. Her demands, coupled with his coaching responsibilities, placed George in a very difficult position; he could reduce the amount of time spent planning and supervising workouts, thus increasing the probability that the team would lose, or he could reduce the amount of time spent with his wife and children, thus increasing the probability that she would ask for a divorce.

The notion that these kinds of stressful experiences can precipitate manic episodes is intuitively appealing, but the research literature does not indicate a clear link between the two events. Consider, for example, the following investigation. Hall and her colleagues studied a group of bipolar patients who had been hospitalized at least once for manic behavior and who were receiving lithium treatment on an outpatient basis (Hall et al., 1977). Each patient was interviewed approximately once each month during his or her visit to the clinic. At each assessment, ratings were made of the patients' mood, and the patients were asked to describe important events that had occurred since their last visit. Twenty-one of the 38 patients remained well over the course of the study (1 year), 6 became manic, 8 became depressed, and 3 experienced both mania and depression. The patients who remained well and those who experienced further episodes did *not* differ significantly in terms of either the number or the type of events that they reported prior to the onset of symptoms. There was a slight trend for the patients who had manic episodes to report more problems with superiors at work in the visit prior to the onset of symptoms, but the difference between these patients and those who remained well was not statistically significant.

George's relationship with his family illustrates the complex interactive nature of affective disorders. Although his marital problems may not have been caused by his affective symptoms, they certainly made an already difficult situation virtually impossible. The marital adjustment of bipolar patients has received considerable attention in the research literature, which indicates that bipolar patients are much more likely to be divorced than unipolar patients or people in the general population. Brodie and Leff (1971) compared 30 pairs of unipolar and bipolar patients. They found that 57% of the bipolar patients were divorced in comparison to only 8% of the unipolar cases. George's situation was probably typical of the problems experienced by manic patients. Cheryl was forced by his erratic behavior to act as a buffer between George and the community. When he acted strangely at work, his colleagues called her to see if she could explain his behavior. She often found herself making up excuses for him in order to avoid the unpleasant necessity of disclosing the personal details of his problems. Her efforts were then "rewarded" by his continued excesses. Cheryl gradually came to see herself as a victim. The incident with the undergraduate student was the last straw. George's behavior was even more difficult for Cheryl to understand and accept because of his inconsistency. She argued that if he were always irrational or out of control, she could easily attribute these problems to a psychiatric disorder. However, between episodes, and most of the time, George was a very reasonable, considerate person. Cheryl found it difficult to believe that he could change so drastically over such a short period of time. Her first inclination was always to attribute his wild, manic behavior to some malicious intent on his part. When he became depressed, she often blamed herself. Eventually, the problem was simply more than she could handle.

TREATMENT

Lithium is the treatment of choice for bipolar affective disorders. The therapeutic effects of lithium salts were first reported in 1949 by John Cade, and Australian psychiatrist. Cade had been studying the toxic effects of uric acid in guinea pigs and the possibility that the lithium ion might reduce this toxicity. He was not initially interested in behavioral effects, but he happened to notice that guinea pigs that had been injected with lithium carbonate became lethargic and unresponsive to stimuli despite remaining fully conscious. This unexpected finding led Cade to wonder whether lithium carbonate might have beneficial effects for psychotic patients who were extremely excited. He used the drug with a sequence of 10 manic patients and obtained remarkable results. Even chronic patients who had been considered untreatable responded favorably within a period of several days. Furthermore, several schizophrenic patients who had previously been markedly restless and excited became quiet and amenable. When lithium was discontinued, the patients generally returned to their previous patterns of wild behavior.

Other clinicians soon began to experiment with the use of lithium and met with similar results. Their favorable impressions of lithium's effects were later confirmed by a number of controlled, double-blind studies (e.g., Schou et al., 1954).

Despite the uniformly positive results of these early investigations, American psychiatrists did not become enthusiastic about the use of lithium until the 1970s. A variety of factors may account for this delay. Perhaps most important were the dangerous side effects associated with the use of lithium. Lithium had been used as a substitute for table salt by patients with heart and kidney problems. A number of severe poisonings and some deaths were reported only a few months before the publication of Cade's report, leading the Food and Drug Administration (FDA) to restrict the use of lithium. The introduction of lithium also coincided with the discovery of the beneficial effects of phenothiazines and the introduction of a series of antipsychotic, antidepressant, and antianxiety drugs in the 1950s. The startling effects of lithium seemed to get lost in the crowd. Nevertheless, a number of investigators continued to examine the therapeutic effects of lithium carbonate, and the evidence was soon overwhelming (Schlagenhauf, Tupin, and White, 1966; Schou, 1968). In addition to its ability to calm patients who were acutely excited, it became clear that lithium was also effective in reducing the risk of future mood swings (Baastrup and Schou, 1967). Many people believed that it was the first prophylactic drug available to psychiatrists in the treatment of abnormal behavior. The FDA finally dropped its restrictions and approved lithium for the treatment of affective disorders in 1970.

In addition to his series of manic patients, Cade also tried lithium with a few depressed patients. His concern was that the apparent tranquilizing effects of lithium might lead depressed patients to become even more depressed and withdrawn. Fortunately, they did not. Subsequent studies have, in fact, demonstrated that lithium can be beneficial for patients who are depressed as well as for those who are manic. This is particularly true for bipolar patients. For example, Baron and his colleagues (Baron et al., 1975) treated 130 depressed patients; 80% of the bipolar patients improved significantly while they were receiving lithium, but only 40% of the unipolar patients showed similar gains. These data indicate that lithium is a reasonable choice in the treatment of bipolar patients who are depressed. They also indicate, once again, that bipolar and unipolar patients seem to be suffering from distinct disorders.

The ability of lithium to prevent future psychotic episodes was first demonstrated by Baastrup and Schou (1967). They compared the behavior of 88 bipolar patients before and after they were treated with lithium. Before treatment, the patients experienced relapses approximately once every 8 months. After they were stabilized on lithium, relapses occurred once every 60 to 85 months. Several subsequent studies that used double-blind procedures and placebo control groups have been examined by Davis (1976) and by Quitkin, Rifkin, and Klein (1976). Both reviews concluded that lithium is clearly effective in preventing the recurrence of manic episodes and probably effective in preventing recurrent depression in bipolar patients.

George's manic episode occurred despite the fact that he was being maintained on lithium carbonate. Nevertheless, it might be argued that the severity and length of this episode were reduced because he was taking lithium. He did respond favorably during his brief stay in the hospital, and he returned to his job very quickly after discharge. It is also possible that the episode might have been triggered by a failure to take the medication regularly. This is a serious problem with all forms of psychopharmacological treatment. It is particularly severe with psychotic patients who characteristically lack insight into the severity of their problems. Every effort is usually made to educate the patient in this regard. The cooperation of family members is often enlisted to assist in the regulation of daily doses. The dangers of lithium also require that patients being treated on an outpatient basis be seen regularly to monitor levels of lithium in the blood. In spite of these precautions, many patients fail to follow medication schedules designed to prevent relapse.

6

SOCIOPATHY

This case differs from most of the others in this book because Bill was never in therapy. One of the authors was acquainted with Bill during childhood and adolescence. The following case history is based on this personal experience.

Bill was the third child in the Wallace family. His parents, originally from Europe, had emigrated when Bill was 9 years old. They rented an apartment on the upper floor of a house in a middle-class neighborhood, and Bill's father got a job in a local factory. His mother worked part-time in a supermarket. No information is available concerning the family's history when they lived in Europe.

Bill and his older brother, Jack, quickly became part of the neighborhood group and participated in the usual run of activities, including baseball, football, outings to the beach, and ball games. Jack became a leading figure in the group and Bill, although not as well regarded as his brother, was always included in its activities.

It was at this time that I began to get to know Bill well. We were the same age; most of the other boys were older. Although we became friends, our relationship was also characterized by a good deal of conflict. When things did not go Bill's way, his response was simple and direct—a fight. My first fight with Bill took place during a baseball game at a local park. We were on opposing teams and were involved in a close play at second base. He slid into the base, I tagged and called "out," and Bill jumped up swinging his fists. Although he lost these fights as often as he won, this became a consistent pattern in his relationships, both with me and with other neighborhood children. Not even an older and obviously stronger opponent could get Bill to back down.

Bill's aggressiveness was not really what led me to regard him as "different" as we grew up together. His escalating daredevil and antisocial behavior seemed more peculiar. One of the first of these episodes occurred when Bill organized a window-breaking competition. He explained to me and three other boys our age that he had recently been walking neighborhood streets at night, throwing rocks through windows. With great enthusiasm he described the excitement this created and how he had easily eluded the few residents who had come out to try to catch him. Bill wanted the four of us to compete in a window-breaking contest. He had worked out a detailed point system—the larger the window, the more points—and wanted to start that night. We all agreed to meet at 7:30 in front of his house.

We met as planned and first filled our pockets with stones. The competition soon began, with Bill clearly in the role of leader, encouraging the rest of us and pointing out windows that would yield many points. My own reaction, as all this began, was extreme fear. All I could think of was "What if we get caught?" Bill, in contrast, showed no signs of apprehension. Indeed, he seemed ecstatic and was virtually bubbling over with enthusiasm. His only negative reaction of the evening was directed toward me when, after "missing" several windows, I emptied my pockets and withdrew from the competition. The other two boys went along with Bill. They also seemed frightened, but they looked up to Bill and may have been more concerned about eliciting his disapproval. Although I was excluded from subsequent nights of competition, Bill eagerly kept me informed of the results. After several months, he was declared the winner when he broke all the large windows of the supermarket in which his mother worked.

At age 10, petty theft replaced window breaking as Bill's major source of excitement. It seemed to me that I was never in a store with him when he did not steal something. He would steal anything—candy, fruit, clothing, toys—not just things he wanted. In fact, he often threw away the things he had stolen. He seemed more interested in the excitement than in any actual material gain. He had discovered several ways of getting money. The first was a Roman Catholic church that had two easy sources of cash—a poor box and a container for donations left by worshippers who had lit a candle. Bill cleaned both out on a regular basis. His second source was a restaurant that had a wishing well, located in a rear garden, whose proceeds were to go to the Salvation Army. Although the wishing well was covered with a metal grate, Bill found that there was one opening that was just large enough to get his hand through. Every couple of weeks, armed with a flashlight and a long stick, he would sneak into the garden at night, move the coins to the right spot, and collect them. Finally, he regularly stole milk money from various neighborhood homes.[1] Bill even stole the milk money from my home. The first time our money was missing, I went directly after him and accused him of the theft. He denied it. The second time, he admitted the theft and offered to cut me in if I would keep quiet!

A final incident, which occurred when Bill and I were both 12, crystalized for me how Bill was somehow different. About a 15-minute walk from our homes was a river that had many expensive houses along its banks. A tremendous rainstorm caused a flood and, tragically, more than 100 people were killed. Early the next morning, with the news of the disaster in the papers and on the radio, Bill set out for the scene, not just to see the devastation but with a plan. Because the victims were wealthy, Bill reasoned, he might strike it rich if he could be the first to find some bodies and take their wallets, watches, and jewelry. He went alone, returned later in the day, and proudly displayed his loot—six watches and several hundred dollars. He returned to the river several more times over the next few days and, although he returned empty handed, he would enthusiastically relate his experiences to anyone who would listen. The excitement and danger seemed more important than the valuables he might find.

During these 3 years, most of the neighborhood youngsters had also received more than a glimpse of the Wallaces' family life. Bill's father was frequently out of work and seemed to have trouble holding a job for more than several months at a stretch. He drank heavily. While we played street ball, we often saw him returning home, obviously drunk. At a first glimpse of their drunken father, both Bill and Jack would get out of his sight as quickly as possible. Both boys reported frequent beatings, particularly when their father had been drinking. At the same time, Bill's father allowed him to get away with things, such as staying out late at night, that none of the other neighborhood children were allowed to do. Bill and Jack both reported that their father was unpredictable in his punishments. Their father and mother also fought often. On many occasions, our play was interrupted by yelling and the sound of loud crashes from their apartment.

The Wallaces eventually moved to an apartment in a lower-middle-class area of the city, about a 30-minute bus ride from their first home. Bill and I were no longer close friends, but I kept track of Bill through Jack, his older brother. According to Jack, Bill's pattern of antisocial behavior began to escalate. He continued to steal regularly, even from members of his family. He was frequently truant from school and got into even more serious trouble for hitting a teacher who had tried to break up a fight between him and another boy. Jack was very concerned about Bill and attempted to talk to

[1]At the time, most homes got daily milk deliveries and people simply left money and empty bottles in a place where the milkman could collect them.

him several times. Jack reported that during these talks, Bill would genuinely seem to agree that he had to change and would express shame and regret about whatever he had done most recently. However, within a few days, the old pattern would be back in full force. Jack eventually came to see Bill's contrition as a con.

We were both 15 the next time I met Bill. Through my continued contacts with Jack, I had learned that Bill had been sent to reform school. I did not know any of the details because Jack had been so ashamed of his brother's behavior that he would not talk about it. One evening, shortly after dinner, the doorbell rang. I answered, and Bill motioned me outside. He had escaped from reform school and wanted me to buy him a meal and loan him some money. Off we went to a local restaurant where I bought him a hamburger and Cokes for both of us. He told me that he had been convicted of car theft and rape the previous year. He had been stealing cars regularly and taking them on joyrides. He was caught when he decided to hold on to a stolen car, one that had particularly caught his fancy. The third day that he had the car, he had parked in a deserted place with a 12-year-old girl he knew from school. He raped her, and she reported him.

As Bill related the story, he became visibly disgusted, not at himself, but at the girl. As he explained it, he was only trying to have some fun and had picked this particular girl because she was only 12 and not likely able to get pregnant. From his perspective, it was an ideal situation. With pregnancy impossible, she should have just lain back and enjoyed it.

I never saw Bill again but, through Jack, learned what happened to him over the next several years. Several weeks after our meeting, he was apprehended by the police. He had again stolen a car; while driving drunk, he had smashed into a telephone poll. After a short stay in a hospital, he was returned to the reformatory, where he spent 2 years. When he was released, Bill had changed greatly. It seemed to Jack that he had now become a real criminal. Car thefts were no longer for joyrides but for profit. Bill became involved in selling stolen cars to others who stripped them to sell their parts. He briefly returned to high school but, with no friends there and little real interest, he soon dropped out. He became a regular at the racetrack and lost money there and with several bookmakers. As had happened before, Jack tried to talk to his younger brother about the trouble for which he seemed headed. But now even the charade of shame and guilt was gone. Bill expressed an "I'll take what I want when I want it" attitude. When Jack tried to point out the likely negative consequences of his behavior, Bill simply shrugged it off, saying that he was too smart ever to end up in jail.

Shortly after his eighteenth birthday, Bill attempted a bank robbery, armed with a 38 caliber automatic pistol. It must have been an incredible scene. Bill was driving a stolen car. On seeing what he thought was a bank, he impulsively decided to rob it. In his rush he had actually undertaken to rob an office of the electric company. Seeing the people lined up at teller's windows to pay their bills had made him think it was a bank. Once inside, although recognizing his mistake, he decided to go through with the holdup anyway and had several tellers empty their cash drawers into a sack. A patrol car passed by the office as the holdup was in progress and, seeing what was happening, the policemen stopped to investigate. Bill ran out of the office directly into the police and was easily arrested. He was tried, convicted, and sentenced to 10 years in the penitentiary.

DISCUSSION

The modern view of the characteristics of sociopathy is due principally to the work of the psychiatrist, Hervey Cleckley. In several editions of his classic text, *The Mask of Sanity*, Cleckley has spelled out the key features of the disorder. The most recent edition (1976 pp. 337–338) lists the following 16 characteristics:

1. *Considerable superficial charm and average or better intelligence.*
2. *Absence of delusions or other signs of irrational thinking.*
3. *Absence of anxiety or other "neurotic" features.*
4. *Unreliability, disregard for obligations.*
5. *Untruthfulness and insincerity.*
6. *Lack of remorse or shame.*
7. *Inadequately motivated antisocial behavior.*
8. *Poor judgment and failure to learn from experience.*
9. *Pathological egocentricity, totally self-centered; incapacity for love.*
10. *General poverty of major emotional reactions.*
11. *Specific lack of insight, unable to see oneself the way others do.*
12. *Unresponsive to special considerations, kindness or trust.*
13. *Fantastic and uninviting behavior after drinking and sometimes with no drinking (e.g., vulgarity, rudeness, quick mood shifts, pranks).*
14. *No genuine suicide attempts.*
15. *Sex life impersonal, trivial and poorly integrated.*
16. *Failure to follow a life plan.*

Cleckley's description of the characteristics of sociopathy, which have been adopted by many researchers, are somewhat similar to one of *DSM-III*'s personality disorders, antisocial personality. The defining characteristics of this disorder are presented in Table 6.1. Sociopathy per se has not appeared in any of the various editions of the *DSM*. It should not be simply equated with antisocial personality disorder. The *DSM-III* definition of antisocial personality disorder, for example, does not mention several of the characteristics that Cleckley would regard as very important. These include superficial charm, lack of anxiety, and failure to experience guilt or shame. The *DSM-III* definition of antisocial personality comes close to being a general description of criminals. Hare (1978), for example, found that fully 76% of a sample of penitentiary inmates met the *DSM-III* criteria for antisocial personality disorder. In contrast, only 33% of these criminals met Cleckley's criteria for sociopathy.

Bill's behavior during childhood and adolescence clearly met many of Cleckley's criteria. He was unreliable, untruthful, lacking in any feelings of shame about his misconduct, and totally without anxiety. His antisocial behavior (such as stealing) was not motivated by any genuine desire to possess the stolen objects, and he often displayed poor judgment, particularly in his escapades of late adolescence. His lack of responsiveness to kindness and friendship was amply demonstrated by his thefts from homes of his friends and by his completely cavalier attitude toward the victim of his rape.

Table 6.1 Diagnostic Criteria for Antisocial Personality (DSM-III, American Psychiatric Association, 1980)

Diagnostic criteria for Antisocial Personality Disorder

A. Current age at least 18.

B. Onset before age 15 as indicated by a history of three or more of the following before that age:

1. Truancy (positive if it amounted to at least five days per year for at least two years, not including the last year of school).
2. Expulsion or suspension from school for misbehavior.
3. Delinquency (arrested or referred to juvenile court because of behavior).
4. Running away from home overnight at least twice while living in parental or parental surrogate home.
5. Persistent lying.
6. Repeated sexual intercourse in a casual relationship.
7. Repeated drunkenness or substance abuse.
8. Thefts.
9. Vandalism.
10. School grades markedly below expectations in relation to estimated or known IQ (may have resulted in repeating a year).
11. Chronic violations of rules at home and/or at school (other than truancy).
12. Initiation of fights.

C. At least four of the following manifestations of the disorder since age 18:

1. Inability to sustain consistent work behavior, as indicated by any of the following: (a) too frequent job changes (e.g., three or more jobs in five years not accounted for by nature of job or economic or seasonal fluctuation), (b) significant unemployment (e.g., six months or more in five years when expected to work), (c) serious absenteeism from work (e.g., average three days or more of lateness or absence per month), (d) walking off several jobs without other jobs in sight (*Note*: similar behavior in an academic setting during the last few years of school may substitute for this criterion in individuals who by reason of their age or circumstances have not had an opportunity to demonstrate occupational adjustment).

2. Lack of ability to function as a responsible parent as evidenced by one or more of the following: (a) child's malnutrition, (b) child's illness resulting from lack of minimal hygiene standards, (c) failure to obtain medical care for a seriously ill child, (d) child's dependence on neighbors or nonresident relatives for food or shelter, (e) failure to arrange for a caretaker for a child under six when parent is away from home, (f) repeated squandering, on personal items, of money required for household necessities.

3. Failure to accept social norms with respect to lawful behavior, as indicated by any of the following: repeated thefts, illegal occupation (pimping, prostitution, fencing, selling drugs), multiple arrests, a felony conviction.

4. Inability to maintain enduring attachment to a sexual partner as indicated by two or more divorces and/or separations (whether legally married or not), desertion of spouse, promiscuity (ten or more sexual partners within one year).

5. Irritability and aggressiveness as indicated by repeated physical fights or assault (not required by one's job or to defend someone or oneself), including spouse or child beating.

6. Failure to honor financial obligations, as indicated by repeated defaulting on debts, failure to provide child support, failure to support other dependents on a regular basis.

7. Failure to plan ahead, or impulsivity, as indicated by traveling from place to place without a prearranged job or clear goal for the period of travel or clear idea about when the travel would terminate, or lack of a fixed address for a month or more.

8. Disregard for the truth as indicated by repeated lying, use of aliases, "conning" others for personal profit.

9. Recklessness, as indicated by driving while intoxicated or recurrent speeding.

D. A pattern of continuous antisocial behavior in which the rights of others are violated, with no intervening period of at least five years without antisocial behavior between age 15 and the present time (except when the individual was bedridden or confined in a hospital or penal instituion).

E. Antisocial behavior is not due to either severe mental retardation, schizophrenia, or manic episodes.

Source: DSM-III, American Psychiatric Association, 1980, pp. 320–321.

ETIOLOGY OF SOCIOPATHY

What causes behavior like Bill's? As with most disorders, the search for the causes of sociopathy has considered both physiological and psychological variables. We will describe research efforts in several areas—the role of the family, genetics, and research on the sociopath's inability to avoid noxious stimuli.

The Role of the Family

Because the family is presumed to play a strong role in teaching children standards of acceptable conduct, it is not surprising that researchers have looked to possible family problems as the causes of the sociopath's failure to abide by society's rules. McCord and McCord (1964) concluded, on the basis of a review of the literature, that lack of affection and severe parental rejection were the primary causes of sociopathic behavior. Several other studies have related sociopathic behavior to the parent's inconsistency in discipline and a failure of parents to teach children their responsibilities to others (Bennet, 1960).

Such data on early rearing must be interpreted with extreme caution because they were gathered by means of retrospective reports. Information about early family experiences and about how the child was taught to behave socially was obtained either from an adult sociopath or from parents, relatives, and friends at a time very much later than when the events actually occurred. The reliability of information obtained in this way is often poor.

One way to avoid the problems of retrospective data is to follow up in adulthood individuals who as children were seen at a child guidance clinic. In one such study very detailed records had been kept on the children, including the type of problem that had brought them to the clinic and information on numerous variables related to the family (Robins, 1966, p. 157). By interviewing the now-adult individuals, the investigators were able to assign diagnoses and describe their adjustment as adults. Adult problems were then related back to the characteristics that these people had had as children in order to determine which of them predicted sociopathic behavior in adulthood. Robins (1966, p. 157) summarized her results as follows:

> *If one wishes to choose the most likely candidate for a later diagnosis of sociopathic personality from among children appearing in a child guidance clinic, the best choice appears to be a boy referred for theft or aggression who has shown a diversity of antisocial behavior in many episodes, at least one of which could be grounds for Juvenile Court appearance, and whose antisocial behavior involves him with strangers and organizations as well as with teachers and parents . . . more than half of the boys appearing at the clinic (with these characteristics were later) diagnosed sociopathic personality. Such boys had a history of truancy, theft, staying out late, and refusing to obey parents. They lied gratuitously, and showed little guilt over their behavior. They were generally irresponsible about being where they were supposed to be or taking care of money. They were interested in sexual activities and had experimented with homosexual relationships. . . .*

In addition to these characteristics, variables related to family life that were mentioned earlier were again found to be important. Both inconsistent discipline and no discipline at all predicted sociopathic behavior in adulthood, as did antisocial behavior of the father.

Note the excellent match between Robins' description of the childhood characteristics of sociopaths and Bill's behavior during childhood. The harsh yet inconsistent disciplinary practices of Bill's father also mesh well with Robins' findings. Both the case history and research findings suggest that child-rearing practices may play an important role in the etiology of sociopathy. It is also clear, however, that parental characteristics cannot provide a complete explanation of the development of sociopathy. Bill's brother, although exposed to a very similar home environment, had no sociopathic traits at all.

Avoidance Learning and Punishment

In defining the sociopathic syndrome, Cleckley pointed out the inability of these persons to learn from experience. In particular, they seemingly feel no need to avoid the negative consequences of social misbehavior. Cleckley also remarked that they were not neurotic and seldom anxious. From these clinical descriptions, Lykken (1957) deduced that sociopaths may have few inhibitions about committing antisocial acts because they experience no anxiety. One of his tests of this hypothesis involved avoidance learning.

A group of male sociopaths was selected from a penitentiary population. Their performance on an avoidance learning task was compared to that of nonsociopathic penitentiary inmates and of college students. It was critical that only avoidance learning and not learning mediated by other possible rewards be tested. If subjects perceive that their task is to learn to avoid pain, they may be motivated not only by the desire to avoid the pain but also by a desire to demonstrate their cleverness to the investigator. To ensure that no other motives would become manifest, Lykken made the avoidance learning task incidental. He used the following apparatus. On a panel in front of the subject there were four red lights in a horizontal array, four green lights (one below each of the red ones), and a lever below each pair of lights. The subject's task was to learn a sequence of 20 correct lever presses but, for each, he first had to determine by trial and error which of the four alternatives was correct. The correct lever turned on a green light. Two of the remaining three incorrect levers turned on red lights, indicating an error. The third incorrect lever delivered an electric shock to the subject. The location of the correct lever was not always the same. The subject was simple told to figure out and to learn the series of 20 correct lever presses. He was not informed that avoiding shock was desirable or possible, only that shock was randomly administered as a stimulant to make him do well. Thus the task yielded two measures of learning: the total number of errors made before the subject learned the correct sequence of 20 presses and the number of errors that produced shock. Avoidance learning was measured by this second index.

In terms of the overall number of errors made, there were no significant differences among any of the groups in Lykken's study. The college students, however, were apparently best able to remember the sequence of presses that produced shock and thus sharply decreased their proportion of shocked errors. The sociopaths made the most shocked errors, but the differences between their shocked errors and those of the other penitentiary inmates only approached statistical significance. The results of Lykken's investigation, therefore, tentatively supported the hypothesis that sociopaths operate under lower levels of anxiety than do normal individuals.

The hypothesis was subsequently given stronger support in a study by Schachter and Latané (1964). The study was much like Lykken's except that all participants were tested twice—once after an injection of a placebo and once after an injection of adrenalin, a drug that mimics the activity of the sympathetic nervous system and thus should increase anxiety. When tested in the placebo condition, the sociopaths avoided the shocks less well than did other subjects. When aroused by the adrenalin injection, however, the sociopaths quickly learned to avoid the shocks, thus supporting the theory.

In the avoidance learning studies discussed thus far, punishment was inevitable if a particular incorrect response was made. But many real-life crimes remain unsolved, so the sociopath is actually in a situation where punishment is uncertain. In these situations of uncertain punishment, according to some clinicians, the psychopath almost magically believes that antisocial behavior will not be punished. Siegel (1978) examined this notion by testing sociopaths, nonsociopathic prisoners, and college students in a card game that involved different probabilities of punishment (losing money). As expected, punishment had the least impact on sociopaths when the probability of punishment was in the middle range (40 to 70%). The sociopaths also underestimated the likelihood of a subsequent punishment after experiencing a trial where the probability of punishment was in the midrange. As in previous studies, then, sociopaths were affected less by punishment and, furthermore, may believe that punishment is unlikely when it is not certain to follow a misstep.

The research findings we have just reviewed seem particularly applicable to Bill. The fear that might prevent stealing, breaking windows, and looting seemed totally absent in him. From his own statements we can conclude that he felt little shame or remorse about his transgressions. Finally, Bill also displayed characteristics similar to those revealed in Siegel's study, thinking that he would never be apprehended for any criminal act.

Physiological Research

Schachter and Latané's work suggests that the avoidance learning deficits of sociopaths may be mediated by some problem in the autonomic nervous system. Because the autonomic nervous system is assumed to play a central role in states of emotion, several investigators have examined sociopaths for both their resting levels of autonomic activity and their patterns of autonomic reactivity to various classes of stimuli. Hare (1978) has summarized the results of many of these investigations. In resting situations, most studies show that psychopaths have lower than normal levels of skin conductance. They are also less reactive when intense or aversive stimuli are presented. Both of these results are consistent with clinical descriptions of sociopaths as being nonanxious. A different picture emerges, however, when heart rate is examined. The heart rate of sociopaths is like that of normal's under resting conditions. Their heart-rate reactivity to stimuli is also unremarkable but, in situations where a stressful stimulus is anticipated, sociopaths show greater than normal increases in heart rate.

These data indicate that we cannot simply speak of the sociopath as being underaroused. To do so we would have needed a pattern of data that showed consistency in both electrodermal and heart-rate measures. Based in part on Lacey's work, Hare (1978) focuses on the *pattern* of psychophysiological differences found in psychopaths. Increased heart rate is viewed as a concomitant of lowered cortical arousal and a gating out of sensory input. Thus the increased heart rate of psychopaths who are anticipating an aversive stimulus would indicate that they are "tuning it out." The lowered levels of skin conductance are then hypothesized to result from the psychopaths' successful coping with the impending aversive stimulus. That is, with skin conductance considered as an index of anxiety, the data indicate that psychopaths are less anxious, perhaps because they have successfully coped with the aversive stimulus by gating it out. This is a plausible interpretation of the data and is consistent with the studies reviewed earlier on avoidance learning.

How do sociopaths acquire this pattern of autonomic responding? One possibility is that it is genetically transmitted. Recent adoptee studies suggest that heredity may play a role in sociopathy. Schulsinger (1972) examined the rate of sociopathy in both the biological and adoptive relatives of sociopaths. He found more sociopathy in the biological relatives than in the adoptive ones. Results favoring this genetic theory have also been found in studies of the adopted children whose biological parents were antisocial personalities (Crowe, 1974; Cadoret, 1978). Thus the evidence suggests that a disposition to become sociopathic, possibly involving the autonomic nervous system, may be inherited.

TREATMENT

There is general agreement that treatment is unsuccessful for sociopaths. Cleckley (1976, pp.438–439) summarized his clinical impressions as follows:

> *Over a period of many years I have remained discouraged about the effect of treatment on the psychopath. Having regularly failed in my own efforts to help such patients . . . I hoped for a while that treatment by others would be more successful. I have had the opportunity to see patients of this sort who were treated by psychoanalysis, by psychoanalytically oriented psychotherapy, by group and by milieu therapy. . . . None of these measures impressed me as achieving successful results. . . . I have now, after more than three decades, had the opportunity to observe a considerable number of patients who, through commitment or the threat of losing their probation status or by other means, were kept under treatment . . . for years. The therapeutic failure in all such patients leads me to feel that we do not at present have any kind of psychotherapy that can be relied on to change the psychopath fundamentally.*

Empirical evaluations of the many treatments that have been employed with sociopaths—psychoanalysis, milieu therapy, group therapy, amphetamines, aversive conditioning, psychosurgery—reach conclusions quite similar to Cleckley's (McCord and McCord, 1964; Suedfeld and Landon, 1978). The inability of sociopaths to form an honest, trusting relationship with a therapist may be a major reason for the ineffectiveness of psychotherapy. A person who lies, cares little for the feelings of others, and has few regrets about personal misconduct is certainly a poor candidate for most forms of psychotherapy. One clinician (Lion, 1978, p. 286), experienced in working with sociopaths, has suggested the following guidelines:

> *First, the therapist must be continually vigilant with regard to manipulation on the part of the patient. Second, he must assume, until proved otherwise, that information given to him by the patient contains distortions and fabrications. Third, he must recognize that a working alliance develops, if ever, exceedingly late in any therapeutic relationship. . . .*

Somatic treatments for sociopathy—psychosurgery, electroconvulsive therapy, and various drugs—have fared no better than psychotherapy. Even the use of stimulants, which Schachter and Latané's data would suggest as of possible benefit, have not produced long-lasting success.

Because many sociopaths spend time in prisons, the discouraging results of imprisonment and the efforts at rehabilitation of convicts are relevant to the treatment of sociopathy. As criminologists have stated repeatedly, prisons operate more as schools for crime (as happened for Bill) than places of rehabilitation. An interesting argument in favor of the incarceration of sociopaths, however, is that sociopaths tend to settle down in middle age (Suedfeld and Landon, 1978). Prisons, then, may protect society from the antisocial behavior of "active" sociopaths.

7

PARANOID PERSONALITY DISORDER

This case study is also based on personal, rather than clinical, experience. Joe Fuller was in treatment for a very brief period of time, but he terminated the relationship well before a therapy plan was formulated. This pattern is, in fact, characteristic of this type of patient. They very seldom seek professional services and, when they do, are very difficult to work with. One of the authors was well acquainted with Joe during high school and college and has stayed in contact with him throughout subsequent years.

SOCIAL HISTORY

Joe was the third of four children. He had two older brothers and a younger sister. His father was a steamfitter and his mother was a housewife. The family lived in a lower-middle-class neighborhood in Providence, Rhode Island. Joe's grandmother also lived with them, beginning when Joe was 11 years old. She was an invalid and could not care for herself after Joe's grandfather died.

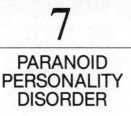

Our first information about Joe comes from his high-school years. Unlike his older brothers, Joe was an exceptionally bright student. On the basis of his performance in elementary school and entrance examinations, he was admitted to a very prestigious public high school in Providence. The school was widely recognized for academic excellence. More than 90% of the graduating seniors went on to college; most went to Ivy League schools such as Harvard, Yale, and Princeton. The school was also known as a "pressure cooker." All of the students were expected to meet very high standards; those who failed were denigrated by their peers. Joe thrived in this intellectually competitive environment. He usually received the highest test scores in his classes, particularly in science. These achievements were based on a combination of intelligence and hard work. Joe was clearly very bright, but so were most of the other students in this school. Joe was a serious student who studied diligently and seemed to be driven by a desire to succeed. While many of the other students worried about examinations and talked to each other about their fear of failure, Joe exuded self-confidence. He knew that the teachers and other students viewed him as one of the best students; he often made jokes about people who "couldn't make the grade." This critical attitude was not reserved for other students alone. Whenever a teacher made a mistake in class, Joe was always the first to laugh and make a snide comment. His classmates usually laughed along with him, but they also noticed a sneering, condescending quality in Joe's humor that set him apart from themselves.

Joe was a classic example of the critic who could "dish it out but couldn't take it." He was extremely sensitive to criticism. It did not seem to matter whether the criticism was accurate or justified; Joe was ready to retaliate at the slightest provocation. He argued endlessly about examinations, particularly in mathematics and science classes. If he lost points on any of his answers, even if he had gotten an "A" on the exam, he would insist that his answer was correct, the question was poorly written, or the topic had not been explained adequately by the teacher prior to the exam. He never admitted that he was wrong. His sensitivity was also evident in interpersonal relationships. Most people are able to laugh at themselves, but Joe could not. His family background was a particular sore spot. Many of the other students in his school were from wealthy homes. Their parents were mostly professionals with advanced degrees. Joe seemed to be self-conscious about his father's lack of formal education and the fact that his family did not live in a large, modern house. He never admitted it openly, but the topic led to frequent arguments. The following example was a typical instance of this sort. Joe had been arguing in class about his grade on a chemistry examination. After class, he overheard another student say to one of his friends, "I don't know why some people have to work so hard for everything." The other boy's father happened to be a very successful businessman. Joe took his comment to mean that Joe was trying to compensate for the fact that his family did not have a lot of money. This implied insult, which may or may not have been a simple comment about Joe's aggressive behavior, infuriated him. Two nights later, while everyone else was watching a school basketball game, Joe sneaked out into the parking lot and poured sugar into the gas tank of the other boy's car so that the engine would be ruined.

Joe did not participate in organized sports or student organizations, and he tended to avoid group activities. He did have a small circle of friends and was particularly close to two other boys. They were people whom he had judged to be his intellectual equals and they were the only people in whom he would confide. He was interested in girls, but his attitude toward women and his interactions with them struck his friends as somewhat odd. The issues of dependence and control seemed to be of central importance to Joe. Whenever one of his friends spent a lot of time with a girl or went out with a girl instead of a group of guys, Joe accused them of being "hen-pecked." Joe seldom dated the same girl twice. He usually insisted that the girl was "weird" or "a drag" but, if the truth were known, most of them would not have gone out on another date with him if he had asked. Most girls found Joe to be rude and arrogant. Conversations with him were one-sided, with Joe trying to impress the girl with his intelligence and simultaneously implying that she was barely worthy of his company. He was not interested in being friends; his sole purpose was to make a sexual conquest. He often bragged about having sex with many girls, but his closest friends suspected that he was still a virgin.

In most respects Joe's relationship with his family was unremarkable. They were not a tightly knit family, but he respected his parents and got along well with his older brothers and his sister. His principal problem at home centered around his grandmother, whom he hated. He complained about her continuously to his friends, saying that she was old and crippled and he wished that his parents would ship her off to an old folks' home. Her inability to care for herself and her dependence on Joe's parents seemed to be particularly annoying to him. He noted on several occasions that if he was ever in a similar situation, he hoped that someone would put him out of his misery.

After graduating from high school, Joe enrolled at Columbia University, where he majored in chemistry and maintained a straight "A" average throughout his first 2 years. He seemed to study all the time; his friends described him as a "workaholic." Everything that he did became an obsession. If he was studying for a particular course, he concentrated on that topic day and night, 7 days a week. If he was involved in a laboratory project, he practically lived in the laboratory. Relaxation and recreation were not included in his schedule. Even if he had the time, there were few leisure activities that Joe enjoyed. He had never been particularly athletic and was, in fact, clumsy. He hated to lose at anything and was also afraid of being ridiculed for looking awkward, so he avoided sports altogether. He was also uninterested in art and films. Joe argued that these activities were a waste of time and a sign of weakness and effeminacy.

Joe's first steady relationship with a woman began during his sophomore year. Carla was a student at a small, liberal arts college in upstate New York. They happened to meet at a small party while she was visiting friends in New York City. Several weeks later, Joe drove to spend the weekend with her. They continued to see each other once or twice a month throughout the spring semester. From Joe's point of view, this was an ideal relationship. He liked Carla; she shared his sarcastic, almost bitter sense of humor, and they got along well sexually. Perhaps most important, the fact that she was not in the same city meant that she could not demand a great deal of his time and could not try to control his schedule or activities. Unfortunately, the relationship ended after a few months when Carla told Joe that she had another boyfriend. Although he was shocked and furious, he made every effort to seem calm and rational. He had always taken pride in his ability to avoid emotional reactions, particularly if they were expected. In discussing the situation with friends, Joe maintained that he had never really cared for Carla and said that he was only interested in her body. Nevertheless, he was clearly interested in revenge. His first plan was to win her back so that he could then turn the tables and drop her. Presumably this process would demonstrate to everyone that he, not Carla, had been in control of the relationship. When this effort failed, he settled for spreading rumors about Carla's promiscuous sexual behavior.

After his breakup with Carla, Joe became even more deeply involved in his laboratory work. He would disappear for days at a time and seldom saw any of his friends. The experiments he was running were apparently based on his own ideas. His assigned work and routine studying were largely ignored; consequently his academic performance began to deteriorate. During the first semester of his junior year, Joe did not receive a grade above a "C."

The experience with Carla also contributed to a decline in Joe's already cynical attitude toward women. He described her behavior as treacherous and deceitful and took the rejection as one more piece of evidence proving that you cannot trust anyone, particularly women. He continued to go out on dates, but he was extremely suspicious of women's intentions and obviously jealous of their attention to other men. On one occasion, he went to a party with a woman he met in one of his classes. They arrived together, but Joe chose to ignore her while he chatted with some male friends in the kitchen. When he later discovered his date talking with another man in the living room, he became rude and offensive. He insulted the woman, making jokes about her clothes and the makeup she was wearing, and suggested that her friend was a homosexual. As might be expected, they never saw each other again. Another time, after he had dated a woman once, he sat in his parked car outside her apartment and watched the entrance for 2 nights to determine whether one of his friends was also seeing her.

LATER ADJUSTMENT

After receiving his B.S. degree, Joe stayed on at Columbia to do graduate work in biochemistry. He continued to work very hard and was considered one of the best students in the department. His best work was done in the laboratory, where he was allowed to pursue independent research. Classroom work was more of a problem. Joe resented being told what to do and what to read. He believed that most faculty members were envious of his intellect. Highly structured reading lists and laboratory assignments, which were often very time consuming, were taken by Joe to be efforts to interfere with his professional advancement. In one case, he became convinced that a professor had cheated him on a final examination. The professor had, in fact, gone out of his way to avoid bias in scoring the examinations; every answer had been typewritten and identified only by social security number. When Joe received a "B+" instead of an "A," he argued that the entire process had been designed to cover up the professor's effort to cheat him. He said that the examination booklets had been decoded *prior* to being read! When his friends asked him why the system was used, he pointed out that the professor was not stupid and, knowing that Joe would discover the plot, had devised a means to make it look as though he had been fair. The chemistry faculty was concerned by this incident but decided to tolerate Joe's eccentricity because he was doing very interesting work and did not present any other problems.

In his second year of graduate school Joe began dating an undergraduate woman in one of his study sections. Ruth was unremarkable in every regard. His friends described her as plain, bland, and mousy. They were surprised that he was even interested in her, but in retrospect, she had one general feature that made her perfect for Joe—she was not at all threatening. He made all of the decisions in the relationship, and she acquiesced to his every whim and fancy. Other men were not interested in her. In fact, they seldom noticed her, so Joe did not have to remain constantly alert to the possibility of desertion. They were perfect complements to each other and were married within a year.

Joe's first job after getting his Ph.D. was as a research chemist for a major drug company. At the beginning, it seemed like an ideal position. He was expected to work somewhat independently doing basic biochemical research. There was no question that he was intellectually capable of the work, and his willingness to work long hours would be beneficial to his advancement, which was closely tied to productivity. Joe expected to be promoted rapidly and was confident that he would be the head of a division within 5 years.

When Joe began working in the company laboratory, he quickly evaluated all of the employees and their relationship to his own position. There were several young Ph.D.s like himself, three supervisors, and the head of the laboratory, Dr. Daniels, a distinguished senior investigator. Joe admired Dr. Daniels and wanted very much to impress him. He did not think much of his young colleagues and particularly resented the supervisors, whom he considered to be his intellectual inferiors. He believed that they had been promoted because they were "yes-men," not because they were competent scientists. He often complained about them to his peers and occasionally laughed openly about their mistakes. When they asked him to perform a specific experiment, particularly if the task was tedious, he was arrogant and resentful, but he usually complied with the request. He hoped that the quality of his work would be noticed by Dr. Daniels, who would then allow him to work more independently. He also worried, however, that the others would notice that he was being subservient in an effort to gain Dr. Daniels' favor. He became more and more self-conscious and was constantly alert to signs of disdain and rejection from the others in the laboratory. The others gradually came to see him as rigid and defensive, and he eventually became isolated from the rest of the group. He interpreted their rejection as evidence of professional jealousy.

Joe's initial work did gain some recognition, and he was given greater independence in his choice of projects. He was interested in the neurochemical basis of depression and spent several months pursuing a series of animal experiments aimed at specific details of his personal theory. Very few people knew what he was doing. He refused to discuss the research with anyone other than Dr. Daniels; even then he was careful to avoid the description of procedural details. His principal concern was that other people might get credit for his ideas. He wanted to impress Dr. Daniels, but he also wanted to take over Dr. Daniels' job. The quickest way to do that was to make a major breakthrough in the laboratory, one for which he alone would receive credit.

Dr. Daniels and the other supervisors recognized that Joe was exceptionally bright and a talented, dedicated scientist. They liked his early work at the company but were dissatisfied with the independent work that he was pursuing. It seemed overly ambitious and, more important, highly esoteric. There were no immediate, practical implications to this line of research, and it did not promise to lead to any commercial results in the near future. Consequently, Joe was told that his work was not acceptable and that he would have to return to doing work that was more closely supervised.

Joe's response to this criticism was openly hostile. He complained bitterly about the imbeciles in company management and swore that he would no longer tolerate their jealousy and stupidity. He was certain that someone had learned about his ideas and that Dr. Daniels and the others were trying to force him out of the company so that they could then publish the theory without giving him credit. Their insistence that he discontinue his work and return to more menial tasks was clear proof, from Joe's point of view, that they wanted to slow down his progress so that they could complete the most important experiments themselves. His paranoid ideas attracted considerable attention. Other people began to avoid him, and he sometimes noticed that they gave him apprehensive glances. It did not occur to him that these responses were provoked by his own hostile behavior; he took their behavior as further evidence that the whole laboratory was plotting against him. As the tension mounted, Joe began to fear for his life.

The situation soon became intolerable. After 3 years with the firm, Joe was told that he would have to resign. Dr. Daniels agreed to write him a letter of reference so that he could obtain another position as long as he did not contest his termination. Joe considered hiring a lawyer to help him fight for his job, but he became convinced that the plot against him was too pervasive for him to win. He also had serious doubts about being able to find a lawyer he could trust. He therefore decided to apply for other positions and eventually took a job as a research associate working with a faculty member at a large state university.

In many ways the new position was a serious demotion. His salary was considerably less than it had been at the drug company, and the position carried considerably less prestige. Someone with Joe's academic credentials and experience should have been able to do better, but he had not published any of his research. He was convinced that this lack of professional success could be attributed to interference from jealous, incompetent administrators at the drug company. A more plausible explanation was that his work had never achieved publishable form. Although the ideas were interesting and his laboratory techniques were technically skillful, Joe was not able to connect the two facets of his work to produce conclusive results. He was also a perfectionist. Never satisfied with the results of an experiment, he insisted on doing follow-up after follow-up and could not bring himself to consider a piece of work finished. The thought of submitting an article and having it rejected by a professional journal was extremely anxiety provoking. Thus, despite his recognized brilliance and several years of careful research, Joe was not able to land anything better than this job as a research associate.

Joe did not like the new job, partly because he thought it was beneath him and also because his activity was even more highly structured than it had been at the drug company. He was working on a research grant in which all of the experiments had been planned in advance. Although he complained a good deal about the people who had ruined his career and expressed a lack of interest in the new line of work, he did high-quality work and was tolerated by the others in the laboratory. The salary was extremely important to Joe and Ruth because they now had a young daughter, Janice, who was 2 years old. There were also some other features about the job that were attractive to Joe. Much of his work was planned, but he was allowed to use the laboratory in his spare time to pursue his own ideas. It was an active research program, and the department included a number of well-known faculty members. Joe believed that these people, particularly his boss, Dr. Willner, would soon recognize his talent and that he would eventually be able to move to a faculty position.

Things did not work out the way Joe had planned. After he had been working at the university for 1 year, Dr. Willner asked him to curtail his independent research. He explained that these outside experiments were becoming too expensive and that the main research funded by the grant would require more of the laboratory's time. Joe did not accept this explanation, which he considered to be an obvious excuse to interfere with his personal work. He believed that Dr. Willner had pretended to be disinterested in Joe's work while he actually kept careful tabs on his progress. In fact, he took this interference to indicate that Dr. Willner believed Joe's research was on the verge of a breakthrough. He continued to work independently when he had the opportunity and became even more secretive about his ideas. Several weeks after these developments, Dr. Willner hired another research associate and asked Joe to share his office with the new person. Joe, of course, believed that the new person was hired and placed in his office solely to spy on his own research.

As the tension mounted at work, Joe's relationship with Ruth became severely strained. While they had never had a close or affectionate relationship, they now seemed on the verge of open conflict. Ruth recognized that Joe was overreacting to minor events; she did not want him to lose another job. She often tried to talk rationally with him in an effort to help him view these events from a more objective perspective. These talks led to arguments, and Joe finally accused her of collaborating with his enemies. He suggested that the people from the drug company and from the university had persuaded her to help them steal Joe's ideas and then get rid of him. As Joe became more paranoid and belligerent, Ruth became fearful for her own safety and that of their daughter. She eventually took Janice with her to live with her parents and began divorce proceedings. Her desertion, as Joe viewed it, provided more evidence that she had been part of the plot all along.

Two weeks after Ruth left, Joe began to experience panic attacks. The first one occurred while he was driving home from work. He was alone in the car, the road was familiar, and the traffic pattern was not particularly congested. Although the temperature was cool, Joe noticed that he was perspiring profusely. His hands and feet began to tingle, and his heart seemed to be beating irregularly. When he began to feel dizzy and faint, he had to pull the car off the road and stop. His shirt was now completely soaked with perspiration, and his breathing was rapid and labored. At the time, he thought that he was going to smother. All in all, it was a terrifying experience. The symptoms disappeared as quickly as they had appeared; within 10 minutes he was able to get back on the road and drive home. He experienced three such incidents within a 2-week period and became so concerned about his health that he overcame his distrust of physicians and made an appointment for a physical examination.

The physician was unable to discover any medical disorder and recommended that Joe consult a psychiatrist about his anxiety. Joe reluctantly agreed that a psychiatrist might be of help and arranged an appointment with Dr. Fein. The issue of Joe's paranoid thinking did not come up during Joe's conversations with Dr. Fein because Joe did not consider it to be a problem. Furthermore, he knew that other people thought that he was overly suspicious and that some people would consider him to be mentally ill. He therefore carefully avoided talking about the efforts to steal his ideas and did not mention the plot involving his wife and former colleagues. He simply wanted to know what was causing the panic attacks and how he could control them. At the end of his second session, Dr. Fein suggested that Joe begin taking Nardil, an antidepressant drug that has also been effective in treating panic anxiety. This suggestion precipitated an extended conversation about the physiological action of mood-stabilizing drugs that escalated into a heated argument. Joe had been disappointed with Dr. Fein; he did not believe that Dr. Fein understood his problem (i.e., the panic attacks) and resented the many open-ended, probing questions that he asked about Joe's personal life. Dr. Fein believed that he was trying to complete a thorough assessment that would allow him to place this specific problem in an appropriate context, but Joe considered this line of inquiry an invasion of privacy regarding matters for which he had not sought advice. The prospect of taking antidepressant drugs further aroused Joe's suspicions. He began asking Dr. Fein about the neurological mechanisms affected by this drug—a topic with which he was intimately familiar because of his own research at the drug company. He was obviously better versed on this subject than Dr. Fein and concluded that Dr. Fein was therefore incompetent because he recommended a treatment that he could not explain completely. Joe finally ended the conversation by telling Dr. Fein that he thought he was a quack. He stormed out of the office and did not return.

The panic attacks continued at the approximate rate of one a week for the next 3 months. Joe also noticed that he frequently felt physically ill and nauseous, even on days when he did not experience a panic attack. Searching for an explanation for these escalating problems, and considering his conviction that other people were trying to harm him, he finally borrowed some equipment from another department and checked the radiation levels in his laboratory. He claimed that he found an unusually high level of radiation coming from a new balance that Dr. Willner had recently purchased.

That was the final piece of evidence he needed. He believed that the people who were conspiring against him, including Dr. Willner, the people from the drug company, and his wife, had planted the radioactive balance in his laboratory so that he would eventually die from radiation poisoning. It struck him as a clever plot. He spent much more time in the laboratory than anyone else and would therefore receive very high doses of radiation. The others were presumably wearing special clothing to screen them from the radiation, thus further reducing their own risk.

Joe confronted Dr. Willner with this discovery; as expected, he denied any knowledge of radioactivity emanating from the balance. Dr. Willner suggested that Joe should take some time away from the laboratory. He had obviously been under a lot of strain lately, considering the divorce proceedings, and could benefit from the rest. Joe was certain that this was a ruse to allow the conspirators to remove the evidence of what he now called the assassination attempt. He refused to take time off and insisted that he would not let the others steal his ideas. The following day he went to the office of the president of the university to demand a formal investigation. An informal series of meetings was eventually arranged involving various members of the laboratory and representatives of the university administration. Joe also contacted the governmental agency that funded Dr. Willner's research, which conducted its own investigation. The result of this time-consuming process was that Joe lost his job. No one was able to find any evidence of a conspiracy to harm Joe or steal his ideas. Both investigations tried to encourage Joe to seek professional help to deal with his unwarranted suspicions.

When he left the university, Joe took a job driving a cab. This final fiasco had ruined his chances of obtaining another research position. No one would write him letters of recommendation. He was, of course, convinced that he had been blacklisted and did not consider the possibility that his problems were created by his own antagonistic behavior. In many ways the change in occupations led to positive changes in Joe's adjustment. He seemed to love driving a cab. He worked very late at night, when most other cabbies were sleeping, and was thus in a noncompetitive situation. The people with whom he interacted were not threatening to his sense of intellectual superiority; in fact, he derived considerable enjoyment from telling his friends stories about the derelicts and imbeciles that rode in his cab. At last contact, Joe was quite content with his situation. He lived by himself in a small apartment, maintained a small circle of friends, and planned to continue working as a cab driver. He was still arrogant and resented his past treatment but seemed resigned to his status as a martyr in the world of chemistry. The need for constant vigilance was greatly reduced because he no longer had access to a laboratory and could not continue to work on his ideas.

DISCUSSION

Personality disorders are defined in terms of stable, cross-situational patterns of behavior that lead to either impairment in social and occupational functioning or subjective distress. These response patterns are exhibited in a rigid and inflexible manner, despite their maladaptive consequences. In paranoid personality, the principal feature centers around unwarranted suspicion and mistrust of other people. These people are often seen by others as cold, guarded, and defensive; they refuse to accept blame, even if it is justified, and they tend to retaliate at the slightest provocation. *DSM-III* lists the following criteria for paranoid personality disorder (p. 309).

A. *Pervasive, unwarranted suspiciousness and mistrust of people as indicated by at least three of the following:*
(1) expectation of trickery or harm.
(2) hypervigilance, manifested by continual scanning of the environment for signs of threat, or taking unneeded precautions.
(3) guardedness or secretiveness.
(4) avoidance of accepting blame when warranted.
(5) questioning the loyalty of others.
(6) intense, narrowly focused searching for confirmation of bias, with loss of appreciation of total context.
(7) overconcern with hidden motives and special meanings.
(8) pathological jealousy.

B. *Hypersensitivity as indicated by at least two of the following:*
(1) tendency to be easily slighted and quick to take offense.
(2) exaggeration of difficulties, e.g. "making mountains out of molehills".
(3) readiness to counterattack when any threat is perceived.
(4) inability to relax.

C. *Restricted affectivity as indicated by at least two of the following:*
(1) appearance of being "cold" and unemotional.
(2) pride taken in always being objective, rational, and unemotional.
(3) lack of a true sense of humor.
(4) absence of passive, soft, tender, and sentimental feelings.

DSM-III emphasizes that these characteristics are not limited to periods of acute disturbance; they are typical of the person's behavior over a long period of time.

Personality disorders are among the most controversial categories included in *DSM-III*. Part of the controversy derives from the debate regarding personality traits and situational specificity of behavior. Social learning theorists have argued that human behavior is largely determined by the situation or context in which it occurs and not by internal personality characteristics (e.g., Mischel, 1968). This position has been supported by studies reporting considerable inconsistency in individuals' behavior measured across different situations. There are, however, other data indicating that cross-situational consistencies in behavior can be identified if the observations are taken on a number of occasions and in a variety of situations (Epstein, 1979). It is possible to recognize the importance of situational variables while also taking into account individual differences in the probability of making a particular response in a given situation. As Epstein (1979, pp. 1122–1123) has argued:

> *The fact that people read in a library and swim in a swimming pool does not establish that there is no generality, or "cross-situational stability," in either swimming or in reading behavior. More to the point is that some people are more prone to swim than others when there is a reasonable opportunity to do so, and this may include swimming in pools, in lakes, and in oceans. Furthermore, one cannot test such a cross-situational proclivity to swim by observing a person once in the vicinity of a swimming pool and once in the vicinity of a lake, as there may be many reasons for that person to forego swimming on a particular occasion. Behavior is obviously determined by more than response dispositions. Given an adequate sample of occasions, however, response dispositions will out.*

The definition of paranoid personality disorder does not assume that these people will always be suspicious, guarded, or tense, regardless of the specific circumstances or people with whom they are interacting, but it does assume that they often behave in this manner and that, given a particular situation, they are more likely than nonparanoid people to behave in this manner.

Personality disorders are also controversial because they are difficult to identify reliably. Interrater reliability during the field trials for the development of *DSM-III* was 0.65 for personality disorders as compared to 0.81 for schizophrenic disorders and 0.83 for affective disorders. Separate figures were not made available for each of the specific forms of personality disorder, thus leaving open the *possibility* that paranoid personality disorder may be a more reliable category than some others, such as borderline personality disorder and passive-aggressive personality disorder. Nevertheless, these data do not inspire overwhelming confidence in the utility of these categories, and they suggest that they should be employed with caution.

The principal issue regarding differential diagnosis and paranoid personality disorders concerns the distinction between this category and paranoid disorders, in which the patients exhibit persistent persecutory delusions or delusional jealousy. The paranoid ideas in paranoid personality disorders are presumably not of sufficient severity to be considered delusional, but the criteria to be used in making this distinction are not entirely clear. Furthermore, the practical utility associated with this distinction has not been established. In other words, it has not been shown that the two categories are etiologically distinct, nor has it been demonstrated that the two carry different treatment implications. *DSM-III* lists the categories separately, but the reliability and validity of the two categories remain an open questions.

Very little is known about the frequency of this disorder because these patients seldom come to the attention of mental health professionals. Although the pervasive suspiciousness, hypersensitivity, and restricted affect are associated with social and occupational impairment, the problems are not of sufficient severity to demand some form of intervention, as in the case of blatant psychoses. The paranoid person's tendency to blame others for their problems and their inability to trust other people also contributes to their failure to seek professional help. In Joe's case, his one brief attempt at treatment was centered around his panic attacks; his defensiveness about other problems, coupled with his sense of intellectual superiority, interfered with any attempt to establish a therapeutic relationship.

PSYCHOLOGICAL THEORIES

Despite this lack of information about the distribution of the disorder within the general population and the fact that large samples of these patients are not available for research purposes, several theories are available that attempt to account for the development of paranoid ideas. Perhaps the earliest hypothesis regarding paranoia was suggested by Freud (1911) in his analysis of the memoirs of Daniel Paul Schreber, an accomplished lawyer who had spent close to 14 years of his life in mental hospitals. Schreber's problems centered around an elaborate set of persecutory and grandiose delusions, including the notion that he would be transformed into a woman. Following this tranformation, Schreber believed that he would become God's mate and that they would produce a better and healthier race of people. Freud argued that the content of Schreber's delusions revealed the presence of an unconscious homosexual wish-phantasy. This hidden desire was taken to be the core of the conflict motivating paranoid ideas. The process presumably begins with the unacceptable thought that "I (a man) love him (a man)." To avoid the anxiety associated with the conscious realization of this idea, the thought is transformed to its opposite.

> *I do not* love *him— I* hate *him.*

This contradiction, which could be expressed in no other way in the unconscious, cannot, however, become conscious to a paranoiac in this form. The mechanism of symptom-formation in paranoia requires that internal perceptions, or feelings, will be replaced by external perceptions. Consequently, the proposition "I hate him" becomes transformed by *projection* into another one: "He hates (persecutes) me, which will justify me in hating him." And thus the unconscious feeling, which is, in fact, the motive force, makes its appearance as though it were the consequence of an external perception: "I do not *love* him—I *hate* him, because HE PERSECUTES ME" (Freud, 1911/1925, pp. 448–449).

There are at least two aspects in Joe's case that might be consistent with this psychodynamic model. He occasionally made comments about other men's sexual orientation, particularly when he was trying to embarrass them. We might infer from these remarks that he was concerned about his own sexual desires, but we do not have any direct evidence to validate this conclusion. His only sexual experiences had been with women, and he did not express any ambivalence about his interest in women. Joe's panic attacks might also fit into Freud's hydraulic model, which suggests that Joe was using the defense mechanism of projection to avoid the anxiety associated with unconscious homosexual impulses. It could be argued that the panic attacks represented a spilling over of excess anxiety that was not being handled efficiently by projection and other secondary defense mechanisms such as repression. Once again, the model seems plausible, but it cannot be tested directly.

An alternative explanation for the development of paranoid delusions was proposed by Cameron (1959). He argued that predelusional patients are anxious, fearful, socially withdrawn, and reluctant to confide in other people. Cameron went on to point out that social isolation leads to a deficiency in social skills. In particular, he argued that predelusional patients are less adept than others in understanding the motivations of other people. They are therefore more likely to misinterpret other people's behavior and, having done so, are also less able to elicit disconfirming evidence from their peers. From time to time most of us have thought that someone else was angry with us or trying to do us harm when, in fact, they were not. We usually come to realize our mistake by talking to our friends about what happened. Cameron's argument was that predelusional patients are even more likely to misinterpret other people's behavior and, given an instance of misinterpretation, are also less able to correct the mistake through interaction with other people. According to Cameron's hypothesis, this cycle is perpetuated by the paranoid person's subsequent behavior. For example, someone who believes that his relatives are plotting against him is likely to behave in a hostile, defensive manner when his relatives are present. They, in turn, may become angry and irritable in response to his apparently unprovoked hostility, thus confirming the paranoid's original suspicion that they are out to get him. Thus Cameron's formulation allows for a complex interaction of personality traits, social skills, and environmental events.

Several elements of Cameron's theory seem applicable in Joe's case. He was not withdrawn and fearful, but he was reluctant to confide in other people. He tended to be a "loner" and felt awkward in social situations such as parties. His habit of laughing at people and provoking arguments would suggest that he was not sensitive to their feelings and point of view, as suggested by Cameron. Perhaps most important is the effect that Joe's behavior had on other people. He was completely unable to consider the possibility that other people talked about him and avoided him because he was initially hostile and belligerent.

Colby (1975; 1977) has proposed an information-processing view of paranoid thinking in which the principal feature is sensitivity to shame and humiliation. The model focuses exclusively on verbal interactions. In the "paranoid mode" of processing, people presumably scan linguistic input for comments or questions that might lead to the experience of shame (defined as "a rise in the truth value of a belief that the self is inadequate"). Faced with the threat of humiliation, the person in the paranoid mode responds by denying personal inadequacy and blaming others. The theory implies that paranoia is associated with a low self-esteem and that episodes of paranoid behavior may be triggered by environmental circumstances that increase the threat of shame (e.g., failure, ridicule). Other negative emotions, most notably fear and anger, are presumably not likely to elicit paranoid responses.

Colby's model provides a plausible explanation for Joe's problems at the drug company and the university laboratory; his paranoid comments provided a rationale for his own failure to succeed. Joe was a brilliant chemist, but he had not developed a successful, independent line of research. The limitations of his work were particularly evident after he had been allowed some independence at the drug company. Joe's supervisors finally became so disappointed with his progress that he was reassigned to more structured projects. Shortly after this demotion his suspicions began to reach delusional proportions. Colby would probably argue that Joe chose to blame his colleagues' interference for failures that would otherwise indicate his own professional inadequacy. The shame-humiliation model also accounts for Joe's later improvement following his change in occupations. As a cab driver, Joe was removed from the field of professional competition in which he was continually exposed to threatening messages. He was reasonably successful as a cab driver, and his self-esteem did not suffer in comparison to the people with whom he usually interacted. There was therefore little need for him to behave in a hostile or defensive manner.

TREATMENT

Psychotherapy is generally of limited value with paranoid patients because it is so difficult to establish a trusting, therapeutic relationship with them. Joe's case is a good example. He expected the therapist to help him cope with his anxiety but was unwilling to discuss his problems at anything other than a superficial level. This defensive attitude would hamper most attempts to engage in traditional, insight-oriented psychotherapy. The client-centered approach developed by Carl Rogers might be more effective with paranoid clients because it fosters a nonthreatening environment. From Colby's point of view, Rogers' emphasis on the provision of accurate empathy and unconditional positive regard would also be likely to bolster the paranoid's fragile self-esteem and thereby reduce his or her sensitivity to potential embarrassment. Unfortunately, there are no data available to support this type of speculation.

Cameron's model might lead to a more directive form of intervention focused on the development of specific social skills. For example, various situations might be constructed in order to demonstrate to the client the manner in which his or her behavior affects other people. Similarly, the therapist might practice various social interactions with the client in an effort to improve his or her ability to discuss initial social impressions. It might also be possible to improve the client's ability to read social cues. This behavioral approach would be used in an effort to expand the client's repertoire of appropriate social behaviors so that the client could respond more flexibly to specific situational demands.

When paranoid ideas reach delusional proportions, the use of antipsychotic medication may also be considered. These drugs are effective in the treatment of schizophrenia, but their effect has usually been measured in terms of global improvement ratings; it is not clear if they have an equally positive effect on all of the symptoms of schizophrenia. In fact, a few studies have examined changes in specific symptoms and concluded that antipsychotic drugs are most likely to have a positive effect on auditory hallucinations and incoherent speech. Paranoid delusions are among the *least* responsive symptoms (Cole and Davis, 1969). Thus, in the absence of other schizophrenic symptoms, patients with paranoid delusions are not likely to benefit from drug treatment.

8

ALCOHOLISM AND MARITAL CONFLICT

After giving her a complete physical examination, Cathy Henry's physician determined that many of her problems were psychological. To be sure, she had reason to be concerned over her medical status because she had been having trouble sleeping for several months, suffered from almost continual diarrhea, felt very fatigued most of the time, and had allowed her once trim body to become flabby and poorly conditioned. One key question that the physician had asked during the examination, however, led him to be concerned about her personal life. "Have you been drinking much alcohol lately?" he had queried, as casually as possible. "No!" she had exclaimed a bit too loudly. She then had burst into tears and recounted the following story.

Twenty-eight years of age, quite attractive, married for 7 years to a successful business executive, and the mother of two children in elementary school, Cathy Henry had watched her drinking patterns change over the previous several years. She had been a social drinker since her college days, but her consumption increased and changed in nature during her first years of marriage. Initially it was the martinis that she would mix for her husband and herself to greet him each evening when he came home from his job in the city after traveling for 1 hour on the commuter railroad. It helps him unwind, she would think to herself, but soon she realized that it was she who looked forward to the drinks. Then there were the parties they would go to or have in their spacious suburban home. She was not particularly fond of the people she met at these gatherings; in fact, when she was honest with herself, she had to admit that she found them aversive. Dick's friends and their wives led lives that were different from the way she thought she would be living. Yes, she did enjoy the affluence, the nice clothes, the obligatory

Mercedes, the private school for the children, the vacations, and all the rest. But she longed for more.

She began to look forward to the numbing effects of that first drink. And then the further numbing of the second. Wasn't booze the social lubricant par excellence? What could be wrong with it if you saw it everywhere you turned? Dick's business lunches, after all, always included a Manhattan or martini before and usually a bottle of wine during the meal. And her lunches with one or two women she had managed to befriend usually followed the same pattern. No, that was not the problem. It was the drink she took by herself before making the early evening batch of martinis to enjoy with her husband before dinner and the drink she poured for herself downstairs in the kitchen while Dick was in the bedroom getting dressed for a party she was not looking forward to. And more and more often it was the second drink she somehow found herself pouring, now secretly, after she had gotten dressed and Dick was picking up the babysitter. Most recently it was the doubts she felt about being sober enough to be the perfect hostess as she sipped a drink while making the canapes on Saturday afternoons in preparation for the dinner party in her home that evening and her husband was at the supermarket with the children for some last-minute shopping.

Different as well was the kind of drink she found herself imbibing. If a dry martini is good, then a very dry one is better. And if there is Tanqueray in the liquor cabinet, why mask its exquisite taste with anything more than a twist of lemon? And why dilute such good liquor with ice cubes if the green bottle can be kept in the back of the refrigerator, next to the long-stemmed goblet that so nicely accommodated a jigger of gin, and later two jiggers and, finally, as much as she felt like pouring without using a measuring glass.

So she awakened one morning and realized that even before she got herself out of bed, she was thinking of that first drink. She also wondered whether she would be able to wait until her husband left for work and her children left for school. And if she had to do the driving for the carpool that day, would she have a few gulps of gin before she left with them to pick up the other children, or would she wait until her return? It seemed to her now that she wanted that first drink not so much to feel better but to avoid feeling worse for not having the drink.

Additional information about her drinking convinced the physician that Cathy might be addicted to alcohol. Clearly her consumption had steadily increased over the past year, the best estimate being at least 15 ounces of 90-proof gin every day. Her drinking almost always began in the morning and continued more or less unabated until she went to bed. If she was out of the house during the day, she often found excuses not to drive. She would drink alcohol in any form available to her, whether it was a fine wine at a restaurant during lunch with a friend or a beer puchased while shopping for groceries and consumed in her car before leaving the supermarket parking lot for an unsteady and dangerous drive home. Especially alarming to both her and her husband was her reaction to being deprived of alcohol for several days during a camping trip. She had dreaded the time away from her cache of liquor (she had a few bottles hidden in her dresser drawers), and the first day had been sheer hell: hands shaking, a feeling of pressure in her head, and an overall feeling that something dreadful was about to happen. Her constant preoccupation was with how and where she was going to get a drink. By the time they returned home several days later, she was a physical and emotional wreck. She had not slept more than a few hours the entire trip and had been abusive to her family during the drive home. Any pretense about not being a problem drinker vanished as she bolted from the car on their arrival home to dash into the house for several gulps of gin right from the bottle.

One final aspect of her predicament worried the doctor. Not surprisingly, Cathy's marriage had been deteriorating as her drinking worsened. Intimacy was gone. Her secretiveness and shame about her drinking, coupled with extreme anger whenever her husband made a comment or suggested she get some help, created a distance between the partners. Dick Henry also resented his wife's increasing unreliability in looking after the children and their home. It was becoming the norm in recent months that he would arrive after work to find the children roaming around the neighborhood unsupervised, dinner unprepared, and the house looking as unkempt as his wife did, propped up on pillows in her room, on the night table next to her a glass filled with gin as she looked idly through magazines or watched whatever mindless program was on television at the time. Sex was infrequent, since Cathy was usually so anesthetized that she made an uninteresting partner in bed, to say the least.

Drinking had become the center of her life. She had denied this for some time, but it no longer seemed possible to continue the charade. Her life was going out of control.

SOCIAL HISTORY

Cathy Henry was raised in a lower-middle-class family in a large city in the northeast. Her parents, both schoolteachers, indoctrinated their four children in the value of higher education; there was seldom any doubt that their daughter would go to college. And, indeed she did—not to the kind of teachers' college her parents had attended but to a private university on the

West coast, far from home. She viewed her college years as difficult but rewarding in that she was exposed to people and ideas that were new and challenging.

One of Cathy's clearest recollections of college were the fraternity parties on "The Row," a street just off campus that was the location for most of the fraternities and sororities. Somehow she had been invited to join one of the more prestigious sororities, a happenstance that opened the doors of the more highly regarded fraternities to her. A very attractive and likable young woman, her main problem was a lack of money relative to the obvious affluence of most of her "sisters." Her roommate, for example, drove a BMW worth at least $25,000 and had a wardrobe that contained the latest in casual and formal wear—just the "right" kind of little animals pressed onto the front of each jersey, just the "right" kind of shoes and jeans. Cathy was able to buy clothing that helped her feel comfortable among her wealthy peers by virtue of the full tuition scholarship she had obtained, a modelling job her roommate had helped her get downtown, and a hefty loan that her father had countersigned for her. Her parents, in fact, had been instrumental in her selecting this university; they viewed it as her ticket of admission into a higher stratum of society. They were not wrong.

It was at the frequent weekend parties that she was introduced to drinking. Back home liquor was a rare accompaniment to socializing, both with her parents and with her high-school friends. At college the situation could not have been more different. A conservative campus, the school was sometimes said to have missed the 1960s; that is, it had not been influenced by the social turmoil on college campuses during the Vietnam protests. Similarly missing on campus was the degree of illicit drug dealing common elsewhere. The favorite drug was drunk, not smoked or snorted, and nowhere with more élan and gusto than at the fraternity parties.

Cathy's first reaction to beer was indifferent, at best. She barely finished her first can, which had been casually handed to her as she entered a party during the second week of her sophomore year. She felt somewhat jaded even holding it but soon relaxed when she saw the group of wholesome-looking young men and women guzzle the brew. By the end of the evening she "had a buzz on," as it had been labelled for her by Dick, the good-looking upper-classman who had flirted with her most of the evening.

Dick was a rambunctious fellow from a well-to-do family. He was majoring in political science and economics and headed for business school and, thereafter, the family firm, which had branches throughout the country. His principal goal in life seemed to be to work harder than his father and be more successful than he, but to do so while appearing to do little work and to care even less about grades. This created a strain in him from which he sought surcease in alcohol. If anyone was Cathy's teacher in the fine art of drinking, it was Dick. They were pinned by Christmas and soon thereafter engaged.

Dick graduated 2 years before Cathy, and they both made the difficult decision that he should accept the offer from the high-powered business school back East while she finished college. They managed to see each other often; Dick flew to the West coast a half dozen times a year. Cathy meanwhile was elected to Phi Beta Kappa, finding more time now for her studies with Dick out of town. She did not go to the parties unless Dick was visiting. Consequently, she had stopped drinking as regularly as she had when Dick was still in school with her. Years later she would comment ruefully to herself that "back then I could really take it or leave it." It seemed impossible that there was ever a time she could actually leave it.

The wedding was a sumptuous gala; the reception was held around the pool of Dick's parents' home. Cathy's family flew out for the occasion, and she hated herself for being a little ashamed of how unsophisticated they seemed compared to the family and friends of her new husband. She herself felt very much on display. It seemed to her that her value to Dick's parents lay less in her intelligence and academic achievements than in her looks, which by now were quite striking. Questions put to her during the reception revolved around starting a family—"When will Dick, Jr., come along, do you think?"—and furnishing her new home in a fashionable suburb outside of Manhattan, where Dick was slated to begin as a vice president in the East coast headquarters of the family business. No consideration was given to any career she herself might have in mind to pursue.

By the end of the first year of marriage they had a baby (named Dick, Jr!). Full-time help was well within their means, but Cathy insisted on caring for the boy and the house on her own. She told Dick and herself that this was what she wanted, but she knew at some level that she was deceiving herself as much as she was fooling Dick.

Her anger and resentment grew. She could not understand why she was not happier; didn't she have it all—a handsome and successful husband, not a hint of financial worry, a lovely home with a summer cottage further east on the bay and, before long, a second child? The other women in the neighborhood were pleasant enough and certainly cordial to "Dick's wife," and the many parties they attended were as lively as those fraternity and sorority affairs. They were similar as well in the lavish availability of alcohol—only the best brands and vintages. Thus it was that alcohol entered her life again, this time in a more serious way.

As already mentioned, Cathy disliked most of the people at the parties she "had to" attend with Dick. She came to realize that it might not be the people themselves whom she found objectionable, but the lack of choice she experienced in attending parties. Their social life revolved around Dick's position. Certainly most of the people she entertained in their home were connected in one way or another with Dick's many business dealings.

CONCEPTUALIZATION AND TREATMENT

"I'm Joe, and I'm an alcoholic." "I'm Nancy, and I'm an alcoholic." Cathy looked uneasily around her at the group of strangers in the basement meeting room of the church. She had decided to attend a meeting of Alcoholics Anonymous after seeing a television commercial earlier that week. The first step, it was said, was to admit to oneself that one was an alcoholic. Like many problem drinkers, Cathy had avoided that frightening confrontation for several years, fooling herself with intellectual games such as the proper definition of alcoholism, the scientific status of alcohol as an addicting drug, and other academic questions that protected her from facing the fact that her drinking was out of control and threatening to ruin her life. She recalled from a psychology course in college that AA helped many people stop drinking, so why not her?

"I'm Cathy, and I'm a. . . a. . . ." She stopped in midsentence, looked beseechingly at the upturned face of an older woman sitting in the row in front of her as if to ask this woman what to say next. The stranger smiled and nodded, somehow helping Cathy take what might be her first step to helping herself: ". . . I'm an alcoholic." She marvelled to herself how relieved she felt just saying these words aloud, words reflecting a thought she had believed would itself spell ruination. But nothing terrible happened. No one in the room laughed, no one cried. They just greeted her by name, and the meeting went on as it had been proceeding before she spoke.

She was told by other members of the group that alcoholism is a disease and that an alcoholic has to learn to abstain entirely. A buddy was assigned to her, a woman whom she could telephone day or night for encouragement not to take a drink. She was pleased and grateful to have someone she could talk to anytime she felt the need, someone who she believed would understand the craving, the almost painful need for a drink.

She drove home that evening feeling more optimistic than she had for years. As she got out of the car, however, she realized that she was already thinking about a drink. Would Dick see her pouring it? Would one of the children? Should she phone her buddy right away? She had been warned that the first few days would be the worst, so perhaps she should call.

She intended to do just that but, as she dialed the number, Dick came into the kitchen and angrily asked her where she had been. Regrettably, Cathy had told him she was going shopping with Ethel, one of her friends, but Ethel had phoned an hour earlier to ask her to have lunch later that week.

Cathy knew she should have told Dick where she was going, but she was so ashamed of her drinking that she did not feel she could even tell him of her resolve to do something about it. As she had learned at the AA meeting, to take that first step meant to admit to others as well as to oneself that one was an alcoholic.

An ugly scene followed. At first Dick did not believe she had gone to AA. He regarded it as "unseemly," as a quasi-religious group for lower-class people, self-help groups being something for those who could not afford professional help. Surely she was having an affair. Cathy could scarcely believe what she was hearing. Things became violent. She punched at Dick, grabbed at his hair. He restrained her as best he could without hurting her and then left the room in a rage. The telephone call to her buddy now forgotten, Cathy downed several ounces of gin from the refrigerator within a few minutes and then collapsed.

She awoke the next day in the hospital. She had hit her head on the edge of a kitchen counter as she fell, opening a deep gash in her scalp. Torn by remorse, guilt, and anger, Dick had rushed her to the emergency room and had her admitted. The x-rays were negative for skull fracture, and her EEG was normal, so she was discharged the following day.

Cathy did not go back to AA, and she wondered years later what course her life might have taken had she returned. She thought many times that the best outcome would have been abstention and a return to her nondrinking days, accompanied by some improvement in her marital relationship. She was not prepared for what did happen, and she was never certain, even years later, about how good the outcome was.

The scene the evening of her return from the AA meeting had frightened both of them. The genteel atmosphere of their lives had no room for shouting and hitting, nor did it allow for open admission of the loss of control that Cathy had confronted at the AA meeting. Dick would not or could not believe it. He pleaded with her not to return to AA. But what was to be done, she pleaded in return. He would do anything to help her with her drinking; he had not known how serious it was (he had unwittingly collaborated with Cathy in hiding the facts both from her and from himself). He would find a therapist for her. No, she said, it was not just her problem. She had begun drinking during the beginnings of their relationship at college, she had stopped when he was away at business school, and she had begun again in earnest soon after their marriage and move to the East coast. No, she said, she could not stop drinking unless there were some fundamental changes in the marriage.

To say that Dick did not want to hear this is an understatement. For him life had been perfect until now—terrific position in the family business, gorgeous wife and children, lovely expensive home. A bad marriage was not part of his version of the American dream. So he resisted for weeks, until Cathy wrecked the stationwagon and almost herself with it.

So it was that the two of them sat next to each other on a sofa in Dr. Seymour's large office a 30-minute drive from their home. Dr. Seymour had a good reputation for dealing with seriously troubled marriages, including those in which alcohol abuse was involved. Neither Cathy nor Dick had ever seen a therapist, although she had thought of it often enough. The first session began as follows.

Dr. Seymour: How can I be of help?

Dick: Well, my wife has this drinking problem. She tried AA but that didn't work. Then she. . . .

Cathy: Wait a minute, Dick. I went to one meeting, and your crummy reaction to it landed me in the hospital with a laceration in my head.

Dr. Seymour: Hold on a minute, please. Cathy, let's hear from Dick and then we'll hear from you. Okay?

Cathy (suspiciously): Okay.

Dr. Seymour: Dick, you were telling me of Cathy's drinking problem.

(Dick spoke for several minutes about his wife's problems, not only her drinking but her grouchiness, her unresponsiveness in bed, and her neglect of household tasks. Dr. Seymour listened attentively, watching both of them closely.)

Dr. Seymour: Okay, Dick, now tell both Cathy and me what *your* problems are.

Dick (taken aback): What do you mean, *my* problems?

Dr. Seymour: I'd like to know how *you* feel about your marriage, about your life. We'll spend time on Cathy's drinking and all the rest, but right now I'd be interested in what you might get out of therapy here.

(Dick continued as he had begun, this time emphasizing how much easier his life would be if Cathy stopped drinking, started preparing meals regularly, and the like.)

Dr. Seymour (sensing he had to do something to get Dick away from concentrating entirely on how Cathy would have to change): Dick, what's happening?

Dick (puzzled, a little nervous): What do you mean, what's happening? I'm telling you what you want to know.

Dr. Seymour: No, I mean, your leg. What's happening to your leg?

(Dick's leg had been shaking for several minutes, unnoticed by him but not by Dr. Seymour.)

Dick: I don't know. I guess it's moving around a little.

Dr. Seymour: Can you say, "*I'm* moving around a little?"

Dick: What?!? What is this bullshit? (Turning to Cathy.) I told you this therapy business was a crock. He tells me I'm doing something when it's my leg that's moving a little

Dr. Seymour: Dick, you talk about your leg as if it belongs to someone else. Just tell me that *you* (pointing at Dick's chest) are moving around, that *you* are moving away from the issue.

Dick (eyes suddenly filling with tears, confused about what was happening inside him, feeling himself on the edge of some sort of emotional release): This whole business is driving me crazy. I'm really angry at Cathy. She's screwing up my life. She. . . .

Dr. Seymour (interrupts): Dick, say anything you want, but begin with the words "I feel. . . ."

(Long pause, Dr. Seymour and Dick looking unflinchingly at each other.)

Dick (suddenly bursts into tears): I feel scared. I feel I am losing it all. I feel like I'm dying. I feel. . . . (Sobs.)

(In the meantime Cathy has been looking alternately at the two men as if watching a tennis match, one moment puzzled, the next hurt, the next expectant, now experiencing a rush of affection and protectiveness for Dick that she had not felt since their engagement 10 years ago.)

Dr. Seymour: Yes, you feel scared. And what do you need?

Dick: I need . . . I need . . . I need Cathy.

Dr. Seymour: Say it again.

Dick: I need Cathy.

(By this point both Cathy and Dick are in tears, but there is some distance between them on the sofa. Dr. Seymour sees Dick's hand inch towards Cathy, then withdraw.)

Dr. Seymour: Dick, what's happening? To your hand?

Dick: It wants to touch Cathy.

Dr. Seymour: Can you take responsibility for that feeling, Dick? What do *you* want? What do *you* need?

Dick (grabbing her hand but still looking at Dr. Seymour): I need *her*!

Dr. Seymour: Tell her. Don't tell me. *Tell her*!

Dick (turning to Cathy): I need you, Cathy!

Dr. Seymour had taken some chances in this first session, but his clinical intuition had told him that this take-charge business executive was terrified at what was happening to his marriage, that he felt he was losing his wife, and that he needed her; Dr. Seymour was less sure why Dick needed Cathy or whether that need could form the basis for a good marriage but, for now, he deemed it necessary to get Dick to acknowledge his own emotional stake and to show Cathy how scared he was about losing her.

Cathy's drinking was not ignored, but it did take some time to attend to it directly. Cathy had been managing to come to the twice-weekly sessions sober, which told Dr. Seymour that her drinking was not as much out of her control as she believed. An agreement had been reached that she be sober during each therapy meeting, and it turned out that Dick was able to help her achieve this subgoal by spending time with her every Saturday and Tuesday morning before their noon sessions. Formal attention to Cathy's drinking began with an exercise that had her and Dick talking to an empty chair.

Dr. Seymour: Okay, we were going to talk about the alcohol today.

Dick: Yes, let me tell you what I think's going on.

Dr. Seymour: Hold on, Dick, let's try it this way. I want you to look at that empty chair and imagine that Cathy's bottle of chilled Tanqueray is in it.

Dick (laughing nervously): Doctor, does your mother know what you do for a living?

Dr. Seymour (smiling): Not a chance. The chair, Dick. Cathy's liquor bottle is in that chair. Talk to it.

Dick (by now accustomed to Dr. Seymour's unorthodox techniques and style): Okay. Let's see. I'd say. . . .

Dr. Seymour: No, don't tell me what you *would* say. Just say it.

Dick: Okay. . . . Listen, you're causing us a lot of problems. . . . You're. . . . (Eyes fill with tears; Dr. Seymour leans forward and whispers encouragingly for him to express the emergent feeling.) You're getting in the way, bottle. You're like an intruder, a home-wrecker. I'm angry at you. No, that's not it. I'm afraid of you. I'm not as strong as you. I'm not as attractive to Cathy as you are. Yes, that's it. I'm afraid Cathy cares for you more than she cares for me. I'm feeling displaced. I almost feel like Cathy's having an affair, right under my nose, right in our own home. She can't wait to get to you when she comes home. She spends more time with you than she does with me. She touches you more. (Begins to cry.)

Dr. Seymour: Cathy, what do you have to say to the liquor in that chair?

Cathy (sobbing): Dick's right. You *are* an intruder. You're my gigolo. You're reliable. I know just what you'll do for me. I know just how to treat you, how much of you to pour, how much of you to take into my body. I've turned to you for help instead of asking Dick for help. I can't love both of you at the same time. But you're always there. I know you won't reject me. I know you so well. And I always know where to find you.

Dr. Seymour developed the clinical hypothesis that Cathy's liquor was like a lover, a threat to their marriage in almost a human sense. Cause and effect were impossible to isolate, but it was clear that the growing distance between the two partners was correlated with Cathy's increasing dependence on the alcohol. Any possible addiction Dr. Seymour conceptualized as the kind of power that a forceful and compelling lover can have over another person. He cared less about whether she was truly addicted than about her inability to turn to her husband for the solace she seemed to find in drink. The fanciful scenario with the empty chair made a profound impression on the couple; they both realized that alcohol was interfering with intimacy in their marriage. And Dick got in touch with his great need for and love of Cathy and of the threat posed by the alcohol. Cathy became more aware of how she turned to the bottle for what she wanted and needed from her husband—not the anesthetizing effects of the drug, but a reliable source of companionship and solace.

Therapy had been progressing well until now, all three parties believing that they were on the right track to improving the marriage and reducing Cathy's reliance on alcohol. But things took an unexpected turn. Dick's fantasy of a favorable outcome to the treatment was a contented Cathy raising their children, tending to the home, and being eager to meet him on his (triumphant) return each day from work. Cathy's ideas were different. The Gestalt approach was helping Cathy discover many of her deepest wants and concerns. She was coming to realize that some of her happiest times had been her last 2 years of college, when she was engaged to Dick and yet separate from him, functioning independently. She had no need for liquor at that time, and she also excelled in her classes, as noted earlier. She abhorred the idea of living like a china doll in her lovely home, her life revolving around ferrying the children and their friends in the stationwagon, shopping for clothes, chatting over lunch with her "girl friends." In short, although she loved Dick, the traditional marriage was suffocating her.

She expressed these "radical feminist" (Dick's terms) ideas during one of the therapy sessions. Dick's reaction was predictable to her, and it seemed that no amount of discussion with the psychologist or at home was going to help him see things her way. For Dick it was a gross violation of the marriage contract; more than that, it was unnatural. On the positive side, he was able to express his fear of being emasculated and humiliated by the fact of his wife working outside the home and having a real say in major family decisions. At least he had some clarification of the issues, and things were being brought out into the open. But change was another matter.

This crisis took place several months after they had begun seeing Dr. Seymour, and it almost drove Cathy back to alcohol. But she realized that to succumb would be tantamount to not taking responsibility for her feelings and for the need to make a choice if she was to continue growing. So she asked that regular sessions be suspended for a month; she needed some time to think by herself. Dick agreed that she would spend a few weeks at her parents' home; the children would be looked after by a family friend. During this time away from her home, her decision to ask Dick for a separation solidified. Paradoxically, this decision was both the most sensible, inevitable one for her and the most unpredicted, rash one. All sorts of issues had to be faced now—change in financial circumstances, the reactions of the children and of the two families, a possible move to another house or even another city. She and Dick had a few more sessions with Dr. Seymour, who respected the decision Cathy had made and agreed to do what he could to help them both adjust to it, even though deep down he felt that marriage itself was too sacred to give up on if there was any hope of accommodation at all.

DISCUSSION

In DSM-III a distinction is made between substance abuse and substance dependence. In the former a person is so involved in drug use that his or her work and other responsibilities suffer. With some drugs, abuse develops into dependence, or addiction; when addicting drugs such as heroin or alcohol are ingested for long periods of time, the body chemistry changes so that the person desperately craves more and more of the substance. Dependence is characterized by tolerance and withdrawal. Tolerance refers to the need to take increasing dosages to achieve a desired state of intoxication; withdrawal refers to the very unpleasant reactions that accompany an attempt to stop taking the addicting drug. Both kinds of disorders, abuse and dependence, can be very serious, and no drug causes more pain and suffering than alcohol.

The use of wines, beers, and other alcoholic beverages dates back thousands of years; their presence is a veritable institution in the United States and other Western countries. In moderation, alcohol has pleasant effects for most people and is widely regarded as a "social lubricant" because of its disinhibiting properties. Conversation seems easier, one's everyday woes recede in importance, and life seems generally cheerier for most individuals who imbibe occasionally. To be sure, many traffic accidents are caused by people who drive when their reflexes, motor coordination, and judgment have been impaired by alcohol, as happened in the case study. But by and large the use of these beverages has some positive effects for the majority of adults.

Problems arise when people drink on a regular basis, even if they have not become addicted. Cathy Henry may not have been truly addicted to alcohol (although she may have been very close to it), yet her life was being seriously affected by her reliance on alcohol to deaden her senses and somehow help the time pass in an otherwise meaningless and aversive existence. It is difficult to meet one's responsibilities to others and even to oneself when our thinking is slowed, our senses dulled, and our memory impaired by the intoxicating effects of a drug such as alcohol. So, even if one's reliance on a drug is "only" psychological, the impairment can be profound.

Addiction is even more serious, of course, because the body so craves the substance that even a resolve to desist from its use is often insufficient. The abuse of the drug increases as one's life revolves around obtaining it and ingesting it. In addition, there are physiological effects of long-term use of drugs. In the case of alcohol, there can be damage to the heart, endocrine glands, and circulatory system, generally through hypertension, or high blood pressure. Cirrhosis of the liver is another consequence of heavy drinking; in this disease active liver cells are replaced by fibrous connective tissue, thereby interfering with blood circulation. Cirrhosis ranks seventh among the causes of death.

For women there is an additional risk: the harm that can be inflicted on a fetus in the womb. Fetal alcohol syndrome has been linked to heavy consumption of alcohol during pregnancy, causing many abnormalities in the developing infant, including mental retardation. So concerned are medical experts that the National Institute on Alcohol Abuse and Alcoholism has recently counseled pregnant women not to drink at all (*Alcohol, Drug Abuse and Mental Health Administration News*, May 2, 1980).

A variety of psychological theories have been advanced in an effort to explain why people start drinking and why they continue even when they realize that it is ruining their lives. Psychoanalytic theory concentrates on fixation at the oral stage of psychosexual development; the mother is believed either to have frustrated or else to have satisfied to too great an extent the dependency needs assumed to be predominant at this earliest stage of life. Other analytic accounts regard excessive drinking as a way to reduce guilt; a common quip is that the superego is the part of the personality that is soluble in alcohol. Little evidence supports these and related views (Davison and Neale, 1982).

Learning accounts have tended to focus on the reduction in distress occasioned by alcohol. Thus we drink because we are negatively reinforced for doing so. Data do support the view that alcohol reduces anxiety (Levenson et al., 1980), but apparently only in the short term. Heavy drinkers, especially those who appear addicted, have been found to feel *worse* after drinking (Nathan et al., 1970). Perhaps it is the social drinker who derives something positive from moderate amounts of alcohol on widely separated occasions, but for the person who drinks every day and in some quantity, the reasons may be quite different. They may have a good deal to do with the fact that the person has become physiologically dependent on the drug.

Although answers continue to be sought for why people drink, other research concentrates on how to help people stop drinking altogether, or at least to achieve better control over their consumption. Millions of dollars are spent each year by the government, private industry, and individuals themselves in efforts to discover effective ways for people to stop their abuse of alcohol. Careful hospital supervision is advised for people who are addicted because the withdrawal can be very dangerous, even fatal, as the person "dries out." Then psychological treatment programs can be undertaken, encompassing many of the following procedures that are also available in noninstitutional settings.

Probably the best-known approach to problem drinking is Alcoholics Anonymous, a self-help group founded in 1935 by two former alcoholics. AA now has more than 30,000 chapters in close to 100 countries; membership totals more than 1 million people. They run regular meetings, like the one Cathy Henry attended. Members provide each other with emotional support and empathy, and especially constant encouragement to lead a life without the drug. AA's central assumption is that alcoholism is an incurable disease marked by a permanent susceptibility to that first drink. Total abstinence, then, is the goal of AA. It will be recalled that one of the features of AA that offended Cathy's husband was its religious tone. Indeed, there is a strong spiritual or religious atmosphere in AA, as can be seen from their 12 suggested steps (e.g., having made a decision that we are powerless to stop drinking on our own and therefore must turn for help to God). Defects of character must also be admitted; resolves must be made to make amends to those we have wronged and to make an ongoing moral inventory of ourselves. There are many who regard AA as the most effective treatment for alcoholism, but adequately controlled research is as yet lacking.

Behavior therapists have paid a good deal of attention to alcoholism and have devised a number of procedures and approaches. Conceptualizing problem drinking as inappropriate attraction to a set of stimulus conditions, workers have designed a variety of aversion therapies to instill in the drinker a distaste for drinking. In fact, one of the earliest articles in behavior therapy concerned aversion therapy with alcoholics (Kantorovich,

1930). In the most general terms, the drinker is shocked on the fingertips or made nauseous by ingesting a drug like apomorphine or by imagining a disgusting scene—all the while confronted by an actual or imagined drinking situation. The assumption is that people can be classically conditioned to fear or otherwise find unpleasant a previously attractive stimulus if that stimulus is repeatedly paired with a negative emotional state. The research is hard to interpret or summarize, but it is fair to say that many drinkers have been helped in this fashion, even though it is far from clear how the techniques work (Wilson and O'Leary, 1980).

A controversial direction in therapy is to encourage controlled drinking. Research has brought into question whether alcoholics really have no control over their imbibing once they take a drink; instead, it has been suggested that their beliefs about themselves and what they are drinking play a central role, may be as important as any physiological addiction (Marlatt, Demming, and Reid, 1973). Add to these findings the realization that it is virtually impossible to avoid alcohol in our society and you come up with the idea that alcoholics might be taught to drink in moderation. A controlled drinking program has the person drink some alcohol and then be informed, by a special monitoring apparatus, what his or her blood alcohol level is. Alcoholics seem to have inordinate difficulty knowing how intoxicated they actually are, so one such treatment program shocks them when they drink more than a moderate amount and teaches them how to cope with problematic situations in a less destructive fashion than retreating into the numbing effects of alcohol. Results are encouraging (Sobell and Sobell, 1976), although people such as those involved in AA decry the idea that an alcoholic can ever become a social drinker; their concern is that this belief is an illusion, a cruel hoax that will discourage alcoholics from trying to abstain altogether.

The therapy for Cathy Henry's problem drinking took a different course from what we have just reviewed. After her husband rejected the idea of her going to AA, she ultimately insisted that they go together to a therapist who would deal with the marital problems Cathy felt were instrumental in her abuse of alcohol. The therapist tacitly agreed with this general conceptualization and, within his Gestalt therapy framework, saw the drinking as a block or intruder between two people who basically loved each other. Gestalt therapy has as its overall goal enabling people to understand what their needs and wants and fears are, to take responsibility for them, and to find ways to incorporate these factors into their whole personality, thereby making themselves whole again (hence the term *gestalt*, the German term for shape). Dr. Seymour pressured Dick Henry to face his own fears and desires squarely, hoping thereby to help both him and his wife see how the drinking was intruding into their lives. Gestalt therapists are very imaginative in devising unusual techniques to make more vivid to clients what they are doing, how they are avoiding feelings. The empty chair technique employed with Cathy and her husband is designed to help people confront their innermost feelings directly; it seemed to have had a profound effect on the Henrys. This therapy is representative of a more clinical and individualized approach to problem drinking, since it appreciates that different people can drink for different reasons. Not only Gestalt therapists but behavior therapists and analytically oriented therapists *in practice* attempt to tailor their interventions to what they believe are the particular needs of the people they are treating. All therapists work within a given theoretical framework, but considerable ingenuity and inventiveness are required to apply the general viewpoint to each client (Lazarus and Davison, 1971).

The Henrys, then, found themselves in a Gestalt-oriented, conjoint marital treatment. Therapists who see couples differ in theoretical orientation, but they do share the basic assumption that a problem apparently in one of the partners is best dealt with by making changes in the relationship. Even if one of the partners brings a particular individual problem into the marriage, anxiety or depression, for example, that problem becomes intertwined in the relationship and, it is assumed, must be worked with in the context of that relationship. Another theme common in marital therapy is communication. Distressed couples are frequently unaware of how their actions affect the other person, and they are often unaware as well of the motivations of their partner. A variety of techniques are employed by marital therapists; illustrated in this case study are some Gestalt techniques designed to help the partners understand themselves and each other better so that their needs could be expressed and satisfied.

This case also highlights a burning issue in the field: the way therapeutic goals are set and the manner by which we evaluate the success of an intervention. Cathy and her husband began seeing the psychologist because of her drinking. Dick had not initially wanted to join Cathy in any therapeutic attempt to control her drinking, but she more or less gave him no choice; her implicit message was "Go see a therapist with me or else. . . ." The "or else" was probably a vague contingency in her mind, but it no doubt included something like " . . . or else I'll keep drinking, and maybe even kill myself as I almost did in the stationwagon the other night."

The choice of Dr. Seymour from all the therapists they might have contacted already biased the direction of treatment because he was known to specialize in marital problems, consonant with Cathy's conceptualization of her drinking. Thus it was not surprising that it was the relationship that was the initial and, ultimately, the principal focus of therapy. Cathy's drinking was not ignored, but it was dealt with as a by-product of a poor relationship. From our earlier discussion it should be obvious that there are many other ways to deal with problem drinking.

How should we think about the outcome of the therapy? It was successful to the extent that Cathy stopped drinking to excess and was abstaining even in the face of tremendous stress—the dissolution of her marriage. But at what cost? Should the separation be viewed as a minor price to pay for reducing her dependency on alcohol? What about Dick's state of mind? He was devastated by the outcome. The children were also put under stress, although it can be argued that they were being compromised earlier by their mother's alcoholism. The answers are not clear.

The selection of Dr. Seymour might have had an additional biasing effect on the outcome of treatment. It has been said that the theories and techniques of a therapist are mere technical aids and that the goals of treatment are separate. In addition, at least in outpatient treatment, the goals are set by the client(s). Consider how valid this argument is in the present case. Dr. Seymour's Gestalt orientation had him train his clients to dig deep into their psyches to uncover feelings of which they were unaware. This was a first step toward owning up to these feelings, acknowledging them as their own and taking responsibility for them. It seemed that Cathy did have some prior awareness of how unfulfilling her suburban mother/housewife life was, but it also seemed that the very training she received in therapy opened up these issues for her in a way that might well not have happened if, for example, she had stayed in AA and concentrated on her drinking. The Gestalt therapy also taught Dick how he truly felt about things; it made him more vulnerable, less macho, and thereby brought him closer to his wife. *But*, from his point of view, what did it get him? He lost his home, his family and, at least in the short run, emerged from therapy in worse shape than before. To be sure, things might have been better for him if he could have met Cathy's needs for greater autonomy, but he did not. Should Dr. Seymour have applied more pressure on him to do so? Perhaps the psychologist's own personal biases discouraged him; he was sad to see the marriage dissolve, but he did agree with the feminist direction Cathy was taking. Had he not opened a Pandora's box by exposing both Cathy and Dick to fears and wants so long denied? Perhaps it was unwise, even unethical, for him to do so without being more certain of the possible outcome. And yet his humanistic orientation has him trust the goodness and "wisdom of the psyche" of his clients, if only the distortions and inhibitions imposed by negative learning can be removed. The implicit tenet of insight therapy, after all, is that knowledge will set you free. It seemed to do so for Cathy, but what about Dick?

9

PSYCHOSEXUAL DISORDER: EXHIBITIONISM

Pete Wilson began therapy in November with a clinical psychologist. During the initial interview, Pete, a 34-year-old white male, explained that he was coming for therapy concerning a sexual problem that he had had for years. The immediate precipitant of entering therapy was that he had been arrested in September for a sexual assault. He had been driving home, taking a shortcut along some back roads, when he saw a car with its hood up and a woman looking at the engine. He stopped to offer assistance. In response to his question about what was wrong, the woman told him that she had stopped because her alternator light had come on. Pete was able to correct the problem by adjusting the fan belt. When the woman thanked him, he pulled her close to him, trying to fondle her buttocks. As she pushed him away, he exposed himself and started masturbating. The woman ran to her car and drove off. Pete made no attempt to follow. Later that night, the police came to his home and arrested him. An initial hearing was held the next day and bail was set. Pete's wife attended the hearing and paid the bail. At his subsequent trial, Pete was allowed to plead guilty to a reduced charge of attempted assault and was put on probation for 2 years. Part of the probation agreement was that Pete seek professional help.

This was not the first time that Pete had done something sexual that could get him into trouble. He had a long history of sexual deviance, dating back to early adolescence, but he had never actually attacked a woman before. His deviant sexual practices took two forms. One was getting himself into crowded places—shopping centers, subway trains, and the like—moving up close behind a woman, and rubbing his pelvis against her buttocks. This type of activity is called frottage. Pete's other deviant sexual practice was exhibitionism. Sometimes he would park his car in a place where many women would be walking and, remaining seated behind the wheel, masturbate as he watched them. He did not expose himself directly but hoped that the passing woman would look into his car and see him. Other times he would masturbate under a raincoat while in a place frequented by women. Teenagers with "cute, little behinds" were the preferred target for both activities.

Pete had engaged in both of these activities since adolescence. The first time he clearly remembered doing either was as a 16-year-old high-school student. He was at a football game on a drizzly Saturday afternoon and had on a raincoat, one in which the pockets allow a hand to go from the outside all the way through the coat to the body. Sitting next to a female acquaintance, he found himself sexually aroused and masturbated to orgasm, apparently undetected by anyone.

When he got his driver's license later that year, he began his practice of openly masturbating in his car. Since then he had engaged in either frottage or exhibitionism fairly regularly—an average of 15 to 20 times per year. Pete reported that the urge to do either usually increased when he was under stress, such as during exams in high school or while under work pressures in adulthood. His sexual behavior had worried him for some time. He had been in therapy for brief periods on three previous occasions. Each time he dropped out after several sessions because it seemed to him that little progress was being made.

Other important facets of Pete's problem were explored over the next several sessions. One of these was his sexual fantasies, which were a mirror of his deviant sexual practices. During the day, he often imagined rubbing against or masturbating in front of young women. His masturbatory fantasies also had the same content. He reported that his sexual fantasies had been increasing lately, stimulated by advertisements for designer jeans in magazines and on television. But there was an important difference between his fantasies and his actual sexual experiences. In real life he had never succeeded in arousing a woman by rubbing against her or publicly masturbating. Women he rubbed against moved away from him or, less frequently, threatened to call for help if he persisted. When women saw him masturbating in his car, their reaction was shock or disgust. In his fantasies, however, Pete's frottage or masturbation usually served as a prelude to intercourse. The young women of his dreams became aroused as he rubbed against them or when they saw his erect penis. His fantasy would then expand to include a more conventional sexual encounter. Fantasies limited only to conventional intercourse, however, were not stimulating to Pete.

Pete also had problems in other areas of his life. Although a college graduate, he had never been able to find a job that he found satisfying. His interests in painting and music had never turned into anything economically viable. He had held a long series of jobs he regarded as dull. The longest period for which he had held the same job was 18 months. He was currently working the day shift in a 24-hour topless bar.

Pete had married his wife, Helen, when he was 24 and she was 22. They had dated for about 6 months before the marriage. Their son, Steve, was now 5 years old. Helen was a high-school graduate who had gone to secretarial school and now worked as an executive secretary for the vice president of an engineering firm. She had held this relatively high-paying and responsible job for the past 4 years. Pete reported that their marriage had gradually gone downhill. It was not so much that they were fighting or arguing a lot but that Helen had become less affectionate, less interested in sex, and did not seem to care as much for him as she once had. Currently, he said, she found excuses to avoid most of his sexual advances. The frequency of intercourse had dropped to about twice per month. He reported that he did enjoy sex with his wife. Foreplay usually involved rubbing his penis on her bare buttocks, and intercourse was in the rear entry position. As with his fantasies, however, frottage was a necessary prelude to arousal and subsequent intercourse. According to Pete, the birth of their son seemed to coincide with the beginning of Helen's decline in interest in him. Pete was initially openly resentful of his son and refused to be involved in feedings, diaper changes, and the like. More recently, his feelings were changing; he was beginning to feel and act more like a father.

SOCIAL HISTORY

The origins of Pete's current problems seemed to lie in his childhood. He reported he had been "emotionally deprived" as a child. His father never held jobs for very long; consequently, the Wilsons moved a great deal. For this reason, Pete felt that he never had a chance to develop close childhood friendships. Furthermore, he felt rejected by his father. He reported that they never played or went on outings together and that his father always seemed cold and distant. Pete's father died when he was 12.

His relationship with his mother was better, but also deviant. Although Pete felt that he and his mother had a warm relationship, he also thought that she was overprotective and somewhat smothering. After the death of Pete's father, his mother never dated and seemed to invest all of her emotional needs in her children, especially Pete. For example, she continued to bathe him until he was 15. During these baths in Pete's early adolescence, she took great care in cleaning his penis, stroking it with the wet bar of soap and seeming to enjoy the erections that were often produced.

When Pete was 13, he and his mother were living in an apartment complex. His principal playmates were three young women, slightly older than himself. The four of them often engaged in rough and tumble play, including wrestling. During one of these play sessions, Pete had his first orgasm. He was wrestling with one of the women and was on top of her, his genitals against her buttocks. While moving, he became erect and continued thrusting until he climaxed.

After this initial pleasurable experience, Pete repeated it with his 8-year-old sister. At night, whenever the opportunity presented itself, he would go to her bed and rub his penis against her bare buttocks until he reached orgasm. He continued this practice regularly for the next couple of years and stopped only after his sister finally threatened to tell their mother. When he stopped the frottage with his sister, he turned to regular masturbation with fantasies of both rubbing and conventional intercourse during his self-stimulation. At 15, an opportunity for conventional intercourse presented itself. Pete had heard stories for some time about the sexual exploits of a 17-year-old girl who lived in the same apartment building as he did. He went out of his way to get to know her, did errands and favors for her and, finally, was invited to have sex with her one night in a nearby park. Although he became aroused as they kissed and petted, he lost his erection when he attempted intercourse. Thereafter Pete reported that he became afraid to approach women. The first instance of public masturbation occurred the next year.

On a social level, adolescence was not much better for Pete than childhood had been. He did hang around with a group, but he did not develop any really close relationships. He did not date much and reported that even being around popular and attractive women made him anxious. He also reported that it was difficult for him to participate in conversations. He felt that most often people talked only about trivialities and that he was just not interested in that.

After graduating from high school, Pete went to a local community college and then to a university, where he graduated with a bachelor's degree in psychology. He then drifted through a series of jobs and casual affairs until meeting his wife. She was the first woman with whom he had ever had a lasting relationship.

Another perspective on Pete, and particularly on his marriage, was gained through a marital assessment conducted in separate sessions with Pete and Helen. Pete's main complaints about Helen centered on her lack of affection and their poor sexual relationship. He also reported that they did argue somewhat about how to spend their leisure time. Helen liked to socialize with friends, but Pete found most of them boring. Helen did not know about Pete's deviant sexuality. She thought that Pete's trouble with the law was the only time he had ever engaged in such activity.

She could not understand why he had done it. She was extremely upset and repulsed by the entire incident, but she had stood by him. She also made it clear that another such incident would end their marriage. Helen's description of the problems in their marriage were similar to Pete's. She recognized that their infrequent sex, absence of affection, and disagreements about socializing with friends were serious problems. Helen also complained about Pete as a father and husband. She resented the fact that he was less than a full partner in the marriage, sharing only minimally in parenting and other household duties. Her resentment was increased because she worked all day and then had to come home to cook, clean, and take care of their son while Pete did little but watch television. Even when Pete was not working, which had occurred often, he made little attempt to help out. She had lost respect for him because of his failure to share in the marriage and because of his job history and consequent inability to make much of a financial contribution. She was currently somewhat ashamed and suspicious about Pete's job as a bartender in a topless bar. Indeed, she attributed most of her inability to be affectionate and her declining interest in sex to this loss of respect. She added that she wished Pete would not always follow the same routine in their sexual encounters. Helen and Pete both completed the Locke-Wallace (1959) marital adjustment test. Each of their scores was in the maritally maladjusted range; Helen indicated substantially more marital dissatisfaction than did Pete.

CONCEPTUALIZATION AND TREATMENT

Initially, Pete's therapist needed to implement some procedures to increase the likelihood that Pete would be able to stop both the public masturbation and the frottage. He had not engaged in either activity for almost 2 months, the longest period for which he had ever refrained since adolescence. But Pete reported that the urges were still there and that they would pop up unexpectedly. Because the frottage and public masturbation were linked to particular situations—parking lots, shopping centers, and subways—Pete was instructed to avoid these situations as much as possible. In addition, Pete was taught how to handle an urge if it arose. He was told to distract himself by imagining that he was on a beach, feeling drowsy, and enjoying the warm sun and then to leave the situation. Pete practiced imagining this scene several times during the session and reported that he was able to visualize it clearly and that he found it calming and relaxing. Neither procedures was viewed as a "cure" for Pete's problems, but the hope was that they would serve as stop-gap measures while more lasting changes were produced by other means.

The plan for therapy involved two components. First, an attempt was made to try to change Pete's sexual fantasies, both when masturbating and when he felt attraction to or arousal by any woman. Second, marital therapy seemed necessary, both for the marriage itself and more specifically, for the sexual relationship between Pete and Helen. Both aspects of the therapy were directed toward increasing the frequency and attractiveness of intercourse.

The first step in trying to make conventional intercourse more attractive to Pete was to have him masturbate while fantasizing only intercourse. Initially, Pete reported that he was unable to develop a full erection unless he imagined frottage or public masturbation. He was first instructed to arouse himself with any fantasy—for him this was most often frottage or public masturbation—to begin masturbating and, when he was close to orgasm, to switch to an intercourse scene. He was able to do this easily. After a week of practice, he was told to switch to the intercourse fantasy closer to the start of masturbation. He was able to do so with no loss of arousal. By the fourth week, he was able to initiate and complete masturbation with no fantasies of frottage or public masturbation.

As this part of the therapy was progressing, Pete also began to work on altering fantasies elicited by women. His usual response to seeing a young woman, particularly in tight jeans, was to begin imagining rubbing against her buttocks. A treatment was devised to help Pete change these fantasies. Initially, during a therapy session, Pete was shown a series of pictures of young women in tight jeans. For each stimulus he was asked to generate a nonsexual fantasy, such as trying to guess the woman's occupation. He was encouraged to focus on the woman's face instead of her buttocks as he thought about the pictures. Over a series of trials, in which Pete verbalized his thoughts, a number of distracting thoughts and fantasies were developed with the therapist guiding Pete and providing feedback. Over the next several weeks, Pete continued to practice his new fantasies, both in session and at home. As this skill became better established, Pete was also encouraged to use it in his day-to-day life.

At this point Pete was able to masturbate with no thoughts of frottage or public masturbation. He reported that he was beginning to have fewer and fewer thoughts of frottage when he encountered attractive young women. Marital therapy was then initiated.

At first the focus was on the nonsexual problems in the marriage. With the therapist functioning as a mediator and facilitator, the couple was instructed to talk about the various difficulties they were experiencing. The first problem they discussed was Pete's failure to help out with household chores. He acknowledged that he had not helped out very much but added also that when he did try to do something, Helen usually found fault with his efforts. Helen agreed, in part, with Pete's analysis. For example, when Pete did the laundry he would leave the clothes in the dryer so they became very wrinkled and would need ironing. From Helen's perspective, she was therefore not really saved from any work; if she had done the laundry herself, she would have quickly folded the clothes and not had to iron them. From Pete's viewpoint, his efforts had gone unappreciated. With the therapist's guidance, Helen and Pete were led to realize the aspects of the situation that were creating the problem. Neither of them was feeling good about what the other person had done. To solve the problem, Pete agreed to do the laundry and fold it immediately after it was dry, and Helen agreed to be sure to let Pete know that she appreciated his efforts. A similar system was instituted for several other household chores (cooking, vacuuming, general cleaning) in which Pete had tried to be helpful, but his efforts had failed to elicit Helen's approval.

Next the therapist tried to move the couple into a consideration of Pete's feeling that Helen was not affectionate toward him. But he was not able to limit the discussion to this problem; Helen was soon talking about her general lack of respect for Pete. The session became highly emotional. Pete, understandably somewhat defensive, argued that he had always done the best he could to be a provider for the family. This issue was not even close to resolution by the end of the session; the therapist instructed Pete and Helen not to talk about it further over the coming week but to think about it and be ready to discuss it the next week.

Two days later, Pete called the therapist to request an extra session. Pete was visibly tense when they met the next day. He said that he had really been shaken by the last session, that he had no idea that Helen had come to see him so negatively. This realization, he said, had a profound effect on him, and he felt compelled to let the therapist know something he had previously not told anyone. Over the past several years he had had a series of casual sexual experiences with young women. During most of them, he had not been able to complete intercourse satisfactorily. The pattern was similar to his initial attempt at intercourse. He would first become aroused and fully erect but later would lose his erection. He said that he wanted to start over now, to stop the affairs, and do more to please Helen.

At the next session with Pete and Helen, Pete quickly announced that he had decided to change jobs, was job hunting, and had several promising leads. Helen was obviously delighted and also reported that Pete was helping out more around the house and that she felt good about expressing her appreciation toward him. The next week, Pete landed a job as a camera salesman in a department store. Helen was very pleased. The two of them stated that they were ready to deal with sex.

Before beginning this phase of therapy, the therapist met individually with Pete to check on his progress in dealing with the urge to masturbate publicly or engage in frottage. Pete had continued to masturbate successfully to fantasies of conventional intercourse. Furthermore, he reported that seeing an attractive young woman no longer led automatically to thoughts of frottage and that he had not really experienced any of his old urges.

From this point on, the therapy progressed quickly. Because Helen was beginning to feel better about Pete, she said that she would not resist his sexual advances. They discussed with the therapist their sexual likes and dislikes and agreed to plan several sexual experiences over the next week. Pete was told to refrain from his usual foreplay (rubbing his penis against Helen's buttocks). The couple agreed on manual and oral stimulation to take its place. They had intercourse four times the next week. Over the next few sessions, the couple continued working on their marital problems. Progress was excellent. They reported that their sexual interactions were both frequent and pleasurable. Occasional sessions with Pete alone revealed that he no longer felt the urge to masturbate publicly or engage in frottage.

DISCUSSION

Pete's problems fall within *DSM-III*'s category of paraphilias, the use of unusual imagery or behaviors to produce sexual excitement. *DSM-III* (pp. 268–275) lists nine paraphilias. These include:

1) fetishism, the repeated use of nonliving objects to produce sexual excitement;
2) transvestism, recurrent cross-dressing to produce sexual arousal;
3) zoophilia, the repeated use of animals for sexual expression;
4) pedophilia, sexual activity with prepubescent children;
5) voyeurism, repetitive looking at unsuspecting people, either while undressing or engaged in sexual activity;
6) sexual masochism, the production of sexual arousal by being made to suffer; and
7) sexual sadism, the production of sexual arousal by inflicting physical or psychological suffering on someone else.

The remaining two paraphilias, exhibitionism and atypical paraphilia, were Pete's specific problems. In exhibitionism, the person repeatedly exposes his genitals to a stranger for the purpose of achieving sexual excitement. Exhibitionism is practiced almost exclusively by men and is the most common sexual offense for which people are arrested. Exhibitionism can involve either the exposure of a flaccid penis or an erect one, accompanied by masturbation, as in Pete's case. At the time of the act, the exhibitionist may feel both cognitive and physiological signs of anxiety—nervousness, palpitations, perspiring and trembling. Many report that the urge becomes so powerful that they lose control and even some awareness of what they are doing. No further sexual contact is sought. The exhibitionist seems to derive at least part of his gratification from the reaction of the victim, which is typically shock, fear, or disgust. According to data from court referrals, exhibitionism usually begins in adolescence, continues into the twenties, and declines thereafter. Whether the frequency truly declines or whether exhibitionists are arrested less frequently is unknown. Educationally and intellectually, exhibitionists seem to be normal (Mohr, Turner, and Jerry, 1964). About 75% of exhibitionists over the age of 21 are married.

Comparing Pete to the usual descriptions of exhibitionists, we can see that he is atypical in some respects. Instead of exposing himself openly, as is usually the case, Pete stayed in his car, hoping that he might be seen. He also indicated that he hoped his exposure would lead to a sexual contact; this is atypical, since most authors regard exhibitionists as actually fearing sexual contact with their victims.

Some features of Pete's background, however, are quite similar to characteristics of exhibitionists in general. Mohr, Turner, and Jerry (1964) report that over 50% of exhibitionists felt that they were distant from their fathers. Furthermore, their marriages tended to be poor, with special difficulties in sexual adjustment. Interpersonally, exhibitionists tended to be socially isolated, with few close friends. And, like Pete, exhibitionists tend to act out more frequently during periods of stress (Witzig, 1968).

Atypical paraphilias include a number of rare activities or practices used to produce sexual arousal, such as necrophilia (sexual activity with corpses), coprophilia (use of feces to produce sexual arousal), and frottage, Pete's problem. Little is known about frottage, although clinical reports indicate that it does not often occur in isolation and more commonly appears in conjunction with other paraphilias such as exhibitionism (Allen, 1969).

THEORIES

In psychoanalytic theory the various paraphilias are viewed as defenses against the anxiety aroused by conventional sexual intercourse. Fenichel (1945), for example, sees the exhibitionist as a person who did not successfully resolve the oedipal conflict. Instead of giving up his mother as his love object, getting over his fear of castration by the father and identifying with him, the exhibitionist continues to fear castration, which is associated with conventional intercourse. According to Karpman (1954), the mother is the villain of the piece. Motivated by unconscious penis-envy, she identifies fully with her son and even may be sexually provocative toward him.

The act of exposing is thought to confirm to the exhibitionist that he does have a penis and has not been castrated. Furthermore, Fenichel believes that the exhibitionist unconsciously hopes that the women to whom he exhibits will expose themselves to him. Seeing that they have no penis is supposed to reduce his own castration anxiety. Other psychoanalytic explanations propose that exhibitionism is a substitute for the true wish to exhibit to mother, an expression of repressed homosexuality, and a substitute for incestuous urges (Karpman, 1954). Similarly, psychoanalytic theory would regard Pete's frottage as a substitute way of expressing sexual impulses. Although some of these speculations ring true for certain aspects of Pete's case (his seductive mother, his early sexual experiences with his younger sister), there are few data that would allow us to evaluate them better. Furthermore, the fact that Pete had been able to complete intercourse successfully is not easily handled by the psychoanalytic position.

The learning-based conceptualization of Pete's case, which guided the therapy that was developed, involved the following considerations. First, during early adolescence Pete experienced a chance conditioning trial in which orgasm was linked to rubbing. Although a single experience like this one would not likely produce a durable effect, the link between rubbing and orgasm may have been strengthened through the many similar experiences he arranged between himself and his sister. His initial failure in conventional intercourse, coupled with his lack of social skills and infrequent dates, maintained his interest in frottage and set the stage for the development of exhibitionism. Finally, his unsatisfactory sexual relationship with his wife did not provide him with an opportunity to give up his old behavior patterns.

This account is still incomplete in many respects. Why did Pete reinforce his habit of frottage with his younger sister? What led him to exhibit instead of trying to develop skills that might have enabled him to date and to enjoy more conventional sexual pleasures? Answers to these questions are not available, either in Pete's case or those of other paraphilias.

TREATING PARAPHILIAS

There are virtually no controlled studies of the effectiveness of particular therapies in treating exhibitionism, frottage, and the other paraphilias. Psychoanalytic therapy follows from the etiological model discussed previously. Using the standard techniques of psychoanalysis—free association, dream analysis, and interpretation—the exhibitionist is encouraged to explore the unconscious impulses (e.g. castration fears or incestuous impulses) that are assumed to be causing the problem. In addition, analysts (e.g., Karpman, 1954) recommend making changes in the patient's life situation, such as moving out of his mother's home or improving the sexual relationship between the exhibitionist and his wife.

Case reports of behavioral approaches to exhibitionism have also appeared in recent years. Wickramsekara (1977), for example, reported on the successful use of systematic desensitization coupled with shaping more appropriate sexual responses. The desensitization aspect of the treatment was oriented toward reducing the young man's anxiety concerning sexual contact. He was first taught deep muscle relaxation and then, while relaxed, imagined a hierarchy of scenes ranging from social contact with a woman to sexual intercourse. As the desensitization progressed, the client was instructed to read erotic material, beginning with lightly sexual material and progressing to *Fanny Hill.* Although he had previously avoided such material for religious reasons, he became more and more involved in his task. Finally, the client was given direct instruction in initiating a sexual relationship with his fiancee. As their sexual relationship progressed, he reported that his desire to exhibit decreased. The case was successfully terminated after the eighteenth session.

Aversion therapies, in which an attempt is made to attach negative properties to exhibiting, have also been employed. MacCullouch, Williams, and Birtles (1977), for example, reported on a case of a 12-year-old exhibitionist whose acts of exposing were limited to older women with well-developed breasts and large buttocks. The procedure involved showing him pictures of women—either of the type linked to his problem or of girls his own age. Slides of the older women were followed by an electric shock that could be avoided if the client pressed a button, turning on a picture of a girl, before 8 seconds had elapsed. The goal of the procedure was to associate fear and anxiety with the stimulus of an older woman and simultaneously to make pictures of young girls a cue for anxiety relief, thereby increasing their attractiveness. After 18 therapy sessions using this procedure, the patient reported that he no longer had urges to exhibit.

A related procedure was developed by Reitz and Keil (1977). They noted that their exhibitionist had rarely been punished for his offenses; the client reported that he had exhibited about 50 times per year for more than 20 years but had only been reported 3 times. The therapists decided to have the patient exhibit himself to psychiatric nurses who would not react at all to him. The patient, however, indicated that he would feel shame and guilt in this situation. The therapy involved the client sitting in an office supplied with magazines for him to read. The nurses came in singly for periods of 15 minutes, during which the client was to expose himself. The client indeed reported considerable embarrassment over these sessions, so much so that he was unable to maintain his erection. After 10 sessions, he requested that he be allowed to talk to the nurses instead of exposing himself. It was also noted that the client was afraid of masturbating and that sexual arousal seemed to elicit exhibitionism automatically. Therefore the patient was instructed to masturbate instead of exposing himself. He subsequently reported that this was a successful substitute for exposure.

The therapy used with Pete was similar to a procedure originally developed by Davison (1968) in treating a case of a young man who required sadistic fantasies to produce sexual arousal. As in the present case, Davison had the client initiate sexual arousal with a sadistic fantasy and then masturbate while looking at a picture of a nude woman. If arousal began to wane, he could return to his sadistic images, but he was told to ensure that orgasm was associated only with the picture. As therapy progressed, the sadistic fantasies were relied on less and less until the client could masturbate to orgasm relying only on the stimulation produced by the nudes. Like Davison's client, Pete learned to become fully aroused and reach orgasm by changing his masturbatory fantasies from exhibiting and frottage to conventional intercourse. In addition, Pete came to change the fantasies that attractive women elicited by practicing new ones, first with pictures and then with women he encountered in the natural environment. Finally, a reduction in marital conflict and an improved sexual relationship between him and his wife were likely contributors to the overall success of the therapy.

10

PSYCHOSEXUAL DISORDER: INHIBITED FEMALE ORGASM

Barbara Garrison was concerned about a number of problems when she arrived for her first appointment at the mental health center. Her principal complaint was an inability to achieve orgasm during sexual intercourse with her husband, Frank. They were both 33 years old and had been married for 15 years. Frank was a police detective, and Barbara had recently resumed her college education. Their children, Bonnie and Dennis, were 15 and 12, respectively.

Barbara's orgasmic problem was situational in nature. She had experienced orgasms through masturbation, and she masturbated an average of once or twice each week; however, she had never reached orgasm during sexual activity with Frank. The problem did not involve sexual drive or arousal. She found Frank sexually attractive, wanted to enjoy a more satisfying sexual relationship with him, and did become aroused during their sexual encounters. They had intercourse two or three times each month, usually late at night after the children had gone to sleep and always at Frank's initiative. Their foreplay was primarily limited to genital manipulation and seldom lasted more than 5 minutes. Frank always reached orgasm within a minute or two after intromission and often fell asleep shortly thereafter, leaving Barbara in a frustrating state of unfulfilled sexual arousal. On many occasions she resolved this dilemma by slipping quietly out of the bedroom to the TV room, where she would secretly masturbate to orgasm. Frank realized that Barbara did not experience orgasms during intercourse but chose not to discuss the problem. He did not know that she masturbated.

This situation was very distressing to Barbara. She felt considerable guilt over her frequent masturbation, particularly after sexual intercourse, because she believed that masturbation was a terribly deviant practice. She was also concerned about the sexual fantasies in which she engaged during masturbation. She often imagined herself in a luxurious hotel room having sexual intercourse with a sequence of 8 or 10 men. They were usually men she did not know, but she would sometimes include men to whom she had been attracted, such as classmates from the university and friends of her husband. Barbara believed that these promiscuous fantasies proved that she was a latent nymphomaniac. She feared that she could easily lose control of her own desires and worried that she might someday get on a train, leave her family, and become a prostitute in a large city. Her anxiety regarding sexual interests and arousal was also a problem during intercourse with Frank. He had, in fact, made an effort numerous times to find out what sorts of things she found arousing, but she remained uncommunicative. She was afraid to tell him what she liked because she thought that he would then realize that she was "oversexed." She was very self-conscious during sexual activity with Frank. She worried about what he would think of her and whether she was performing adequately. Questions were continually running through her mind, such as "Am I paying attention to the right sensations?" or "Will it happen this time?" The combination of fear of loss of control of her sexual impulses and continual worry about her inadequacy as a sexual partner finally persuaded Barbara to seek professional help.

In addition to Barbara's inability to reach orgasm during intercourse, Barbara and Frank were not getting along as well as they had in the past. Several factors were contributing to the increased strain in their relationship. One involved Barbara's decision to resume her education. Frank had not completed his college education, and the possibility that Barbara might finish her degree was threatening to him. He was also uncomfortable around the friends Barbara met at the university. His job as a detective seemed to increase this tension because relations between students and the police had been strained by several years of demonstrations on the campus. Frank believed that Barbara's younger classmates saw him as a fascist, or an agent of the establishment. He resented changes in the way she dressed (she often wore blue jeans) and also attributed their increasingly frequent political disagreements to the subversive influence of the university environment.

They also had more financial concerns than in previous years. Barbara's tuition and other fees amounted to a considerable amount of money each semester and, within 3 years, their daughter, Bonnie, would be old enough to go to college. They had also taken out a substantial loan to build an addition onto their home. In order to make more money Frank had been working many more overtime hours. Considering that he was away from home so often, Barbara resented the fact that he spent most of his spare time working on the new rooms in their house.

Bonnie and her friends were another major problem. She was a freshman in high school, and her boyfriend, John, was a senior. Barbara did not like most of Bonnie's friends. She wanted Bonnie to be one of the leaders of the school—a good student, popular, active in school organizations—but Bonnie did not fit that mold. She was a marginal student, did not care for sports or group activities, and spent most of her time with John and her other friends at a local pinball alley. John was not a good student either. He worked part-time at a service station and planned to become a mechanic after graduation. Barbara and Bonnie argued continuously, mostly about Bonnie's relationship with John. Barbara was preoccupied with the possibility that Bonnie might get pregnant. They did not talk about sex openly because the topic was too anxiety provoking for Barbara. She did make every effort, however, to prevent them from being by themselves. Bonnie had asked on several occasions whether John could come over to their house to watch television and listen to records. Barbara would only allow John to be in the house if she or Frank were in the same room with them. The net effect of this rule was to ensure that Bonnie and John spent most of their time away from the Garrison's home. It also led to arguments between Barbara and Frank because he felt that Barbara was being too severe. Frank believed that the problem was mostly in Barbara's imagination. These problems were, in most ways, typical of the conflict that parents experience with teenage children. In the Garrison's case the tension was compounded by Barbara's sexual difficulty and their financial and educational worries.

Despite their frequent arguments and differences of opinion, Barbara and Frank were both seriously committed to their marriage. Neither of them were particularly happy, but they were not considering a divorce. Barbara believed that their relationship would be markedly improved if she could overcome her orgasmic dysfunction. Frank was less concerned about that particular issue but agreed that Barbara might feel better if a therapist could "help her understand *her* problem." He hoped that a psychologist might be able to improve the relationship between Barbara and Bonnie.

SOCIAL HISTORY

Barbara's parents were both in their middle forties when she was born. They had one other child, a boy, who was 10 years older than Barbara. Her father was a police officer, and her mother was a homemaker. They were conservative, devoutly religious people. In addition to taking care of the children and her other household responsibilities, Barbara's mother spent a considerable amount of time in volunteer roles at their church. She was a Sunday school teacher for many years and always took Barbara with her to her classes. Barbara's parents clearly cared for each other and for the children, but they were not openly affectionate. She could not remember seeing them embrace or kiss each other except for frequent pecks on the cheek or top of the head nor, on the other hand, could she remember hearing them argue. It was a quiet, peaceful household in which emotional displays of any kind were generally discouraged.

Barbara's parents and her older brother were very protective of her. She was "the baby of the family" and was always closely supervised. It usually seemed to Barbara that she was not allowed to do many of the things that her friends' parents permitted. When she was very young, she was not allowed to leave their yard. When she was older and in high school, she was not allowed to go out on school nights and had to be home by 10 P.M. on weekends. Her parents insisted on meeting all of her friends and, in some cases, forbade her to associate with certain other children. Until she was 16 years old, Barbara was not allowed to go to parties if boys were also invited. She remembered her first date as an awkward experience that occurred during her junior year in high school. A boy whom she had admired for several months had finally asked her to go to a movie. Her parents agreed to allow her to go after her father asked several of his friends about the boy and his parents. When he picked her up before the movie, Barbara's parents asked so many questions that they were finally late for the show. Later, as they were leaving the theater, Barbara realized that her brother and his girlfriend, who both attended a local junior college, had been sitting several rows behind them. Their parents had called him and asked if he would keep an eye on her "to be sure everything was okay." He did not intend to be secretive and, in fact, asked Barbara if she and her friend would like to go out for hamburgers and cokes after the show. This carefully arranged supervision did not ruin the experience. Everyone had a good time, and Barbara went out with this same boy several times in the next year. Nevertheless, the protective manner in which Barbara was treated by her family prevented her from developing close relationships with boys her own age and later left her feeling uncomfortable when she was alone with men.

Barbara's knowledge about and experiences with sexual activity were extremely limited during childhood and adolescence. Neither of her parents made an effort to provide her with information about her own body or reproductive functions. Her mother did discuss general issues such as romance and marriage with Barbara, but only at the most abstract level. All of the books and magazines in their home were carefully screened to avoid exposing the children to suggestive literature or photographs. Barbara was not able to learn much about these matters from her friends because she was so closely supervised. After she began menstruating at the age of 11, her mother gave her a book that explained the basic organs and physiology associated with the human reproductive system and, once again, avoided any personal discussion of Barbara's concerns about sexuality. The implicit message conveyed by her parents' behavior and attitudes was that sex was a mysterious and dangerous phenomenon.

After she graduated from high school, Barbara began taking classes at the local junior college. She continued to live at home with her parents and maintained several of the same friends she had had in high school. During her first semester, Barbara met Frank, who was then a student at the police academy. After several weeks, they began to see each other regularly. Her parents liked Frank, perhaps because her father was also a policeman, and they gradually began to allow her greater freedom than they had when she dated in high school. Frank and Barbara were both 18 years old, but he was much more mature and experienced. He had been dating regularly since he was 15 and had had sexual intercourse for the first time when he was 17. Their sexual relationship progressed rapidly. Although she was initially apprehensive and shy, Barbara found that she enjoyed heavy petting. She refused to have intercourse with Frank for several months; finally she gave in one evening after they had both been drinking at a party. She later remembered being disappointed by the experience. Frank had climaxed almost immediately after intromission, but she had not reached orgasm. Her guilt was replaced by utter shock when she recognized several weeks later that she was pregnant. They did not discuss the pregnancy with her parents and agreed that they should be married as soon as possible. Bonnie was born less than 6 months after their marriage. Despite the obvious "prematurity" of the birth, Barbara's parents never mentioned the issue of premarital intercourse or pregnancy. She dropped out of college before Bonnie was born and did not return to school for many years.

Barbara and Frank's sexual relationship did not change very much over the next few years, although their frequency of intercourse declined markedly during their second year of marriage. Intercourse continued to be a pleasurable experience for both of them, even though Barbara was not able to experience orgasm. Her first orgasm occurred after they had been married for more than 3 years and both of their children had been born. Following their typical pattern, Frank had fallen asleep after intercourse and Barbara was lying in bed, half awake and very much aroused. She was lying on her stomach and some of the blankets happened to be bunched up under her pelvis and between her legs. Without recognizing what she was doing, Barbara began rocking rhythmically from side to side. She was very relaxed and noticed that this motion created a very pleasurable sensation. Several minutes after she began rocking, she experienced an intense, unmistakable orgasm. It was an extremely pleasurable phenomenon restrained only by her fear of waking Frank. After this accidental discovery of masturbation, Barbara experimented further with various styles of self-manipulation and was soon masturbating regularly. Unfortunately, she was afraid to describe these experiences to Frank because she believed that it was an immoral and selfish act, and her ability to reach orgasm by self-stimulation did not generalize to coital situations with Frank. Barbara also avoided conversations about sex when she was talking with other women. She believed that masturbation and sexual fantasies were sinful behaviors and was convinced that none of her friends had ever had such an experience.

CONCEPTUALIZATION AND TREATMENT

In approaching the sexual problem described by Barbara, the therapist focused on Barbara and Frank as a couple, not on Barbara as an individual. He was principally concerned with the things they did and said when they were together. It was clear from Barbara's description of the problem that she knew very little about sexual behavior. Her reports also indicated that she and Frank were not communicating effectively during sexual activity and were not engaging in effective sexual behaviors. Because of the focus on the relationship and not on Barbara alone, the therapist asked Barbara to bring Frank with her to the second treatment session.

Frank was initially reluctant to join Barbara in treatment because he had always believed that the problem was primarily hers. Nevertheless, he agreed to talk to the therapist at least once and, during this interview, he indicated that he was also dissatisfied with their sexual relationship. On further questioning, he even admitted that he had secretly worried that he was to blame for Barbara's orgasmic difficulty. This thought had caused him considerable anxiety from time to time, particularly when he was also worried about his performance in other roles such as work and his relationship with the children. The therapist asked Frank to describe their sexual activity from his perspective and noted, as Barbara had previously indicated, that there was very little emphasis placed on foreplay. Two considerations seemed to be particularly important in this regard. First, Frank said that he did not know what sorts of activity might be more pleasurable for Barbara, since she had never expressed any feelings in this regard. Second, Frank indicated that he generally felt unsure of his own ability to delay ejaculation and therefore preferred to insert his penis in Barbara's vagina before he "lost control." This concern was related to his belief that intercourse was the most mature form of sexual activity and his fear that Barbara would begin to question his virility if he were unable to accomplish intercourse. Although he realized that Barbara was not entirely happy with their sexual relationship, Frank privately conceded that he would rather not draw attention to his own difficulty. The therapist responded in a reassuring manner, emphasizing that he did not want to ascribe responsibility to either partner. The primary concern of treatment, he said, would be to increase both partner's satisfaction with their sexual relationship. He also noted that most forms of sexual dysfunction, particularly premature ejaculation, are easily amenable to brief, learning-based forms of therapy. Given this explanation of the problem and considering the optimistic prognosis, Frank agreed to work together with Barbara toward a solution of their problem.

During his initial interviews with both Barbara and Frank, the therapist made an effort to consider various factors that might contribute to sexual dysfunction, such as depression, fatigue, and marital dysharmony. None of these seemed to account for the problem. Both partners were somewhat unhappy, but neither was clinically depressed. Although their relationship had been strained by the sexual problem, they were both committed to the marriage. Neither was involved in an extramarital relationship, which might detract from their involvement in treatment or their interest in change, and both Barbara and Frank expressed affection for one another. It was interesting to note that they were more willing to express their positive feelings for the other person when they were talking with the therapist than when they were interacting directly. Overall, the sexual dysfunction did not seem to be secondary to other adjustment problems.

Before beginning a psychological approach to their sexual problem, Barbara and Frank were also asked to obtain complete physical examinations. This assessment was recommended in an effort to rule out the possibility that their difficulty could be traced to a physical disorder. Various diseases that affect the central nervous system, hormone levels, and vascular functions can influence sexual arousal and performance. Abnormalities in the musculature and tissue structure of the genital area can also be problematic. None of these factors were evident in this particular case.

During the third session, the therapist explored many of Barbara's and Frank's attitudes and beliefs about sexual behavior. His purpose was to improve their communication with each other about sexual matters and to open a discussion in which they could acquire additional knowledge and correct mistaken beliefs. Several issues were particulaly important and seemed to be related to their failure to engage in more effective sexual behavior. For example, both Barbara and Frank believed that vaginal stimulation should be the principal source of sexual pleasure for women and that orgasm during coitus is dependent solely on such stimulation. The therapist explained that the clitoris is, in fact, more sensitive than the vagina. Female orgasm seems to depend on both direct and indirect stimulation of the clitoris during both masturbation and intercourse. Considerable time was also spent discussing the Garrison's attitudes toward and use of sexual fantasies. The topic was broached cautiously by the therapist. He commented in a matter-of-fact tone that most normal adults engage in sexual fantasies; he then asked Frank to describe one of his favorite fantasies. Despite some initial embarrassment, and much to Barbara's surprise, Frank told Barbara and the therapist that he often pictured himself working late at night and being seduced in the detectives' lounge by an attractive female colleague. This was the first time that Barbara and Frank had discussed sexual fantasies. While Barbara expressed some mild jealousy that Frank would think about another woman, she was very relieved to learn that he also used sexual fantasies. His self-disclosure lowered her anxiety on the topic. She then shared a description of one of her own fantasies—admittedly one that was less provocative than her thoughts of having intercourse with several men in a row. Having explored these and other issues at some length, the therapist recommended a few books that the Garrisons should read in order to learn more about human sexuality. It was hoped that this information would reduce their anxiety about their own interests and practices and, at the same time, suggest new activities that they had not yet tried.

The next step in treatment was to eliminate some of the obstacles that were interfering with Barbara's ability to become totally aroused and to teach her and Frank to engage in more effective sexual behavior. This could only be accomplished in a totally nondemanding atmosphere. Because of their history of sexual difficulty and dissatisfaction, Barbara and Frank had become self-conscious about their sexual behavior. Barbara felt considerable pressure, which was mostly self-imposed, to reach orgasm; Frank was secretly concerned about whether he could delay ejaculation long enough for Barbara to become more aroused. From the point at which Frank initiated sexual activity, both of them tended to assume a detached perspective as they observed what they were doing and how they were feeling. The therapist attempted to eliminate pressure to perform by telling Barbara and Frank that they were *not* to attempt sexual intercourse under any circumstances during the next few weeks. He told them that he was going to ask them to practice an exercise known as "sensate focus" in which their only goal would be to practice giving and receiving pleasurable sensations.

Sensate focus is a simple touching exercise in which the partners take turns gently massaging each other's bodies. The therapist instructed them to begin by finding a quiet time when they would not be disturbed or distracted and they were not overly tired. Having removed their clothes, Barbara was to lie on her stomach across their bed while Frank massaged her back and legs. She was encouraged to abandon herself to whatever pleasures she experienced. Barbara's instructions were to concentrate on the simplest sensations—warm and cold, smooth and rough, hard and soft—and to let Frank know what she enjoyed and what she wanted to change. Stimulation of Barbara's breasts and genital area was expressly prohibited to avoid the demand for increased sexual arousal. They were asked to practice sensate focus at least four times before their next session.

Barbara and Frank both responded very positively to this initial exercise. They described these extended periods of touching and caressing as very relaxing and pleasurable; they both said that they had felt a sense of warmth and closeness that had disappeared from their relationship years ago. Barbara also expressed some relief that she was able to focus on the pleasure of his touch without worrying about whether she would have an orgasm or whether he would ejaculate quickly and leave her stranded in a state of unfulfilled arousal. With this positive beginning, the therapist suggested that they move on to the next step. They were to change positions for the next week. Frank would sit on the bed with his back against the headboard and his legs spread apart. Barbara would sit in front of him, facing in the same direction, with her back resting against his chest and her legs resting over his. In this position, Frank would be able to touch and massage the front of her body; the restriction against touching her breasts and genitals was removed. He was told, however, to avoid direct stimulation of the clitoris because it can be irritating and in some cases painful. She was instructed to rest her hand gently on his and to guide his touch to convey the sensations that were most pleasurable to her, including location, pressure, and rhythm of movement. The therapist emphasized that Barbara was to control the interaction. As before, they were asked to practice at least four times in the following week.

At the beginning of the next session, minor problems were noted in the progress of treatment. Barbara reported that she had become somewhat self-conscious with the new exercise. She found the experience pleasant and arousing, but her mind wandered and she was unable to achieve a state of total abandon. Frank had also encountered some difficulty with ejaculatory control. On the third evening of practice, he had become totally absorbed in the process and, without completely realizing what he was doing, he had rubbed his erect penis against Barbara's back and reached orgasm. The therapist reassured Frank that this experience was not unexpected and could, in fact, be seen as the predictable outcome of his immersion in the sensate focus exercise. It was also clear, however, that some additional changes should be made in the process to help Frank gain more control and to reduce Barbara's tendency toward detachment.

The therapist decided to address the issue of ejaculatory control by recommending that Barbara and Frank practice the "start-stop" procedure. Frank was instructed to lie on his back so that Barbara could stimulate his erect penis manually. His task would be to concentrate on his own level of arousal and signal Barbara when he experienced the sensation that immediately precedes ejaculation. At this point, Barbara would discontinue stimulation. When Frank no longer felt that ejaculation was imminent, she would resume stimulation until he again signaled that he was experiencing the urge to ejaculate. They were asked to repeat this cycle four or five times initially and to work toward achieving 15 to 20 minutes of continuous repetitions.

The sensate focus exercise was also continued with additional instruction. Barbara was specifically encouraged to engage in her favorite sexual fantasies while guiding Frank's hands over her body. Frank's acceptance and support were particularly helpful in this regard because of Barbara's guilt about the use of sexual fantasies. By concentrating on these images, she would be able to avoid other mental distractions that had impaired her ability to become completely involved in the sensate focus exercise.

The next 2 weeks of practice were very succesful. Frank was able to control his ejaculatory urges within 4 or 5 days of practice; Barbara found that the start-stop exercise was also quite pleasurable for her. In the past Frank had always discouraged her from stroking or playing with his erect penis because he was afraid that he would ejaculate prematurely. It was becoming clear that their improved communication about what they enjoyed and when to start and stop various activities resulted in considerably greater freedom and pleasure than their previously constricted interactions had allowed. Barbara was now able to reach orgasm through Frank's manual stimulation of her breasts and clitoris. She was much less inhibited about directing his touch, and he noted he had learned a lot about Barbara's erotic zones. Much of the tension and inhibition had been reduced.

The final step was to help Barbara experience orgasm during coitus. The prohibition against intercourse was lifted, and a new procedure was introduced. As before, they were instructed to begin their exercises by alternating in sensate focus. When they were both moderately aroused, Frank would lie on his back and Barbara would sit on top of him with her knees drawn toward his chest and insert his penis into her vagina. She would then control the speed and rhythm of their movements. Emphasis was placed on moving slowly and concentrating on the pleasurable sensations associated with vaginal containment. If Frank experienced the urge to ejaculate, Barbara was instructed to withdraw his penis until the sensation had passed. If she became less aroused during coitus, they would also separate, and Frank would once again employ clitoral stimulation until Barbara reached a stage of more intense arousal, at which point they would resume coitus.

Barbara and Frank practiced this procedure many times over the next few weeks. It was an extremely pleasurable experience, and they noticed that they had made considerable progress, most notably Frank's ability to delay ejaculation throughout 20 to 30 minutes of intercourse with Barbara in the superior position. Nevertheless, Barbara was not able to reach orgasm through penile stimulation alone. They continued to alternate periods of insertion with manual stimulation of the clitoris, but Barbara's orgasms were limited to the latter intervals. The therapist noted that this was not uncommon and encouraged them to begin experimenting with other positions for intercourse that would also allow manual stimulation of her clitoris during coitus. The Garrisons were perfectly satisfied with this solution.

Fifteen weeks after their initial visit, Barbara and Frank had made very significant changes in their sexual adjustment. Both of them were pleased with these developments, which included Frank's confidence in his ability to control ejaculation and Barbara's ability to reach orgasm during intercourse. Perhaps most important, these changes were not specifically limited to their sexual interactions. They reported that they also talked more frequently and openly about other areas of their lives and felt closer to each other than they had at the beginning of treatment. Thus the new lines of communication that had been developed in sexual activities did generalize, or transfer, to some other situations.

Even though some of the Garrisons' peripheral problems were resolved spontaneously after the successful treatment of Barbara's orgasmic inhibition, other difficulties remained. Several were addressed directly in further treatment sessions. Their relationship with Bonnie, for example, continued to be a source of frequent aggravation. They argued with her individually and as a couple and sometimes fought with each other when she was not present. Most of these arguments centered around the issues of freedom and responsibility. Could Bonnie stay out past 10 P.M. on weekdays? Should she and her boyfriend be alone in the house when Barbara and Frank were out? What chores was she expected to do, and how often should she do them? All of these questions were addressed in conjoint family sessions in which the therapist served as a mediator. Bonnie and her parents negotiated a mutually acceptable contract that specified what she could expect from them and, in turn, what they could expect from her. The agreement also included contingencies that would go into effect when and if anyone failed to fulfill his or her commitments. The level of conflict in the Garrison home was substantially reduced after the negotiation of this contract.

DISCUSSION

Psychosexual disorders are defined in terms of interference with any phase of the human sexual response cycle. This cycle may be thought of as a continuous sequence of events or sensations, beginning with sexual desire and ending with the decrease in tension following orgasm. Masters and Johnson (1966) have suggested that this cycle may be roughly divided into four phases that are characteristic of both men and women. During the *excite-*

ment phase, the person begins to respond to sexual stimulation with increased flow of blood to the genital area. This engorgement leads to erection in the male and vaginal lubrication in the female. Continued stimulation leads to increased levels of sexual tension, known as the *plateau phase* of sexual arousal. Various physiological changes, including more rapid breathing and an increase in heart rate and blood pressure, occur throughout the excitement and plateau phases. These changes reach their maximum intensity during the *orgasmic phase*, a very brief period of involuntary response. In males the orgasmic phase occurs in two stages, beginning with the collection of sperm and seminal fluid in the urethra (creating a sensation of inevitability, or "point of no return") and ending with ejaculation. In females the orgasmic phase involves rhythmic contractions in the outer third of the vagina. From a subjective point of view, the orgasmic phase is the point of peak physical pleasure. It is followed by a rapid dissipation of tension. The period following orgasm, known as the *resolution phase*, encompasses the return of bodily functions to a normal resting state.

Interference with sexual response may occur at any point and may take the form of subjective distress (such as the fear of losing ejaculatory control) or disrupted performance (such as the inability to maintain an erection sufficient for intercourse). In males the most common forms of sexual dysfunction are inhibited sexual excitement (formerly known as impotence) and premature ejaculation. *DSM-III* defines inhibited sexual excitement as "recurrent and persistent inhibition of sexual excitement during sexual activity, manifested by partial or complete failure to attain or maintain erection until completion of the sexual act" (p. 279). Premature ejaculation is defined as being present when "ejaculation occurs before the individual wishes it, because of recurrent and persistent absence of reasonable voluntary control of ejaculation and orgasm during sexual activity" (p. 280). In females the most common problems include inhibited sexual excitement ("failure to attain or maintain the swelling response of sexual excitement until completion of the sexual act" (*DSM-III*, p. 279), functional dyspareunia (genital pain associated with coitus), functional vaginismus (involuntary spasms of the vaginal musculature that interfere with coitus), and inhibited orgasm. *DSM-III* defines inhibited female orgasm as "recurrent and persistent inhibition of the female orgasm as manifested by a delay in or absence of orgasm following a normal sexual excitement phase during sexual activity that is judged by the clinician to be adequate in focus, intensity, and duration" (p. 279). All of these problems may be general or situational in nature. In the case of inhibited sexual excitement in a male client, for example, he may never have been able to attain or maintain an erection until completion of the sex act. On the other hand, he may have been able to do so in the past, or with a different partner, but not be able to do so presently.

Kaplan (1979) has drawn attention to another general area of sexual dysfunction, inhibited sexual desire. It is clear that a lack of interest in sexual activity may be an important source of distress, particularly for the spouse or partner of such an individual, but it is also a difficult problem to define. What is a normal sexual appetite? Instead of establishing an arbitrary standard, *DSM-III* has opted for a flexible judgment in this area that depends on a consideration of "factors that affect sexual desire such as age, sex, health, intensity and frequency of sexual desire, and the context of the individual's life" (p. 278). In fact, *DSM-III* notes that this diagnostic category should be used infrequently and only when the lack of desire is a major source of subjective distress.

Diagnostic judgments in the area of sexual dysfunction often depend on subtle considerations. Is the problem sufficiently persistent and pervasive to warrant treatment? And, if it is, does the problem center around one partner or the other? These may be difficult questions. In the Garrison's case, for example, it was not clear whether Barbara's inability to reach orgasm during orgasm could be attributed to Frank's difficulty in delaying or controlling his ejaculatory response. On the other hand, if she had been able to reach orgasm quickly, he might not have worried about the question of control. Two conclusions can be drawn from these considerations. First, sexual dysfunction is most easily defined in the context of a particular interpersonal relationship. The couple, not either individual, is the focus for assessment and treatment. Second, the identification of sexual dysfunction rests largely with the couple's subjective satisfaction with their sexual relationship and not with absolute judgments about typical, or normal, levels of performance.

Few data are available regarding the prevalence of the various forms of psychosexual dysfunction, but most are not uncommon. With the exception of marital conflict, sexual dysfunction does not seem to be associated with impairment in other areas of occupational and social functioning. There is no evidence to indicate that individuals suffering from sexual dysfunction also exhibit other forms of disturbance such as personality disorders, although persistent sexual problems may lead to depression or anxiety.

ETIOLOGY

Some cases of sexual dysfunction may be the result of other forms of physical of mental disturbance. Human sexual response is a very complicated and delicate system that may be disrupted by any number of factors. Various physical conditions, including diseases of the central nervous system, drug ingestion, and fatigue, can impair the person's interest in sexual activity or the ability to perform sexual responses. Other psychological adjustment problems can also lead to disturbances in sexual activity. Depression, for example, is commonly associated with a drastic decline in the person's interest in sex. These types of considerations should be considered before a direct treatment approach is attempted, but most instances of sexual dysfunctions are not simple by-products of physical or mental disorders (Masters and Johnson, 1970).

Various psychological explanations have been proposed to account for the development and maintenance of sexual dysfunction. Psychoanalytic theory traces sexual problems to an inadequate resolution of the oedipal conflict. In Barbara's case, for example, a psychoanalyst might have argued that her inability to reach orgasm during intercourse was associated with fear of success in the sense that being successful in her adult sexual relationship might be analogous to succeeding in the oedipal situation. According to this notion, Barbara wanted to have intercourse with her father and was thus in competition with her mother. But she was also afraid that if she succeeded her mother would punish her severely. To the extent that her husband was symbolic of her father and reaching orgasm during intercourse with him was equivalent to "winning" the struggle with her mother, Barbara's orgasmic inhibition could be determined by this unconscious mental conflict. The treatment approach that follows from this theoretical position would involve long-term, individual psychotherapy with Barbara in which the goal would be to help her achieve insight into her frustrated sexual desire for her father, her consequent fear of her mother, and the relationship between this conflict and her current relationship with her husband.

Certain aspects of this theory are consistent with the present case. Most notable might be the resemblance between her father and her husband, Frank. They were both police officers and shared various interpersonal characteristics, such as conservative social and political beliefs. On the other hand, they did not resemble each other physically, and Frank's behavior toward Barbara and their children was much less stern and protective than her father's had been. Barbara's current relationship with her mother might also be raised as evidence in support of a psychoanalytic approach to the case. Her father had died shortly after Barbara and Frank were married. Barbara's mother moved into an apartment near the Garrison's home, and she and Barbara continued to see each other often. Barbara admitted privately that her mother was usually more of an annoyance than a help, meddling in their daily activities and criticizing the manner in which Barbara and Frank handled the children. Nevertheless, Barbara was markedly unassertive with her mother and usually acquiesced to her demands. A psychoanalyst might have argued that this close, ongoing interaction exacerbated and maintained Barbara's rivalry with her mother and that her submissive yet covertly hostile attitude was mostly motivated by her fear of retaliation. Barbara's problems with her teenage daughter, Bonnie, could also be explained in psychoanalytic terms. Without much difficulty, Barbara's exaggerated concerns about Bonnie's sexual behavior could be seen as the projection of her fear that she would lose control of her own sexual desires (e.g., as was evident in her discussion of her sexual fantasies and the fear that she might flee to Los Angeles to become a prostitute). There are, however, more parsimonious explanations for these phenomena. Her parental behavior may have been a simple reflection of the pattern modeled by her parents; they were very protective of her when she was young, and she was now protective of Bonnie.

Learning theorists have also stressed the importance of past events in determining present sexual adjustment, but they have emphasized the importance of conditioning procedures, not unconscious mental conflict and sexual desire for one's parents. From a behavioral perspective, many forms of sexual dysfunction can be seen as the product of learned inhibitions that are acquired as a result of unsuccessful, early sexual experiences. In some cases, these may have been traumatic events such as being raped or molested. They may also include more typical situations. Consider, for example, an adolescent boy who is discovered masturbating by his mother, particularly if she responds with anger or disgust. The boy may develop, through classical conditioning, an association between the stimuli that lead to sexual arousal (say he was looking at pictures of nude women at the time) and shame or anxiety. Subsequent anticipatory anxiety may interfere with his ability to maintain an erection during sexual intercourse. Operant learning principles may also play a similar role. For example, many teenagers have their first sexual experience in the back seat of a parked automobile, a situation in which they run the risk of being discovered and possibly humiliated. In this situation, the male may be reinforced for ejaculating quickly after intromission by escape from the anxiety-provoking situation of being partially exposed to any curious passerby who happened to peer in the window. In general, behavioral models of sexual dysfunction emphasize the importance of learned, anticipatory anxiety that is associated with sexual stimulation and the development of avoidance responses that serve to reduce this anxiety. They also stress the importance of knowing how to engage in effective sexual behaviors; they focus on what the people do during sexual activity instead of on the symbolic meaning of the act.

The learning perspective is also compatible with several elements of Barbara's case. Her parents' inability to display physical affection (at least in front of the children), their failure to provide her with any information about sexual behavior, and the implicit message that sexual activity was somehow shameful or disgusting were all important factors that contributed to both her anxiety regarding sexual activity and her lack of appropriate heterosexual social skills. Prior to her relationship with Frank, Barbara had no sexual experience beyond very brief kisses and hugs after dates. She and Frank, at his insistence, progressed very rapidly in their own sexual relationship without giving Barbara any time to extinguish gradually her fear of physical intimacy. Furthermore, their first experience with intercourse was generally unpleasant. This unfortunate event, coupled with their subsequent realization that Barbara had become pregnant, contributed to furthering her discomfort in sexual activity. Instead of addressing the problem directly and learning more enjoyable ways of interacting sexually, Barbara and Frank tried to ignore the problem and eventually came to avoid sexual intercourse as much as possible and to shorten the occasions when they did have sex to the briefest possible intervals.

Whether or not sexual inhibitions are learned through classical or operant learning procedures is a matter of controversy. Perhaps the most important consequence of the general behavioral approach to sexual dysfunction has been the emphasis that is placed on the current, situational determinants of the problem. Kaplan (1974) has summarized these factors under four general headings. The first is "failure to engage in effective sexual behavior." This category includes practices such as rushing to the point of intromission before the woman is sufficiently aroused, as was the Garrisons' habit. Kaplan points out that this sort of error is almost always the result of ignorance about human sexual responses and not the product of deeply ingrained neuroses or personality disorders. Frank and Barbara did not know that most women take longer than men to reach an advanced stage of sexual arousal and, as a result, neither of them had made a serious effort to improve or prolong their activity during foreplay.

The second category listed by Kaplan is "sexual anxiety," which includes problems associated with subjective factors such as the pressure to perform adequately and fear of failure. This type of interference was clearly present in the Garrisons' case. Frank had been concerned for a number of years about losing control of his ejaculatory response. Because of this fear, he continued to rush through the initial stages of sexual activity and resisted any subtle efforts that Barbara made to slow things down. She, on the other hand, was troubled by a double-edged concern. Although she always *tried* very hard to have an orgasm (and was, in fact, quite self-conscious about her failure to reach a climax), she was simultaneously worried about getting carried away. Barbara was convinced that if she really abandoned herself completely and followed her "raw sexual instinct," she would lose control of herself. In so doing, she feared that she would risk losing Frank completely because he would be repulsed by her behavior. This was truly a vicious dilemma. If she did not relax and let herself go, she would not have an orgasm, thus perpetuating her own unhappiness as well as Frank's conviction (as she imagined it) that she was an inadequate lover. On the other hand, if she did relax and let herself go, she would lose control and run the risk of alienating him completely.

Kaplan's third category includes "perceptual and intellectual defenses against erotic feelings." Sexual responses are not under voluntary control. The surest way to lose an erection, for example, is to think about the erection instead of the erotic stimuli. Nevertheless, many people engage in a kind of obsessive self-observation during sexual activity and, as a result, become spectators, not participants, in their own lovemaking. Masters and Johnson (1970) refer to this pattern of behavior as the "spectator role," noting that it is among the most common deterrents to successful sexual response. This problem was particularly characteristic of Barbara's behavior. She often found herself ruminating during sexual activity and asking herself questions about her own performance and desires (Will I come this time? What would happen if Frank knew what I have been thinking about?).

"Failure to communicate" is the final category of immediate causes of sexual dysfunction. As Kaplan has noted: "Trying to be an effective lover for oneself and one's partner without communicating is like trying to learn target shooting blindfolded (1974, p. 133)." The Garrisons' failure in this regard was painfully obvious. Neither was willing to talk to the other person about their desires and pleasures. In Barbara's case, her inhibitions could be traced to the environment in which she was raised. Her parents conveyed very explicitly the message that decent people did not talk about sex. If she could not talk to her own mother about basic matters such as menstruation and pregnancy, how could she expect to discuss erotic fantasies with her husband? Consequently, Barbara and Frank knew very little about the kinds of stimulation and fantasies that were most pleasing to their partner.

TREATMENT

Largely because of the pioneering work of Masters and Johnson (1970), most forms of sexual dysfunction can now be treated successfully through a direct, psychological approach. Instead of treating the problem as a symbol of unconscious turmoil, Masters and Johnson are concerned with the problem itself and the current, situational determinants that serve to maintain it. Their approach is clearly behavioral. They seek to eliminate sexual anxiety by temporarily removing distracting expectations (they forbid intercourse during the first several days of treatment) and substituting competing responses. The sensate focus exercise, for example, is employed to create an erotic atmosphere, devoid of performance demands, in which the couple can learn to communicate more freely. In later sessions they instruct the couple in the use of specific exercises designed to foster skills related to their specific sexual problem.

The "start-stop" procedure, which was originally introduced by Semans (1956), is a good example of this approach. The male partner is taught to attend to important sensations that signal the imminence of ejaculation and to interrupt further stimulation until the urge passes. Frank's experience indicates that there are important cognitive changes that accompany the physiological and behavioral components of this technique. As he became more successful in controlling his ejaculatory responses, Frank experienced less apprehension during extended periods of foreplay. His increased confidence and willingness to communicate were, in turn, very important assets in addressing Barbara's orgasmic difficulty. Tremendous success has been achieved with this approach. Semans reported success with 8 out of 8 cases of premature ejaculation. Masters and Johnson[1] treated 186 men for premature ejaculation and found that 182 were able to learn to control ejaculation so that their partners could achieve orgasm during coitus at least 50% of the time. Furthermore, in a 5-year follow-up of 74 of these men, Masters and Johnson identified only one instance of relapse. Very few forms of treatment in the field of abnormal behavior can claim such impressive rates of documented success.

The prognosis for orgasmic dysfunction in women is also quite good, but not as optimistic. Masters and Johnson reported an 80% rate of success with 106 women who had been unable to reach orgasm during intercourse (but had been able to reach orgasm through masturbation). Kaplan (1974) has pointed out that the criteria for success are somewhat ambiguous in this kind of problem. With very few exceptions, all women can learn to experience orgasm, but a substantial percentage cannot reach climax through the stimulation afforded by intercourse alone. As in Barbara's case, many women require additional stimulation beyond that associated with the motion of the erect penis in the vagina. In the absence of information to the contrary, these women should not be considered treatment failures and they should not be encouraged to believe that they are settling for "second best." Barbara and Frank were very happy with their sexual relationship despite the fact that she could not achieve orgasm through intercourse alone. They had made remarkable changes in their ability to communicate and share sexual pleasure and were content to utilize positions that allowed either Frank or Barbara to stimulate Barbara's clitoral area manually while they were having intercourse. With this quasi-limitation in mind, direct approaches to orgasmic dysfunction have been very successful.

[1]Masters and Johnson used a variant of Semans' procedure known as the "squeeze technique," in which the wife also squeezes the end of the penis between her thumb and forefinger during interruptions of sexual stimulation.

11

SCHIZOPHRENIA: PARANOID TYPE

Bill McClary made his first appointment at the mental health center reluctantly. He was 25 years old, single, and unemployed. His sister, Colleen, with whom he had been living for 18 months, had repeatedly encouraged him to seek professional help. She was concerned about his peculiar behavior and social isolation. He spent most of his time daydreaming, often talked to himself, and occasionally said things that made very little sense. Bill acknowledged that he ought to keep more regular hours and assume more responsibility, but he insisted that he did not need psychological treatment. The appointment was finally made in an effort to please his sister and mollify her husband, who was worried about Bill's influence on their three young children.

During the first interview, Bill spoke quietly and with frequent hesitations. The therapist noted that Bill occasionally blinked and shook his head as though he were trying to clear his thoughts or return his concentration to the topic at hand. When the therapist commented on this unusual twitch, Bill apologized politely but denied that it held any significance. He was friendly yet shy and clearly ill at ease. The discussion centered around Bill's daily routine and his rather unsuccessful efforts to fit into the routine of Colleen's family. Bill assured the therapist that his problems would be solved if he could stop daydreaming. He also expressed a desire to become better organized.

Bill continued to be very guarded throughout the early therapy sessions. After several weeks, he began to discuss his social contacts and mentioned a concern about sexual orientation. Despite his lack of close friends, Bill had had some limited and fleeting sexual experiences. These had been both heterosexual and homosexual in nature. He was quite concerned about the possible meaning and consequences of his encounters with other males. This topic occupied the next several weeks of therapy.

Bill's "daydreaming" was also pursued in greater detail. It was a source of considerable concern to him, and it interfered significantly with his daily activities. This experience was quite difficult to define. At frequent, although irregular, intervals throughout the day, Bill found himself distracted by intrusive and repetitive thoughts. The thoughts were simple and most often alien to his own value system. For example, he might suddenly think to himself, "Damn, God." Recognizing the unacceptable nature of the thought, Bill then felt compelled to repeat a sequence of self-statements that he had designed to correct the initial intrusive thought. He called these thoughts and his corrective incantations "scruples." These self-statements accounted for the observation that Bill frequently mumbled to himself. He also admitted that his unusual blinking and head shaking were associated with the experience of intrusive thoughts.

Six months after Bill began attending the clinic regularly, the therapist received a call from Bill's brother-in-law, Roger. Roger said that he and Bill had recently talked extensively about some of Bill's unusual ideas, and Roger wanted to know how he should respond. The therapist was, in fact, unaware of any such ideas. Instead of asking Roger to betray Bill's confidence any further, the therapist decided to ask Bill about these ideas at their next therapy session. It was only at this point that the therapist finally became aware of Bill's extensive delusional belief system.

For reasons that will become obvious, Bill was initially reluctant to talk about the ideas to which his brother-in-law had referred. Nevertheless, he provided the following account of his beliefs and their development. Shortly after moving to his sister's home, Bill realized that something strange was happening. He noticed that people were taking special interest in him and often felt that they were talking about him behind his back. These puzzling circumstances persisted for several weeks during which Bill became increasingly anxious and suspicious. The pieces of the puzzle finally fell in place late one night as Bill sat in front of the television. In a flash of insight, Bill suddenly came to believe that a group of conspirators had secretly produced and distributed a documentary film about his homosexual experiences. Several of his high-school friends and a few distant relatives had presumably used hidden cameras and microphones to record each of his sexual encounters with other men. Bill believed that the film had grossed over $10 million at the box office and that this money had been sent to the Irish Republican Army to buy arms and ammunition. He therefore held himself responsible for the deaths of dozens of people who had died as the result of several recent bombings in Ireland. This notion struck the therapist and

Bill's brother-in-law as being quite preposterous, but Bill's conviction was genuine. He was visibly moved as he described his guilt concerning the bombings. He was also afraid that serious consequences would follow his confession. Bill believed that the conspirators had agreed to kill him if he ever found out about the movie. This imagined threat had prevented Bill from confiding in anyone prior to this time. It was clear that he now feared for his life.

Bill's fear was exacerbated by the voices that he had been hearing for the past several weeks. He frequently heard male voices discussing his sexual behavior and arguing about what action should be taken to punish him. They were not voices of people with whom Bill was personally familiar, but they were always males and they were always talking about Bill. For example, one night when Bill was sitting alone in his bedroom at Colleen's home, he thought he overheard a conversation in the next room. It was a heated argument in which one voice kept repeating, "He's a goddamned faggot and we've got to kill him!" Two other voices seemed to be asking questions about what he had done and were arguing against the use of such violence. Bill was, of course, terrified by this experience and sat motionless in his room as the debate continued. When Roger tapped on his door to ask if he was all right, Bill was certain that they were coming to take him away. Realizing that it was Roger and that he had not been part of the conversation, Bill asked him who was in the next room. Roger pointed out that two of the children were sleeping in the next room. When Bill went to check, he found the children asleep in their beds. These voices appeared at frequent but unpredictable intervals almost every day. It was not clear whether or not they had first appeared before the development of Bill's delusional beliefs.

The details of the delusional system were quite elaborate and represented a complex web of imaginary events and reality. For example, the title of the secret film was supposedly *Honor Thy Father*, and Bill said his name in the film was Gay Talese. *Honor Thy Father* was, in fact, a popular novel that was written by Gay Talese and published a few years prior to the development of Bill's delusion. The actual novel was about organized crime, but Bill denied any knowledge of this "other book by the same title." According to Bill's belief system, the film's title alluded to Bill's disrespect for his own father and his own name in the film was a reference to his reputation as a "gay tease." He also maintained that his own picture had been on the cover of *Time* magazine within the past year with the name Gay Talese printed at the bottom.

An interesting array of evidence had been marshaled in support of this delusion. For example, Bill pointed to the fact that he had happened to meet his cousin accidentally on a subway in Brooklyn 2 years earlier. Why, Bill asked, would his cousin have been on the same train if he were not making a secret film about Bill's private life? In Bill's mind, the cousin was clearly part of a continuous surveillance that had been carefully arranged by the conspirators. The fact that Bill came from a very large family and that such coincidences were bound to happen did not impress him as a counterargument. Bill also pointed to an incident involving the elevator operator at his mother's apartment building as further evidence for the existence of the film. He remembered stepping onto the elevator one morning and having the operator give him a puzzled, prolonged glance. The man asked him if they knew each other. Bill replied that they did not. Bill's explanation for this mundane occurrence was that the man recognized Bill because he had obviously seen the film recently; he insisted that no other explanation made sense. Once again, coincidence was absolutely impossible. His delusional system had become so pervasive and intricately woven that it was no longer open to logical refutation. He was totally obsessed by the plot and simultaneously so frightened that he did not want to discuss it with anyone. Thus he had lived in private fear, brooding about the conspiracy and helpless to prevent the conspirators from spreading knowledge of his shameful sexual behavior.

SOCIAL HISTORY

Bill was the youngest of four children. He grew up in New York City where his father worked as a fire fighter. Both of his parents were first-generation Irish Americans. Many of their relatives were still living in Ireland. Both parents came from large families. Bill's childhood memories were filled with stories about the family's Irish heritage.

Bill was always much closer to his mother than to his father, whom he remembered as being harsh and distant. Being the youngest child, he was treated protectively. His mother doted on him and did not encourage social activities with other children. When his parents fought, which they did frequently, Bill often found himself caught in the middle. Mr. McClary accused his wife of lavishing all her affection on Bill and seemed to blame Bill for their marital disharmony. Mrs. McClary, on the other hand, pointed out that her husband spent all of his time with their oldest son and excluded Bill from their activities. Neither parent seemed to make a serious effort to improve their relationship. Bill later learned that his father had carried on an extended affair with another woman. His mother depended on her own mother, who lived in the same neighborhood, for advice and support and would frequently take Bill with her to stay at her parents' apartment after particularly heated arguments. Bill grew to hate his father, but his enmity was tempered by guilt. He had learned that children were supposed to respect their parents and that, in particular, a son should emulate and revere his father. Mr. McClary became gravely ill when Bill was 12 years old, and Bill remembered wishing that his father would die. His wish came true. Years later, Bill looked back on this sequence of events with considerable ambivalence and dismay.

Bill could not remember having any close friends as a child. Most of his social contacts were with cousins, nephews, and nieces. He did not enjoy their company or the games that other children played. He remembered himself as a clumsy, effeminate child who preferred to be alone or with his mother instead of with other boys.

He was a good student and finished near the top of his class in high school. His mother and the rest of the family seemed certain that he would go on to college, but Bill could not decide on a course of study. The prospect of selecting a profession struck Bill as an ominous task. How could he be sure that he wanted to do the same thing for the rest of his life? He decided that he needed more time to ponder the matter and took a job as a bank clerk after graduating from high school.

Bill moved to a small efficiency apartment and seemed to perform adequately at the bank. His superiors noted that he was reliable, although somewhat eccentric. He was described as quiet and polite—his reserved manner bordered on being socially withdrawn. He did not associate with any of the other employees and rarely spoke to them beyond the usual exchange of social pleasantries. Although he was not in danger of losing his job, Bill's chances for advancement were remote. This realization did not perturb Bill because he did not aspire to promotion in the banking profession. It was only a way of forestalling a serious career decision. After 2 years at the bank, Bill resigned. He had decided that the job did not afford him enough time to think about his future.

He was soon able to find a position as an elevator operator. Here, he reasoned, was a job that provided time for thought. Over the next several months, he gradually became more aloof and disorganized. He was frequently late to work and seemed unconcerned about the reprimands that he began receiving. Residents at the apartment house described him as peculiar. His appearance was always neat and clean, but he seemed preoccupied most of the time. On occasion he seemed to mumble to himself, and he often forgot floor numbers to which he had been directed. These problems continued to mount until he was fired after working for 1 year at this job.

During the first year after finishing high school, while working at the bank, Bill had his first sexual experience. A man in his middle forties who often did business at the bank invited Bill to his apartment for a drink, and they became intimate. The experience was moderately enjoyable but primarily anxiety provoking. Bill decided not to see this man again. Over the next 2 years, Bill experienced sexual relationships with a small number of other men as well as with a few women. In each case, it was Bill's partner who took the initiative. Only one relationship lasted more than a few days. He became friends with a woman named Patty who was about his own age, divorced, and the mother of a 3-year-old daughter. Bill enjoyed being with Patty and her daughter and occasionally spent evenings at their apartment watching television and drinking wine. Despite their occasional sexual encounters, this relationship never developed beyond the casual stage at which it began.

After he was fired from the job as an elevator operator, Bill moved back into his mother's apartment. He later recalled that they made each other very nervous. Rarely leaving the apartment, Bill sat around the apartment daydreaming in front of the television. When his mother returned from work, she would clean, cook, and coax him unsuccessfully to enroll in various kinds of job-training programs. His social isolation was a constant cause of concern for her. She was not aware of his bisexual interests and encouraged him to call women that she met at work and through friends. The tension eventually became too great for both of them, and Bill decided to move in with Colleen, her husband, and their three young children.

CONCEPTUALIZATION AND TREATMENT

Bill's adjustment problems were obviously extensive. He had experienced serious difficulties in the development of social and occupational roles. From a traditional diagnostic viewpoint, Bill's initial symptoms pointed to a schizotypal personality. In other words, before his delusional beliefs and hallucinations became manifest, he exhibited a series of peculiar characteristics in the absence of floridly psychotic symptoms. These included several of the classic signs outlined by Meehl (1964): anhedonia (the inability to experience pleasure), interpersonal aversiveness, and ambivalence. Bill seldom, if ever, had any fun. Even his sexual experiences were described in a detached, intellectual manner. He might indicate, for example, that he had performed well or that his partner seemed satisfied, but he never said things like, "It was terrific," or "I was really excited!" He strongly preferred to be alone. When Colleen and Roger had parties, Bill became anxious and withdrew to his room, explaining that he felt ill. Bill's ambivalence toward other people was evident in his relationship with his therapist. He never missed an appointment; in fact, he was always early and seemed to look forward to the visits. Despite this apparent dependence, he seemed to distrust the therapist and was often guarded in his response to questions. He seemed to want to confide in the therapist and was simultaneously fearful of the imagined consequences. Bills pattern of cognitive distraction was somewhat difficult to interpret. His scruples were, in some ways, similar to obsessive thoughts, but they also bore a resemblance to one of Schneider's first rank symptoms of schizophrenia—thought insertion. Considering this constellation of problems, it was clear that Bill was in need of treatment, but it was not immediately obvious that he was psychotic. The therapist decided to address Bill's problems from a social learning perspective. The ambiguity surrounding his cognitive impairment seemed to warrant a delay regarding biological interventions such as medication.

The first several therapy sessions were among the most difficult. Bill was tense, reserved, and more than a bit suspicious. Therapy had been his sister's idea, not his own. The therapist adopted a passive, nondirective manner and concentrated on the difficult goal of establishing a trusting relationship with Bill. In the absence of such an atmosphere, it would be impossible to work toward more specific behavioral changes.

Many of the early sessions were spent discussing Bill's concerns about homosexuality. The therapist listened to Bill's thoughts and concerns and shared various bits of information about sexuality and homosexual behavior in particular. As might be expected, Bill was afraid that homosexual behavior per se was a direct manifestation of psychological disturbance. He also wondered about his motivation to perform sexual acts with older men and expressed some vague hypotheses about this being a reflection of his desire to have a closer relationship with his father. The therapist assured Bill that the gender of one's sexual partner was less important than the quality of the sexual relationship. In fact, the therapist was most concerned about Bill's apparent failure to enjoy sexual activity and his inability to establish lasting relationships. Instead of trying to eliminate the possibility of future homosexual encounters or to impose an arbitrary decision based on prevailing sexual norms, the therapist tried to: (1) help Bill explore his own concerns about the topic, (2) provide him with information that he did not have, and (3) help him develop skills that would improve his social and sexual relationships, whether they involved men or women.

As their relationship became more secure, the therapist adopted a more active, directive role. Specific target problems were identified, and an attempt was made to deal with each sequentially. The first area of concern was Bill's daily schedule. The therapist enlisted Colleen's support. Together with Bill they instituted a sequence of contingencies designed to integrate his activities with those of the family. For example, Colleen called Bill once for breakfast at 7:30 A.M. If he missed eating with everyone else, Colleen went on with other activities and did not make him a late brunch as had been her custom prior to this arrangement. In general, the therapist taught Colleen to reinforce appropriate behavior and to ignore inappropriate behavior as much as possible. Over the initial weeks, Bill did begin to keep more regular hours.

The Premack principle was also used to encourage more involvement in household chores; high probability behaviors were made contingent on the emission of low probability behaviors in an effort to increase the frequency of the low probability behaviors. Unfortunately, this phase of the treatment program met with limited success because of a lack of appropriate high probability behaviors. High probability behaviors are the things that the person prefers to do when he or she is given a free choice (when there are no explicit contingencies in effect). Whenever he had a chance, Bill spent most of his time daydreaming. There were few specific activities that he enjoyed. Indeed, this relative inability to experience pleasure was one of the most troublesome aspects of Bill's behavior. The most appropriate activity in this regard involved Colleen's youngest daughter, Susan. Bill enjoyed helping Susan with her homework after dinner. The therapist considered making this activity available to Bill only if he had just cleared the table and loaded the dishwasher. While this contingency may have been effective, it seemed somewhat shortsighted. Bill's very low level of social contact was a major source of concern. The therapist decided against using a procedure that might further reduce this activity. Instead, he simply tried to encourage Bill to work with the children as much as possible and continued to coach Colleen and her husband in the use of praise and ignore procedures.

After several weeks of work, this home-based program began to produce positive changes. Bill was following a schedule closer to that of the rest of the family and was more helpful around the house. At this point, the therapist decided to address two problems that were somewhat more difficult: Bill's annoying habit of mumbling to himself and his lack of social contacts with peers. Careful interviews with Bill and his sister served as a base for a functional assessment of the self-talk. This behavior seemed to occur most frequently when Bill was alone or thought he was alone. He was usually able to control his scruples in the presence of others; if he was particularly disturbed by a distracting thought, he most often excused himself and retired to his room. Colleen's response was usually to remind Bill that he was mumbling and occasionally to scold him if he was talking loudly. Given the functional value of Bill's scruples in reducing his anxiety about irreverent thoughts, it seemed unlikely that the self-talk was being maintained by this social reinforcement. The therapist decided to try a stimulus control procedure. Bill was instructed to select one place in the house in which he would daydream and talk to himself. Whenever he felt the urge to daydream or repeat his scruples, he was to go to this specific spot before engaging in these behaviors. It was hoped that this procedure would severely restrict the environmental stimuli that were associated with these asocial behaviors and thereby reduce their frequency. Bill and the therapist selected the laundry room as his daydreaming room because it was relatively secluded from the rest of the house. His bedroom was ruled out because the therapist did not want it to become a stimulus for behaviors that would interfere with sleeping. Colleen was encouraged to prompt Bill whenever she noticed him engaging in self-talk outside of the laundry room. The program seemed to have modest, positive results, but it did not eliminate self-talk entirely.

Interpersonal behaviors were also addressed from a social learning perspective. Since moving to his sister's home, Bill had not met any people his own age and had discontinued seeing his friends in New York City. Several avenues were pursued. He was encouraged to call his old friends and, in particular, to renew his friendship with Patty. The therapist spent several sessions with Bill rehearsing telephone calls and practicing conversations that might take place. Although Bill was generally aware of what things he should say, he was anxious about social contacts. This form of behavioral rehearsal was seen as a way of exposing him gradually to the anxiety-provoking stimuli. He was also given weekly homework assignments involving social contacts at home. The therapist discussed possible sources of friends, including a tavern not far from Colleen's home and occasional parties that Colleen and Roger had for their friends. This aspect of the treatment program was modestly effective. Bill called Patty several times and arranged to stay with his mother for a weekend so that he could visit with Patty and her daughter. Although he was somewhat anxious at first, the visit was very successful and seemed to lift Bill's spirits. He was more animated during the following therapy session and seemed almost optimistic about changing his current situation.

It was during one of their visits to the neighborhood tavern that Bill first mentioned the imagined movie to Roger. When the therapist learned of these ideas, and the auditory hallucinations his treatment plan was modified. He had initially rejected the idea of antipsychotic medication because there was no clearcut evidence of schizophrenia. Now that evidence was available, an appointment was arranged with a psychiatrist who agreed with the diagnosis and prescribed a moderate dosage of Mellaril, one of the standard phenothiazines. Because Bill's behavior was not considered dangerous and his sister was able to supervise his activities closely, hospitalization was not necessary. All of the other aspects of the program were continued.

Bill's response to the medication was positive but not dramatic. The most obvious effect was on his self-talk, which was reduced considerably over a 4-week period. Bill attributed this change to the virtual disappearance of the annoying, intrusive thoughts. His delusions remained intact, however, despite the therapist's attempt to encourage a rational consideration of the evidence. The following example illustrates the impregnable quality of delusional thinking as well as the naiveté of the therapist.

One of Bill's ideas was that his picture had been on the cover of *Time* magazine. This seemed like a simple idea to test, and Bill expressed a willingness to try. Together they narrowed the range of dates to the last 8 months. The therapist then asked Bill to visit the public library before their next session and check all issues of *Time* during this period. Of course, Bill did not find his picture. Nevertheless, his conviction was even stronger than it had seemed. He had convinced himself than the conspirators had seen him on his way to the library, beaten him there, and switched magazine covers before he could discover the original. Undaunted, the therapist recommended two more public libraries for the next week. As might have been expected, Bill did not find his picture at either library but remained convinced that the cover had appeared. Every effort to introduce contradictory evidence was met by this same stubborn resistance.

Overall, the medication had a positive effect on Bill's behavior, but it also produced some bothersome side effects. Many of these were minor in nature, such as dry mouth and drowsiness. The latter problem was handled by adjusting the schedule for Bill's daily dosage so that he took most of the Mellaril 2 hours before bedtime. The most annoying side effect involved muscular rigidity. Bill said that his arms and legs felt stiff and that his hands sometimes trembled involuntarily. Colleen noted that his movement and posture appeared somewhat more awkward than usual. These motor disturbances, which are known as extrapyramidal effects, were counteracted by having Bill supplement his Mellaril with an anti-parkinson drug, Cogentin. Despite the annoying side effects, Bill expressed satisfaction with the antipsychotic medication because it cleared his thinking and thus eliminated a major source of personal distress.

Over the next several weeks, Bill became somewhat less adamant about his beliefs. He conceded that there was a *chance* that he had imagined the whole thing. It seemed to him that the plot probably did exist and that the movie was, in all likelihood, still playing around the country, but he was willing to admit that the evidence for this belief was less than overwhelming. Although his suspicions remained, the fear of observation and the threat of death were less immediate, and he was able to concentrate more fully on the other aspects of the treatment program. Hospitalization did not become necessary, and he was able to continue living with Colleen's family. Despite important improvements, it was clear that Bill would continue to need a special supportive environment and it seemed unlikely that he would assume normal occupational and social roles, at least not in the near future.

DISCUSSION

The diagnostic hallmarks of schizophrenia are hallucinations, delusions, and disorganized speech. The criteria listed in *DSM-III* (pp.188–189) require at least one of the following symptoms, or sets of symptoms, to support a diagnosis of schizophrenic disorder.

(1) bizarre delusions (content is patently absurd and has no *possible basis in fact), such as delusions of being controlled, thought broadcasting, thought insertion, or thought withdrawal.*
(2) somatic, grandiose, religious, nihilistic, or other delusions without persecutory or jealous content.
(3) delusions with persecutory or jealous content if accompanied by hallucinations of any type.
(4) auditory hallucinations in which either a voice keeps up a running commentary on the individual's behavior or thoughts, or two or more voices converse with each other.
(5) auditory hallucinations on several occasions with content of more than one or two words, having no apparent relation to depression or elation
(6) incoherence, marked loosening of associations, markedly illogical thinking, or marked poverty of content of speech if associated with at least one of the following:
  (a) blunted, flat, or inappropriate affect
  (b) delusions or hallucinations
  (c) catatonic or other grossly disorganized behavior.

In addition to these criteria, *DSM-III* requires that the patient exhibit some deterioration from a previous level of occupational or social functioning and that some continuous signs of the disorder must have been evident for at least 6 months at some time during the patient's life. The required 6-month period may include a prodromal, or preliminary, phase that is evident before the onset of active hallucinations or delusions. *DSM-III* (p. 189) defines a prodromal phase as a clear deterioration in functioning that is not due to a mood disturbance or substance abuse and that involves at least two of the following symptoms.

(1) social isolation or withdrawal.
(2) marked impairment in role functioning.
(3) markedly peculiar behavior (e.g. collecting garbage, talking to self in public, or hoarding food).
(4) marked impairment in personal hygiene and grooming.
(5) blunted, flat, or inappropriate affect.
(6) digressive, vague, overelaborate, circumstantial, or metaphorical speech.

(7) odd or bizarre ideation, or magical thinking.
(8) unusual perceptual experiences, e.g. recurrent illusions, sensing the presence of a force or person not actually present.

Bill clearly fits this set of criteria for schizophrenia. Prior to the admission of his complex, systematized delusional scheme, he exhibited several of the characteristics of a prodromal phase. He had been socially isolated ever since moving to his sister's home. Although he did interact with his sister and her family, he made no effort to stay in touch with the few friends he had known in New York City, nor did he attempt to meet new friends in the neighborhood. In fact, he had never been particularly active socially, even during his childhood. His occupational performance had deteriorated long before he was fired from his job as an elevator operator. Several neighbors had complained about peculiar behavior. For example, one of Colleen's friends once called to tell her that she had been watching Bill as he walked home from the grocery store. He was carrying a bag of groceries, clearly mumbling to himself, and moving in a very strange pattern. He would take two or three steps forward, then one to the side onto the grass next to the sidewalk. At this point, Bill would hop once on his left foot, take one step forward, and then step back onto the sidewalk and continue the sequence. Thinking that this behavior seemed similar to games that are common among children, Colleen asked Bill about his walk home. He told her that each of these movements possessed a particular meaning and that he followed this pattern to correct scruples that were being placed in his head as he returned from the store. This explanation, and his other comments about his scruples, would also fit the *DSM-III* notion of magical thinking. Overall, the onset of Bill's delusional beliefs and auditory hallucinations can be seen as an extension of the deterioration that began much earlier.

Bill's case also provides an interesting opportunity to describe the use of *multiaxial* evaluation as it is employed in *DSM-III*. This system provides for the evaluation of the client in each of five different areas. Axes I and II include the disorders usually associated with psychopathology. Personality disorders and specific developmental disorders (e.g., developmental reading disorder) are coded on Axis II. All other disorders (for both adults and children) are coded on Axis I. Bill would receive a diagnosis of schizophrenic disorder on Axis I and schizotypal personality disorder on Axis II. The *DSM-III* criteria for schizotypal personality disorder are listed in Table 11.1.

Axis III provides for the description of physical disorders or conditions that might be relevant to either understanding the person's adjustment problems or the development of a treatment plan. Examples might be thyroid conditions, which sometimes result in psychotic symptoms, and

Table 11.1 Diagnostic Criteria for Schizotypal Personality Disorder

The following are characteristic of the individual's current and long-term functioning, are not limited to episodes of illness, and cause either significant impairment in social or occupational functioning or subjective distress.

A. At least four of the following:

1. Magical thinking, e.g., superstitiousness, clairvoyance, telepathy, "6th sense," "others can feel my feelings."
2. Ideas of reference.
3. Social isolation, e.g., no close friends or confidants, social contacts limited to essential everyday tasks.
4. Recurrent illusions, sensing the presence of a force or person not actually present (e.g., "I felt as if my dead mother were in the room with me"), depersonalization, or derealization not associated with panic attacks.
5. Odd speech (without loosening of associations or incoherence), e.g., speech that is digressive, vague, overelaborate, circumstantial, metaphorical.
6. Inadequate rapport in face-to-face interaction due to constricted or inappropriate affect, e.g., aloof, cold.
7. Suspiciousness or paranoid ideation.
8. Undue social anxiety or hypersensitivity to real or imagined criticism.

B. Does not meet the criteria for schizophrenia.

Source: DSM-III, American Psychiatric Association, 1980, pp. 312-313.

hypertension, which might affect the use of certain forms of medication. No such conditions were present in Bill's case. The severity of recent stressful experiences can be rated on Axis IV. Consideration is given to the events that might have precipitated or exacerbated the problems listed on Axes I and II. Bill would be given a rating of 1 (no apparent psychosocial stressor); he had already lived with his sister for more than 1 year, so his change of residence would not be considered, and no other major events had occurred that might have caused problems for him. Axis V, the final category, lists the patient's highest level of adaptive functioning in the past year. Bill would receive a rating of 6 (very poor) on a 7-point scale because he exhibited marked impairment in both social relations and occupational functioning. The purpose of this multiaxial evaluation is to provide a more thorough picture of the patient's problems than would be evident in the provision of a single diagnostic category. In Bill's case, the lack of significant stressors to which his problems might be attributed, the presence of schizotypal personality features, and his relatively poor level of adjustment throughout the past year are all indicative of a poor prognosis.

The specific criteria listed in *DSM-III* represent a major change from the definition of schizophrenia that was listed in *DSM-II* (APA, 1968). The earlier definition was much more general and did not specify the boundaries of the diagnostic category. Following the lead established by Eugen Bleuler at the beginning of the twentieth century, American psychiatrists came to rely on subtle judgments regarding affective and cognitive functioning instead of on specific statements about hallucinations and delusions. Bleuler argued that there were four primary symptoms of schizophrenia: loosening of associations (disorganized speech), blunted or inappropriate affect, ambivalence (the simultaneous expression of opposite emotions, attitudes, or wishes toward a given person or object), and autism (a preference for fantasy over reality). These came to be known as the four As. Unfortunately, they are all somewhat difficult to identify with an acceptable level of reliability. It is very difficult, for example, to decide whether a patient's mood is blunted, slightly depressed, or contemplative. In fact, the patient may be either preoccupied or bored. Because of the ambiguity surrounding these kinds of criteria, schizophrenia came to be a very broad, poorly defined category. *DSM-III* has reversed that trend.

Schizophrenia is a relatively common disorder, affecting approximately 1 to 2% of the population (Zerbin-Rüdin, 1972). It is found equally in men and women. Onset usually occurs during adolescence or early adulthood, but somewhat later for women than for men. The prognosis is mixed. When Kraepelin first defined the disorder (originally known as dementia praecox), he emphasized its chronic deteriorating course. Many patients do, in fact, show a gradual decline in social and occupational functioning and continue to exhibit psychotic symptoms either continuously or intermittently throughout their lives. However, a substantial number of patients seem to recover without signs of residual impairment. Among the most informative data pertaining to prognosis have come from the World Health Organization's International Pilot Study of Schizophrenia (1975). Compared to other diagnostic categories such as affective disorders, schizophrenics tended to have a worse outcome 5 years after being hospitalized. There was substantial overlap between the groups, however, and considerable variability within the schizophrenic patients. The results of this study and several others indicate that roughly 33% of schizophrenic patients recover, 33% continue to experience some kind of impairment, and the remaining patients follow the severe, chronic pattern initially described by Kraepelin (Strauss and Carpenter, 1979).

Although schizophrenics share some important common characteristics, they are also an extremely heterogenous group. This feature was emphasized in the title of Bleuler's classic monograph, *Dementia Praecox or the Group of Schizophrenias* (1911/1950). Kraepelin and Bleuler both outlined subtypes of schizophrenia, including catatonic, paranoid, hebephrenic, and simple types. Each of these subtypes was defined in terms of a few characteristic types. Catatonic patients were identified by their bizarre motor movements and the unusual postures they would assume. Their motor behavior might include either a rigid posture with total immobility or undirected, maniclike excitement. Paranoid patients were those who expressed delusions of persecution and reference. The primary feature of hebephrenia was taken to be wildly inappropriate affect and florid symptomatology (e.g., bizarre delusions and hallucinations). Simple schizophrenia was a category originally proposed by Bleuler to describe patients without the more obvious symptoms such as hallucinations and delusions. The latter category has been eliminated from the schizophrenic disorders in *DSM-III* and is now listed as schizoid personality disorder. Bill would clearly be included in the paranoid subcategory of schizophrenic disorders.

Differential diagnosis has often been a difficult problem in schizophrenia. As noted earlier, many American clinicians came to use the term very broadly prior to the publication of *DSM-III*. Patients who would have been diagnosed as affective or neurotic disorders in Europe were considered schizophrenic by the criteria listed in *DSM-II*. The current trend is to be more conservative in the use of schizophrenia (see also the discussion of bipolar affective disorders in Chapter 5). Patients who meet the criteria for major affective disorders are excluded from schizophrenia in *DSM-III*. Substance abuse and organic brain syndrome should also be ruled out, since hallucinations and delusions may also appear in association with these disorders.

Symptomatically defined subgroups possess a certain intuitive appeal, but they have not proved to be particularly useful in other respects. One major problem has been a lack of reliability in assigning patients to subcategories. Because of problems in identifying the general category of schizophrenia, it is not surprising that the subtypes present further difficulties. Inconsistency is another drawback; patients who exhibit one set of prominent symptoms at one point in time may exhibit another set of features during a later episode. The symptomatically defined subgroups have also not been shown to possess either etiological or predictive validity. For example, a specific treatment has not been found that is more or less effective with catatonic patients in comparison with hebephrenics.

Another way of subdividing schizophrenic patients is on the basis of their premorbid pattern of adjustment. Good premorbid patients are those who attained a relatively adequate level of adjustment prior to the onset of symptoms. Social activities, particularly with members of the opposite sex, are usually taken to be particularly important in making this judgment. Poor premorbid patients, on the other hand, were never able to achieve satisfactory interpersonal relationships and were socially isolated from a relatively early age. A number of studies published during the 1960s indicated that this distinction between good and poor premorbid patients may be a more meaningful way of subdividing schizophrenics than were the traditional subtypes. Bill's behavior prior to the actual onset of psychotic symptoms would place him in the poor premorbid group and suggest that his long-term prognosis was not particularly favorable.

ETIOLOGY

Various psychological and environmental events have been suggested as playing an important role in the development of schizophrenia.[1] Psychoanalytic theory included the first psychological model of psychotic symptoms. Bill's concern about homosexuality is particularly interesting in light of Freud's view of paranoid ideas. Freud (1911/1925) argued that paranoid beliefs were the product of the ego's attempt to control anxiety associated with unconscious homosexual desires. According to this model, homosexual desires are unacceptable to the ego, which employs the defense mechanisms of reaction formation and projection to convert the impulse to a more acceptable form. The logic is as follows. The notion that "I, a man, love him, another man" is converted, through reaction formation, to "I hate him." Since this is also an unacceptable idea, it is converted to "He hates me." This notion may be a source of concern, but it is supposedly less anxiety provoking than the original homosexual impulse. Concerns about homosexuality and paranoid ideas do seem to be associated in many cases of paranoid schizophrenia (see *DSM-III*), but many paranoid clients are *aware* of their homosexual impulses. Bill realized that he was attracted to other men and had, in fact, engaged in sexual relations with other men. Psychoanalytic theory argues that the paranoid ideas are the result of complex efforts to avoid the conscious realization of these impulses, but Bill was openly struggling with the issue of sexual orientation. If the homosexual desires have already reached the level of conscious awareness, there should be no further need for the defense mechanisms of reaction formation and projection.

Several offshoots of psychoanalytic theory have focused on the role of the family in producing schizophrenia. Following the lead of Freud and based on their own clinical experience, many therapists argued that schizophrenics had been adversely affected during early childhood by their relationships with their mothers. These mothers were reportedly cold, overprotective, and domineering. As a result, the child's ego was not adequately

[1]These clearly operate in interaction with biological variables, which are reviewed in Chapter 12.

developed. Subsequent stressful experiences encountered during adolescence and early adulthood were then likely to precipitate severe regression to the primitive state of primary process thinking and narcissism, which was seen as characteristic of schizophrenic behavior (Fenichel, 1945).

Among the most prominent family models of schizophrenia is that proposed by Lidz and his colleagues (Lidz, 1973; Lidz et al., 1957). The structure of the schizophrenic's family, Lidz argues, is unable to foster the development of a mature personality. Normal families provide for the nurturance of their offspring within the context of a general organization that includes a mutually supportive alliance between the parents and the retention of boundaries between generations. Within this structure, each of the parents provides an appropriate role model with whom same-sexed offspring may identify. This organization is absent in the family of the preschizophrenic. In its place, Lidz and his colleagues have identified two deviant forms of family structure—marital schism and marital skew—that seem to be responsible for many of the problems exhibited by schizophrenic patients. Both of these family types include parents who are peculiar, immature, and who use their children to fulfill their own needs and to combat an alienated spouse.

Bill's family fit Lidz's description of marital schism. In a schismatic family, the personality problems of both parents are exacerbated by a lack of reciprocity and mutual support in their marriage. Each parent attempts to coerce the other for his or her own satisfaction, but neither is willing to cooperate in the pursuit of mutual goals. The parents compete with each other for the children's loyalty and attempt to form alliances with the children, or other relatives, that will subvert their spouse's position. Lidz and his colleagues noted that most partners in these marriages maintain very strong ties outside the marriage, most often with their own parents. These relationships interfere with their desire, or need, to cooperate with their spouse.

Skewed marriages present a somewhat different pattern. These families are dominated by the serious psychopathology of one of the parents. In contrast to the conflict and withdrawal seen in schismatic marriages, the submissive spouses in skewed families tend to complement and support their disturbed partner. Despite the apparent cooperation, skewed relationships still foster a pathological family environment. The submissive parent covers up the bizarre behavior of the dominant partner, and the children are taught to participate in this pattern of denial, which Lidz refers to as *folie à famille*. In one case, for example, the patient's father believed that he was one of only a few souls who were chosen for salvation. His wife shared this belief. The children were encouraged to view their father in divine terms. This practice no doubt isolated them culturally from their peers at the same time that it may have fostered the development of irrational thinking. Thus, overall, the disturbance present in the skewed marriage is as detrimental to the children as is the open hostility of a schismatic relationship.

Some empirical studies have supported this view of schizophrenics' families (e.g., Waring and Ricks, 1965), but serious methodological problems have plagued this area of research (Fontana, 1966; Mishler and Waxler, 1968). Perhaps the most difficult issue concerns the direction of influence between parents and children. Many studies have shown that the parents of schizophrenics behave differently than do the parents of non-schizophrenics, particularly in the presence of their disturbed offspring. But can we conclude that the parents' unusual behavior *caused* the children to become schizophrenic? It is just as reasonable to suggest that the parents' deviance represents a *response* to their children's unusual behavior. Some data have been reported that are consistent with this alternative explanation (Liem, 1974). Thus, at the present time, research studies have not provided convincing evidence that the family environment plays a central role in the etiology of schizophrenia.

One final area of investigation is relevant to Bill's case. A considerable body of evidence indicates that schizophrenia and social class are inversely related; a disproportionately large percentage of schizophrenics fall into the lowest social class on the basis of occupational and income ratings (Kohn, 1968). There are two competing explanations for this phenomenon. Some investigators have taken these data to indicate that the increased stresses associated with life in low-income homes are causally related to the development of schizophrenia. This is known as the sociogenic model. An equally reasonable explanation holds that schizophrenics drift into the lowest social classes as a result of the problems associated with the onset of the disorder. In other words, schizophrenia leads to educational failure and unemployment, not the other way around. Both explanations have received some empirical support (e.g., Turner and Wagonfeld, 1967). Bill was clearly an example of the drift hypothesis. He was raised in a middle-income family and had been expected to go on to college in preparation for a professional career. His indecision at the end of high school led him to delay college enrollment. Beginning with his job at the bank, Bill moved to an unskilled position as an elevator operator and eventually became unemployed. His occupational decline was related to his growing preoccupation with unusual ideas and increased interference with his cognitive functions.

TREATMENT

Snyder (1974) has referred to the discovery of antipsychotic medication as "a story of serendipity." It was perhaps the most important advance that had been made in our knowledge of schizophrenia. In the late 1940s Henri Laborit, a French surgeon, was experimenting with the use of an antihistamine, promethazine, to prevent surgical shock. Although the drug did not achieve the desired effect, Laborit noted that it was able to induce a state of disinterest without putting the patient to sleep. For this reason he suggested that this and similar drugs might be useful in psychiatry. Following his advice, Delay and Deniker administered chlorpromazine to various psychiatric patients and quickly noted a dramatic response among schizophrenics (see Deniker, 1970). Their success was confirmed by other clinicians. In a matter of months chlorpromazine was being used at hospitals throughout Europe and the United States.

There are several important variables to consider in selecting a treatment for acute schizophrenic disturbance. Antipsychotic drugs have become the principal form of intervention since their introduction in the 1950s. A large number of carefully controlled studies have demonstrated that these drugs have a beneficial effect for many acute schizophrenics (e.g., Cole, 1964). There are other patients, however, who do not respond to antipsychotic medication. Unfortunately, investigators have thus far been unable to identify patient characteristics that will reliably predict response to antipsychotic drugs. Psychosocial programs are also used extensively, but their utility is questionable. Traditional psychotherapy has not been shown to be more effective than medication (e.g., May et al., 1976), and its high cost in terms of therapists' time makes it a poor choice for most patients. More direct, efficient interventions centering around the patients' family and the development of specific interpersonal skills may eventually prove to be more helpful.

The utilization of inpatient services has been seriously questioned in recent years. Although many patients must be hospitalized, others can apparently be treated successfully while they remain in the community. When patients cannot remain at home, brief periods of hospitalization seem to be as effective as long-term confinement (Caffey, Galbrecht, and Klett, 1971).

Given the demonstrated value of antipsychotic medication and the promise of social learning programs, it seems reasonable to conclude that a combination of the two approaches would provide the most beneficial treatment package for schizophrenic patients. This is the kind of program that was followed with Bill. There are, however, some interesting data suggesting that directive forms of psychosocial treatment may *not* enhance the results achieved with medication alone, at least not with all patients. Hogarty and his colleagues (1974) conducted a long-term treatment study with schizophrenic patients who had been discharged from psychiatric hospitals. Patients were randomly assigned to one of four different treatment groups in order to evaluate the separate and combined effects of antipsychotic medication and a directive, problem-oriented form of counseling. These groups were: (1) drug alone, (2) drug plus sociotherapy, (3) placebo alone, and (4) placebo plus sociotherapy. Outcome was measured in terms of the percentage of patients who relapsed (had to be returned to the hospital). At the end of a 2-year follow-up period, 80% of the placebo patients had relapsed compared to only 48% of the patients receiving medication. The placebo patients who received psychotherapy did not have a better outcome than did the placebo patients who did not receive psychotherapy. Furthermore, the addition of psychotherapy to the medication program did not have a significantly beneficial effect on the patients' outcome. Only medication was effective in reducing the rate of relapse.

An even more interesting result was obtained when the investigators examined the adjustment of patients who survived the 2-year follow-up. The patients who had been readmitted to the hospital were excluded from all four groups for the purpose of this analysis. Within this subset of patients, there was an interaction between the effects of medication and sociotherapy. Patients who were receiving medication were better adjusted if they also received sociotherapy than if they received only medication. This result provides support for the notion that at least *some* schizophrenic patients can benefit from directive forms of psychosocial intervention. But the results from the placebo patients indicate that this suggestion should be treated with caution. Within the group of patients who received only a placebo, those who also participated in sociotherapy were *less* well adjusted than the patients who received a placebo alone. In other words, sociotherapy was beneficial for patients who were receiving medication and apparently harmful for those who were not receiving medication. It may be that patients who are not on medication cannot handle the increase in stress that is probably associated with an active, directive form of social intervention. This phenomenon may have been evident in Bill's case. He was not receiving medication until after the therapist became aware of his extensive delusional system. His response to the behavioral program seemed to be more positive after the introduction of antipsychotic medication. In fact, prior to that point, the role-playing that was attempted during sessions and the homework assignments during the week actually seemed to increase his level of anxiety.

The social support provided by Colleen's family was obviously very important to Bill. Whereas early research studies concerning the role of the family in schizophrenia were concerned with the *causes* of the disorder, more recent work has stressed the family's influence on the *course* of the disorder. Brown and his colleagues in England have studied schizophrenic patients and their families from the point at which the patient is discharged from the hospital (Brown, Birley, and Wing, 1972; Vaughn and Leff, 1976).

The families have been separated into two groups based on the degree of expressed emotion (EE) prior to the patient's release. High EE families are those in which at least one family member was extremely critical of the patient and his or her behavior. None of the members of low EE homes expressed hostility toward the patient. The patients were followed up for 9 months after discharge, with the dependent variable being the percentage of patients who returned to the hospital for further treatment. Relapse rates were much higher for patients who returned to high EE homes. In the first 9 months, 51% of the patients from high EE homes relapsed and only 13% of the patients in low EE homes returned to the hospital. These data are also consistent with Bill's experience. If he had been living with his mother, who was at least aloof and probably a constant source of irritation, it is unlikely that he would have been able to remain outside of a hospital throughout this extended psychotic episode. The supportive environment provided by Colleen and her family and their willingness to tolerate many of Bill's idiosyncrasies were undoubtedly helpful in preventing a more serious deterioration in his behavior.

12

SCHIZOPHRENIA: UNDIFFERENTIATED TYPE

Margaret Willoughby arrived at the psychiatric hospital with her husband, Ray. She was 39 years old and the mother of a 7-year-old son, Michael, and a 4-year-old daughter, Susan. Margaret had a long history of psychological disturbance and had been hospitalized many times—three in the 8 years that she and Ray had been married. For the past week, Margaret had refused to let Michael go to school, insisting that he and Susan stay at home with her and read aloud from the Bible. The children were quite upset by this unusual behavior, and Michael's teacher was beginning to question the excuses that Ray had been making for his son's absence from school. Ray had always tried to tolerate Margaret's idiosyncratic behavior. He had grown accustomed to her religious preoccupations, her occasionally odd speech and mannerisms, and her habit of locking herself alone in her room for hours, and sometimes days, at a time. But her interference with the children's behavior and Michael's education had become too much for him to handle. After a long and heated argument, in which Ray threatened to call the police if she did not cooperate, Margaret reluctantly agreed to accompany him to the hospital.

An involuntary admission procedure was necessary because Margaret did not believe that she needed psychiatric care. She told the psychiatrist that her problem was strictly between her and God. Margaret believed that because she had never been in love with Ray she had committed a mortal sin by marrying him and bringing children into the world. Now, as punishment, God had made her and her children immortal, so that they would have to suffer in their unhappy home life forever. She had come to this realization one evening while she was washing the dishes. Looking down into the sink, she saw a fork lying across a knife in the shape of a cross; suddenly she knew that she had become immortal. There were two other pieces of evidence that Margaret used to support her belief. One was that a local television station had recently begun to rerun old episodes of "The Honeymooners," a 1950s situation comedy in which the main characters, Ralph and Alice Cramden, often argue and shout at each other. Margaret interpreted the reappearance of this series as a sign from God indicating that her own marital conflict would go on forever, just as the Cramdens' fights were replayed time after time. The other clue to Margaret's and the children's immortality was her contention that the pupils of their eyes were now fixed in size and would neither dilate nor constrict. This was, of course, not the case, but Margaret insisted that it was true. She explained that ever since she had recognized the punishment that had been imposed, she and the children had been reading from the Book of Revelations in the Bible and praying that God would have mercy on them.

Throughout this interview, Margaret's face remained blank and expressionless. She spoke in a dull monotone that was punctuated by occasional, involuntary protrusions of her tongue and lip-smacking movements. Her posture was stiff, and her hands trembled slightly as she spoke. Her speech was, for the most part, relevant and coherent, but her answers were sometimes loosely related to the question that had been asked; she occasionally slipped from one topic to another without reason or warning. For example:

Psychiatrist: When you realized that you were immortal, were you afraid?

Margaret: No. You see, the sun to me is the sun to people, but it's God to me. When I look up to the sun, it's God, not the sun anymore. See what I mean? God took over my life because I didn't deserve to live it myself. I've got to get out of here so that I can be closer to Him.

At a later point in the interview, the psychiatrist asked:

Psychiatrist: In the past month, have you heard any voices that weren't really there?

Margaret: I don't think so. No, I haven't. . . . (Pause.) My husband sometimes sings to himself when he's in the shower, but that's not what you wanted to know. The kids also make a lot of noise in the bathroom. . . . (Pause.) I used to be jealous of women who wore bikinis.

Based on these and other signs of formal thought disorder, her blunted affect, and her delusional belief about immortality in the absence of symptoms of affective disorder or organic impairment, the psychiatrist reached a diagnosis of schizophrenia.

Margaret had been taking antipsychotic medication (primarily phenothiazines such as Mellaril, Thorazine, and Stelazine) since her first psychotic episode at the age of 16. These drugs had a positive effect on several of her more dramatic problems, such as formal thought disorder and auditory hallucinations (which she had experienced in the past), but they also made her feel lethargic and had gradually led to the development of the movement disorder that was now evident in her peculiar facial tics and the trembling of her hands. Because of these unpleasant side effects, and perhaps because of her tendency toward disorganization and erratic behavior, Margaret occasionally discontinued taking her medication. These interruptions were usually followed, within a month or two, by the reappearance of florid psychotic symptoms. This was what had happened in the present episode. After she was admitted to the hospital, Margaret was given an intramuscular injection of Prolixin, a long-acting antipsychotic drug. Prolixin injections can be given once every 2 to 4 weeks and are particularly useful with patients such as Margaret, who are unreliable in taking oral doses.

Within 2 weeks she had stopped talking about her delusional ideas; signs of formal thought disorder were no longer present in her speech. Considering this general improvement in her condition, the physician in charge of her care arranged for her discharge from the hospital, despite the persistence of several residual problems. Her affect was still blunted, and she continued to remain aloof from the other patients. There was also little change in the neurological symptoms, such as her involuntary facial movements and the shaking of her hands and feet.

After her return home, Margaret continued to visit the hospital's outpatient clinic on a biweekly basis to receive further medication. Although she was no longer blatantly psychotic, she continued to exhibit serious occupational and social role impairment. Most of her time was spent aimlessly, watching television or sitting alone in her room. Ray was a full-time postal worker and also took care of almost all of the household and parental responsibilities. Ray seemed to assume these added responsibilities without resentment; he truly believed that Margaret had an illness and was therefore less able to perform many tasks that would have otherwise been expected of her. Their marriage had reached a kind of impasse. Recognizing that she would have a difficult time living on her own and caring for the children, Margaret no longer asked for the divorce that she had demanded for several years. Ray no longer expected conventional behavior from Margaret, whom he considered to be "an emotional invalid." He seemed resigned to caring for her and the children as best he could.

SOCIAL HISTORY

Margaret was the youngest of three children. Her family was well off financially; during Margaret's infancy, they lived in an expensive apartment in New York City. Her father was a successful corporate lawyer. He was bright, ambitious, and worked long hours, rising quickly to the top of his firm. Margaret's mother was a talented dancer and actress who was also described by her family and friends as being high-strung, nervous, and somewhat eccentric. She worked intermittently in off-Broadway theater productions, but she was not particularly well known. She had been in long-term psychoanalysis with a private psychiatrist for many years and had been hospitalized for a very brief period of time shortly after Margaret's birth. Although the details of her problems were not available, her hospital diagnosis had been emotionally unstable personality.[1]

Neither of Margaret's parents had much time for the children, who were sent to boarding schools as soon as they reached the third grade. Records obtained from Margaret's elementary school indicated that she was unusually passive and socially withdrawn. She did not enjoy the company of other children, preferring instead to spend her time in isolated play and wandering alone around the wooded campus. From an academic standpoint, her early performance was adequate, but not exceptional.

The only time that Margaret spent with her family was during holidays. They gathered at the family's summer home at the lake for Thanksgiving, Christmas, and the Fourth of July. For the most part, these were uneventful visits. They were pleasant, although not particularly joyful, occasions, marred only by her mother's usual irritability and intermittent outbursts of anger, which were usually directed at Margaret's father. Margaret did look forward to seeing her two older brothers, Jonathan and Peter, who attended an academy several hours' drive from Margaret's school. She was particularly fond of Jonathan, who was already a talented pianist and spent long hours performing for her during these visits. He was the only person with whom she talked openly and with whom she felt comfortable.

Margaret's academic performance declined steadily between the fifth and ninth grades, as did her scores on standardized achievement tests. Her teachers attributed the problem to her obvious lack of interest in her studies. Their comments on her report cards also frequently expressed concern about her introverted manner. In the seventh grade, when she was 12 years old, Margaret's teacher referred her to the school psychologist

[1]This was a category included in *DSM-I* that no longer appears in *DSM-III*. It applied roughly to individuals who would now be described as either histrionic personality disorder or borderline personality disorder.

because he was worried about her lack of friends and the great amount of time that she seemed to spend daydreaming. Her scores on the verbal and performance scales of the Wechsler Intelligence Scale for Children (WISC) were both within normal limits (99 and 107, respectively). The psychologist interpreted her drawings on the House-Tree-Person test as indicating poorly developed ego boundaries and considerable hostility toward her mother. He encouraged her to attend individual counseling sessions with him, which she did for the next several weeks. Unfortunately, Margaret was extremely uncommunicative during these visits; despite the therapist's persistent efforts to establish rapport with her, she soon stopped coming for her appointments.

When Margaret was old enough to attend high school, her parents arranged for her to enroll in an exclusive New England prep school. She was accepted in spite of her undistinguished academic record because her father made substantial contributions to the school's endowment. Her well-established pattern of social isolation persisted, as did her marginal classroom performance. She also became the object of jokes and teasing by some of her peers. Her somewhat unusual appearance and idiosyncratic mannerisms had been ignored by the other children at her previous schools, but the social life at her prep school was governed by several cliques whose members were often intolerant of outsiders.

Margaret's first episode of psychotic behavior occurred when she was 16 and in her third year at the prep school. She was taking a psychology course from a young male teacher, Mr. Loftin, with whom she became preoccupied. Although she had never shown any interest in boys her own age, she began to demonstrate an unusual fascination with Mr. Loftin. He later reported that he had sometimes noticed her watching him from a distance when he was walking on the campus. He also noted that her direct, unflinching stares in class frequently made him feel uncomfortable. Despite these signs of interest, she never spoke to him directly. Shortly before the end of the spring semester, Mr. Loftin began receiving anonymous notes which he later realized were from Margaret. They were mostly concerned with metaphysical issues such as the nature of the universe and extrasensory perception. At some points, they lapsed into incoherent rambling. Two weeks after the notes began to appear, Margaret went to the school's headmaster to complain about Mr. Loftin. She believed that he was inserting obscene thoughts into her head. At unpredictable intervals throughout each day, Margaret suddenly found herself thinking about performing oral sexual acts with Mr. Loftin. She insisted that these ideas were not her own and were not under her control.

The headmaster referred Margaret to the school psychologist, who met with her to discuss this unusual report. His initial impression was that she had made a simple error in attributing her own previously inhibited sexual desires to Mr. Loftin. The psychologist spent several hours with Margaret discussing her interest in Mr. Loftin and her own sexual desires. Despite all efforts to reach a rational explanation for Margaret's subjective experience, she continued to insist that she was the unwilling recipient of alien, intrusive ideas. Her mood was becoming increasingly unpredictable during these days, and she was visibly agitated following the school officials' refusal to report Mr. Loftin to the police. Her parents were finally called; they arranged for her to be admitted to a private psychiatric hospital.

TREATMENT AND SUBSEQUENT COURSE

Upon admission to the hospital ward, she was angry and argumentative. Margaret insisted that she did not need help and that she was not mentally ill. Her problem, she insisted, was the simple product of Mr. Loftin's attempt to influence her thoughts. Her appearance was somewhat disheveled, and her posture seemed stiff and awkward. She avoided eye contact with the psychiatrist during the intake interview, directing most of her comments to her father, who had accompanied her to the hospital. She said that she had not experienced auditory hallucinations and denied the use of drugs. Her answers to questions were generally coherent, although they were sometimes vague and tangential. On more than one occasion, she shifted from one topic to another in the middle of a sentence. Based on these indications of formal thought disorder and her report of thought insertion, the psychiatrist reached a diagnosis of schizophrenia.

Phenothiazine medication was prescribed. Margaret was encouraged to participate in various social and therapeutic activities that were available at the hospital. In fact, she spent most of her time sitting alone under trees and wandering around the hospital grounds. She cooperated with the ward routine and gradually stopped talking about the thoughts that Mr. Loftin had been inserting in her head. When she was asked about these phenomena, Margaret explained that Mr. Loftin must have lost interest in her after she left the school. Her condition seemed greatly improved after 3 weeks in the hospital, and she was discharged to return to her parents' apartment.

Margaret spent the following summer with her mother at their vacation home, and returned to school in the fall. Mr. Loftin had resigned to accept a position at another school, thus reducing one major source of stress from her environment. Margaret earned passing grades in all of her subjects during her senior year and seemed somewhat brighter emotionally and more outgoing than she had been in previous years. Some of this improvement might have been related to the development of an interest in English literature, which she pursued with ardent fervor. Another student in her

English class, who shared her interest in the poetry of Shelley and who was also something of an outcast, became Margaret's companion and a possible source of social support. They ate meals together, talked about their readings, and occasionally went to movies on weekends. Unfortunately, neither girl took the initiative to maintain contact following their graduation in the spring; they subsequently lost touch with each other.

Margaret enrolled at a large state university the following fall (her grades were not adequate to permit entrance to a more prestigious school). She lived in a single room in a dormitory and continued to spend most of her time by herself. Her studies seemed to be progressing satisfactorily until shortly before the end of the first semester, when she suddenly stopped attending classes and began spending all of her time in her room. Her only ventures outside were to eat occasional meals in the cafeteria. The other women residents became extremely concerned about her bizarre appearance and unusual behavior. She had taken to wearing double layers of clothing, did not bathe, and sometimes muttered incomprehensibly to herself while she stood in line for food. After she was served, she returned to her room with her tray instead of sitting with the other people in the cafeteria. This behavior was brought to the attention of one of the resident counselors, who went to Margaret's room to find out what was troubling her. She found Margaret sitting in her bed, surrounded by notebooks, volumes of poetry, rumpled clothes, and dirty dishes from the cafeteria. The counselor tried to ask Margaret how she was feeling or if she could help in any way, but Margaret was largely unresponsive. She had been writing for several days; crumpled sheets of paper were strewn over the top of the desk and about the floor of the room. When she did speak, her answers were accentuated by silly giggling that was inappropriate to the topic at hand. For example, Margaret seemed unable to restrain her laughter as she tried to explain that her classes no longer seemed meaningful. The counselor could easily recognize that Margaret was seriously disturbed and persuaded her to come along to the student health center, where she was admitted to their small inpatient unit on a temporary basis.

Her parents were contacted; within 2 days she was transferred to the private psychiatric hospital where she had been treated 2 years previously. The admitting psychiatrist noted the presence of complete auditory hallucinations and delusional thinking as well as formal thought disorder. For the past 3 weeks, she had been hearing a voice telling her to stab her mother. The voice was male and spoke in a whisper; it came from behind her right shoulder. It appeared at frequent intervals throughout each day and was occasionally accompanied by another male voice that argued against such violent action. She believed that these voices and her other thoughts were being monitored by the campus police, who were waiting to see whether she would follow the voice's instructions. The following conversation is an excerpt from her intake interview.

Psychiatrist: Why had you been thinking about stabbing your mother?

Margaret: Because the voice was telling me I could have two rounds or four rounds, and I didn't know if they were talking about clocks, or what time it was, or anything. . . .

Psychiatrist: Why were the voices saying these things?

Margaret: Because of the pig. The . . . like white light is pure, right? Well, I was fighting the, ah, thought that. . . . You see, I went over to another woman's room and I saw this guy who's going to be a computer programmer. And the woman said that her uterus is out of place, and I said, "You must have a sugar daddy or something." I guess it's all right. Everybody's got to survive.

As in her previous episode, Margaret's speech was often difficult to follow. She answered questions tangentially and seemed to lose track of the goal for her speech within even brief comments, such as her preceding second answer. The notes that the counselor had observed in her room and that her family later read were similarly disjointed and incomprehensible.

This time Margaret was hospitalized for 15 months. The treatment program involved the use of antipsychotic medication (Mellaril) and involvement in the social milieu of her ward. Group psychotherapy sessions were held daily, but Margaret refused to participate. Despite the continued use of medication, Margaret's condition did not improve significantly during the first 6 months of her hospitalization. She continued to dress in an unusual fashion, wearing two and sometimes three dresses at a time. Although she was reluctant to discuss the voices that she had described hearing on admission, she often seemed to be responding to hallucinations. She would sit for hours staring out the window and mumbling to herself in a low voice. On occasion, she would suddenly stop whatever she was doing and turn to look at an empty hallway or room, as though someone had spoken to her when, in fact, no one was there. Her giggling diminished gradually, and her affect eventually became flat and blunted. When she did speak to staff members or other patients, her comments were sometimes difficult to follow. She continued to complain that her thoughts were being monitored by the police. This surveillance caused her considerable distress; she argued that it continually interfered with her ability to organize and express her own thoughts.

In the seventh month of her hospitalization, Margaret began to make noticeable improvements. The most obvious change occurred in her general physical appearance. She began dressing appropriately, bathed regularly without prompting from the staff, and combed her hair. Her facial expression seemed less dull and apathetic. She became more active physically. Although she continued to isolate herself, she did respond coherently to the comments of staff members and other patients.

Shortly after these changes began to develop, Margaret received word from her brother, Jonathan, that their father had told their mother that he wanted a divorce. The news had a dramatic effect on Margaret's behavior. She became agitated and restless, refused food and, once again, began talking openly about people interfering with her thoughts. The day after she talked to her brother, she cornered one of the other female patients in the hospital's recreation room and threatened to hit her with a chair. Margaret claimed that she had heard the other woman talking about her and laughing at the way she dressed. The other woman was 67 years old, socially withdrawn, and essentially mute. The hapless, bewildered victim of this attack was rescued by two attendants, who restrained Margaret and took her to her room, where she was secluded for a few hours. Margaret's behavior stabilized within several days. She continued to make modest improvements in her adjustment and did not engage in any more violent outbursts. In her ninth month in the hospital, she entered an occupational training program in medical technology. She attended classes during the day and returned to the hospital ward at night. She also began to leave the hospital for occasional weekends, which she spent with her brother Jonathan at his apartment in New York. At the end of the 6-month training program, her level of adjustment was stable and much improved, so she was discharged from the hospital.

After her discharge, Margaret continued to take antipsychotic medication on a maintenance basis. Her prescription was renewed at weekly, 10-minute visits that she made to the office of her private psychiatrist, who also checked for the development of side effects and asked a few perfunctory questions about her adjustment. She no longer reported hallucinations or delusions; her speech was coherent and relevant, although somewhat lacking in spontaneity. The only obvious sign of residual impairment was a marked constriction of Margaret's emotional responses. She continued to seem apathetic and lifeless and reported that she had never been able to experience real pleasure or excitement.

Her father had remarried very shortly after the divorce and moved to California. Her mother was still living in New York, but Margaret decided not to see her because their visits always seemed to lead to arguments and unpleasant scenes. Margaret stayed with Jonathan until she found a job as a medical technician at a nearby hospital. She then moved to a small studio apartment, where she lived alone and seemed to manage quite well. Unfortunately, she found her work in the hospital laboratory to be stressful. Her responsibilities were, in fact, simple and routine, but Margaret complained that the medication made her drowsy and interfered with her ability to concentrate. She therefore discontinued the antipsychotic medication, against the advice of her psychiatrist and her brother. Shortly after doing so, she reported feeling less fatigued, but her ability to concentrate did not improve. Furthermore, several weeks after she stopped taking medication, Margaret started hearing the voices again. This time they sounded like the whispers of other people in the laboratory, talking about her appearance and commenting on her inadequate performance. One particularly frequent and persistent voice, which sounded to Margaret like that of an older woman, kept mumbling, "We don't want crazies like her working with us. Listen to what she's thinking. She's as nutty as they come. Stay away from her!"

The stress and confusion quickly overwhelmed Margaret, and she quit her job 3 months after it began. At this point, Jonathan read about the use of large doses of vitamins to treat schizophrenia. He found the name of a psychiatrist who claimed remarkable success with this procedure and persuaded Margaret to pay him a visit. This psychiatrist prescribed a standard dose of antipsychotic medication to be supplemented by a daily dose of 20,000 milligrams of niacin. She continued this treatment program for the next year.

After her return to medication, Margaret's adjustment restabilized. She continued to live by herself and seldom ventured far from her apartment. Jonathan, who was now an accomplished concert pianist, visited her regularly and tried to encourage her to become more active and continue taking her medication. She did, in fact, begin doing some volunteer work for the Red Cross at a clinic in her neighborhood. This pattern of marginal social and occupational adjustment continued for several months.

Margaret's third hospitalization occurred at the age of 22, approximately 1 year after she had begun megavitamin treatment. Although she had continued to take the phenothiazines and vitamins that were prescribed for her, her behavior had become more disorganized over a period of several weeks. She was once again experiencing auditory hallucinations, dressing strangely, and spending long hours staring out her apartment window, mumbling to herself. Jonathan called her psychiatrist; together they persuaded her to admit herself voluntarily to a state psychiatric hospital. She was treated and discharged after 3 months.

This pattern of brief hospitalizations, separated by periods of marginal adjustment in the community, repeated itself several times over the next few years. Margaret lost touch with everyone in her family except Jonathan, who continued to visit her regularly, whether she was in the hospital or living in her apartment. He also provided her with considerable financial support. She worked at various jobs as a hospital aide, a waitress, and a retail clerk, but she never held one position longer than 1 year.

Margaret met Ray when she was 30 years old. He was a 38-year-old bachelor. She was working as a waitress at the restaurant where he ate most of his meals. Ray was, in some ways, similar to Margaret. He was quiet, shy, and without many friends. They slowly became acquainted and eventually began meeting when Margaret was not working. They went for walks and saw movies together. Ray also took her to several concerts in which Jonathan was playing. Margaret was a passive participant throughout this courtship period. Her feelings about Ray were ambivalent. She sometimes enjoyed the change from her usual lonely routine, and she believed that Ray was a nice person, but she did not find him physically attractive and was not in love with him. His intrusion into her carefully developed, isolated existence was also anxiety provoking because she now felt some pressure to behave more appropriately.

Ray was very persistent, despite Margaret's reluctance, and they gradually came to spend more and more time together. He was aware of her history of adjustment problems and managed to convince himself that he would be able to help her through his devotion and support. Jonathan liked Ray and also believed that this relationship would be beneficial for Margaret. Ten months after they met, Ray suggested to Margaret that they should get married. After several weeks of gentle persuasion and persistent coaxing from both Ray and Jonathan, she agreed. Her major motivation was the recognition that her marriage would relieve much of the burden that her problems had placed on Jonathan over the years.

Contrary to Ray's initial expectations, their marriage did not have an obviously positive effect on Margaret's adjustment. If anything, she went downhill. She became pregnant shortly after they were married. The pregnancy was a difficult one; the usual nausea and fatigue were compounded by Margaret's poor physical condition and her inability to relax. Although she continued to visit a psychiatrist regularly and take her antipsychotic medication, she suffered a symptomatic relapse and had to be admitted to the hospital again. Michael was actually born in an obstetric wing of the psychiatric hospital. The baby was cared for by Ray's sister, who had several children of her own, until Margaret was discharged from the hospital, 2 months after the birth.

Margaret regretted her decision to get married from the beginning. When Michael was 1 year old, she began asking Ray for a divorce. He refused, saying that she would not be able to care for herself or the baby without him. She confessed to her brother and her therapist that she did not love Ray and that she never had. Nevertheless, Ray remained committed to the relationship, and Margaret did not press the issue further.

Three years after their marriage, when Margaret was 34, she developed a sudden fanatic devotion to religion. Her family had never been religious, and Margaret had never been a member of a formal church. She had, however, been interested in religious issues, particularly during her last year in high school and her brief college career when she was absorbed in romantic literature. Her conversion occurred after she was visited by two members of an evangelical Christian sect noted for its fundamentalist beliefs. They were canvasing her neighborhood door to door. Margaret let them into the apartment and listened as they spoke about the imminence of Christ's second coming. They left considerable literature with her, which she later read. She also began watching religious programs on a special television channel. Within 2 or 3 days, she became completely preoccupied with her newly developed faith and began talking constantly to Ray about the wonders of eternal salvation. This change in Margaret was initially distressing to Ray, who preferred the quiet, withdrawn wife to whom he had grown accustomed. He refused to become an active participant in her religious activities; as a result, they grew even further apart.

Perhaps most distressing about Margaret's religious conversion was the fact that other members of her church group, with whom she began meeting regularly, convinced her that she should discontinue her medication. They argued that God would protect her from the devil, who had, in their view, been responsible for the voices that she had heard intermittently over the past 15 years. Unfortunately, Margaret followed their advice; within several weeks she experienced another relapse. This time she was hospitalized for only 12 days. Her medication was resumed, and she was soon discharged to Ray's care.

Margaret stopped going to church meetings after the psychotic episode; she did agree to continue taking medication, but she remained a devout believer in the teachings of her religious group. She and Ray continued living together despite Margaret's increased emotional estrangement from their relationship, and Susan was born the following year. It was after Susan's birth that Margaret once again began to worry about her inability to love Ray. She brooded about the sinfulness of their relationship and continually expressed the belief that she was going to be punished by God.

DISCUSSION

At various points, Margaret exhibited several of the classic symptoms of schizophrenia; she clearly fit the *DSM-III* criteria for that disorder (these criteria are listed in Chapter 11). Formal thought disorder and flat or inappropriate affect were among her most persistent problems. Judgments regarding thought disorder are based on the listener's perception that the patient's speech is difficult to follow. Margaret's comments were often disjointed and elusive in meaning, as illustrated by the examples provided earlier. Her affective responses were also disturbed. During her earliest episodes, she was frequently observed giggling to herself for no apparent reason. Between periods of acute psychosis, particularly as she grew older, her emotional responses seemed flattened or totally absent. Her face was usually expressionless, even when she discussed topics that would provoke happiness, fear, or depression in other people. Both of these symptom categories—associative and affective disturbances—were among the cardinal features outlined by Bleuler (1911) when he originally described schizophrenia.

Margaret also experienced some of the 11 symptoms that Schneider (1959) listed as being of first-rank importance in the diagnosis of schizophrenia. Schneider's first-rank symptoms include a variety of specific forms of hallucinations and several types of disturbed thinking, many of which have been included in the *DSM-III* criteria for schizophrenia. Examples are auditory hallucinations in which either a voice keeps up a running commentary on the person's behavior or thoughts, or two or more voices converse with each other. Margaret experienced the latter phenomenon. Her complaint about her high-school psychology teacher's interference with her thoughts was an example of a first-rank symptom known as "thought insertion"—the belief that alien thoughts were being projected into her mind against her will.

The delusional beliefs that Margaret expressed from time to time were not typical paranoid or grandiose delusions (as illustrated in Chapter 11). She did not believe that people were plotting against her or that she had special powers or abilities. The statement that she and her children had become immortal is an example of the first-rank symptom that Schneider called "delusional perception." Delusional perception is defined as the attachment of abnormal, personal significance to a common and otherwise harmless perceptual experience. As Schneider (1959) explained:

> *A furniture van stands before a house and to the typical passer-by is nothing but a furniture van with the added implication that someone is moving. This is a legitimate interpretation and there are reasonable grounds for it. There is nothing special about the interpretation, no self-reference, nothing personal. A schizophrenic would, if this were the occasion for a delusional perception, recognize that this particular moving van had another and deeper import for him and was of abnormal significance; he would thus construct a "delusional" meaning, a delusional significance. (p. 111)*

Margaret's belief in her immortality and that of her children, following immediately from the sight of the knife and fork crossed in the shape of a crucifix, was a delusional perception. Another person would not have attached special significance to this trivial experience, but Margaret was convinced that it held an urgent, personal meaning.

Schneider's first-rank symptoms are useful diagnostically because they have been specifically defined and can therefore be identified reliably. They are also clearly distinct from more common experiences that are not indicative of schizophrenia. In the case of hallucinations, for example, it is important to distinguish between the kind of complete hallucinatory experiences described by Schneider, which are almost always associated with some form of psychosis, and illusions or pseudohallucinations. From time to time, most people think that they have heard their names being called when they were not or hear a bump or squeak that sounds like a word. These experiences should not be confused with complete auditory hallucinations because they are not psychotic in nature and do not indicate a need for treatment.[2]

Margaret's subtype diagnosis was "undifferentiated" because she did not meet the specific criteria for the other types listed in *DSM-III*. Her delusions were not predominantly persecutory or grandiose, so she would not fit in the paranoid type, and none of the typical features of catatonic type (motor rigidity, posturing, excitement, and stupor) were present. The criteria for disorganized type include (1) frequent incoherence, (2) absence of systematized delusions,[3] and (3) blunted, inappropriate, or silly affect. Margaret did exhibit occasional speech disturbances (incoherence), and her affect was often blunted, but she also expressed a systematic delusion regarding immortality. Her diagnosis was therefore schizophrenic disorder: undifferentiated type.

The development of Margaret's problems followed a common course. Before the onset of overt psychotic symptoms, there was clear evidence of a decline in intellectual performance, and her behavior was markedly passive and introverted. Both of these phenomena have been observed in research studies employing a follow-back methodology in which the investigator starts with adult schizophrenics and then locates archival data pertaining to their behavior during childhood (prior to the onset of symptoms). Lane and Albee (1964, 1965), for example, were able to examine the results of standardized intelligence tests that had been administered to children who later became schizophrenic. Their scores were compared to those of their siblings, who did not become schizophrenic, thus controlling for nuisance variables such as social class and family mobility. The preschizophrenics' scores were significantly lower than those of their siblings. A similar pro-

[2]The pseudopatients in the Rosenhan (1973) study of psychiatric diagnosis, for example, would not have been considered schizophrenic if the clinicians involved had followed Schneider's criteria for auditory hallucinations. The pseudopatients reported indistinct voices in which only single words ("empty," "hollow," and "thud") were audible.

[3]Systematized delusions, in contrast to fragmented delusions, are well-organized, pervasive beliefs. *DSM-III* defines them as either "a single delusion with multiple elaborations or a group of delusions that are all related by the individual to a single event or theme" (p. 358).

cedure has been used to study the premorbid social behavior of schizophrenics. Watt and his colleagues have analyzed information obtained from teachers' comments that were recorded in the children's school records and found that the premorbid behavior of schizophrenic males may be different than that of schizophrenic females. Watt's preschizophrenic boys were described as disagreeable and emotionally unstable more often than control subjects; preschizophrenic girls were more likely to be described as being introverted and passive (Watt, 1978; Watt & Lubensky, 1976). This general characterization fits Margaret's childhood behavior well.

The problems that Margaret continued to experience between her episodes of acute symptomatology are also characteristic of a substantial proportion of schizophrenic patients. When Kraepelin (1919) proposed the diagnostic category of *Dementia praecox*, which we now call schizophrenia, he emphasized the chronic, deteriorating course that most patients followed. Bleuler (1911) painted a somewhat more optimistic picture, which has been supported by follow-up data from the International Pilot Study of Schizophrenia (Strauss and Carpenter, 1979; WHO, 1975). Approximately 33% of schizophrenic patients show no evidence of continued impairment 5 years after their first hospitalization. The remaining patients, however, are either still hospitalized or demonstrate residual signs of disturbance. *DSM-III* defines this residual phase of schizophrenia in the following manner.

> *Persistence, following the active phase of the illness, of at least two of the symptoms noted below, not due to a disturbance in mood or to a Substance Use Disorder.*

(1) social isolation or withdrawal.
(2) marked impairment in role functioning as wage-earner, student, or homemaker.
(3) markedly peculiar behavior (e.g. collecting garbage, talking to self in public, or hoarding food).
(4) marked impairment in personal hygiene and grooming.
(5) blunted, flat, or inappropriate affect.
(6) digressive, vague, overelaborate, circumstantial, or metaphorical speech.
(7) odd or bizarre ideation, or magical thinking, e.g., superstitiousness, clairvoyance, telepathy, "sixth sense," "others can feel my feelings," overvalued ideas, ideas of reference.
(8) unusual perceptual experiences, e.g. recurrent illusions[4], sensing the presence of a force or person not actually present (p. 189).

[4]An illusion is a misperception of a real external stimulus (e.g., the creaking of stairs sounds like a voice); a hallucination is a perceptual experience that occurs in the *absence* of any external stimulation.

Margaret clearly exhibited several of these problems between episodes, including social isolation, impaired role functioning, and blunted affect. Her problems were chronic and showed no signs of significant improvement over the years following her first episode.

ETIOLOGY

There is no longer any question about the fact that genetic factors are involved in the transmission of schizophrenia. In fact, Seymour Kety, one of the leading investigators of biochemical and genetic factors in schizophrenia, has quipped, in response to Thomas Szasz, that "If schizophrenia is a myth, it is a myth with a strong genetic component" (Kety, 1974). The most persuasive data supporting this conclusion come from twin studies and investigations following various adoption methods. Twin studies depend on the following reasoning. Monozygotic (MZ) twins develop from a single zygote, which separates during an early stage of growth and forms two distinct but genetically identical embryos. In the case of dizygotic (DZ) twins, two separate eggs are fertilized by two sperm cells, and both develop simultaneously. Thus DZ twins share only 50% of their genes, the same as siblings not sharing the same prenatal period. Based on the assumption that both forms of twins share very similar environments, MZ twins should manifest a higher concordance rate (i.e., more often resemble each other) for traits that are genetically determined. This is, in fact, the pattern that has now been reported for schizophrenia over a very large number of studies (Gottesman and Shields, 1972, 1976). One of the most careful and informative twin studies has been reported by Fischer (1973). She found concordance rates of 0.48 in MZ twins and 0.20 in DZ twins.[5] This very substantial difference betwen MZ and DZ concordance indicates the influence of genetic factors. On the other hand, the absence of 100% concordance among the MZ twins also indicates that genetic factors do not account for all of the variance. The development of the disorder must therefore depend on an interaction between a genetically determined predisposition and various environmental events. This general view is known as a "diathesis-stress" model and is currently the most widely accepted notion regarding the etiology of schizophrenia. Unfortunately, neither the exact nature of the genetic component nor the specific type of environmental events has been determined.[6]

[5]Actual concordance rates vary depending on a number of methodological factors. These are pairwise rates using "schizophreniclike psychosis" in the proband's cotwin as the criterion for concordance. All of the twins had passed through the standard age of risk so that age-correction procedures were unnecessary.

[6]Some of the more popular environmental considerations are discussed in Chapter 11.

The earliest twin studies were subjected to a number of criticisms (Jackson, 1960). Among the most persuasive was the argument that twin studies do not adequately control the influence of environmental events; if MZ twins are more similar than DZ twins from a physical standpoint, their parents may be more likely to treat them in the same way. Therefore their environments may, in fact, be more similar than those of DZ twins, and the higher concordance rates observed among MZ twins may reflect the influence of environmental variables and not genetic factors. Adoption studies were initiated in an attempt to rule out more completely the influence of environmental factors. The first such study was reported by Heston (1966), who began with a sample of children who were born to schizophrenic mothers and then adopted within days after birth. A control sample of adopted children whose biological mothers were not schizophrenic was matched to the schizophrenics' children with regard to age, sex, age at separation from mother, type of foster care placement, and so on. All of the children were then followed up and interviewed many years later, at the average age of 36 years. The age-corrected risk for schizophrenia among the children of the schizophrenic mothers was 16.6%. In contrast, *none* of the children in the control sample had become schizophrenic as adults. Once again, the clear influence of genetic factors was apparent.

Adoption studies such as Heston's and studies of the families of schizophrenic patients have also drawn attention to two related points of interest. First, the biological relatives of schizophrenics may be at risk for other psychological adjustment problems in addition to schizophrenia. In Heston's study, for example, the offspring of the schizophrenic mothers were also more likely than the control subjects to exhibit signs of mental deficiency and personality disorder, most notably sociopathy.[7] It also may be the case that, in the absence of behavioral disturbance, the genetic factors related to schizophrenia are linked to positively valued traits such as creativity. Heston, for example, noted that the most interesting people he interviewed were among the children of schizophrenic mothers who had not become mentally ill themselves. They were more spontaneous when interviewed, had more colorful life histories, worked at more creative jobs, and followed the most imaginative hobbies. This impression was also reported in another adoption study conducted in Iceland (Karlsson, 1966). Both of these phenomena were evident in Margaret's family. Her mother was a talented actress and dancer who also exhibited obvious signs of personality disorder, although she was not schizophrenic. Margaret's brother, who did

[7]Even though this pattern may indicate that disorders such as sociopathy are genetically related to schizophrenia, it may also reflect the genetic influence of the target children's fathers, whose diagnostic status was unknown to Heston.

not manifest signs of psychological disturbance, was widely recognized as a talented musician.

TREATMENT

Since the advent of antipsychotic medication (see Chapter 11), most other biological forms of intervention, including electroconvulsive therapy (ECT) and psychosurgery, have fallen into disfavor in the treatment of schizophrenia. New methods are still introduced from time to time, but none of them have been proven to be effective in controlled investigations. Megavitamin therapy, which Margaret received for a period of several months, is an example of such an innovative approach that has gained some popular support from both clinicians and patients. Unfortunately, controlled investigations have failed to demonstrate a beneficial effect following this form of treatment, which involves the consumption of 3000 to 30,000 milligrams of nicotinic acid or niacin daily (e.g., Ban and Lehmann, 1970; McGrath, 1974). Used as a supplement to antipsychotic drugs, megavitamin treatment does not lead to shorter or less frequent periods of hospitalization, nor does it produce greater improvement in particular symptoms than the use of antipsychotics alone. The fact that some patients have shown remarkable improvement using this approach may mean that some subgroup of patients will respond favorably to megavitamin treatment. Nevertheless, the studies reported thus far have not been able to identify such a group of patients, and the improvement of individual patients may be attributed to any number of factors unrelated to the specific action of vitamins themselves. Thus, other than sporadic clinical reports, there is no support for the use of this procedure.

Antipsychotic medication remains the treatment of choice for schizophrenic disorders. It seems to have a specific effect on many psychotic symptoms, such as hallucinations and incoherent speech. Taken on a maintenance basis, it also reduces the probability of symptomatic relapse. In Margaret's case, medication did seem to have a positive effect. On many occasions, the administration of phenothiazine medication was associated with an improvement in her most dramatic symptoms. It was also clear that she often relapsed soon after discontinuing the medication that she was taking on an outpatient basis.

Despite these positive effects, there are also several limitations and some problems associated with the use of antipsychotic drugs. One is that many schizophrenic patients fail to improve even after they have taken medication for a long period of time; we do not know how to predict which patients will respond positively. Several groups of investigators have attempted to identify patient characteristics such as premorbid adjustment and the presence of particular symptoms that are associated with drug-related improvement, but the results of these studies have been inconclusive (e.g., Hollister et al., 1974; May et al., 1976).

Another problem, which was evident in Margaret's case, is that medication is only a partial solution. Once the most dramatic symptoms have improved, most patients continue to suffer from role impairments that are not the direct product of hallucinations and delusions. In short, medication can sometimes relieve perceptual aberrations, but it does not remove deficiencies in social and occupational skills.[8]

A final problem, which has only recently been recognized, is the frequent development of long-term side effects, most notably a serious, involuntary movement disorder known as tardive dyskinesia. Margaret had been taking antipsychotic medication for several years and was beginning to manifest obvious signs of tardive dyskinesia, such as trembling of the extremities, lip-smacking, and protrusions of the tongue. These symptoms can be very disconcerting both to patients and those with whom they interact. Perhaps most disturbing is the fact that the disorder is often irreversible. Unfortunately, the patient and clinician are often in a difficult bind; if medication is continued on a long-term basis, the probability increases that the patient will develop serious side effects such as tardive dyskinesia; if the medication is discontinued, the patient may relapse. The problem has not been resolved. Most therapists now agree that long-term medication should be used judiciously and that drug-free intervals should be scheduled to determine whether or not maintenance medication is, in fact, beneficial for each particular patient.

[8]Psychosocial approaches to the treatment of these problems are discussed in Chapter 11.

13

ATYPICAL PSYCHOSIS AND FETISHISM

Mark Randolph, 26, was involuntarily committed to an inpatient unit at a local mental health facility following an incident at a home for senior citizens. Mark had been employed as a janitor at the home for 3 months. He performed his duties satisfactorily, but several residents at the home thought he behaved strangely. Mark rarely spoke to anyone. When he did, it was usually to make some bizarre comments about women and sex such as, "smelly women really turn me on." Mark's comments about women were often followed by the interjection "phew" used as an exclamation, such as "Cheryl Ladd, . . . phew!", "Farrah Fawcett, . . . phew!" Mark not only behaved strangely; with an ever-present farmer's cap pulled down around his eyes and a shirt pocket full of pens and pencils, he looked weird.

Mark's mannerisms and appearance were disturbing to the residents at the home for senior citizens but were tolerated. More disturbing behaviors, which led to his confinement at the mental health facility, surfaced later.

Mark became sexually aroused and experienced an urge to masturbate when he heard static from any source. He liked to place pictures of women next to a radio and masturbate while the radio produced static. Mark had recently purchased a video recorder with which he recorded television programs featuring attractive women. (He could construct very exact hierarchies of attractiveness of the various female television personalities.) The programs were replayed later while Mark masturbated after turning on electrical appliances that caused interference with the video recorder. Mark experienced his most intense arousal during severe thunderstorms. With great anticipation he would ready the video recorder and then masturbate to orgasm as often as seven times while watching prerecorded television programs disrupted by the storm's electrical activity. If Mark became aroused to static in a public situation, he would make inappropriate sexual advances toward women or find a woman to look at while he masturbated. Some of Mark's more daring sexual escapades occurred during spring break at a nearby state university. He would cruise major thoroughfares hoping to pick up female hitchhikers. After picking up a woman, Mark would turn on the car radio, which he had tuned between stations, and masturbate by rubbing his thighs together. Mark's masturbatory behavior in the car with female hitchhikers sometimes became more intense. More than one hitchhiker had reported him to the police after experiencing a harrowing ride down the highway with Mark masturbating vigorously and the car radio blaring static. The police rarely acted on the reports because they considered Mark harmless; a verbal reprimand was the most severe punishment he had ever received. Unfortunately, similar behavior one day at the home for senior citizens got Mark into a great deal of trouble.

Mark had spent the morning emptying wastebaskets and cleaning rest rooms. He particularly enjoyed mornings on the job because his rest room chores included cleaning urinals, which he liked to sniff. In one of the rooms at the home, Mark found an old radio. The radio was of a type popular in the 1940s; it was powered by vacuum tubes and housed in a large wooden cabinet. Mark turned on the radio, which produced a roar of static. He immediately became sexually aroused and began to rummage through the belongings of the occupant of the room to find a picture of a woman to look at while he masturbated. Several residents heard the commotion and went to the room to investigate. Looking in, they saw Mark masturbating while rapidly paging through a magazine. Realizing that he had been discovered, Mark did not stop masturbating; instead, he turned toward the residents and began laughing maniacally. The residents were frightened by his behavior and called the police. After a short conversation among police and local mental health professionals, Mark was placed in the inpatient unit at the mental health facility for observation.

In a number of intervews with the therapist, Mark expressed bizarre beliefs concerning his attraction to static and heterosexual relationships. He believed that everyone became sexually aroused to static and that persons used this source of arousal for their own pleasure and to make others jealous (i.e., Mark believed that persons became extremely jealous if they learned that others got sexually aroused without them). He was convinced that a woman who lived next door to him was being made jealous in this manner by a man who lived down the street. It was Mark's contention that the man would purposely drive past the woman's home at the same time each night so that she would think he was going home to be aroused by static while watching a local female newscaster on the television. Mark also believed that the woman sent out her brothers at specific hours to see if the man was at home so she would know to which television personalities he was becoming aroused. The brothers supposedly passed in front of Mark's house in their car as they circled the block to spy on the man. Mark was upset by the woman's supposed preoccupation with the man's activities. He took it as a rejection of his own unexpressed interest in her. Because he could not stand to be hurt by the alleged scheming of his neighbors, Mark moved out of the house he shared with his mother and rented a room across town. He rarely returned to the old neighborhood except to have breakfast with his mother.

At his new location, Mark planned his activities around the daily television schedule. He believed that some programs were particularly good for making his female neighbors jealous. It was important for him to be at home during these programs so that his neighbors would think he was getting sexually aroused to attractive women on the television. This was Mark's way of showing his female neighbors that he did not need them sexually. When Mark got a job hauling trash in a truck and could not be in his rented room during particular daytime programs, he went to great lengths to cover up his absence. He left his room at 5 A.M. before his neighbors were up. He returned after work at 6:30 P.M., a "safe" time to be seen because the national news was on all channels. One day when Mark was hauling trash in an area near the new neighborhood, he warned his boss not to drive past the house in which his room was located. Mark feared that his female neighbors would see him and realize he was not at home getting aroused. When his boss ignored the warning and drove past the house, Mark literally ripped apart the inside of the truck.

Mark was fired from his job hauling trash after the incident in the truck. Shortly thereafter he got a job as a janitor at a sawmill. Instead of leaving for work before his neighbors were up and returning during the news, Mark started to wear a bag over his head when he was in the vicinity of his room. Although he admitted that the bag drew attention to him, he was convinced that his neighbors did not know it was he wearing it; therefore they would not know when he was absent from the room and missing daytime programs.

The job at the sawmill lasted only a few weeks. Mark was convinced that a secretary at the sawmill was taunting him by getting aroused to static from a radio on her desk. Mark confronted his boss and insisted that the radio be removed or he would quit. The boss said he was crazy. Mark quit but returned at the lunch hour and broke the plug on the radio so the secretary could not use it to get aroused. Several weeks later Mark got the job at the home for senior citizens, where his behavior finally led to his commitment at the mental health facility.

SOCIAL HISTORY

Mark was the first of two children of a lower-class family; his sister, Lois, was 2 years younger. He and his sister were raised by their mother after their father died when Mark was 8. Mark remembered little about his father. He described his relationship with his mother as good but noted that she was a cold, domineering woman who was very strict with him when he was a child and still told him what to do.

Mark contracted a case of encephalitis at the age of 7. He was sick for 2 months and apparently near death on at least one occasion. At the age of 9, Mark experienced a prolonged period of high fever, the cause of which was never diagnosed. An electroencephalogram (EEG) given during the period of high fever was abnormal. The EEG is a gross measure of brain activity and is not always easy to interpret. In Mark's case, the abnormalities appeared to be localized in the left hemisphere.

Mark had a vivid recollection of the origin of his attraction to static. He reported that at approximately 6 years of age he began to listen to static on the radio while rocking on a hobbyhorse. He described this activity as pleasurable and noted that before the pairing of static with rocking he found static aversive. Shortly thereafter, Mark began to enjoy placing model horses and pictures of horses next to a radio producing static. During a meeting of his mother's card club when Mark was approximately 11 years old, he discovered that he became sexually aroused around women after several of the women had good naturedly patted him on his behind. Mark also discovered that he could intensify the arousal by turning on a radio in the next room. He subsequently began masturbating with pictures of both horses and women placed next to a radio producing static. According to Mark, his sexual attraction to horses, and especially women on horses, has persisted to adulthood.

During adolescence, Mark was a loner with few if any friends. He was not interested in athletics or social functions. He spent a great deal of time with his mother and sister because they seemed to be the only persons who did not ridicule him for behaving strangely. Although he had a strong early interest in sex, he rarely approached girls for fear they would reject him. Mark claimed he had a "relationship" with one "special" girl throughout high school. Actually, he merely sat behind her on the school bus and fantasized that she cared for him as much as he did for her. He obtained her picture from someone else one day when the students on the bus exchanged class pictures. Mark took the picture home and locked it in a fireproof strongbox in which he kept his favorite pictures for masturbating. The strongbox held pictures of other female classmates, but these were cut out of the high-school yearbook when he could not obtain them otherwise.

Mark's "relationship" with the girl on the school bus ended abruptly one day when he confronted her and expressed his desire for a more physical relationship. The girl was appalled by this suggestion and made it clear that she wanted nothing to do with him. Mark was devastated by the girl's reaction. Over a period of a few weeks, he slipped into a severe depression and admitted himself to a state psychiatric hospital. While in the hospital, Mark underwent a series of electroconvulsive treatments that seemed to relieve his depression but left him confused and disoriented for several weeks after he was released.

Mark joined the navy after graduating from high school. He took his collection of pictures in the strongbox with him on cruise. Before long, his attraction to static and his strange behavior were subjects for ridicule among the men on the ship. One or two men apparently threatened to throw him overboard. After enduring what he perceived to be constant tormenting for almost 1 year, Mark was given a mental discharge from the navy.

Mark's first sexual encounter occurred while he was in the navy. He paid a prostitute in San Diego $20 to have intercourse with him. Mark found the experience extremely enjoyable and said that he was not anxious with the prostitute as he was with other women. He greatly appreciated the fact that with a prostitute money was the only prerequisite to physical intimacy. Upon returning home after his discharge, Mark began to frequent a notorious truck stop in a major city close to his hometown. Prostitutes at the truck stop provided a variety of services. If he could get enough money, Mark went to the truck stop every couple of weeks. There, he would pay a prostitute to spend the night with him in a rented trailer. Mark and the prostitute would have sex in the trailer while a radio, which he brought along, produced static. These biweekly trips to the truck stop were Mark's only "social" interactions with women.

Five years after returning home, Mark filed for disability payments from the navy on the advice of a local mental health official. He was awarded the payments, the first of which came in a large lump sum. Although Mark wanted to buy a new car with the money, his mother took it and made a down payment on the house in which they now live.

CONCEPTUALIZATION AND TREATMENT

Mark's behavior presented a complex and difficult diagnostic picture. A psychiatrist involved in the case believed Mark was schizophrenic. This diagnosis was made on the basis of Mark's elaborate delusional belief system concerning static and heterosexual interactions. However, because there was not a discernable deterioration from a previous level of functioning, Mark did not clearly meet the *DSM-III* criteria for schizophrenia (described in Chapter 11). The psychiatrist prescribed antipsychotic medication, which had no effect on Mark's behaviors or delusional beliefs.

After the failure of antipsychotic medication, Mark was placed on imipramine (Tofranil), an antidepressant. Imipramine has been thought to be effective in treating obsessive-compulsive disorder. Mark was suspected to be obsessive-compulsive because he was "obsessed" with sex and static. Actually, because his "obsessions" were voluntarily produced and enjoyed, Mark did not meet the *DSM-III* criteria for obsessive-compulsive disorder (described in Chapter 1). Imipramine had no effect on Mark's behavior.

The therapist (who is the author of this case study) chose to ignore the problem of diagnosis. There was agreement among those involved in the case that Mark's most problematic behavior, at least in a legal sense, was his sexual arousal response to static. Prior to the therapist's involvement, several treatment approaches to this particular problem, including hypnosis, were tried without success. The therapist's first concern was identifying the specific situations in which Mark became sexually aroused.

Mark was asked to keep a daily record describing situations in which he became sexually aroused and how often orgasm resulted. The record was kept in a small notebook that he carried with him at all times. Over a period of 4 weeks, Mark recorded an average of three to four orgasms a day in situations that always included static and a woman's image. In several situations, Mark was in public when he suddenly heard static and could not, or would not, control his behavior. Once while walking through the electronics department of a large store, Mark heard static coming from several radio scanners placed on shelves as demonstrators. Instead of removing himself from the situation, he turned up the volume on two of the radios and masturbated behind a stereo display while looking at women in the store. Mark reported that the number of times he became sexually aroused was too large to record because he was always "turned on." Mark attributed his constant state of arousal to chance encounters with static and his preoccupation with women.

Physiological assessment of Mark's sexual behavior followed a procedure suggested by Tollison and Adams (1979). Mark was brought into the laboratory and seated in a chair. A penile strain gauge was properly placed to measure changes in penile circumference, which is one of the most accurate measures of male sexual arousal. After a 20-minute habituation period in which Mark became more comfortable with the laboratory surroundings, a baseline of "0% full erection" was marked on one channel of a polygraph. Mark was then asked to masturbate to just short of orgasm, at which point "100% full erection" was marked. The penile response was allowed to return to baseline, and a randomized presentation of various stimulus conditions was begun.

Mark chose from his collection two pictures of women for use in the assessment. Interestingly, neither picture was sexually explicit. A radio tuned between stations provided static, and a picture of a tree was used as a neutral stimulus. Stimulus conditions to be presented included: the radio off, the radio producing static, each picture alone, and each picture with radio producing static. By presenting the pictures alone and in combination with static, the contribution of each stimulus to Mark's level of arousal could be assessed. Stimulus conditions were presented for 3 minutes while the penile response was recorded as a percentage of full erection. At 1-minute intervals during stimulus presentation, Mark was asked to report verbally his level of arousal in increasing steps from 1 to 10. After presentation of a stimulus condition, a neutral picture (car) was presented until the penile response returned to baseline, at which time the next stimulus condition was presented. To ensure that Mark was not manually stimulating himself during stimulus presentations, body movement was detected by a stabilometer located under his chair and recorded on one channel of the polygraph.

The physiological assessment showed no penile response to the radio off, a somewhat surprising finding considering the number of associations between radios and sexual arousal in Mark's history. There was also no penile response to the neutral picture, and the penile response to the neutral picture plus static was similar to that to static alone. The penile response to static was slightly greater than that to a picture of a woman but did not exceed 40% full erection. A simultaneous presentation of static and a picture of a woman, however, resulted in a penile response approaching 90%. Mark's self-report of sexual arousal to the problematic stimulus conditions was similar to his physiological response except that he reported more arousal to a picture of a woman than to static. In either case, static enhanced Mark's arousal to heterosexual stimuli, represented here by pictures of a woman. Based on this assessment, Mark's problem seemed to be that static increased his sexual arousal response to heterosexual stimuli to such an extent that he had little control over his behavior. In addition, if either static or heterosexual stimuli were absent, his attempts to fill in the "missing component" would be reinforced by increased arousal and orgasm. For example, if Mark saw an attractive woman, he would try to locate a source of static to increase his arousal to the woman. The increase in arousal would, in turn, reinforce the behavior of locating a source of static. The same can be said for behaviors that locate a woman's image when static is already present. This interpretation may explain Mark's so-called "obsession" with static and sex; in combination, they were extremely reinforcing.

A technique was designed to decrease directly Mark's sexual arousal response to static and thereby lessen its enhancing potential for responses to heterosexual stimuli. In addition, a heterosocial skills training program was planned to teach Mark requisite skills for interacting with women or at least to behave a little less strangely. The rationale for the heterosocial skills training program was simple. If Mark's deviant outlet for sexual arousal was to be supressed, access to more appropriate outlets must be learned. A person gains access to normal heterosexual outlets through a variety of skilled behaviors, such as conversational and dating skills. These skills, which collectively are called heterosocial skills, must be taught to those individuals who, for whatever reason, have never learned them.

The current treatment of choice for eliminating deviant sexual arousal seems to be aversion therapy with electric shock used as the aversive stimulus (Tollison and Adams, 1979). The rationale for aversion therapy is based on conditioning principles; aversive experiences are associated with stimuli that elicit deviant arousal by pairing the stimuli with an aversive stimulus. The development of the association should be followed by a cessation of the problem behavior. This particular technique is called *counterconditioning.* Aversive experiences may also be associated with deviant arousal itself by pairing the arousal with an aversive stimulus. Since the presentation of the aversive stimulus is contingent or dependent on a response by the individual (in this case, sexual arousal), this is a *punishment* procedure. The therapist decided to combine components of punishment with flooding and response prevention in treatment. Flooding and response prevention are terms used to describe the technique of exposing an individual to situations in which problem behaviors occur (flooding) while preventing the occurrence of these behaviors (response prevention). The situations that elicited deviant sexual arousal in Mark were identified by the formal assessment. An aversive stimulus would be used to prevent or inhibit the occurrence of sexual arousal during exposure to these situations if Mark could not inhibit arousal by himself.

In order to find an effective inhibitor of sexual arousal, Mark was brought into the laboratory and exposed to static while penile responses were recorded. It was determined that cognitive strategies, such as imagery and self-distraction, had little inhibitory effect on arousal. Lavender smelling salts not only failed to inhibit arousal to static but actually significantly increased it. (It is informative to recall here that Mark enjoyed sniffing urinals at the home for senior citizens.) Electric shock delivered to the wrist proved to be an effective inhibitor of sexual arousal as measured by penile response.

Treatment of Mark's deviant sexual arousal consisted of one session each day for 4 days. Within each session, three treatment periods were scheduled. A treatment period consisted of a 30-minute presentation of static during which sexual arousal was prevented and a 20-minute presentation of pictures from Mark's collection during which sexual arousal was allowed. Mark was presented with pictures of women during treatment to encourage arousal to these more appropriate stimuli, although it is unclear whether preventing deviant arousal increases appropriate arousal (Tollison and Adams, 1979).

Penile responses were recorded throughout the treatment periods. The maximum penile response allowed to static was set at 20% full erection because Mark reported an initial awareness of sexual arousal at approximately this level. This level of arousal was about 50% of that in response to static during the formal assessment. A shock of 1/2-second duration was delivered contingent on a 20% full erection response to static and, thereafter, at 5-second intervals as long as the response was greater than 20%.

The order of presentation of static and pictures was changed for each session. This was done so that decreases in penile response to static due to fatigue were not confused with decreases due to possible treatment effects. At the end of each session, Mark was asked to masturbate at home without static. This was a form of masturbatory reconditioning in which an attempt was made to have Mark associate orgasm with stimuli other than static.

Mark's sexual arousal to static decreased both within and across the treatment sessions. Within treatment sessions, both fatigue and treatment effects seemed to have been factors influencing penile response. Treatment effects were demonstrated in several treatment periods when a decrease in response to static (indicated by a decrease in the number of shocks) was not followed by a decrease in response to pictures. Across the four treatment sessions, the mean number of shocks decreased from 22 in the first session to 2 in the fourth session; the mean penile response to pictures increased from 13% full erection to 59%. Mark was not only learning to control his arousal to static in the laboratory; he was also increasing his arousal to more appropriate stimuli.

Mark expressed surprise at his increasing success in suppressing his arousal to static in the laboratory. He reported that he had masturbated with static once between sessions but otherwise had been able to resist any urges for the first time in memory. Two more treatment sessions were scheduled before a second formal assessment. If the second formal assessment showed that static no longer enhanced heterosexual arousal, the frequency of treatment sessions would have been decreased to a point where, ideally, treatment gains could be maintained with occasional "booster" sessions. Assuming that the second formal assessment showed significant improvement in control of deviant arousal, emphasis in treatment was to shift to the heterosocial skills training program. Unfortunately, circumstances beyond the control of the therapist brought treatment to a halt.

After the fourth session, Mark told the therapist that he was determined to put an end to the alleged activities of his neighbors at home. Mark had recently returned home to live with his mother because he could no longer afford his rented room after losing his job at the home for senior citizens. Mark described two incidents that had occurred the previous evening. He had thrown a rock and hit a car passing in front of his home. Mark believed that the car was driven by the brothers of the woman who lived next door; the brothers were supposedly on another spying mission for their sister. Mark then broke out the basement window of the house of the man who lived down the street. Mark confronted the man and said that he, Mark, knew what was going on in the neighborhood and it had better stop. Incredibly, the man said that even though he had no idea what Mark was talking about, he understood Mark's "confusion" because they were both Christians, a disarming comment in what was surely an explosive situation. Mark repeatedly threatened to harm his neighbors while relating these incidents to the therapist. He smacked his hand into his fist and laughed maniacally as he warned that he had had enough. Even his "phew!" took on a sinister tone.

The therapist contacted the psychiatrist in charge of the case and recommended that Mark be hospitalized or put into a sheltered environment while treatment continued. The therapist's immediate concern was to get Mark out of an environment that had become extremely provocative as a result of his delusional beliefs. The psychiatrist responded by withdrawing Mark from treatment. He believed that the aggressive acts were the result of symptom substitution. That is, treatment had supposedly removed a symptom—arousal to static—that Mark had used as a defense mechanism against his hatred of his mother. This hatred was now presumably directed against his neighbors.

Mark resumed his masturbation ritual with static shortly after treatment was terminated. In a couple of months, he seemed to have regained the level of arousal to static that he had demonstrated prior to the treatment. The psychiatrist had encouraged this development after deciding to ignore the deviant arousal and concentrate on "dynamic" issues in therapy, such as Mark's relationship with his mother.

As part of the new orientation in therapy, Mark was given a job in a sheltered workshop where his odd behavior would be tolerated. At the workshop, Mark met a girl with whom he struck up a "relationship." The girl was mentally retarded and did not object to Mark's preferences for static with sex. Mark, in turn, did not feel threatened by a girl "no one else would want." Although hardly the basis for an ideal relationship, there was some talk of marriage over the objections of the girl's father who was understandably apprehensive.

DISCUSSION

Although not directly dealt with in therapy, some aspects of Mark's behavior met the *DSM-III* criteria for schizotypal personality disorder (described in Chapter 11). These criteria were the following: (2) ideas of reference—actually a *delusion* of reference in Mark's case because the beliefs were more firmly held than those characterizing *ideas* of reference. The activities of neighbors and others had a particular and unusual significance for Mark; (3) social isolation, for example, no close friends or confidants, social contacts limited to essential, everyday tasks; (5) odd speech (without loosening of associations or incoherence), e.g., speech that is digressive, vague, overelaborate, circumstantially metaphorical. Mark's painstaking descriptions of the attractiveness of the various female television personalities, "phew!", was one example; (7) suspiciousness or paranoid ideation. Mark believed that the secretary at the sawmill was taunting him by becoming aroused to static from a radio on her desk; (8) undue social anxiety or hyperanxiety to real or imagined criticism. Other than prostitutes, for whose services he paid, Mark would not approach women for fear they would reject him. As noted in Chapter 11, the diagnosis of personality disorders is coded on Axis II in *DSM-III*.

The disorders coded on Axis I in *DSM-III* are more florid or "showy" than those coded on Axis II. This is true in Mark's case; his delusion about static and heterosexual relationships, a prominent and bizarre feature of his behavior, had been used by different clinicians to arrive at diagnoses of schizophrenia and obsessive-compulsive disorder. As stated previously, Mark's behavior did not meet the criteria for a diagnosis of schizophrenic disorder on Axis I. The exclusion of a diagnosis of schizophrenia became more credible with the failure of antipsychotic medication to have any effect on his behavior. It was also stated previously that Mark's behavior did not meet the criteria for obsessive-compulsive disorder in that his preoccupation with women and static was not a true obsession. The appropriate *DSM-III* diagnosis coded on Axis I would seem to be atypical psychosis. "This is a residual category for cases in which there are psychotic symptoms (delusions, hallucinations, incoherence, loosening of associations, markedly illogical thinking, or behavior that is grossly disorganized or catatonic) that do not meet the criteria for any specific mental disorder" (p. 202).

Multiple diagnoses may be made on Axes I and II when necessary to describe problem behavior more fully. Mark's attraction to static could be coded as a psychosexual disorder on Axis I. Psychosexual disorders are divided into four groups in *DSM-III*. One of these groups, the paraphilias, consists of disorders in which sexual arousal becomes attached to an inappropriate object, situation, or activity. When describing a particular type of paraphilia, the preface "para-" is often dropped and replaced with the Greek word for the object to which sexual arousal (or abnormal liking, "philia") is attached. For example, *zoo*philia is a term that described the use of animals to produce sexual excitement; in *pedo*philia the "love object" is a child; a *necro*philiac (atypical paraphilia in *DSM-III*) obtains sexual gratification from corpses.

Fetishism is a type of paraphilia in which sexual arousal becomes attached to an inanimate object or a particular part of the body. The name of the object or part of the body is used as an adjective when describing the fetish. Thus sexual attraction to boots is a boot fetish, to feet, a foot fetish, and so on. The term "fetish" originated as a reference to an idol or an object with magical significance (Delora and Warren, 1977). It keeps a flavor of its original meaning in present-day usage as seemingly neutral objects "magically" elicit sexual arousal. Although some fetish objects, such as articles of female clothing, are more common than others, the number of possible fetish objects is probably infinite (Tollison and Adams, 1979).

DSM-III lists two criteria for a diagnosis of fetishism (p. 269).

A. The use of nonliving objects (fetishes) is a repeatedly preferred or exclusive method of achieving sexual excitement.

B. The fetishes are not limited to articles of female clothing used in cross-dressing (transvestism) or to objects designed to be used for the purpose of sexual stimulation (e.g., vibrator).

Mark's problem meets both criteria if static is considered a nonliving *object*. If not, the formal diagnosis coded on Axis I would be atypical paraphilia. "This is a residual category for individuals with Paraphilias that cannot be classified in any of the other categories" (p. 275).

Regardless of the formal diagnosis, Mark's deviant sexual arousal is probably best conceptualized as a fetish. He definitely showed a preference for the use of static as a method of enhancing sexual arousal; static was used for this purpose in every orgasmic experience Mark recorded over a 4-week period. Related to this issue is the frequent observation that fetishists start collections of their fetish objects. Mark had a collection of favorite pictures of women that he used for masturbation, but this collection of pictures was not used exclusively or even preferably; he also used videotapes of women and unsuspecting "live" women, which were his preferred heterosexual stimuli. Mark could not, of course, collect static but, interestingly, he had acquired a sizable collection of electronic parts such as diodes, transistors, and wiring. Mark claimed he did not know why he started the collection of electronic parts other than that he found such "stuff" fascinating. The electronic parts were also kept locked in a fireproof strongbox but were not used in the masturbation ritual.

Physiological theories of fetishism assume some kind of organic pathology. The psychiatrist involved in Mark's case attributed the origin of Mark's static fetish to a neurological disorder indicated by the abnormal EEG at the age of 9. The neurological disorder presumably resulted from the encephalitis contracted at the age of 7. Theories attributing fetishism to neurological disorders indicated by an abnormal EEG have had some support in the literature. Epstein (1961) described four patients with fetishes who showed abnormal EEGs. He suggested that indications of dysfunction in the temporal lobe seem to be associated with fetish behavior. Recent advances in neurological diagnostic techniques do not usually support Epstein's work (Tollison and Adams, 1979). Also of interest here were the results of a second EEG given to Mark after the incident at the home for senior citizens. Inexplicably, this second EEG was normal.

Psychoanalytic formulations of fetishism view the fetish object as a substitute penis that the fetishist, as a child, believed his mother possessed (Freud, 1928). A variation of this dynamic theme in which fetishism is a sign of "something else" occurred in the rationale expressed by the psychiatrist for withdrawing Mark from treatment. The psychiatrist believed that although Mark's static fetish was the result of a neurological disorder, its present function was as a defense mechanism against his hatred for his mother. According to the psychiatrist, Mark hated his mother but *displaced* this hatred onto other women. This hatred was in turn transformed into sexual arousal by a *reaction formation* and static. When treatment removed the fetish, the hatred was still displaced onto other women but was no longer transformed into sexual arousal—thus the two aggressive acts by Mark against his neighbors.

Psychoanalytic interpretations direct treatment only to the extent that underlying conflicts ("something else") are recognized. Recognizing the underlying conflict becomes a formidable task because of the myriad defense mechanisms that mask its "true" character. Even after the true character of the underlying conflict is supposedly recognized, the specific treatment approach is unclear. For these reasons, a more direct approach centered on the problem behavior itself is often more reasonable.

The behavioral formulation of the development of fetishism was outlined by Tollison and Adams (1979). The first prerequisite seems to be some kind of conditioning experience—the fetish object must be paired with stimuli that elicit sexual arousal. An experiment by Rachman (1966) illustrated the conditioning component in fetishism. Several male graduate students were repeatedly presented with pictures of women's boots followed by pictures of nude females that the subjects had chosen as sexually stimulating. As a result of their pairing with pictures of nude females in the conditioning paradigm, pictures of women's boots acquired the potential to elicit sexual arousal as measured by changes in penile volume. Interestingly, penile response also generalized to other types of women's footwear.

The conditioning experience in the development of Mark's static fetish probably occurred as he rocked on his hobbyhorse while listening to static. In this manner, static was paired with stimulation that presumably elicited sexual arousal.

According to Tollison and Adams (1979), the second prerequisite for the development of fetish behavior seems to be the strengthening of the initial conditioning experience through masturbation and orgasm. That is, as the fetish object is repeatedly paired with masturbatory behavior, the association between the fetish object and behavior leading to orgasm is strengthened. Thus the fetish object acquires an increased potential to elicit sexual arousal. Mark strengthened his initial conditioning experience with static in just this manner. By repeatedly pairing static with masturbation, Mark strengthened the association between static and sexual stimulation originally learned on the hobbyhorse.

Finally, Tollison and Adams (1979) point out that heterosocial and heterosexual skills deficits frequently play a role in the etiology and maintenance of fetish behavior. A number of case studies, including this one, have reported deficits in heterosocial skills among individuals exibiting fetish behavior. The process or mechanism by which these deficits influence the strength of fetish behavior is unclear. Heterosocial skills deficits may contribute directly to the strength of the fetish by some process that "channels" sexual arousal to fetish behavior when deficits prevent its expression in more appropriate ways. Heterosocial skills deficits may also make an indirect contribution to the strength of the fetish when they lead to increased masturbatory behavior that strengthens the initial fetish conditioning experience.

The behavioral formulation of the development of fetishism suggests a specific treatment approach. First, the conditioned association between the fetish object and stimulation leading to orgasm must be disrupted or "deconditioned." The principal methods for accomplishing this end are the techniques of counterconditioning and punishment described earlier. Theoretically, it should also be possible to extinguish deviant arousal by presenting the fetish object and preventing the occurrence of masturbatory behavior that stengthens the conditioned association. As described, this is a straightforward Pavlovian extinction procedure. The fetish object is the conditioned stimulus, masturbatory behavior is the unconditioned stimulus, and sexual arousal is the response conditioned to the fetish object, which extinguishes when masturbatory behavior is prevented. The treatment applied to Mark's static fetish was conceptually a variant of a Pavlovian extinction procedure in which extinction was presumably accelerated by the active prevention of sexual arousal by an aversive stimulus.

The second component of treatment suggested by a behavioral formulation of fetishism is a heterosocial and heterosexual skills training program. Through methods such as reinforcement, modeling, and instruction, the patient is taught appropriate interpersonal skills to initiate and maintain relationships with the opposite sex; the same methods are used to teach specific behaviors and techniques required for successful sexual experiences. It is this second component of treatment that was most often ignored by early behavioral approaches to fetishism and that now adds to the efficacy of a behavioral approach.

14

INFANTILE AUTISM

SOCIAL HISTORY

Sam Williams was born in 1974, the second child of John and Carol Williams. The couple had been married for 5 years; he was a lawyer, and she a homemaker. Sam weighed 7 pounds, 11 ounces at birth, which had followed an uncomplicated, full-term pregnancy. Delivered by Caesarean section, he came home 6 days after the delivery.

His parents reported that Sam's early development seemed quite normal. He was not colicky, and he slept and ate well. During his first 2 years, there were no childhood illnesses except for a mild cold at age 14 months. After Sam's second birthday, however, his parents began to become somewhat concerned. He had been somewhat slower than his older sister in achieving some developmental milestones (such as sitting up alone and crawling). Furthermore, his motor development seemed uneven. He would crawl normally for a few days and then not crawl at all for awhile. Although he made babbling sounds, he had not developed any speech and did not even seem to understand anything his parents said to him. Simple commands such as "Get the ball," "Come," or "Do you want a cookie?" elicited no response. Initially, the Williamses thought Sam might be deaf. Later they vacillated between this belief and the idea that Sam was being stubborn. They reported many frustrating experiences in which they tried to force him to obey a command or say "mama" or "dada." Sometimes Sam would go into a tantrum during one of these situations, yelling, screaming, and throwing himself to the floor. That same year, the Williams' pediatrician told them that Sam might be mentally retarded.

Toward his third birthday, Sam's parents also began to notice him engaging in more and more behavior that seemed strange and puzzling. Most obvious were his repetitive hand movements. Many times each day he would suddenly flap his hands for several minutes. Other times he rolled his eyes around in their sockets. He still did not speak, but he made smacking sounds and sometimes he would burst out laughing for no apparent reason. He was walking now and often walked on his toes. Sam had not been toilet trained, although his parents had tried to do so. Sam's social development was also beginning to concern his parents. Although he would let them hug and touch him, he would not look at them and generally seemed indifferent to their attention. He also did not play at all with his older sister, seemingly preferring to be left alone. Even his solitary play was deviant. He did not really play with his toys, for example, pretending to drive a toy car into a service station. Instead, he was more likely to just manipulate a toy, such as a car, holding it and repetitively spinning its wheels. The only thing that really seemed to interest him was the family stereo. He was content to sit for as long as permitted, watching intently as a record spun on the turntable. Temper tantrums often ensued when the stereo was turned off.

At age 3 years, the family's pediatrician recommended a complete physical and neurological examination. Sam was found to be in good health, and the neurological examination revealed nothing remarkable. A psychiatric evaluation was performed several months later. Sam was brought to a treatment facility specializing in behavior disturbances of childhood and was observed for a day. During the day, the psychiatrist was able to see firsthand most of the behaviors that his parents had described—hand flapping, toe walking, smacking sounds, and preference for being left alone. When the psychiatrist evaluated Sam, she observed that a loud slapping noise did not elicit a startle response as it does in most children. The only vocalization she could elicit that approximated speech was a repetitive "nah, nah." Sam did, however, obey some simple commands such as "Come" and "Go get a potato chip." The psychiatrist diagnosed Sam as autistic and recommended placement in a day-treatment setting.

CONCEPTUALIZATION AND TREATMENT

Sam was 4 years old by the time there was an opening for him at the treatment center. He was bused to and from a special school 5 days a week, spending the remainder of his time at home with his parents and sister. The school provided a comprehensive educational program conducted by specially trained teachers. The program was organized mainly along operant conditioning principles. In addition, Sam's parents attended classes once a week to learn operant conditioning so they could continue the school program at home. The school's personnel conducted another evaluation of Sam, observing him in the school and later at home. Interviews with the parents established that they were both well adjusted and that their marriage was happy.

One of the first targets of the training program was eye contact. When working with Sam, his teacher provided small food rewards when Sam spontaneously looked at him. The teacher also began requesting eye contact and again rewarded Sam when he complied. Along with this training, the teacher worked on having Sam obey other simple commands. The teacher would try to select a time when Sam seemed attentive and would then, establishing eye contact, say the command and at the same time show him what was meant (i.e., model the desired behavior). For example, the teacher would say, "Sam, stretch your arms up like this," and then the teacher would lift Sam's arms up and reward him with praise and a small amount of food, such as a grape. This procedure was repeated several times. Once Sam began to become more skilled at following the command, the teacher stopped raising his arms for him and let him do it entirely for himself. These training trials were conducted daily. As the response to a particular command became well established, the command would be made in other situations and by other people. Sam's progress was slow. It often took weeks of training to establish his response to a simple command. After his first year in the school, he did respond reliably to several simple requests such as "Come," "Give it to me," and "Put on your coat."

At the same time that Sam was learning to respond to commands, other aspects of the training program were also being implemented. While Sam was in the classroom, his teacher worked with him on trying to develop skills that would be important in learning, for example, sitting in his seat, maintaining eye contact, and listening and working for longer periods of time. Each activity was rewarded in much the same way as his performance of simple behaviors had been. As these skills became better established, the teacher also began working on expanding Sam's vocabulary by teaching him the meaning of pictures of common objects. A picture of one object, such as an orange, was placed on a table in front of Sam. Once Sam had looked at the object, the teacher said "This is an orange. Point to the orange." When Sam pointed to the orange, he was rewarded. If necessary, the teacher would move his hand for him at first. Next, another picture, such as a cat, was selected and the same procedure followed again. Then the two pictures were placed in front of Sam and the teacher asked him to point to one of them: "Point to the orange." If Sam pointed correctly, he was rewarded. If he did not, the teacher moved his hand to the correct object. After Sam had correctly pointed to the orange several times in a row, the teacher asked him to point to the cat. With that response established, the teacher switched the position of the pictures and repeated the process. When Sam had begun to point correctly to the orange and the cat, a third picture was introduced and the training procedure was started anew. During 1 year of training, Sam learned the names of 38 common objects with this procedure.

Sam's speech therapist, whom he saw daily, was also working with him on language skills. Initially they worked on getting Sam to imitate simple sounds. Sitting across a table from Sam and waiting until Sam was looking (or prompting him to look by holding a piece of food near his mouth), the teacher would say "Say this, ah," taking care to accentuate the movements required for this sound. At first Sam was rewarded for making any sound. Subsequently, rewards were only forthcoming as Sam's productions approximated more and more closely the required sound. As sounds were mastered, Sam was trained to say simple words in a similar fashion. Over the course of a year, Sam learned a few words—"bye-bye," "no more," and "mine"; however, overall, his verbal imitation remained poor.

Having Sam learn to dress and undress himself was another target during the first year. Initially, his teacher helped him through the entire sequence, describing each step as they did it. Next, they would go through the sequence again, but now Sam had to do the last step himself (taking off his shoes, putting on his shoes). More difficult steps (tying shoes) were worked on individually to give Sam more practice on them. Once some progress was being made, this aspect of the treatment was carried out by the parents. They first observed the teacher working with Sam and then discussed the procedure and were shown how to make a chart to record Sam's progress. Over a period of weeks, the number of steps that Sam had to complete by himself was gradually increased, moving from the last toward the first. Sam was rewarded each time he dressed or undressed, usually with a special treat (e.g., a favorite breakfast food). In this case, the training was quite successful. By midyear Sam had mastered dressing and undressing.

Toilet training was another area that Sam's parents and teachers worked on. At home and at school, Sam was rewarded for using the toilet. He was checked every hour to see if his pants were dry. If they were, he was praised and reminded that when he goes to the toilet he will get a reward. Shortly thereafter, Sam would be taken to the toilet, where he would remove his pants and sit. If he urinated or defecated, he was given a large reward. If not, he was given a small reward just for sitting. As this training was progressing, Sam was also taught to associate the word "potty" with going to the toilet. Progress was slow at first, and there were many "accidents," which both teachers and parents were instructed to ignore. But Sam soon caught on and began urinating or defecating more and more often when he was taken to the bathroom. Then the parents and teachers began working on having Sam tell them when he had to go. When they checked to see if his pants were dry, they would tell him to let them know, by saying "potty" when he had to go to the toilet. Although there were many ups and downs in Sam's progress, by the end of the year he was having an average of less than two accidents per week.

One reason for Sam's relatively slow progress during his first year in the special school was his temper tantrums. These occurred sometimes when he was given a command or when a teacher interrupted something he was doing. Not getting a reward during a training session was another common cause. Sam would scream loudly, at the top of his voice, throw himself to the ground, and flail away with his arms and legs. Several interventions were tried. It had been observed that Sam's tantrums usually led, particularly at home, to getting his own way. For example, a tantrum had often been a successful device for having his parents keep a record spinning on the turntable even when they did not want to listen. Thus, ignoring the tantrum was the first approach. Sam's teachers simply let the tantrum play itself out, acting as if it had not happened. The procedure had no apparent effect. Next, time-out was tried. Every time a tantrum started, Sam was picked up, carried to a special room, and left there for 10 minutes or until the screaming stopped. This procedure also failed to have an effect on the tantrums and screaming, even with several modifications such as lengthening the time-out period.

During the second year of Sam's treatment, many of the first year's programs were continued. The range of commands to which Sam responded was expanded, and his ability to recognize and point to simple objects increased. In his speech therapy he learned to imitate more sounds and some new words ("hello," "cookie," and "book"). His progress in speech therapy, however, remained slow and uneven. He would seem to master some sound or word and then somehow lose it. He was, however, still dressing and undressing himself and going to the toilet reliably.

Feeding skills were one of the first targets for the second-year program. Although his parents had tried to get him to use a knife, fork, and spoon, Sam resisted these attempts and ate with his fingers or by licking the food from his plate. Drinking from a cup was also a problem. Sam still used a baby cup with only a small opening at the top. As in some of the previous programs, this one was implemented by both Sam's teachers and parents and involved a combination of modeling and operant conditioning. Training sessions conducted at mealtime first involved getting Sam to use a spoon. Sam was shown how to hold the spoon; then the teacher picked up the spoon, saying "Watch me. You push the spoon in like this and then lift it up to your mouth. Now you push the spoon in. Yes, that's right. Now lift it up to your mouth." Sam did not initially imitate, so the teacher had to guide him through the necessary steps, moving his hand and spoon to pick up food and then raising his arm until the spoon was at his mouth, telling him to open his mouth and guiding the spoon in. Praise was provided as each step in the chain was completed. After many repetitions, Sam was required to do the last step by himself. Gradually, more and more of the steps were done by Sam himself. Successes were followed by praise and failures by saying no or removing his meal for a short time. When eating with a spoon was well established, the training was expanded to using a fork and drinking from a cup. In several months, Sam was eating and drinking well.

Sam's failure to play with other children also was a major focus during the second year. The first step was to get Sam to play near other children. Most of his playtime was spent alone, even when other children were in the playroom with him. So his teacher watched Sam carefully and rewarded him with small bits of food whenever he was near another child. A procedure was also used to force Sam to interact with another child. Sam and another child would be seated next to one another and given the task of stacking some blocks. Each child was, in turn, given a block and prompted to place it on the stack. In addition to praising them individually as they stacked each block, both children were rewarded with praise and food when they had completed their block tower. After repeating this process several times, the program was expanded to include the cooperative completion of simple puzzles. "Sam, put the dog in here. Okay, now Nancy, put the cat here." Gradually, the prompts were faded out and the children were simply rewarded for their cooperative play. Although this aspect of therapy progressed well, transferring these skills to the natural play environment proved difficult. Attempts were made to have Sam and another child play together with toys such as a farm set or a small train. The teacher encouraged them to move the objects around, talking to them about what they were doing and rewarding them for following simple commands. Although Sam would usually follow these commands, his play remained solitary, with little eye contact or cooperation with the other child.

Sam's self-stimulatory behavior was a final target worked on during the second year. Sam's hand-flapping and eye-rolling had already decreased somewhat over the past year, perhaps because more of his day was being filled with constructive activities. Now a specific intervention, to be used by Sam's teachers and his parents, was planned. Whenever Sam began hand-flapping, he was stopped and told to hold his hands still, except when told to move them, for 5 minutes. During the 5-minute period he was told to hold his hands in several different positions for periods of 30 seconds. If he did not follow the command, the teacher or parents moved his hands into the desired position; if he did not maintain the position for 30 seconds, the teacher or parents held them still. Food rewards were provided for succesful completion of each 30-second period. Gradually, the teacher and parents were able to get Sam to comply without moving his hands for him or holding him. Then they turned to the eye-rolling and implemented a similar program, having Sam fix his gaze on certain objects around his environment whenever he began to roll his eyes. Over a period of several months of training, Sam's self-stimulatory behavior decreased by about 50%.

At the beginning of his third year in school, Sam, now 7 years old, was tested with the Stanford-Binet and achieved an IQ of 30. The language and speech training continued, as did the attempt to reduce the frequency of his self-stimulatory behavior. His tantrums, which had not responded to previous interventions, were becoming worse. In addition to screaming and throwing himself on the floor, he now became violent at times. On several occasions he had either punched, bitten, or kicked his sister. His parents reported that during these tantrums he became so much out of control that they feared he might seriously injure someone. Similar episodes occurred in school, usually when an ongoing activity was interrupted or he failed at some task. Trouble had also emerged on the bus that brought him to and from school. All the children were required to keep their seat belts on, but Sam would not do so and was often out of his seat. Twice in one week the bus driver stopped the bus and tried to get Sam buckled back into his seat. She was bitten once the first time and five times the second. The bus company acted quickly and suspended service for Sam. In an initial attempt to resolve the problem, Sam was put on Thorazine, a drug widely used in the treatment of schizophrenia. But after a month of the drug and no apparent effect, it was stopped. In the meantime, Sam's mother had to drive him to and from school. He was beginning to miss days or be late when his mother's schedule conflicted with the school's.

Because of the seriousness of the problem and the fact that other treatments had not worked, a punishment system was implemented. Because Sam's tantrums and violent outbursts were almost invariably preceded by loud screaming, it was decided to try to break up the usual behavior sequence and punish the screaming. Whenever Sam began to scream, a mixture of water and tabasco sauce was squirted into his mouth. The effect of this procedure, which was used by both his teachers and parents, was dramatic. The first day of the treatment, Sam began screaming six times. His response to the tabasco mixture was one of shock and some crying, which stopped quickly after he was allowed to rinse out his mouth. For the next 3 days, he experienced the tabasco twice each day, went 2 days with no screams, and then had one screaming episode; thereafter he neither screamed nor had a severe temper tantrum again for the rest of the year.

Sam's progress in other areas was not so dramatic. He continued to expand his vocabulary slowly, learning to say more words and recognize more and more objects. But his performance remained highly variable from day to day. His self-stimulatory behavior continued, although at a level below that which had been present earlier. He still remained isolated, preferring to be alone rather than with other children.

DISCUSSION

In 1943 Kanner described a group of 11 children who had not developed relationships with other people and had severe language deficits and obsessional features. He proposed the term autism to describe this disorder. Autism did not appear in *DSM-I* (1952) or *DSM-II* (1968), but it is included in *DSM-III* as one of the pervasive developmental disorders.

Autism is distinguishable from the other pervasive developmental disorder, childhood onset pervasive developmental disorder, on the basis of specific symptoms and because it begins before the age of 30 months (Kolvin, 1971). There is a good deal of confusion in the classification of these major disorders of childhood. *DSM-II* used the diagnosis of childhood schizophrenia for the later onset (after 30 months) conditions. The implication was that it was simply an early onset form of adult schizophrenia. But the available evidence did not support this supposition and instead demonstrated many differences between child and adult schizophrenia. For example, delusions and hallucinations do not seem to be prevalent among schizophrenic children. Although the sex ratio is about equal among adult schizophrenics, childhood schizophrenia is more common among males (Lotter, 1966). Moreover, unlike adult schizophrenia, there is no preponderance of childhood schizophrenia among the lower classes. Finally, in a well-executed 10-year follow-up study of psychotic children, many of whom could be regarded as childhood schizophrenics, Lockyer and Rutter (1969) did not find that they had become adult schizophrenics. We must therefore conclude that the evidence does not favor viewing child and adult schizophrenia as two closely related disorders.

Therefore, *DSM-III* proposed the new diagnosis, childhood onset pervasive developmental disorder. The diagnosis is to be applied to disorders, beginning after 30 months but before 12 years of age, that involve both deficits in social relationships and "oddities of behavior." The disturbances in the realm of social relationships include lack of appropriate emotional responsivity, lack of interest in social relationships, and inappropriate clinging. The oddities of behavior include sudden episodes of intense anxiety, peculiar motor behaviors such as stereotyped finger or hand movements, either over- or underresponsiveness to environmental stimuli, self-mutilation, speech abnormalities, and obsessional insistence on maintaining sameness in routines.

Autism begins earlier than childhood onset pervasive developmental disorder and also has somewhat different symptoms. A major feature of autism is "extreme autistic aloneness," an inability to relate to people, or to any situation other than being alone in a crib, that is found from the very beginning of life. Autistic infants are often reported to be "good babies," apparently because they do not place many demands on their parents. They do not coo or fret or demand attention, nor do they reach out or smile or look at their mothers when being fed. When they are picked up or cuddled, they often arch their bodies away from their caretakers instead of molding themselves against the adult as normal babies do. Autistic infants are content to sit quietly in their playpens for hours, never even noticing other people. After infancy they do not form attachments with people but, instead, may become extremely dependent on mechanical objects such as refrigerators or vacuum cleaners. Because they avoid all social interaction, they rapidly fall behind their peers in development. Clearly, this feature is very characteristic of Sam. Although he did not actively avoid human contact or develop an attachment with a mechanical object, he was almost totally asocial.

Even before the period when language is usually acquired, autistic children show deficits in communication. Babbling, a term used to describe the utterances of children before they actually begin to use words, is less frequent in autistic children and conveys less information than does that of other children (Ricks, 1972). Even on a nonvocal level, autistic children manifest a communication deficit. They do not, for example, use gesture as a substitute for speech, and it has proved difficult to try to train them to do so (Bartak, Rutter, and Cox, 1975).

The difficulties that older autistic children have with language are even more pronounced. Mutism, complete absence of speech, is prevalent, as was true with Sam. About 50% of all autistic children never learn to speak (Rutter, 1966). When they do speak, peculiarities are often found, including echolalia. The child echos, usually with remarkable fidelity, what he or she has heard another person say. In delayed echolalia the child may not repeat the sentence or phrase until hours or weeks after hearing it.

Another abnormality common in the speech of autistic children is pronoun reversal. The children refer to themselves as "he," "you," or by their own proper names; the pronouns "I" or "me" are seldom used and then only when referring to others. Pronoun reversal is closely linked to echolalia. Since autistic children often use echolalic speech, they will refer to themselves as they have heard others speak of them; pronouns are, of course, misapplied. This pronoun reversal might be expected to disappear as normal speech is built up, but it is apparently highly resistant to change

(Tramontana and Stimbert, 1970). Some children have required very extensive training even after they have stopped parroting the phrases of other people.

Communication deficiencies are clearly one of the most serious problems of autistic children. The fact that about 75% of autistic children score in the mentally retarded range on IQ tests is undoubtedly a reflection of these deficiencies. They may also leave a lasting mark of social retardation on the child. The link between social skills and language is made evident by the often spontaneous appearance of affectional and dependent behavior in these children after they have been trained to speak (Churchill, 1969; Hewett, 1965).

An autistic child's ability or inability to speak is often an effective means of predicting later adjustment, an additional indication of the central role of language. Rutter (1967) found that of 32 autistic children without useful speech at 5 years of age, only seven had acquired speech when followed up about 9 years later. Eisenberg and Kanner (1956) had earlier followed up a sample of 80 autistic children classified according to whether or not they had learned to speak by age 5. Fifty percent of the children who had been able to speak at this age were later rated as showing fair or good adjustment, but only 3% of the nonspeaking children were so rated. More recent studies have also shown a close link between the acquisition of language and later adjustment (Lotter, 1974; Treffert, McAndrew, and Dreifuerst, 1973). Based on these findings, we would predict a relatively poor outcome for Sam.

The third major feature of autism is that these children become extremely upset over changes in daily routine and their surroundings. An offer of milk in a different drinking cup or a rearrangement of furniture may make them cry or bring on a temper tantrum. Even common greetings must not vary. Sam did not exhibit this symptom.

In addition to the three major signs just described, autistic children have problems in eating, often refusing food or eating only one or a few kinds of food. They may also have difficulty walking but be quite proficient at twirling and spinning objects and in performing ritualistic hand movements. Other rhythmic movements, such as endless body rocking, seem to please autistic chilren. They may also become preoccupied with manipulating a mechanical object and be very upset when interrupted. Often the children have sensory problems. Like Sam, some autistic children are first diagnosed as being deaf because they never respond to any noise; some even seem to be insensitive to noise or light. Bowel training is frequently delayed, and head banging and other self-injurious behaviors are common (Rutter, 1974). Autistic children have been shown to be negativistic, turning their backs on others and actively resisting whatever is expected of them (Cowan, Hoddinott, and Wright, 1965). Finally, other features of autistic children's behavior also have an "obsessional" quality, similar to the preservation of sameness. In their play, they may continually line up toys or construct intricate patterns out of household objects. They may become preoccupied with train schedules, subway routes, or number sequences. Clearly, Sam displayed many of these behaviors.

What happens to such severely disturbed children when they reach adulthood? Kanner (1973) has reported on the adult status of 9 of the 11 children whom he had described in his original paper on autism. Two developed epileptic seizures; by 1966 one of them had died and the other was in a state mental hospital. Four others had spent most of their lives in institutions. Of the remaining three, one had remained mute but was working on a farm and as an orderly in a nursing home. The last two have made at least somewhat satisfactory recoveries. Although both still live with their parents and have little social life, they are gainfully employed and have some recreational interests. From his review of all published follow-up studies, Lotter (1978) concluded that 5 to 17% of autistic children had a relatively good outcome in adulthood. Most of the remaining children had a poor outcome, and 50% were institutionalized.

PHYSIOLOGICAL CAUSES

Several considerations make physiological accounts of autism plausible. First, the age of onset is very early. If a psychological stress were to precipitate such disorders, it would indeed have to be a particularly noxious event. Yet the available evidence does not indicate that autistic chilren are reared in especially unpleasant environments or that they have suffered some severe trauma. This point was certainly true in Sam's case. Second, a syndrome quite similar to autism may develop in the aftermath of brain diseases such as encephalitis. Third, mental subnormality is often associated with some kind of brain dysfunction; the majority of children with autism have low levels of intelligence.

If autism is related to abnormal brain functioning, this should be detectable in EEGs or through a neurological examination. Most studies of the electrical activity in the brains of autistic children have found abnormal brain rhythms. One early study (Kanner and Eisenberg, 1955) found that only 3 of 28 cases had abnormal EEGs, but more recent studies have reported a higher incidence. Hutt and his colleagues (1964) reported low-amplitude, high-frequency waves and used them as evidence in proposing an overaroused cortex as the cause of autism. Others have failed to find this specific pattern, however, detecting instead slow-wave activity (Hermelin and O'Connor, 1968). Lotter (1974) reports that 33% of autistic children seem to have a neurological dysfunction, either seizures or an abnormal

EEG. Similarly, Rutter and Lockyer (1967) reported that 14 to 20% of autistic children eventually develop seizures.

Genetic studies of autism are difficult to conduct because the disorder is so rare. Indeed, the family method presents special problems because autistic persons almost never marry. Nonetheless, the rate of autism in siblings of autistic children is about 2% (Rutter, 1967). Although this is a small percentage, it indicates a fiftyfold increase in risk as compared to the morbidity risk in the general population.

Early twin studies of autism were seriously flawed, principally because of sampling bias. But evidence of the importance of genetic factors in autism is provided by a methodologically sound study conducted by Folstein and Rutter (1978). Of 10 DZ pairs, there was no concordance for autism; in the 11 MZ pairs, the concordance rate was 36% (4 of 11 pairs). In addition to examining concordance for autism, Folstein and Rutter also looked at concordance for cognitive disabilities (e.g., delayed speech, articulation problems, low IQ) in the twins. Concordance for cognitive impairment was 82% in the MZ and 10% in the DZ pairs. This finding indicates that the nonautistic cotwins in MZ pairs are much more likely to be cognitively impaired than are the nonautistic cotwins in DZ pairs. The implication is that autism may be genetically linked to a broader deficit in cognitive ability.

In Sam's case there was no evidence of any neurological abnormality, nor was there any family history of autism. Consistent with Folstein and Rutter's findings, however, Sam's older sister did have a learning disability.

PSYCHOLOGICAL CAUSES

As might be expected, theorists of a psychogenic bent attribute autism to early experiences, especially those shared by the mother and child. Inadequate mothering is considered to bring on childhood psychoses. Perhaps the best known of the psychological theories was formulated by Bruno Bettelheim (1967). The basic supposition of Bettelheim's theory is that autism closely resembles the apathy and hopelessness found among inmates of German concentration camps during World War II. Bettelheim hypothesizes that the young infant is able to perceive negative feelings from his rejecting parents. The mother, on the one hand,may expect too much of the infant and be easily disappointed. Or the mother may expect too little, treating the child as a passive object. In either case the child comes to believe "that one's own efforts have no power to influence the world, because of the earlier conviction that the world is insensitive to one's reactions" (p. 46).

This experience of helplessness is viewed as extremely frustrating for the child. But he is unwilling to communicate his frustration because he feels that nothing good can come from it. He continues to withdraw from the world, his only activities—his ritualistic hand movements and echolalic speech—being more a means of shutting out the world than truly meeting it. An elaborate fantasy life is created, and insistence on sameness is the rule that brings permanence and order to the world. Autistic children remain safe only if everything about them stays put. Since the essential purpose of activity is to bring about change, autistic children avoid any sort of action; their universe centers on a static environment, beyond which they will not move.

Bettelheim's theory rests primarily on the hypothesis that at early critical periods, when the effect on the child is profound, the parents reject him. In his early papers Kanner described the parents of autistic children as cold, insensitive, meticulous, introverted, distant, and highly intellectual (Kanner and Eisenberg, 1955). He summed up his theory of how such traits affect the children by saying that they are reared in "emotional refrigeration." Others (e.g., Singer and Wynne, 1963; Rimland, 1964) have also noted the detachment of parents of autistic children.

Social-learning theorists have also postulated that certain childhood learning experiences cause psychotic childhood disorders. Ferster (1961), in an extremely influential article, suggested that the inattention of the parents, especially of the mother, prevents establishment of the associations that make human beings reinforcers. Because the parents have not become reinforcers, they cannot control the child's behavior. Ferster's reasoning is as follows.

1. Behavior is controlled primarily by its consequences.
2. Initially, the young child responds only to primary reinforcers, such as food and milk.
3. As children grow older, their behavior comes more under the control of secondary and generalized reinforcers, such as praise and love, and these social rewards acquire their reinforcing properties through contiguous association with primary rewards.
4. The behavior of severely disturbed children is a consequence of inadequate secondary and generalized reinforcers.
5. The parents of disturbed children, especially those of autistic children, neglect the child, for example, by being involved in professional and other nonfamily-oriented activities.
6. Thus the child learns to function alone or autistically and never becomes responsive to human contact, having been deprived of it during the earlier stages of life.

Both Bettleheim and Ferster imply that parents play the crucial role in the etiology of autism. Thus many investigators have studied the characteristics of these parents. Recent investigations (e.g., Cox et al., 1975) have failed to confirm earlier reports. When the parents of autistic children were compared to those of children with receptive aphasia (a disorder in understanding speech), the two groups did not differ in warmth, emotional demonstrativeness, responsiveness, and sociability. Similarly, DeMyer et al. (1972) did not find that parents of autistic children were rejecting and Cantwell, Baker, and Rutter (1978) and McAdoo and DeMyer (1978) did not observe parental deviance using standard measures such as the MMPI. The weight of the evidence is overwhelming: the parents of autistic children are unremarkable, as was the case with the Williams.

Even if we were to ignore these recent findings, the direction of a possible correlation between parental characteristics and autism is not easily determined. The deviant parental behavior that has been reported could easily be a reaction to the child's abnormality rather than the other way around. And if parental behavior causes autism, why is the incidence of similar difficulties so low in siblings? Moreover, although autism is a severe disorder, the parental behavior that has been discussed does not seem likely to be more than mildly damaging. It would seem that only very gross mistreatment, such as keeping the child in a locked closet, could precipitate such severe problems so early in life.

TREATMENT

Numerous therapeutic approaches have been tried with autism. None of them have met with great success. On a physiological level, autistic children have been treated similarly to adult psychiatric patients. Common procedures include electroconvulsive therapy, psychosurgery, vitamins, and various drugs, particularly the phenothiazines. None has proved to be highly effective.

A number of different psychological approaches have been proposed. One of the most famous is Chicago's Orthogenic School, founded by Bruno Bettelheim (1967). Based on his theory of autism, he developed a residential treatment center in which the autistic child could overcome fear and mistrust of the environment and begin the process of development anew. The child, isolated from his or her parents, is provided with a person who satisfies all needs and reduces any environmental pressures. The therapy, conducted by paraprofessionals, is meant to encompass the child totally.

Somewhat similar is Mahler's (1965) program, which is also based on the notion that autism develops from an inadequate mother-child relationship. In Mahler's procedure, an attempt is made, in some sense, to have the mother and child relive the period during which development went astray. The child is encouraged to regress (e.g., by eating and acting in a babylike fashion or through more symbolic representations of regression); the mother, with instruction from the therapist, tries to meet the child's emotional needs.

Unfortunately, the effectiveness of the treatments we have just discussed (and many other procedures as well) is difficult to evaluate. Many studies have examined the effects of psychotherapy in poorly defined groups of psychotic children, thus precluding definitive statements about autism. Furthermore, a basic requirement for statements concerning therapeutic effectiveness—an untreated control group—is lacking in almost all studies. Finally, the reported rates of success are difficult to evaluate because objective criteria for improvement are usually not specified.

Like the psychotherapeutic approaches, behavior therapy with autistic children requires a great expenditure of time and effort. This point is well illustrated by our description of the therapy program that was developed for Sam. Results of behavior therapy studies, however, are much easier to evaluate because the researchers have typically paid attention to the basic rudiments of experimental design. In general, behavior therapists focus on reliably assessed, observable behaviors and manipulate the consequences these behaviors elicit from the environment. As in Sam's case, desirable behaviors (e.g., speech, playing with other children) are rewarded, and undesirable ones (e.g., hand-flapping, screaming) are either ignored or punished. The desired behaviors are broken down into smaller elements that are learned first and then assembled into a whole. A good example of this procedure was seen in the procedures used to try to get Sam to speak. Modeling is a frequent adjunct in these operant behavior therapy programs.

Although based on data from small numbers of cases, the behavior therapy literature clearly indicates that many aspects of autism can be changed with such programs. Self-care skills, social behavior, and language have all shown improvements in controlled studies. Undesirable behaviors such as self-stimulation and self-injurious behavior have been decreased (Ross and Nelson, 1979). Unfortunately, maintenance of these gains once the therapeutic program ends has been a problem (Lovaas et al., 1973). Furthermore, it would be inaccurate to say that behavior therapy "cures" autism. The children's deficits are partly overcome, but most autistic children remain severely disturbed.

15

ATTENTION DEFICIT DISORDER WITH HYPERACTIVITY

Ken's mother telephoned the clinic in the middle of November. Ken was 7 years old and in the first grade at the time. His mother explained that he was having trouble at school, both academically and socially. The school psychologist had said that Ken was either brain damaged or hyperactive. An initial appointment was scheduled for the following week for Ken and both parents.

SOCIAL HISTORY

The case was assigned to an intern in clinical psychology who met the family in the clinic's waiting room. After a brief chat with all of them, he explained that he would first like to see the parents alone and later spend some time with Ken. Mr. and Mrs. Wilson, a white, middle-class couple, had been married for 12 years. He was 37, she 36. Ken was the middle of three children; an older sister was 9 and a younger brother 4. There were no apparent problems with either sibling. Mrs. Wilson experienced a full-term pregnancy with Ken. The actual delivery was without complication, although labor was fairly long (14 hours). After collecting this background information, the therapist explained that he would like to get an overview of the problem as it existed now.

According to the parents, Ken's problems began in kindergarten. His teacher frequently sent notes home about disciplinary problems in the classroom. In fact, there had been considerable question about promoting Ken to the first grade. The final result was a "trial promotion." Everyone hoped that Ken would mature and do much better in first grade, but his behavior became even more disruptive. Ken's mother reported that she had heard from his teacher several times over the first 2 months of school. Ken's teacher complained about his failure to get work done, classroom disruption, and aggressiveness.

Finally, Ken was evaluated by the school psychologist, who administered the Children's Apperception Test, a series of pictures to which the child is to make up stories, and the Bender-Gestalt, a test in which the child copies a standard series of geometric designs. According to the school psychologist, Ken's stories indicated a good deal of emotional turmoil and a lack of "impulse control." His drawings on the Bender-Gestalt were "immature." This was the basis for the diagnosis of possible brain damage.

The therapist then turned to evaluate the parents' perception of Ken at home and his developmental history. They described him as a difficult infant, much more so than his older sister. He cried frequently and was described as a colicky baby by their pediatrician. He did not eat well, and his sleep was often fitful and restless. As Ken grew, his mother reported even more difficulties with him. He was into everything. Verbal reprimands, which had been effective in controlling his sister's behavior, seemed to have no effect on him. When either parent tried to stop him from doing something (e.g., playing with an expensive vase, turning the stove off and on), he would often initiate a temper tantrum, throwing things, breaking toys, and screaming. His relationship with his sister was poor. He bit her on several occasions and seemed to take delight in trying to get her into trouble.

A similar pattern emerged with neighborhood children. Many neighborhood parents no longer allowed their children to play with Ken. During this period, Ken's parents also reported that he had low frustration tolerance and a short attention span. When the therapist asked what they meant, they were able to provide concrete examples. For example, Ken could not stay with puzzles and games for more than a few minutes and often reacted angrily when his brief efforts did not produce success. Going out for dinner had become impossible because of Ken's misbehavior in restaurants. Even mealtimes at home had become unpleasant. Indeed, Ken's parents had begun to argue frequently about how to deal with him.

Toward the end of the first session, the therapist brought Ken to his office while his parents remained in the clinic waiting room. Ken initially maintained that he did not understand why he was at the clinic, but later he allowed that he was getting into a lot of trouble at school. He agreed that it would probably be a good idea to try to do something about his misbehavior.

Ken and his parents were brought together for the final minutes of the first session. The therapist explained that the next several sessions would be devoted to conducting a more thorough assessment, including visits to the Wilsons' home and Ken's school. The parents signed release forms so the therapist could obtain information from their pediatrician and the school. The following information was gathered through these sources and from further interviews from the parents.

THE CURRENT PROBLEM

School records generally corroborated Ken's parents' description of his experience in kindergarten. His teacher described him as being "distractible, moody, aggressive," and a "discipline problem." Toward the end of kindergarten, he had been given the Peabody Picture Vocabulary Test (PPVT) and the California Achievement Test (CAT). Although his IQ (as estimated from the PPVT) was 120, he did not perform very well on the reading and mathematics subsections of the CAT.

An interview with Ken's first-grade teacher revealed a picture that agreed with other reports. Ken's teacher complained that he was frequently out of his seat and unable to sit still, he did not complete assignments, and his peer relations were poor. Ken seemed indifferent to efforts at disciplining him. Ken's teacher also completed a short form of the Conners Rating Scale (Sprague, Cohen, and Werry, 1974) on Ken. The instrument corroborated the hyperactive picture that had already emerged (see Table 15.1).

Table 15.1 Teacher's Rating of Ken's Behavior on the Short Form of the Conners Rating Scale

	Degree of Activity			
Observation: Classroom Behavior	**(0) Not At All**	**(1) Just a Little**	**(2) Pretty Much**	**(3) Very Much**
Constantly fidgeting			X	
Demands must be met immediately—easily frustrated				X
Restless or overactive				X
Excitable, impulsive			X	
Inattentive, easily distracted				X
Fails to finish things he starts—short attention span				X
Cries often and easily		X		
Disturbs other children				X
Mood changes quickly and drastically		X		
Temper outbursts, explosive and unpredictable behavior				X

Source: Sprague, Cohen, and Werry, 1974.

The therapist also arranged to spend a morning in Ken's classroom. During the morning, Ken was out of his seat inappropriately six times. On one occasion, he jumped up to look out the window when a noise, probably a car backfiring, was heard. He went to talk to other children three times. Twice he got up and just began walking quickly around the classroom. Even when he stayed seated, he was often not working and instead was fidgeting or bothering other children. Any noise, even another child coughing or dropping a pencil, distracted him from his work. When his teacher spoke to him, he did not seem to hear; it was not until the teacher had begun yelling at him that he paid any attention.

Subsequent sessions with Ken's parents focused on his current behavior at home. The pattern of behavior that had begun earlier in Ken's childhood had continued. He still got along poorly with his sister, had difficulty sitting still at mealtimes, and reacted with temper tantrums when demands were made of him. His behavior had also taken on a daredevil quality, as illustrated by climbing out of his second-story bedroom window and racing his bicycle down the hill of a heavily trafficked local street. Indeed, his daring acts seemed to be the only way he could get any positive attention from his neighborhood peers, who seemed to be generally afraid of him. He had no really close friends.

Mr. Wilson missed two of these sessions because of his business schedule. Most days he had to commute to work, a 2-hour train trip each way. During one of the sessions with just Mrs. Wilson, a hint of marital discord emerged. When this was brought up directly, Mrs. Wilson agreed that their marriage was not as good now as it once had been. A major source of their arguments centered around how to handle Ken. Mrs. Wilson had come to believe that severe physical punishment was the only answer. She described an active, growing dislike of Ken and feared that he might never change. The next time Mr. Wilson was present, he was asked about his child-rearing philosophy. He admitted that he took more of a "boys will be boys" approach. In fact, he reported that as a youngster he was rather like Ken. He had "grown out of it," and he expected that Ken would too. As a result, he let Ken get away with things for which Mrs. Wilson would have punished him. The couple's arguments, which had recently become more heated and frequent, usually occurred after Mr. Wilson had arrived home from his 2-hour commute. Mrs. Wilson, after a particularly exasperating day with Ken, would try to get Mr. Wilson to do something. He would refuse, accuse his wife of overreacting, and the battle would begin.

The therapist's visit to the Wilson's home began at 3 P.M. just before Ken and his sister would get home from school. The first part of the visit was uneventful but, at about 4:30, Ken and his sister got into a fight over who was winning a game. Ken broke the game, and his sister came crying to her mother, who began shouting at Ken. Ken tried to explain his behavior by saying that his sister had been cheating. His mother ordered him to his room; shortly thereafter, when she heard him crying, she went up and told him he could come out. The children were served their dinner at 5:30; Mrs. Wilson planned to wait until her husband came home later to have hers. The meal began with Ken complaining that he did not like anything on his plate. He picked at his food for a few minutes and then started making faces at his sister. Mrs. Wilson yelled at him to stop making the faces and eat his dinner. When she turned her back, he began moving food from his plate onto his sister's. As she resisted, Ken knocked over his glass of milk, which broke on the floor. Ken's mother was enraged at this point. She looked like she was ready to hit Ken, but she calmed herself, perhaps because of the therapist's presence. Although she told Ken that he would be in big trouble when his father got home, nothing happened. When Mr. Wilson came home, he made light of the incident and refused to punish Ken. Even though Mrs. Wilson's exasperation was obvious, she said nothing.

In subsequent direct evaluations of Ken, the therapist administered the Wechsler Intelligence Scale for Children (WISC) and the Lincoln-Ozeretsky Test of motor development, which is thought to provide information relevant to the possible presence of a neurological dysfunction. Ken's full-scale IQ was slightly above average (106), and he performed at age level on the various subtests of the Lincoln-Ozeretsky.

CONCEPTUALIZATION AND TREATMENT

The therapist conceptualized Ken's problem in an operant conditioning framework. Although open to possible biological causes of Ken's behavior, the therapist believed that a structured program of rewards and punishments would help. Treatment would then involve trying to increase the frequency of positive behaviors (complying with parental requests, interacting positively with his sister, staying in his seat in the classroom) by providing positive consequences for them. Similarly, undesirable behaviors should be followed by negative consequences. It was explained to Ken's parents that many of these undesirable behaviors actually produced positive results for him. His tantrums, for example, frequently allowed him to have his own way. The complicating feature was the attitude of Ken's parents. Would either of them be willing to engage in the considerable effort that is required to make a contingency management system work? To try to counter this potential problem, the therapist, after explaining the results of his overall assessment and the broad outlines of his treatment plan, asked both parents to try to put aside their existing attitudes for a brief period while they implemented a simple, scaled-down version of the overall plan. The hope was that a simple intervention, directed at only a couple of problem areas, would produce visible, quick results. This small change might be sufficient to increase the parents' enthusiasm and allow a complete therapeutic package to be instituted later.

Two target behaviors were selected—out of seat in the classroom and inappropriate behavior at mealtimes at home. The latter category was further defined as meaning no complaining about the food served, no kicking his sister under the table, staying in his chair, and no laughing, giggling, or making faces. During the next week, the parents were instructed to record the frequency of disruptive behavior at mealtimes as well as several other target behaviors (temper tantrums, fights with siblings, and noncompliance with parental requests) that could be targets for later interventions. The next day, Ken's teacher was contacted. He agreed to keep a record of the number of times Ken was out of his seat each day.

During the next session, an intervention was planned. The records of the past week indicated that every meal had been problematic. Ken had also been out of his seat when he was supposed to be working at his desk an average of 9 times per day. The therapist explained to Ken and his parents that in the next week daily rewards would be made available if Ken was not disruptive at mealtimes and if he reduced the number of times he was out of his seat at school. After discussion with all parties, it was agreed that Ken would be allowed to select either an extra half-hour of television watching, a favorite dessert, or playing a game with one of his parents if his behavior met an agreed on criterion. The initial criterion was being out of his seat less than 5 times per day and being nondisruptive for at least one of the two meals eaten at home. (On weekends, only the mealtime criterion was in effect.) Ken's parents were shown how to make a chart that was to be posted on the refrigerator. His teacher would send a daily note home indicating how many times he was out of his seat and that number, along with checks for a "good" meal, would be entered on the chart. Ken's teacher was telephoned after the session, and the program was explained. He agreed to keep sending home a daily record of the number of times Ken was out of his seat.

Ken's parents were obviously excited as they met the therapist at the beginning of the next session. They had brought their chart with them; some changes had obviously occurred. Ken met criterion on 6 of the 7 days. His average number of times out of his seat reduced from 9 to 3.6, and he had been unpleasant at mealtimes only 5 times (2 of these occurred on Saturday, resulting in his single failure to obtain a reward).

During the next several sessions, the parents and the therapist worked on expanding the program. Temper tantrums, fighting with his siblings, and noncompliance with parental requests had all been frequent the previous week. Ken's parents now seemed eager to attempt to deal with them. Of the three targets, noncompliance proved to be the most difficult to deal with. It presented such a large array of possibilities that a specific description of a criterion was problematic. The program that was developed involved the following components. Temper tantrums were to lead to a time-out procedure in which Ken would have to go to his room and remain there quietly for 10 minutes. Fighting was handled first by a simple request to stop. If that was ineffective, the time-out procedure would be employed. To try to get Ken to comply with parental requests (e.g., to go to bed, to stop teasing his sister), the parents were instructed to make the requests calmly and clearly to be sure Ken had heard them. If he did not comply, they were to give him one reminder, again in a calm fashion; if that failed, he would be sent to his room. The therapist stressed to the parents that their requests to stop or to do something had to be made calmly and that time-out should also be administered calmly. Finally, the parents were instructed to provide social reinforcement for cooperative play and being pleasant at meals (e.g., by simply telling Ken how pleased they were when they saw him playing nicely with his siblings). Based on the records from the previous weeks, it looked as though Ken would have experienced about 20 time-outs if the new system had been in effect. It was therefore decided that if Ken was sent to his room less than 10 times, he would receive a special end-of-week reward, a trip to the theater to see *Mary Poppins*. The mealtime procedure was kept in effect and, as before, a chart was to be completed showing school behavior, mealtimes, and frequency of time-outs. This time the parents were also asked to keep a log of the number of times they praised Ken and of the specific details of instances of noncompliance. The latter feature was included so the therapist could be assured that the parental requests were not unreasonable.

In the interim, the therapist contacted Ken's teacher and increased the scope of the school program. The teacher was told to maintain his record keeping of Ken being out of his seat, but he was also instructed to try to praise Ken as often as possible when Ken was working appropriately. The daily report card was expanded to include number of assignments completed and aggressive interactions with peers, defined broadly to include both physical and verbal aggression. Other instances of disruptive behavior (being noisy, making faces) were also to be recorded in this manner. The records from this week of recording were to be used in planning another intervention during the next session with the parents.

At the session following the implementation of the time-out procedure, the parents were decidedly less enthused than they had been the previous week. Although the improvement in mealtime behavior had been maintained, Ken had been sent to his room 17 times over the course of the week and thus did not get his Sunday trip to see *Mary Poppins*. It seemed that time-out was not an effective consequence for Ken. The therapist asked the parents for more details on how they were using the procedure. It turned out that Ken had lots of toys in his room, so the therapist decided to change the system. In an effort to increase the effectiveness of time-out, Ken's toys was put away so that time-out consisted of sitting on his bed with no toys to play with or books to look at. Furthermore, all the at-home targets were linked to a daily reward (one of the three described earlier). Specifically, Ken was to get 2 points for each pleasant meal, 2 points if he had only one time-out before dinner, and 2 points for none after dinner. The expanded school program was also converted to a point system. The teacher's records for the previous week indicated that Ken had been out of his seat an average of 3 times per day, had completed 55% of his assignments, and was either aggressive or disruptive 5 times during the average day. A set of new criteria were adopted for school and linked to points: 2 points for out of seat less than 3 times per day, 2 points for completing 70% or more of his assignments, and 2 points for reducing the frequency of aggression or disruptiveness to less than 3 times per day. Thus, overall Ken could earn 12 points on each school day and 6 on weekends. The criterion for one of the daily rewards was set at 8 points on a school day and 4 points on weekends. In addition, a weekly total of 54 points would result in a movie; *Mary Poppins* was still playing.

The system now appeared to be working well. During one typical week, Ken earned 58 points and thus got his trip to the movie. In addition, he met the criterion for a daily reward each day. At home, he had averaged only one time-out per day, and 12 of 14 meals had been without incident. At school, he had been out of his seat slightly less than twice per day, completed an average of 70% of his assignments, and was either aggressive or disruptive less than 3 times per day.

For the following week, the criteria were increased again. At school, points could be earned for out of seat less than twice per day, completing 80% of his assignments, and being aggressive or disruptive less than twice per day. At home, the point system was left unchanged. The criterion for a daily reward was raised to 10 for school days and 6 on weekends; the criterion for the end-of-week reward was raised to 66. In addition, a new daily reward was added to the program—a bedtime story from Ken's father. The parents were also encouraged to continue providing praise for good behavior. Ken's teacher was telephoned to discuss a similar tactic for the classroom.

The program continued to evolve over the next few weeks, and Ken made steady progress. By the fourteenth week, it was clear that Ken's behavior had changed greatly. At this point, sessions were spaced to once every 2 weeks, and the family was followed for 3 more months. Increased emphasis was placed on teaching Ken's parents the general principles that they had been following—that when problems arose they would be able to handle them on their own by making the necessary modifications in the system. Both Ken's parents and his teacher were also reporting changes in Ken that had not been targets of the intervention. He was described as being less moody, more pleasant, and more able to deal with frustration. He had also begun to form some friendships and was being invited to other children's homes to play. Although Ken was still reported to be somewhat difficult to handle, his parents now felt that they had some skills they could use. Ken's mother reported that she now felt much more positively toward him. The couple also indicated that their arguments had become much less frequent. Two steps remained. First, the daily rewards were phased out. Instead, the parents were to provide social reinforcement for good behavior during the day. The rewards were still provided, but in a less formal manner in which they were not linked explicitly to the number of points earned during the day. Finally, the formal contingency aspect of the weekend reward was dropped. A "good week" still led to a special treat or activity but was not linked specifically to a particular criterion. Ken's behavior remained stable; the family terminated treatment.

DISCUSSION

Problems such as Ken's have been described by a number of different diagnostic terms over the past two decades. Minimal brain dysfunction, hyperkinesis, and hyperactivity have been the most commonly applied terms. According to *DSM-III*, Ken's diagnosis would be attention deficit disorder with hyperactivity, one of the subcategories in the manual's section headed "Disorders Usually First Evident in Infancy, Childhood or Adolescence." This large section encompasses disorders of the intellect (e.g., mental retardation), emotions (e.g., anxiety disorders), overt behavior (e.g., attention deficit disorder), and pervasive disorders of development (e.g., infantile autism).

The current diagnostic term, attention deficit disorder, reflects the prevailing view that problems in attention are the principal aspect of the disorder. These difficulties include failure to finish tasks, not listening, being easily distracted, and having problems concentrating and maintaining attention. This description fits Ken well. Attention deficit disorder can be diagnosed as with or without hyperactivity. When hyperactivity is present, the child has problems in staying seated in school, fidgets when seated, and is often described as "always on the go." Hyperactivity is especially evident in any situation that requires controlling activity level, such as school and mealtimes. Ken's behavior in the classroom and at home was consistent with *DSM-III*'s description of the features of hyperactivity.

In addition to their core problems, children with attention deficit disorder with hyperactivity have a number of difficulties. As evidenced by poor academic and test performance (Weiss et al., 1971), between 40 and 50% have learning problems. Misconduct at school is found in about 80% (Satterfield et al., 1972). They are commonly described by adults as immature. They may choose to play with children younger than themselves and with toys inappropriate to their age; they also persist in baby talk (Weiss et al., 1971). They are often described as stubborn, have low frustration tolerance, and throw temper tantrums frequently.

The problems of these children begin in early infancy. They are more likely than their peers to develop colic (Stewart et al., 1966), and they fail to reach developmental milestones at the expected ages (Denhoff, 1973). Furthermore, even during infancy there are deviations in activity level; some are overactive; interestingly, others are too passive (Werry, Weiss, and Douglas, 1964). By the preschool years, their overactivity and inattentiveness are evident. At this stage in their lives, they are often considered temperamental and emotional children (Schain and Reynard, 1975). But their problems continue into the elementary school years; eventually most of them come to the attention of mental health professionals.

It is estimated that 8 to 9% of elementary school boys and 2 to 3% of girls have the disorder (Miller, Palkes, and Stewart, 1973). At one time it was thought that the problem simply went away by adolescence. Difficulties with activity level do diminish somewhat, but adolescent youngsters still have difficulty maintaining attention (Weiss et al., 1971; Hoy et al., 1978). Deficits in learning and perception remain (Mendelson, Johnson, and Stewart, 1971), and social relationships at home and with peers are still problematic (Huessy, Metoyer, and Townsend, 1974). Some problems remain in young adulthood, although they are of lesser magnitude. Impulsivity continues, as evidenced by more frequent changes in residence and car accidents; a minority show signs of antisocial behavior. On the brighter side, many attain equal job status and satisfaction to controls and are only slightly below average in educational level (Weiss et al., 1979).

PHYSIOLOGICAL THEORIES

A predisposition toward the disorder may be inherited. Morrison and Stewart (1971), for example, found that 20% of hyperactive children had a parent who had been hyperactive. The corresponding figure for control children was 5%. Similar results have been reported by Gross and Wilson

(1974), and the findings have held up in more methodologically sophisticated adoption studies (Morrison and Stewart, 1973; Cantwell, 1975). Reports from Ken's father indicate that he may have had attention deficit disorder as a child, but the information is too sketchy to be sure.

A biochemical theory of hyperactivity, proposed by Feingold (1973), has enjoyed much attention in the popular press. Based on one of his earlier clinical cases, Feingold concluded that attention deficit disorder might be caused by food additives. He embarked on a study in which children were kept on a diet free of food additives. Many children responded favorably. Feingold's work was subsequently replicated (Hawley and Buckley, 1974). Thus it is possible that the central nervous systems of some hyperactive children, perhaps through a genetically transmitted predisposition, are upset in some way by food additives. It is unlikely, however, that all cases of attention deficit disorder are caused by sensitivity to food additives. Well-controlled studies of the Feingold diet have found that only a minority of such children respond positively (Goyette and Conners, 1977).

Although Ken did not exhibit signs of possible brain damage, some children with attention deficit disorder do show such signs. Their mothers often have difficult pregnancies (Pasamanick, Rogers, and Lilienfeld, 1956). In infancy they are more likely to have had seizures, encephalitis, cerebral palsy, and head injury (Conners et al., 1972). The disorder can also be brought on by lead poisoning (Wiener, 1970). Some of the affected children show abnormal EEGs (Gross and Wilson, 1974) in addition to the soft neurological signs already mentioned. All this evidence points to some brain malfunction, but what parts of the brain might be impaired? Or is the problem biochemical, not structural? Unfortunately, currently available data do not allow a more meaningful specification of the vague term "brain damage" (Sroufe, 1975).

PSYCHOLOGICAL THEORIES

Bettelheim (1973) suggests that hyperactivity develops when a predisposition to the disorder is coupled with unfortunate rearing by parents. A child with a disposition toward overactivity and moodiness is stressed further by a mother who easily becomes impatient and resentful. The child is unable to cope with the mother's demands for obedience, the mother becomes more and more negative and disapproving, and the mother-child relationship becomes a battleground. With a disruptive and disobedient pattern already established, the demands of school cannot be handled, and the behavior of the child is often in conflict with the rules of the classroom.

The Fels Research Institute's longitudinal study of child development supplies some evidence that is consistent with Bettelheim's position (Battle and Lacey, 1972). Mothers of children with attention deficit disorder were found to be critical of them and relatively unaffectionate, even during the children's infancy. These mothers continued to be disapproving of their children and dispensed severe penalties for disobedience. The parent-child relationship, however, is bidirectional; the behavior of each is determined by the actions and reactions of the other. The influence of the child's behavior on changing the actions of mothers has recently been demonstrated (Barkley and Cunningham, 1979). In Ken's case it seemed that his mother's negative attitude toward him was principally a response to his disruptive behavior. Nevertheless, her negative attitude, coupled with the inconsistent disciplinary practices of the parents, may have exacerbated Ken's disorder.

Finally, although no comprehensive theory has been proposed (O'Leary, 1980), two ways in which learning might figure in hyperactivity should be mentioned. First, some of the child's undesirable behavior could be directly reinforced. In Ken's case, his daredevil acts and classroom clowning did elicit attention from his peers, and his negative behaviors gained considerable attention from his parents, peers, and teacher. Ken's temper tantrums also allowed him to get his own way. Second, as Ross and Ross (1976) suggest, hyperactivity may be modeled in the behavior of parents and siblings. This did not seem to be the case in the Wilson family.

TREATMENT

One of the major therapies used for children with attention deficit disorder is the administration of central nervous system stimulants such as dextroamphetamine (Dexedrine) and methylphenidate (Ritalin). Although it may at first seem strange to stimulate further a child who may already be having problems with overactivity, research indicates that these drugs both improve attention and lower activity level. Their main therapeutic effect may be to improve attention; activity level then decreases because the child is able to stay with various activities for longer periods of time.

The available research clearly indicates that stimulants, particularly methylphenidate, are effective in treating attention deficit disorder. From 33 to 50% of treated children show an immediate positive response to stimulants. Another 10 to 20% show moderate improvement. Short-term side effects of stimulant treatment, principally insomnia and loss of appetite, usually disappear quickly. However, possible long-term risks of treatment with stimulants have not been well researched, so the decision to use them should be weighed carefully (Ross and Ross, 1976). Furthermore, the drugs have not been shown to affect all the problems associated with the disorder. Academic achievement and social problems, for example, may not improve (O'Leary and Pelham, 1978).

A variety of psychological therapies have also been employed for attention deficit disorder, but the one that has been most thoroughly studied is an operant learning approach such as that used in Ken's case. Positive reinforcement is used to increase on-task behavior, remaining seated, and positive interactions with peers, teachers, and parents; negative consequences follow undesirable behaviors such as being disruptive in the classroom. Such programs have been used successfully to treat outpatients on an individual basis as well as with children in special classrooms (O'Leary, 1980). In a direct comparison of behavioral procedures and stimulants, Gittelman-Klein et al. (1976) evaluated the effectiveness of the following three treatments: behavior therapy plus a placebo drug, behavior therapy plus Ritalin, and behavior therapy alone. All treatments led to significant improvements in the children's behavior. The combination of behavior therapy and Ritalin, however, was the most effective. At the end of the 8-week treatment program, children treated in this way were indistinguishable from their normal classmates and more improved than children who received either treatment alone.

16

SCHOOL PHOBIA

Mr. and Mrs. Berg had taken Robert to doctors and clinics repeatedly. One Sunday night they even took him to the emergency room of the city hospital after they found him panic-stricken, writhing in bed with pain. A nice-looking, curly haired, underweight 8-year-old, Robert, now in second grade, had always been very much afraid of school. Recently, his fears were becoming tinged with a morbid depression that had begun to alarm his parents.

The child sat in an overstuffed chair in the office of the family doctor, someone who did not take an especially psychological approach to his patients. Had the warm Ovaltine she had suggested helped?, she asked the skeptical Robert, who shook his head sheepishly, looking all the while to his mother. She was sitting nearby with an expression of desperation and love that only made the boy feel even more guilty about the pain he was causing his family. If only he could stop being a baby, Robert thought to himself, as the doctor and his mother discussed the latest pattern of school morning and evening "shenanigans."

Without fail, Sunday through Thursday evenings found the boy eating little at dinner, staring morosely at his plate, picking idly at his food, and wondering whether it was really worth eating, since he would probably be vomiting it all 1 to 2 hours later. His skinny little body was beset with a host of twitches and rituals that simply became more pronounced if someone commented on them. Robert felt as ill equipped to resist them as he felt helpless to control the anxiety that mounted as the evening wore on.

Bedtime offered little solace; Robert found it necessary to observe whether he would fall asleep before 9 P.M.; when that did not happen before 9:30 P.M., and on late into the evening, he would sometimes break into tears that brought his mother into bed with him. In a fruitless effort to distract his worrying mind and ease him into sleep, she told Robert fanciful stories and promised him rewards if he would manage to go to school the following day without the usual somatic complaints and pitiful entreaties that he be allowed to stay home "just for today."

But it was the morning that really threw the household into total chaos. Rising by 6:00 A.M., Robert would pace the floor of the small apartment, causing the boards to creak and usually waking up his older brother. By 7:00 A.M. everyone was awake. While preparations for the day occupied everyone else, Robert spent the time groaning in a corner of the kitchen, rubbing his stomach, and occasionally dashing into the bathroom to throw up in the toilet. His mother would plead, cajole, insist that he at least drink a glass of milk for breakfast, but Robert would generally refuse, whining that it would only make him vomit more.

When it was time to set out to school, Robert had to be pushed out of the apartment. His tearful pleading and complaints of stomach upset and all manner of bodily ills were many times met by relenting on his mother's part, and she would let him remain at home. (The fact was that Robert, an unusually bright child, did not get much out of school scholastically, a fact that his mother had come to use to justify to herself the frequent decision to let Robert stay with her instead of insisting he go to school.) Much of the time, however, Robert's entreaties were rebuffed, especially when his stern father had not yet left for work. He would make his way miserably to school, trying to hide his tears from schoolmates.

Once at school, Robert usually settled down by lunchtime, but not without a visit from his mother, who would come to the school yard at recess with encouraging and loving words to her little boy and a container of milk and some cookies. This midmorning contact with mother was an implicit part of the "deal" Robert had struck with her for his going off to school. She continued these visits even though she admitted to herself that it was probably not in her son's best interests. It was, she knew, in her own interests; she would otherwise be nervous and upset about Robert's well-being in her absence.

Robert's peer relationships were surprisingly good. He was well liked by his schoolmates and by neighborhood friends, in spite of the fact (it seemed to Robert) that he acted like a baby as far as school was concerned. Although thin, almost emaciated in appearance from all the vomiting and his generally lackluster appetite, Robert was healthy and possessed an above-average athletic prowess. If he could not get to school without crying and vomiting, he could at least play stickball with enthusiasm and distinction.

But he had no way to express adequately to another human being, even to his mother, how terrified school made him. It was not just the separation from home that frightened him—although, to be sure, he did not ever stray far from his neighborhood or even spend much time at friends' houses. There was something particular about *school.* Yes, his present teacher in second grade was not an especially warm person, but she was always nice to Robert, both out of pity and out of appreciation for how good a student he was. The building itself seemed to him as cheery and attractive as a haunted house from a Boris Karloff movie, and the authoritarian atmosphere did little to make the boy feel better. It is not an exaggeration to say that Robert's sorrowful walk to school in the morning resembled that of a convicted murderer as he made his way from his death cell to the room being readied for him with cyanide gas.

SOCIAL HISTORY

Robert was the younger of two sons; his brother was 6 years his senior. The mother and father were second-generation Jews, and Mr. Berg was a self-employed insurance broker. He had graduated from a business school and worked for several years in a large agency downtown before striking out on his own. Mrs. Berg did not attend college; she married her husband soon after her graduation from high school and became pregnant 3 months after. Years later Mr. Berg angrily told her that he would have gone into another line of work if he had not been saddled so quickly with family responsibilities. For some time Mrs. Berg blamed herself for having prevented her husband from pursuing a vocation he might have been better suited for than selling insurance.

Money was a constant worry for the household. Suppertime conversation revolved around things the family needed but (apparently) could not afford, and particularly around the importance of higher education for the two boys. It was never a question of *whether* Robert and his brother would go to college and to some professional school afterward but of *which* college and *which* type of postgraduate training. For many lower-middle-class Jewish families, education was viewed as *the* golden opportunity for advancement. Even though it had been 60 years since Robert's great-grandparents had fled from Russia to the United States to escape tsarist pogroms, the youngster had already incorporated these values and anxiety-laden goals.

Robert and his older brother were very different from each other—Robert tense and nervous much of the time, his older brother jovial and optimistic, at least outwardly. They were alike, however, in that they were both very intelligent and serious about their schooling. Indeed, Robert's recollections years later were that he viewed kindergarten as the first difficult and challenging step toward making his way in life.

But Robert's home life was hardly an unmitigated disaster, even if he sometimes acted as if it were. Both boys were the recipients of a seemingly boundless outpouring of love and approbation from grandparents and parents alike, none more effusive than from their mother. An overweight woman, she constantly hugged and kissed her two boys, showering praise and food on them whenever they were near her, which was often. Robert's brother seemed to respond positively to this affection (and his rotund, cherubic appearance attested to his enjoyment of the food), but somehow Robert experienced it as yet another source of tension. In his worrying mind, every display of love and every word of approval only reminded him of the possibility of *not* having the love and approval. Even though praise and affection seemed to be constantly available, Robert began, even in earliest childhood, to worry if his mother would still love him if he was not "good." When he began school, there suddenly seemed to be countless hoops to be jumped through in an unending effort to retain the closeness and approbation that, already by age 5, he had developed a strong need for, especially from his mother.

Another aspect of Robert's home life that assumed significance for him was the comparison he made between the modest, lower-middle-class surroundings in which he was growing up and the relative affluence of his cousins. His uncle was an extroverted lawyer who had built a lucrative general practice. He was not above "chasing ambulances," but other clients also came his way with more dignified and expensive legal needs. As far back as Robert could remember, the visits to his cousins' home (in "the better" section of town) were an admixture of gleeful enjoyment of expensive and elaborate toys and a spacious house, and a brooding envy and resentment that these "nice things" were not his. The return to the small, crowded apartment on a Sunday evening, after an afternoon of temporary immersion in the material things that only money could buy, oppressed Robert for reasons his young mind could not grasp. All he knew was that he felt tense, angry, and hurt.

Robert was afraid of school from the very outset. His extreme fear and avoidance, however, were almost less remarkable than something else, an attitude that was apparent on the days he managed to get to school. His kindergarten teacher noted to herself the first few days of school that this little boy was so serious. While the other children would act like the 5 and 6-year-olds they were, Robert behaved more like a goal-oriented first-year medical student. He always sat with his hands tightly folded on the table in front of him looking attentively at the teacher, eager to do her bidding, even trying to anticipate her wishes—anything to be patted on the head, assured that he was a good boy, a smart boy, not prone to make mistakes or to give cause for a cross word or rebuke. So sensitive had he become by then to criticism and disapproval that it would wound him deeply even when some other child was spoken to sternly. So he was on edge continuously, lest he himself fall short in the teacher's eyes or lest a classmate be victim of such a disaster.

This pattern persisted until the middle of second grade, when a visit to the family doctor—who by now was at her wits' end with Robert—resulted in a promising referral. At the nearby university, a professor visiting from another country was teaching a seminar on child psychotherapy. Word was disseminated in the professional community that childhood psychological problems were being sought for practicum work for the graduate students under the professor's supervision. This referral led to the following intervention.

CONCEPTUALIZATION AND TREATMENT

The way therapy was planned and implemented was unusual in that Robert's case was discussed intensively in the clinical seminar of Professor Long. The more behavioral members of the group argued that Robert's school phobia be handled straightforwardly, as a fear and avoidance of school and therefore amenable to a graduated exposure therapy regimen, modeled on a case report by Lazarus, Davison, and Polefka (1965). According to these authors, a counterconditioning approach is appropriate in the earliest stages of treatment, when fear and avoidance are so high that virtually no approach responses are being performed. The strategy is to expose the child gradually to school, all the while trying to induce states antagonistic to anxiety by comforting him, hugging him, and the like, even if it means reinforcing avoidance. Later on, as the child is more and more able to attend school, rewards can be made contingent on varying degrees of school attendance.

But other, less behavioral students suggested a more complex and less strictly behavioral intervention. First, it was noted that Robert was subject to anxieties other than those surrounding school, although his school phobia was obviously a dominating force in his life and that of his family. He showed anxiety and extreme reluctance about venturing far from home for *any* reason unless in the company of a family member, especially his mother. Notice was also taken of the mother's apparent need to have the boy overly dependent on her. She seemed to accede too readily to the child's demands to stay home; if he made it to school, she would visit during recess and lovingly hand milk and cookies to Robert through the bars of the school fence (even though he could have brought the snack with him). In addition, Robert's unusual seriousness and concern about doing perfect work in school were believed to play a part in the phobia; school seemed to represent a grave and weighty affair at an age when most children have fun and enjoy the simple pleasures of childhood. Robert's resentment and envy at his wealthy uncle also seemed relevant, perhaps highlighting the material benefits that awaited those who would work instead of play. Finally, since the household had been organized around Robert's timorousness, it was thought that adjustments would be necessary in order to support whatever improvement Robert might show in going to school regularly and without duress.

Therapy proceeded along several fronts, often simultaneously—an intensive approach made feasible by virtue of Robert becoming a teaching case for the graduate students. Professor Long and one of his students conducted office sessions with Robert alone, with Robert accompanied by his parents, and with the parents by themselves; another student worked with the boy directly on the school phobia every weekday.

The latter, as the most straightforward and behavioral aspect of the treatment program, can be described first. The overall goal was to expose Robert gradually and steadily to more and more of the school situation. For the first few mornings, the student-therapist would come to the apartment about 30 minutes before Robert's scheduled departure, talk soothingly with him, trying to point out the fun aspects of school, and then leave with him to walk a few blocks, but not all the way, to school. Robert knew, in other words, that he would not attend school the first few days but would just practice walking there in the company of the therapist (whom he grew quickly to like). By the end of the week, Robert felt he was ready to enter the school yard with the therapist and decide only then whether to proceed to the classroom. By this point the school administration and Robert's teacher had been apprised of the graduated exposure program, the consequence being that, for a while, Robert would not be attending regularly (not much of a change, to be sure); when present, he would be accompanied by an adult. It was also explained to the other children in his class that Robert's "friend" was someone who was trying to make him more at ease in school. Fortunately, the children showed understanding and support; they liked Robert, even with his occasional vomiting and erratic attendance, and hoped that the man with him would succeed in making him more comfortable in school.

After 2 weeks, Robert was able to leave his house by himself, walk to school, and enter the school yard to see the therapist waiting for him. A few days later he was able to make it into the classroom, with the therapist waiting for him there; 2 weeks after that, he could remain at school all day, meeting the graduate student as he left the building for the walk home. During these weeks, the emphasis was on rewarding approximations to school attendance; it was necessary to caution his mother against coming to school at recess or being (overly?) willing to allow the boy to remain home if he expressed a desire to do so. Dealing with the mother's reluctance to stay away from school at recess was something that occupied the other therapist team, as will be seen shortly.

What was regarded as a breakthrough occurred 7 weeks after the beginning of therapy. The therapist was waiting for the boy to come out of the school building and then accompany him home when Robert appeared with several classmates who lived in his neighborhood. In a serious manner, more appropriate for a child several years older, Robert asked the therapist if he would mind not walking him home because he would rather be in the company of his friends.

The preceding exposure regimen was sufficient for eliminating the phobia of the child reported by Lazarus et al. However, it can never be known whether or not it would have sufficed as well for Robert; as indicated, Professor Long's seminar elected to have different therapists work simultaneously with Robert and his parents.

Without necessarily implicating the mother as the cause of the boy's dependency and school avoidance, Professor Long and his student cotherapists decided that her attitudes and needs should be examined. Perhaps Mrs. Berg had to have Robert be fearful; at the very least, she put up with monumental disruption in her own life just to cater to Robert's wishes and anxieties.

The first few sessions in Professor Long's office were with Robert and his parents. The therapists asked each of them for their perspectives on what was going on and what might help the situation. Robert was fairly uncommunicative, looking frequently at his parents for help in answering even the simplest and most mundane questions, such as what his teacher's name was and how many pupils were in his class. The mother sighed a great deal during the sessions, occasionally weeping and declaring that she would lay her life down for Robert, would do anything "just to make my little boy happy." The father was distant in the sessions, seeming acutely uncomfortable about discussing things of an emotional nature. His was a very traditional marriage, and the raising of the children was entirely the mother's responsibility. In the case of Mrs. Berg, it became more and more clear that this was a responsibility she treasured and was reluctant to share with her husband, even though she complained now and then that he did not take enough of an interest in the children.

Two sessions were spent with Robert alone, and the therapists were pleasantly surprised at how loquacious and insightful he was when his parents were absent. He was able to express that he dreaded making a mistake at school, that he desperately needed the approval of his teacher even as he needed that of his mother, that "perfect" performance at school seemed to him the best and most reliable way to obtain this approbation, without which existence itself seemed doubtful. In Robert's eyes, entrance into college also depended very much on his work in second grade. The pressure this created made going to school a dreaded duty, an awesome task. At the same time, Robert expressed, albeit vaguely and unclearly, a sense that his mother was almost as anxious about his leaving her side as he was. Even when she pleaded with him to set out for school or to play in a friend's house on a Saturday morning, he somehow felt that she would rather he not do so. At the very least, he felt confused about what his mother actually wanted. Not wishing to disappoint her, the boy was made even more nervous by this ambiguity. He also wondered how she could be so accepting of his frequent vomiting and complaining. He experienced himself as a burdensome individual and found it hard to believe that she did not occasionally resent his "antics" as well. (Several weeks into therapy Robert got his mother to admit that, indeed, she had often been angry at him for his dependency and angry at herself as well for needing it.)

The student-therapist who saw Robert alone considered the boy intelligent enough to attempt some rational-emotive therapy with him (Ellis, 1962), so he engaged him in the following dialogue:

Therapist: Okay, Robert, can you tell me what makes you nervous when Ms. Zeiss returns the test papers?

Robert: I dunno . . . maybe it's because my grade won't be good.

Therapist: How good is good?

Robert (smiling sheepishly): Well . . . kind of like . . . uh . . . having everything right.

Therapist: That must be hard to do all the time.

Robert: Naw, not that hard, not if I think real well on the test.

Therapist: But can't it happen that you make a mistake?

Robert: Yup, I once did.

Therapist (restraining himself from laughing): Well, what happened?

Robert: I felt really awful when I saw my paper.

Therapist: What did the teacher say? Did she say anything to you as she handed it to you?

Robert: No, she kind of smiled. But I just knew she was disappointed in me. That's why she smiled.

Therapist: Is that the only reason she could have smiled?

Robert: Well. . . , yah, I think so.

Therapist: Okay, I'm going to play a little game with you about what we say to ourselves. Will you do it with me?

Robert (unenthusiastically): I guess so, if we have to.

Therapist: Well, I think it might help you. So let's give it a try. Let's pretend I'm your teacher, and I am smiling at you while I hand you a test that you made a mistake on. What I want you to do is talk out loud about whatever comes into your mind. You know, tell me what you are saying to yourself.

Robert: Isn't it nutty to talk to yourself?

Therapist: Nope, I do it all the time. Don't you?

Robert: Hmm, yah. But I didn't know if it was normal.

Therapist: Sure it is. Everyone does it. And the kind of stuff I'm learning from Professor Long shows me that what people talk about with themselves has a lot to do with how they feel. Does that make any sense to you, Robert?

Robert: Yah, I guess so.

Therapist (not wanting to push the issue): Okay, let's just see what comes up. (Pretends to hand Robert his test that has an error on it.).

Robert (forehead furrowed): Oy, I made a mistake. She thinks I'm a jerk, a dope. She doesn't like me anymore. I can't stand this.

Therapist: Hmm, that's heavy stuff, little friend. Is that what you'd really think to yourself?

Robert: Well, I think so. I give myself a hard time when I make a mistake, and I'm sure other people think I'm a jerk.

Therapist: Do *you* think other people are jerks when they make mistakes?

Robert: Well, sometimes I do. I mean, if you're careful about what you do, won't you always be right?

Therapist: I don't think so. I make lots of mistakes, but I don't think I'm a jerk for doing that. That's part of being a human being. Aren't you one of those? (Pokes Robert playfully in the ribs.)

Robert (laughs, in spite of himself): Yah, I guess so. I'm sure no angel!

Therapist: That would be kind of boring, don't you think?

Robert: I guess so.

Therapist: Listen, Robert. I think that the kind of hard time you give yourself when you make a mistake is what makes you feel bad. Ms. Zeiss's smile can't make you feel bad, can it?

Robert: No, I guess not.

Therapist: And even if she frowned at you, would that make you a total jerk? Wouldn't there be good things about you, like all the other things you do nicely? And how nice you are to other kids? And other stuff?

Robert: Well, I guess so.

Therapist: Let's try this. I'm going to pretend I'm your teacher again, giving you back that same test. This time instead of telling me what you'd usually think, I want you to try to tell yourself something that might make you not feel so bad. Can you try?

Robert: Okay. (Takes imaginary test paper from T.) Oy—I mean, oh. A mistake. Poo. I don't like making mistakes. Hmm. She's smiling at me. Maybe she likes me even though I made a mistake. Come to think of it, she always tells us kids that as long as we do our best, she isn't going to be disappointed or mad.

Therapist: How do you feel?

Robert: A little better, I guess. But I don't think I can do that at school.

Therapist: Well, we'll do lots of practice here, and you can try these new things out at school, and at home, and anywhere you like. And we can see how it works for you.

Such dialogues were repeated many times in the six sessions the graduate student-therapist had alone with Robert; they were also discussed in the conjoint family sessions with Robert's parents. It required a fair amount of explaining and "selling" for the parents to accept the viability of the approach. To no one's surprise, Mr. and Mrs. Berg found that their own self-talk bore similarities to that of their son.

In the family sessions the mother's needs and fears also came up for discussion. The professor and his cotherapist encouraged her to talk about how she felt on mornings that Robert left the house for school. At first insisting that she was grateful and delighted to have him out of the house, she slowly came to admit that her own anxieties would mount within minutes of Robert's departure. "What if he falls down? What if some bully picks on my little Robert? What if Robert begins to vomit—will he be okay? What if he gets upset by something the teacher says?" She began to muse about how she was getting herself worked up by dwelling on these remote negative possibilities. She also came to realize that there was an emptiness in her life at home. An intelligent woman, she had not attended college but, instead, married right out of high school and quickly became pregnant with Robert's older brother. Her home life was not terribly exciting; her husband worked long hours and played a very small role in household activities, including the rearing of his two sons. The marital relationship was impoverished, and Mrs. Berg lavished her considerable affection on her boys, especially little Robert who, "after all," needed extra love and affection.

After several sessions that included Robert, therefore, it was decided that the parents come without him to work on improving their communication with each other. There turned out to be a number of unresolved issues in their marriage, among them Mr. Berg's feelings of having let his family down by not earning as much money as he felt he should be earning, Mrs. Berg's guilt about having (in her eyes) deprived Mr. Berg of a more satisfying career by getting married early and beginning a family right away, and other problems that had developed over the years and underlay the remoteness each felt from the other.

Fortunately, these marital therapy sessions took place at the same time Robert began to show some significant improvement in school attendance. His mother was thus able to support Robert's leaving the house in the morning and endure not seeing him again until he returned home. The midmorning visits to the school yard seemed less necessary to Mrs. Berg as her relationship with her husband improved. She even began to go to his office several mornings a week to help out with some clerical chores, something that brought the two people together in a way that was new to each of them and rekindled some of the personal interest they used to have in each other.

An interesting development took place regarding Robert's love-hate attitudes toward his wealthy uncle. Prior to treatment, Mrs. Berg would complain periodically at dinner about the family's marginal financial picture. Mr. Berg's reaction would be to withdraw into sullen silence. Robert's anxieties would mount, fearing in some inchoate way that a disaster was about to befall the household. His reaction would quickly turn to anger at what was viewed to be an unfair attack on his father—anger, however, of which he was barely aware, so quickly was it avoided or repressed by his love for his mother. Yet, how could his beloved mother do anything so wrong as attack her husband? Somehow in Robert's young mind these feelings took the form of violent envy of his uncle's affluence tinged with resentment at the uncle and at his father as well. These revelations emerged at one of the closing individual sessions the boy had with the therapists in which his fears of failing at school were linked to the belief that he had to do well at this early stage of his education if he were to succeed financially later in life. Nondirective discussions helped the child elaborate on these concerns and see their origins more clearly. At the last therapy session, a conjoint one with Robert and his parents, each family member used the opportunity to talk openly about the financial worries each had been harboring for several years. Ironically, it turned out that Robert's father was doing a good deal better in his insurance business than the mother or Robert believed. Robert himself was becoming less anxious about his need to succeed in elementary school; the rational-emotive treatment seemed to have helped him view things in general as less serious and forbidding.

Two months after the initial contact with Professor Long, Robert was managing to attend school regularly, with only an occasional bout of nervousness in the morning. When he did report reluctance to leave for school, his mother matter-of-factly informed him that she would not be able to look after him at home because of a prior commitment, usually to go to Mr. Berg's office. Robert's father, on his part, made it a point not to leave for work until Robert had left for school, enabling him to support his wife in the firm decision that weekday mornings were a time for children to go to school and parents to begin their own activities. There was overall much less tension in the household as the parents' relationship improved; this improvement in emotional tone apparently lessened Robert's general anxiety level and helped him regard school as less threatening, even as inviting. Robert's brother, who had played little role in the treatment, proved to be very helpful in providing rewards to his younger brother, such as taking him to a nearby park on Friday afternoons after a week of regular school attendance.

DISCUSSION

Even though Robert sometimes felt that he was the only little boy with the kind of problem from which he had been suffering, school phobia is not uncommon, estimated at 17 per 1000 children per year (Kennedy, 1965). Unlike other childhood fears, school phobia does not have a good prognosis without intervention; it does not seem to be a problem that children grow out of. But the intervention itself does not have to be professional; many school phobic children get over the problem if they are somehow forced to attend school, regardless of their misery. Repeated exposures to school, as is the case with most fears, tend to extinguish the fear if nothing traumatic occurs during an exposure.

School phobia does not formally appear in *DSM-III*; it is discussed as one facet of the separation anxiety disorders which, in turn, are among the anxiety disorders of childhood or adolescence. The essential feature of separation anxiety disorder ". . . is a clinical picture in which the predominant disturbance is excessive anxiety on separation from major attachment figures or from home or other familiar surroundings" (p. 50). In a footnote, *DSM-III* does state that a pure school phobia is indicated when a child fears school whether in the company of a parent or not, but the implication is that most children who refuse to go to school are basically reluctant to leave a parent or other caretaker. The *DSM-III* description clearly characterizes Robert, who manifested reluctance to be away from his mother under various circumstances. School itself becomes a serious issue because (1) it is a regular event, and (2) it is expected that children go. Unlike staying overnight at a friend's house or going to a neighborhood party without one's mother, going to school is something that is to take place most weekdays, rain or shine.

The principal theories of the etiology of phobias come from psychoanalytic writers and from workers in the behavioral camp. Still accepted by psychoanalytically oriented clinicians is Freud's view that phobias are a defense against the anxiety produced by repressed id impulses. The anxiety linked to a particular id impulse is said to be displaced to an object or situation that has some symbolic connection to the impulse. By avoiding the phobic object, the person avoids dealing with repressed conflicts. Another way to state this is to say that neurotic anxiety—of which the fear of school is one example—is the fear of the disastrous consequences that are expected to follow if a previously punished and repressed id impulse is allowed expression. The therapeutic implication of this theory is that a direct approach to alleviating the fear should not be undertaken; that would leave the person defenseless against a terrifying confrontation with repressed id impulses. Instead, psychoanalytic treatment of phobias attempts to uncover the repressed conflicts gradually, helping the person examine them in the light of present-day reality. The person has to be taught not to fear his or her impulses.

A wide range of techniques, such as free association, dream analysis, and interpretation, is used by analysts. For a child like Robert, a clinician would probably employ play therapy. Children are usually less able and willing to express their concerns verbally to adults. The work of Klein (1932) and Anna Freud (1946) provides a vehicle to delve into the child's unconscious. A play therapy room is equipped with toys such as puppets, puzzles, sand and water, and rubber clowns. The child might be asked to arrange little dolls to represent dinnertime at home. The way the youngster does this is interpreted by the analytic clinician in an effort to understand what is really bothering the child. What little evidence is available on play therapy, however, does not find it to be notably effective (Barrett, Hampe, and Miller, 1978).

A particular treatment can be effective even if the etiological theory from which it arises lacks supporting evidence. That is, analytic play therapy could one day be found effective for some children's fears even if the analytic theory of the development of fears is found wanting. This distinction between etiology and treatment is important when we examine behavioral viewpoints on phobias because there is far more evidence supporting behavior therapy for eliminating phobias than there is evidence supporting the etiological views favored by behavioral workers.

It is widely assumed by behavioral theorists that phobias are acquired by classical conditioning, as seems to have happened in a well-known case by Watson and Rayner (1920). A young child, little Albert, was shown a white rat, to which he evidenced no signs of fear. Then a loud noise was created during several presentations of the animal. After five such associations between the rat and the frightening noise, Albert came to fear the creature.[1] In classical conditioning terms, the child acquired a conditioned response to a previously harmless stimulus, the conditioned stimulus, by virtue of its being paired with an intrinsically noxious event, the loud tone, or the unconditioned stimulus. Subsequent attempts (e.g., English, 1929) to replicate this notorious demonstration have not been successful, however, warranting considerable caution in believing that phobias usually develop in this manner.

A variation of straightforward classical conditioning might provide a better account of how phobias develop. Perhaps certain kinds of neutral stimuli are more likely than others to be conditioned to fear. That is, it may be that people are physiologically predisposed to acquire classically conditioned fear responses to certain types of events. This notion of preparedness was originally proposed by Garcia (Garcia, McGowan, and Green, 1972) to explain experimental findings that rats more readily associate visual stimuli with fear produced by electric shock and taste stimuli with nausea produced

[1]See Harris (1979) and Samelson (1980) for discussions of the limitations of this study and the curious role it has played in the development of learning models of phobias.

by radiation. In fact, the rats learned to avoid the taste of a particular food even if they became nauseated several hours after eating; by contrast, pairing food taste with pain from electric shock did not lead to a conditioned fear and avoidance of the food. Based on this research, Seligman (1971) has hypothesized that human beings may be "prepared" to acquire classically conditioned fear and avoidance to certain types of objects and situations. Consonant with this view is the finding that people tend to have phobias for animals such as cats and dogs, but not lambs. Moreover, few people are phobic about electrical outlets, even though they present greater dangers than do most domesticated animals. Some human experimental evidence lends support to this preparedness idea (Öhman, Erixon, and Löfberg, 1975). Perhaps this extension of learning theory will provide a fruitful link with the emphasis psychoanalytic theory places on the symbolic significance of phobias.

Another behavioral view hypothesizes that phobic reactions can be learned by imitating others. Laboratory research does confirm that a wide range of behaviors and emotions can be acquired through modeling (see Bandura, 1977) but, as with the classical conditioning view, there is a dearth of evidence that modeling accounts for the origins of most phobias. In Robert's case, for example, the therapists did not find instances of other school phobic children whom Robert knew; the youngster with whom he had the closest relationship, his older brother, seemed to be an unusually happy child, not one who could provide a model for fearfulness.

A third behavioral hypothesis concerns operant conditioning. Perhaps phobic avoidance is directly rewarded. For whatever reason, the child begins to shy away from school; this behavior is reinforced by the parents. There is suggestive evidence for this in Robert's case; his mother seemed to give in readily to Robert's pleas to remain by her side instead of setting out for school and, even when he made it to school, she would visit during recess, perhaps communicating to the boy that leaving the situation would be okay. But such an account does not explain the initial avoidances of school, nor does it help us understand the great fear that accompanies the avoidance of a school phobic child.

Despite the questions raised about these behavioral views on the development of phobia, behavior therapies based on these ideas have been found to be very successful in reducing or eliminating groundless fears (Wilson and O'Leary, 1980). The treatment described for Robert contains a number of elements that were combined to provide a broad-spectrum approach to the several facets of his problem.

School phobics often have other fears as well. Robert fit this description, too, although the concerns uncovered by the therapists focused on his extreme need for approval and perfection. Indeed, the judgment of the therapy team and clinical seminar was that Robert's fear of school had a great deal to do with his extreme sensitivity to criticism, his inordinate desire to do well and not to make mistakes in a setting that he had learned to construe as vital for his ultimate ability to be a success in life. Thus, while Robert experienced anxiety whenever he had to be away from a family figure, especially his mother, the therapists nonetheless attended to his fears of making mistakes in the belief that improvement here would complement other efforts to get him to attend school in a normal fashion.

The treatment undertaken individually with Robert was consistent with the need to expose him to what he feared and with the desirability of dealing with particular sensitivities that could be seen as contributing to the phobia—in Robert's case, the demands he placed on himself never to err. Exposure to school was accomplished by gradually bringing the boy into more and more contact with the school situation, initially while trying to reduce his anxiety (through the comforting presence of the therapist); in the later stages of treatment, when he seemed capable of actually approaching the school and remaining there on his own, attendance was treated more as an operant, reinforced by praise at home and from the therapist.

Robert's perfectionism was conceptualized as due to self-statements that informed him of how catastrophic it was to make a mistake. Following Ellis (1962), the therapist taught Robert to say different things to himself, along the lines of it not being so essential to perform flawlessly. Coupled with the graduated *in vivo* exposure regimen, Robert's fear and avoidance of school diminished steadily over the 2 months of intensive therapy.

The separation anxiety component of the phobia was not overlooked by the therapy team. Robert's extreme dependency on his mother seemed to be a major contributing factor to the avoidance of school and other "away-from-mother" situations. The initial interviews with Robert and his parents suggested that Mrs. Berg was, as it were, conspiring to keep Robert near her, both because of her own morbid fears of something dreadful befalling him and because he had become the center of her existence. Her relationship with her husband was found wanting, especially in honesty and depth of communication. Several sessions of training the two people to express their concerns and feelings to the other helped reestablish the intimacy that was once there and shifted the mother's attentions to someone other than Robert: to her husband and to herself. This seemed to help the boy in another way; he found it hard to believe that his mother did not resent his fearfulness at least a little, and her protestations that she would do "anything" for Robert's well-being were as suspicious to Robert as they were false to the mother herself. Her increased honesty with the boy helped solidify the gains in his attending school because she was better able to resist his pleas to stay at home with her; she now had other things to turn to and felt more justified than before in asserting her own needs. Fortunately for Robert, the satisfaction of those needs was inconsistent with Robert remaining at home any weekday he did not feel like going to school. Mrs. Berg's constant availability had, it seemed, undermined attempts by Robert to get himself to school.

A caution is in order vis-a-vis Mrs. Berg's role in her son's school phobia. For many years Mom has been the "villain" in theories of psychopathology (Davison and Neale, 1982). Either her overprotectiveness, as in the present case, or her neglect, as in the case of autistic children (Ferster, 1961), has been designated a major pathogenic factor, that is, a variable causing the disorder in question. In most instances the validity of the claim is impossible to evaluate; in some cases it is almost certainly untrue. Schizophrenia, in particular, is linked much more to a genetic predisposition than to any harm inflicted on the child by a parent.

And yet the way parents or primary caretakers deal with children is likely to be important, if not in the genesis of a disorder then at least in the course of the disorder. In Robert's case the therapists hypothesized that Mrs. Berg's own dependency on Robert and the exclusive focus he provided in her otherwise uninteresting life were reducing still further whatever inclination and capacity the boy had to make it to school. The reinforcement she provided for avoidance would be expected to help maintain the problem by diminishing Robert's opportunities to be exposed to the school situation. And whatever their theoretical differences, therapists and parents have for thousands of years recognized the need for people to face up to their fears if they hope to conquer them.

So the therapists realized that Mrs. Berg would have to change her reactions to Robert's early morning activities if therapy was to proceed. She would have to stop relenting when Robert pleaded with her to stay at home, and she would have to allow the student-therapist to apply some pressure as well as encouragement in getting the youngster out of the apartment and at least partway to school.

On the surface this seems to be a straightforward matter, but it is not. The graduated exposure regimen, as benign and gentle as it was, nonetheless required the child to urge himself on to do things that he would have preferred not to do; it would have been easier for him to fall back and stay at home. On some mornings the therapist did not easily get him to leave the house; the conduct of treatment seldom is as smooth as it sometimes seems in case reports. On one morning in particular Robert's mother tugged at the therapist's sleeve, her eyes moist, and whispered to him that Robert be allowed to remain at home "just this one time more." The therapist empathized with her pain but saw it as his professional responsibility to apply more pressure than the mother would. Not being as emotionally involved with the boy as the mother was, he was able to overlook the boy's pathetic and pained entreaties and nudge him out of the door. (It is not without good reason that most professionals avoid treating their own kin—there is such a thing as caring too much.)

There is a further moral to this story. Mental health workers, especially if they themselves have never raised children, must appreciate the torment a parent goes through when a child suffers, whether it is psychologically or physically. Children have fewer emotional resources than adults to cope with pain and difficulty. This vulnerability elicits protectiveness from adults, especially from parents, and considerable empathy and mature judgment are called for by therapists in deciding when to break those strong ties of dependency to urge the child to move forward even when that means he or she moves away from the parent.

When a child is referred for treatment, the impetus usually comes from an adult. This is natural; one can hardly expect a youngster to understand as well as an adult can that he or she needs professional assistance for a psychological problem. But this points out an issue for those working with childhood problems: the tendency for the child to be designated as the one having the problem and as the only family member in need of change. If the therapists in our case study had employed only a graduated exposure regime with Robert without involving the parents at all, Robert might have been rid of his school phobia. But, for reasons already stated, it seemed unlikely that attending only to Robert would have a positive outcome because the child was inevitably enmeshed in the parents' relationship to each other. The therapists therefore wisely considered how Mrs. Berg's marital problems might be influencing her dealings with Robert. On the assumption that she was unwittingly reinforcing the boy's school avoidance and that her doing so arose from her own excessive dependency on Robert for life satisfaction, Professor Long and his cotherapist helped her make beneficial changes in her marital relationship, the result being that she could focus on things other than her total absorption in and devotion to her younger son. It is conceivable that treatment could have been initiated by the parents for their marital problems, with Robert's phobia of school regarded as a secondary problem that would have been remedied by improving the relationship between mother and father. Here, too, however, some special attention to Robert, perhaps along the lines reported here, would probably have been needed.

In general terms, any therapy for a child usually must involve the child's caretakers, who are most often the parents. An adult's life is bound up with other people, but children are particularly intertwined with others; they are under more constant surveillance and are subject to more control by others than are most adults. To intervene only with a child, keeping the parents uninvolved in and even ignorant of the treatment, is not seen by most contemporary child clinicians as a prudent or productive course.

A case study, as has been mentioned, cannot provide scientifically acceptable evidence. Robert's school phobia was indeed eliminated during the 2 months of treatment, but it is not possible to know which aspect of the multifaceted therapy was most important or which was even superfluous. For example, the case reported by Lazarus, Davison, and Polefka (1965) emphasized the importance of graduated exposure to school, with little if any explicit attention paid to familial or marital factors or to the boy's self-talk as something in need of change. Would Robert have fared as well without the conjoint sessions? Like all clinicians, the professor and his students made the conservative judgment that family factors should be considered. Robert's mother seemed so very dependent on the boy—in some ways even more than Robert was dependent on her—that the concern was that she would undermine the attempts to help the boy leave home each morning. As much as she sincerely wished for Robert to attend school normally, his presence with her at home seemed so reinforcing to her that denying her that without helping her find some adequate substitute might have been poor clinical practice. But this was not a wealthy family, it should be remembered, and it was fortunate for them that Robert's problem was used as a teaching case for the graduate students in Professor Long's seminar. Over the 2 months of treatment, it was estimated that 25 hours of professional time were devoted to the Berg family; in many communities in the 1980s, this could cost upwards of $1500. Even with some assistance from health insurance, this expenditure might have been beyond this family's means.

17

BULIMIA

Gary Robbins, a 27-year-old white male, came to the county clinic in late October. He was somewhat sloppily dressed, but spoke well and quickly launched into a vivid description of his current problems. At the time Gary entered therapy, his life seemed to be coming apart at the seams. He was moderately depressed, low in self-esteem, and had even thought of suicide. During the first session, he explained that his most pressing problem was staying out of jail, a real enough threat considering the 20 or so bad checks he had written in the last few weeks. To cover these checks, Gary explained that he had taken several advances on his salary, had borrowed money from close family and friends, and had furthered his indebtedness by borrowing from high-interest, short-term lending institutions. All of this resulted in outstanding debts totaling $12,000. The possibility of borrowing additional funds to cover the checks was bleak.

Supermarket, restaurant, and fast-food purchases were responsible for Gary's financial predicament. During the course of a weekday, he would spend between $20 and $50 on groceries and prepared foods. On weekends the figure would rise to upward of $100 in a single day. Gary explained that these vast quantities of foodstuffs were quickly consumed, usually at home, but sometimes at restaurants or in his automobile. He was able to eat all of this food only by regurgitating several times during a "meal."

Further details concerning these gastronomical binges were discussed in later therapy sessions. On weekdays, trying to conserve money, Gary would not eat anything until lunchtime. Lunch might consist of a dozen MacDonald's hamburgers, five jumbo orders of french fries, four chocolate shakes, and several single-portion apple pies. If time permitted, Gary said that more enjoyable lunches were leisurely ones at "all you can eat" restaurants offering spreads of unlimited pastas, salad, fried fish, or chicken. These meals could easily last for 2 hours during which several whole pizza pies, many orders of fish or chicken, or plate upon plate of pasta were consumed. Several trips to the bathroom, during which he would vomit, allowed him to consume these vast quantities of food. Perhaps fortunately for Gary, although to his dismay, these "all you can eat" establishments recognized his voracious appetite; many banned him from partaking of their specials.

Gary usually left work about 6:00 P.M. On his way home, he would stop at a supermarket to buy his groceries for the evening. Ten pounds of potatoes, two quart jars of mayonnaise, several quarts of club soda, four heads of lettuce, bags of potato chips and pretzels, and bottles of salad dressing to accompany them was a routine shopping list for dinner. Once home at his one-bedroom apartment, located only a few miles from his office, Gary would spend as little time as possible transforming his raw groceries into edible fare. With the ingredients just described, the meal would consist of about 10 pounds of potato salad and many large bowls of green salad, accompanied by glasses of club soda to, as Gary explained, facilitate eating and vomiting. If potatoes were not purchased, several large boxes of rice or many loaves of bread might replace them. The volume of food was Gary's overriding concern.

With the television tuned to his favorite programs and surrounded by several of the day's newspapers, Gary would settle down to dinner in his living room. He reported that he ate rapidly and that satisfaction was not derived from the food's taste but, instead, from a sensation that was related to filling himself up. When too full to continue eating, he retired to his bathroom and regurgitated. The soda water and judicious selection of foods enabled him to do this easily; by the time Gary came to the clinic, he could vomit voluntarily without putting his finger down his throat. This binging and purging combination was repeated as often as necessary until all of the food was consumed. Occasionally, he would finish "too early" and would have to go out to buy more food. During the evening, Gary required from 5 to 15 trips to the bathroom, depending on the amount and type of food consumed.

This pattern of behavior was very distressing to Gary, not only because of the financial problems it was creating but also because it was associated with a sense of helplessness. Often, he would resolve to eat normally during the day but, when evening came, he would be unable to resist. His thoughts would turn more and more to food, and his desire to binge strengthened and became irresistible. Hunger did not seem to play a significant role in his binging. The urge to fill himself simply increased as evening approached.

As for his financial condition, Gary reported that weekends and paydays were especially costly periods for him. With a pocketful of money, he would forego preparing all his own meals and eat some of them at diners and restaurants instead. He would eat at several restaurants during a single evening and, although the tab was moderate at each place (about $10), stopping at five or six restaurants quickly ate into his paycheck. Weekends were also problematic because he had more time available. Binging could start before noon and continue well into the night. Gary said that on these all-day eating and purging sprees he would be left physically exhausted, to the point of falling asleep in front of the television with half-empty bowls and plates surrounding him.

Gary was employed as an electronics engineer in a large manufacturing firm specializing in aerospace navigation equipment. During his 6 years of employment, he had received two promotions, each with substantial salary increases, for his innovations in design and his devotion to the job. In later sessions Gary reported he often worked long hours on the job, coming in early and staying until quite late in the evening, to avoid eating. The engineering work that Gary did was on the solitary side; he was given an assignment and returned a finished design to his supervisor. Gary indicated that working alone was to his liking and that on occasions when a project required the collaboration of several design specialists, animosities between him and the group inevitably developed. Dr. Black, Gary's supervisor, had nonetheless taken a liking to Gary and had supported Gary's salary advances without question.

Gary's social life was almost nonexistent. There were very few single women working in his section at the firm, and he did not care to frequent bars and discos as a way of meeting people. He did not enjoy either loud music or alcohol. Although he did say he had a few casual male friends, he saw them infrequently. Besides working and eating, the only other waking activity that Gary engaged in regularly was swimming at a local YMCA. He swam with the same intensity that he applied to his job. His early morning swims were comprised of 85 laps of the olympic-size pool while he raced against the clock. He reported feeling deprived and angry with himself whenever he had an off day at the pool. Such disappointments usually led to an even longer and more intense eating binge later in the day.

Swimming was also a means of keeping fit and trim. Gary mentioned in several of the early therapy sessions that he had an intense fear of becoming overweight and flabby, although he was actually somewhat underweight for his height. He attributed his regurgitation to this fear and recognized that it created a serious threat to his physical health. Because meals were rarely eaten without subsequent regurgitation, Gary was satisfying very few of his body's nutritional needs. He occasionally ate a sandwich and kept it down, but this was not done on a regular basis. Frequent exposure of his upper digestive system to stomach acids was also a problem; he had stomachaches often. Because of his embarrassment about his binging, he had not consulted a physician recently.

SOCIAL HISTORY

Gary was raised in an affluent suburb of Chicago where his father was vice president of a large investment firm. His childhood was unremarkable. Gary said he got along fine with his two older sisters and had an "Okay" time growing up. Gary's mother was described as overprotective and stern. His father was rarely present due to frequent business trips and long hours at the office. Gary reported that his mother was obese and that she dieted frequently, lost weight, and then regained it. He recalled how his mother would often complain about her weight problem and warn her children about never becoming fat. All of the children in the Robbins family attended a prestigious private school; like his father, who had attended the school, Gary excelled academically.

Gary's history of vomiting and purging dated back to his high-school days. He was not able to remember specific events that triggered unusual eating behavior, but he clearly recalled an instance of overeating that occurred during the summer between his junior and senior high-school years. It happened the first time that Gary was away from home for an extended period at a summer camp for teenagers gifted in science. Camp activities included morning classes, followed by nature hikes in the early afternoon, more traditional recreational activities later in the afternoon, and movies or stargazing at night. It was hardly a fun-filled summer, but a highly competitive, intellectual atmosphere—one that he did not enjoy. In August, he recalled sneaking off to a small grocery store in town and buying 9 or 10 candy bars, finding a secluded spot in the woods, and consuming all of the candy. When asked why he did this, Gary admitted that it had puzzled him somewhat at the time but, since it did not do anyone harm and seemed to lift his spirits, he thought little of it.

Several months later, in his senior year, Gary recalled stuffing himself with pizza at a party held by one of his classmates. Because he was watching his weight for the swimming team and realized how fattening the pizza was, he reasoned that the simplest way to prevent weight gain was to induce vomiting. As soon as he returned home, he went to the bathroom, stuck his fingers down his throat, and regurgitated the food. He said he felt a bit disgusted with himself but that, after all, he had prevented weight gain. Gary found himself in the same situation several weeks later. Feeling stressed by college applications and all of the choices that entailed, he purchased five jumbo bags of potato chips one afternoon and ate them in his bedroom. Regurgitation was easier the second time, and Gary had few second thoughts about the episode. Soon he found himself regularly eating larger dinners to the point that his mother remarked about his "healthy" appetite, attributing it to her son's vigorous athletics. Gary now had a way of enjoying as much food as he liked without concern for his weight.

Gary was accepted to the engineering college of a prestigious Midwestern university several hundred miles from his home. Adjusting to college life presented some problems for him. Making new friends was somewhat difficult. For the first time he felt challenged by his course work. Initially, he binged very infrequently—most often when stressed in some way. However, during his first 2 years in college, his frequency of binging began to increase.

Two years later, when Gary was home from college during a midsemester break, Mrs. Robbins no longer felt that her son's appetite was healthy. During that 2-week period, Gary's mother noticed that her refrigerator was emptying out at a distressingly rapid rate. At first she thought it was friends whom Gary had over late in the evenings; by the end of his vacation, she suspected that something was wrong. When she asked him about the food, he denied overeating and tried to pass the blame off to his sisters and their boyfriends. Back at school, Gary was forced to limit his binging to weekends for financial reasons. He continued to have a few buddies from the swimming team, but he saw less of them on weekends because the binging was beginning to occupy all of his time. Although he limited his binging to several times per week, each binge involved the consumption of vast quantities of food. Between binges he watched his diet very carefully.

When he graduated *summa cum laude*, several engineering firms offered him responsible, high-paying jobs. He accepted one and began to work for a large engineering firm in Indianapolis. For the previous 9 months he had been dating a young woman, Glenda. In late May they decided to live together. With a new job to contend with and a life-style that did not afford him much privacy, Gary's eating habits were normal for several months. Indeed, he reported that he was hardly troubled by the desire to binge. However, as Glenda's and Gary's situation became more routine, his binging and vomiting slowly returned. He tried to eat when he was out of the house or when Glenda was not at home or asleep. But, like Gary's mother, Glenda soon noticed that after the weekly shopping the cupboard was bare in a matter of a few days.

Inevitably, Glenda discovered Gary's secret. He reported that at first she was disgusted and angry. But a few days later she became more sympathetic, and they both decided that he should seek help. Gary's visit to a psychiatrist that year was the first of many such professional consultations.

Ten sessions with a dynamically oriented psychiatrist who probed Gary's childhood, did not relieve the problem; in fact, it seemed to get out of hand during those months. Unable to accept Gary's "bizarre eating," Glenda left him.

Feeling depressed by Glenda's absence, Gary took solace in eating. His savings account was quickly depleted by his dietary excesses, and soon he was requesting advances from his employer. At first, these were forthcoming without question. After several months of advances, sensing his employer's suspicions, Gary sought help to stall what seemed to be impending financial ruin and embarrassment. He went to his physician and told him the entire story. A 3-week stay at a nearby private hospital was the result. To Gary's surprise, the hospital stay relieved many of the pressures resulting from his excessive spending. Going into the hospital with a "medical" problem seemed, in his mind, to provide an excuse for his borrowing; he was isolated from creditors, and his company-supplied insurance paid the bills. While in the hospital Gary was permitted to eat only three meals a day. Opportunities to acquire extra food (e.g., by visiting the hospital cafeteria and shops) were limited. His behavior after meals was carefully monitored to ensure that no vomiting was induced. Gary found that he could eat normally in the hospital, and that brightened his spirits. Life seemed considerably brighter when Gary left the hospital; he had high hopes of maintaining a regular eating routine. Within 15 days of discharge, however, Gary was back to binging and purging. This pattern of economic distress arising from bad checks at grocery stores, brief hospitalization to relieve pressure, and a temporary normalization of his eating had occurred three more times in the next 5 years.

CONCEPTUALIZATION AND TREATMENT

The first problem dealt with in therapy was eliminating the threat of imprisonment, which was imminent if Gary continued to write bad checks. Several supermarket chains had already hired collection agencies, and they were hounding Gary. Furthermore, all possibilities of borrowing money had been exhausted several months ago, so it was, Gary felt, a desperate situation. His therapist agreed that an immediate step should be taken to prevent further excessive spending and binging. An unusual primary intervention was implemented: Gary was to destroy his checkbook and to deposit his payroll check into an account that required both his and his therapist's signature for withdrawals. The intent of this move was obvious. If Gary had no checks or cash readily available to him, he would not be able to incur further indebtedness, thus reducing the likelihood of imprisonment.

The therapist did not view this intervention as a cure, but only as a means of creating an atmosphere where more traditional psychotherapeutic techniques could be effective. With some relief of the financial pressure, Gary's eating patterns might be modified to the point where he could manage his own finances. Within 2 weeks, Gary's daily spending was cut by approximately two-thirds, and he was able to make substantial payments to creditors and friends from whom he had borrowed money. These payments lifted Gary's spirits considerably, and the therapist felt more basic causes of the binging and purging pattern could be addressed.

There were several areas for possible intervention. Gary felt that even small amounts of food would make him fat. It was difficult for him to eat regular meals without vomiting because of his intense fear of becoming obese. Socially, Gary had withdrawn from all interpersonal contacts with the exception of on-the-job contact with co-workers. Eating had become his main source of reinforcement. Because he was almost always eating and purging in his apartment, it was also likely that those surroundings had acquired stimulus control properties that would make it difficult for him to avoid eating in that environment. Finally, over the past several years, Gary's self-esteem had waned markedly, and he had become more and more depressed. The therapist felt these problems could hinder progress in the other areas of intervention.

The therapist decided to begin by addressing Gary's irrational belief that if he ate regular meals he would become obese. Playing the "devil's advocate," the therapist agreed with Gary that eating regular meals would indeed lead to his being overweight; moreover, the therapist contended that eating only two regular meals a day could lead to overweight. Gary also agreed with this argument, thus confirming the presence of an irrational belief. The therapist went one step further. He suggested that eating a very small lunch and dinner would also lead to obesity. "Even if you ate a half grapefruit and small salad for lunch and a small piece of broiled fish and another small salad for dinner, you'd probably gain weight." Gary admitted that no one could possibly gain much weight on such a diet. With a foothold achieved, the therapist further cajoled Gary with extreme examples. Ultimately, he seemed to convince Gary that with reasonable eating one could maintain a trim figure.

To encourage social participation, Gary was given a specific plan for activities that involved meeting people. Community meetings, including town hearings and local political committees, religious groups, and organizations for the improvement of the environment were all discussed, with particular emphasis on how to make initial contact. During the session where these plans were discussed, the therapist and Gary role-played possible approaches to strangers at these meetings. Specifically, Gary played the part of a man or woman while the therapist demonstrated how to begin a conversation with the stranger. After several demonstrations, the roles were reversed, and Gary played himself attempting to start a conversation with a stranger, played by the therapist. After he adjusted to the initial anxiety of the situation, Gary quickly learned how to approach people. These social activities would not only encourage more social contacts and perhaps lessen his depression, but they would also keep Gary out of his apartment and cut down on his binging.

In order to break the almost automatic chain of events leading to binging, the therapist carefully examined Gary's actions during his free time: lunchtimes and evenings after work. He discovered that Gary had tremendous difficulty passing a grocery store or a fast-food restaurant without going in and buying something. New routes for coming home from work that did not have any markets or fast-food chains along the way were devised. Gary used them instead of his normal routes. The idea was, simply, to eliminate the temptation to stop.

Over the last few years, Gary's self-esteem had suffered markedly. He felt bad about harassing his family and friends for money. They in turn had come to treat him as an outcast. Gary also reported that he sometimes despised himself because his eating habits were disgusting and he felt out of control. After weekends of especially excessive binging, the therapist observed temporary changes in Gary's mood. He was much more subdued than usual, and his affect was depressed. During the previous financial crises, Gary mentioned that he had contemplated taking his life as a way out, but he had never made any concrete plans or attempted to do so. Considering the lack of positive, encouraging feedback that Gary's environment provided, it was not surprising that the therapist's genuine concern about Gary, expressed in his willingness to see Gary frequently and his warmth during sessions, had increased Gary's self-esteem.

Considerable progress in reducing Gary's eating was made in the first 2 months of therapy. His average daily expense was down to $7, and the amount of time spent binging and purging had been reduced by about 75%. Additionally, at least twice a week, Gary was attending a group concerned with preventing the opening of a local nuclear power station and had met several interesting people. He felt much better about himself because he no longer was borrowing money and because he was not binging as much.

Despite these positive changes, virtually all progress was eradicated in one weekend. Gary had been working for 17 months on the design of a component that was the heart of the navigational system for a new commercial airliner. On the Friday morning prior to the weekend, the company was notified that production of the airliner had been scrapped. All of Gary's efforts for the past 1½ years had been wasted. Gary left work at 1 P.M. and began a 3-day binge; during that time he wrote nearly $350 in bad checks. During his session with the therapist the following week, Gary said he wanted to stop therapy for an indefinite period while he "got himself together." The therapist's phone call to Gary several months later revealed that he had declared bankruptcy and was continuing to binge.

DISCUSSION

Gary's disorder, bulimia, is one of several eating disorders described in *DSM-III*'s major section on "Disorders Usually Arising During Childhood and Adolescence." The other eating disorders include:

1. Anorexia nervosa: an intense fear of becoming obese resulting in reduced intake of food and severe weight loss.
2. Pica: the persistent eating of nonnutritive substances in infancy.
3. Rumination disorder of infancy: the repeated regurgitation of food, resulting in weight loss.

The key to the diagnosis of bulimia is recurrent episodes of binge eating. Literally, bulimia means "ox hunger," or voracious appetite, but it now refers to binging. The binges typically involve eating high-calorie, easily ingested food, usually in secret. The binges end when abdominal pains become severe or when the person is interrupted. Vomiting frequently follows the binge, either terminating it or allowing further eating to take place. Bulimics are usually intensely concerned about their weight, which may show fairly dramatic fluctuations. They realize that their eating is abnormal but report that they cannot control themselves. Their inability to control their eating often leads to feelings of depression and low self-esteem.

Bulimia can occur either by itself, as in Gary's case, or as an accompanying symptom of anorexia nervosa. In anorexia nervosa, which begins in adolescence and is much more common in women than in men, the person severely restricts his or her food intake and loses a significant proportion of his or her body weight. In addition, anorexics show distorted attitudes toward eating, food, and weight. They may, for example, deny that anything is wrong, even when their emaciated state is obvious to everyone else. A distorted body image is common. Anorexics think that they are too fat, even though objective data indicate otherwise.

Some anorexics report that they have no appetite but, among anorexics with bulimic episodes, 69% report strong urges to eat. Somewhat more than 50% of anorexics also have bulimia. The frequency of binges and vomiting in these patients, however, is less than was true for Gary. Anorexics with bulimia differ in several ways from those without this feature. Before the onset of the disorder, bulimic patients are more likely to be overweight, and many of them report that their mothers were obese. Bulimics are also more likely to be depressed, to use alcohol and drugs, and to display impulsive behavior such as stealing (Casper et al., 1980; Garfinkel, Moldofsky, and Garner, 1980).

Russell (1979) has reported on the characteristics of a group of 30 patients with bulimia, collected over a 6½-year span. All patients were currently bulimic but *not* anorexic. Twenty-eight were women. Seventeen had previously had definite anorexia and another seven may have had a mild form of anorexia (e.g., moderate weight loss). Comparing Gary to Russell's figures clearly shows how unusual his problems were. First, he was male; second, he did not have anorexia before the onset of bulimia.

Russell's patients all met the common criteria for bulimia—episodes of binge eating followed by self-induced vomiting, laxative use, or both, and an intense fear of becoming fat. Vomiting was typically induced by sticking fingers or a toothbrush down the throat, although six patients had acquired the ability to vomit voluntarily. Thirteen patients were heavy laxative users (e.g., 12 to 20 tablets per day). The patients reported that they continually thought about food, even to the extent that their eating fantasies interfered with completing daily activities. Their dreams were often of food and eating! The patients reported that they did not eat to satisfy hunger. "It is not hunger. Hunger is a feeling of a gap inside of you. You eat something small to stop that feeling. I go on eating after I've satisfied that hunger. I want to keep eating till I feel full—it's the final limit—you can then eat no more" (pp. 434–435). The frequency of binging varied greatly in Russell's sample. Some patients would only do so every week or so, but others were more like Gary, with daily binging, particularly in the evening. Depressive symptoms were very common. Thirteen patients had moderate depression, as indicated by one or more of the following symptoms: severe, persistent gloom with suicidal ideas; minor suicidal gestures; irritability; and impairment of concentration. Another thirteen patients were so severely depressed that, in addition to their symptoms, they were either unable to work or cope with daily activities, had a serious suicide attempt, or had a course of electroconvulsive therapy.

Several serious physical complications may result from bulimia. The repeated vomiting can lead to potassium depletion which, in turn, can produce epilepsy. Urinary infections and kidney failure also occur in some patients.

On a theoretical level, bulimia is poorly understood. Two components of the disorder seem central, however. The first is the fear of becoming fat. Some psychoanalytic writers have proposed that eating disorders generally occur in people who fear sex and symbolically equate sex with eating.

Anorexia then is a symbolic means of avoiding pregnancy, and binging occurs when the repressed sexual urges can no longer be held in check. This account does not fit Gary well. The theory is meant to apply to women, who are much more likely than men to have eating disorders. Furthermore, Gary's relationship with Glenda did not indicate any serious conflicts over sex. In Gary's case, it may have been his mother's obesity that triggered his extreme concerns about being overweight.

But even with an understanding, albeit speculative, of Gary's fear of becoming fat, we still must account for his binging. What function did it serve for him? By his own report, it was not the taste of food that appealed to him. He was neither a gourmet nor a gourmand! Instead, Gary, like Russell's patients, reported that the feeling of fullness was what he desired. Several processes could be involved. First, Gary's early binges seemed, at least in part, to be stress related. Binging could have been established as a way of coping with stress. Second, his binging may have filled up a life that was devoid of many other pleasurable activities.

Little is known about the treatment of bulimia. Russell (1979) recommends hospitalization as an initial step, followed by psychotherapy. But no information is really available about exactly how the therapy should proceed. As in Gary's case, an attempt to change the bulimic's irrational beliefs about eating and weight gain may be a valuable area for intervention. Of even greater potential, however, would be a therapy based on an understanding of the functional significance of binging. Unfortunately, we do not understand exactly what the binge eating does for the bulimic.

Little information is available on the prognosis for bulimia. Anorexics with bulimia, however, have poorer prognoses than anorexics without this feature, suggesting that successful management of the disorder is difficult. Indeed, Gary's relapse seems similar to what often happens in the treatment of addictions. Marlatt and Gordon (1978) have noted that about 67% of alcoholics, smokers, and heroin addicts relapse within 90 days following the end of treatment. These relapses are precipitated by life stresses or social pressure to resume the old habit. A single violation of abstinence is usually sufficient to wipe out totally the treatment gains that had occurred. Marlatt and Gordon refer to this as the abstinence violation effect. They argue that when a person violates his or her commitment to abstinence, a state of dissonance is created between the behavior and the self-image of the person. This dissonance motivates attempts to reduce it, for example, by changing the self-image "I guess I haven't really recovered." Furthermore, the transgression is attributed to personal weakness and thus the person is likely to expect future failures.

This analysis seems highly relevant to Gary, who relapsed in a situation of stress and whose first binge reinstituted the full-blown pattern. Treatment, then, should include components to deal with relapse. Gary might have first been trained to recognize situations that could create pressure for him. Furthermore, he could have been given specific training in coping, either skills to handle problematic life situations or dealing with negative emotional states. Finally, he might have been told that relapse is likely, that it does not indicate that the treatment has failed or that he is a weak person. Within this framework, he could also have been instructed on how to cope with a single binge to reduce the likelihood that one abstinence violation would lead to a complete resumption of his old pattern.

18

DEPRESSION AND A SUICIDAL ATTEMPT IN AN OLDER ADULT

Helen Kay, age 73, had been found at 4:00 A.M. by a city policeman during his routine patrol of the beach near the amusement pier. She was huddled against a wooden piling, an empty pint of whisky in her left hand. He thought at first that she was dead, but she was still breathing, faintly. Hustling her into his car, he took her to the emergency room of the county hospital.

When they arrived, Mrs. Kay was mumbling incoherently to herself, occasionally jumping up to run wildly about the examining room. The physician in charge was tempted to administer a tranquilizer just to quiet her down but wisely refrained from doing so, given her state of apparent alcohol intoxication and his awareness of the ultrasensitivity many old people have to drugs.

Information gleaned later from acquaintances at the hotel she lived in provided the following picture of the previous 2 days. Mrs. Kay failed to show up in the dining room of the retirement hotel for breakfast on a Monday morning. The manager, careful about such incidents among his elderly clientele, sent one of the waiters upstairs to check on her; he returned 30 minutes later to report that Mrs. Kay had pulled him into her room with a frightened look on her face and then proceeded to scream at him: "I did what I could!" The waiter managed to extricate himself to report the situation to his boss, who went to her room himself. He had known Mrs. Kay since she took up residence a few months earlier and felt he could deal with her better, which indeed turned out to be the case. She refused to come downstairs to eat, but she did agree to eat the breakfast that was brought up to her room.

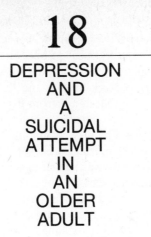

This incident was not totally unexpected. Over the preceding months Mrs. Kay had occasionally acted peculiarly, her moods shifting from elation one moment to utter lethargy and despondency the next. These mood swings seemed to be related to her shopping trips to a nearby liquor store. She had, in fact, begun to drink heavily and by herself in her room. The staff had come to expect verbal abuse from her within a few hours of her return from the store. On this particular morning, the manager noticed a strong odor of alcohol when he was persuading her to eat some breakfast; he concluded that she had been drinking earlier that morning.

Later that evening Mrs. Kay was herself again, sober and, unfortunately, very depressed. Despondency was not unheard of among other residents of the hotel, but Mrs. Kay's sadness had a morbidity and oppressiveness that worried and angered the other guests. For example, at dinner the same day, Mrs. Kay went on and on about her aching back and feet, her poor eyesight, and generally about the woes that God had inflicted on her as punishment. A woman sitting beside her walked only with the aid of a four-pointed cane, was almost completely blind, and was otherwise in poorer physical health as well as more problematic financial straits than Mrs. Kay—and exclaimed that to her angrily. Mrs. Kay's reaction was to sulk and brood even more, eventually excusing herself before dessert was served and retreating to her room to drink herself into a stupor once again.

The following morning saw a repeat of her refusal to come down for breakfast, but this time she also refused to open her door to the manager. A tray was left outside her door but remained untouched the rest of the morning. In the early afternoon Mrs. Kay was seen leaving the hotel and heading in the direction of the liquor store. Just before dinnertime, a couple from the hotel saw her walking morosely by herself in the park across the street from the hotel. Occasionally stopping to gaze at the ocean, with a liquor bottle dangling from one hand, she seemed altogether miserable. Their impulse to approach was suppressed by their expectation of verbal abuse from her.

Mrs. Kay did not return to her hotel that evening. Instead, at twilight, she unsteadily negotiated the wooden stairs leading down to the beach and walked along the water's edge until it grew dark. Suddenly chilled by the night ocean breezes, she found her way to the pier and settled herself against a piling to finish her bottle. Hours later she was discovered by the police officer.

SOCIAL HISTORY

Mrs. Kay had led an interesting and rewarding life. The daughter of a well-to-do family from the Midwest, she had grown up amid the warmth and friendliness of a small town. She was popular with peers and successful in school. Influenced by an English teacher in her junior year of high school, she applied to some private colleges in the East in addition to the nearby state university, where most of her classmates would go. At the end of her senior year she elected to attend Radcliffe.

Her years in Cambridge were pivotal for her. Although subject to the sexism taken for granted in the 1920s, she nonetheless learned to value her own intelligence and drive, deciding—to her family's dismay—that she would forge a career for herself after college instead of immediately marrying the law student who had proposed to her.

But it was not just her ambitiousness that characterized her college years. She found herself subject to occasional profound depressive episodes, some of them serious enough to have her roommates take her to the university health service. She declined to see a psychiatrist, believing in spite of her growing worldliness that "shrinks" were only for crazy people. She believed that she could, and should, deal with her moodiness on her own, and she somehow managed to do this. She excelled at Radcliffe socially and academically and easily obtained a position with a prestigious literary monthly in New York City immediately after graduation. Her law school beau, Harold Kay, visited her often. After his own graduation, he got a job with a good firm in New York City. Two years later they married.

The marriage was a generally happy one: three children, all of them bright and beautiful and ultimately successful in their respective careers and lives; two careers, not a common occurrence at that time; considerable income from both their jobs; and reasonably good physical health. Three years after they married, they moved to Los Angeles, where Mr. Kay had received an offer from a noted law firm, and Mrs. Kay an editorial position with a leading city newspaper. Trying during the days after Mrs. Kay's near death under the pier to understand how she could have come so close to drinking herself to death, her oldest son reflected on his mother's recurrent depressions and on the seemingly inordinate responsibility she took for anything bad that happened to her children or to her husband. The depressive episodes she had experienced since her husband's death a few years ago were not new, nor was the blame she heaped on herself for Harold's condition during his final years.

Mr. Kay retired from his lucrative law practice at 72 years of age. He had intended to continue working, slowing his pace only a little as he broke in a new young partner. But the morning cough and increasing forgetfulness thwarted those happy plans. A cancerous lung had to be removed, regrettably without halting the spread of the disease. His intellectual deterioration, diagnosed as senile dementia, progressed month after month. Mr. Kay became bedridden for the remaining 3 years of his life. His wife, devoted to him as ever, insisted against her children's wishes on looking after him at home. She rearranged furniture in their house so that she was seldom more than a few feet from his bedside. Her books, typewriter, and sewing machine were nestled into a corner of the master bedroom, and there was even a hotplate on the dresser so that she could make tea for the two of them without leaving the room. Her depressions were coming upon her more often now and with frightening intensity, accompanied by sleeplessness, poor appetite, and thoughts of suicide. Still, she nursed her ever-deteriorating husband.

Mrs. Kay began to notice her husband being less responsive than usual. In one horrible moment of insight she confessed to herself that he had no idea who she was or who he was. She had been warned of this occurrence in senile dementia; the brain wastes away inexorably and inevitably, and the worsening memory eventually obliterates the person's sense of identity. She was forced to realize that she was looking after a man whose resemblance to the person she had been married to for over 50 years was becoming more and more remote.

She hated herself for having these thoughts. Who knows what is going on in his mind, she would ask herself. Surely he needs and appreciates my personal care each day and night. Surely he will die if I let him go into a hospital. Family, friends, and Mr. Kay's own physician had been urging that decision on her for months, but she could not bear the image of his being lifted from bed to stretcher, and then to an ambulance, and then into a hospital corridor and, ultimately, into a strange bed in which he would be placed to die.

But that is exactly what happened. She was persuaded to allow his hospitalization on the basis of medical needs that the physician insisted, almost angrily now, could not be met at home. The dreaded scene of transfer to the hospital took place in a fashion eerily similar to her nightmare fantasy. One day later he died.

Although the death was hardly unanticipated, Mrs. Kay was devastated. At the funeral, she interrupted the minister's eulogy repeatedly with declamations of her responsibility for her husband's death. The other mourners, familiar with the actual circumstances of Mr. Kay's illness, shook their heads in sadness. At the gravesite, she had to be physically restrained from falling on top of the casket as it was lowered. Even though she insisted that she wanted to return to her home that evening, she was taken by her son to his home. He arranged in the following weeks to sell his parents' house and have his mother live with him and his family.

Her welcome into the five-bedroom house of her son was genuine. Mrs. Kay's daughter-in-law was a caring person. Even though the routine of her household had to be altered to accommodate the presence of another person, she was sincere in efforts to make her mother-in-law feel at home. But these efforts were largely unnoticed. The woman complained at meals every day of what a burden she was to the family, and no amount of reassurance changed her mind. Ironically, her very act of complaining was the most burdensome aspect of her living with them. She began, several months after her husband's death, to beseech her son to find her a place where she could live on her own; he reluctantly did so. Consulting with a social service agency, he was referred to several retirement hotels along a pleasant boulevard and across the street from a lush city park overlooking the ocean. There were palm trees and green grass all year round and many other older people living in the neighborhood. Mrs. Kay's good physical health and her favorable financial circumstances made entry into one of the hotels feasible. The social worker assured Mr. Kay that such a move was the best alternative for his mother. An inspection of the hotel by the entire family confirmed all of this. A week later Mrs. Kay moved some of her belongings into a spacious single room on the fourth floor of the Hotel Gregorian. A sign over the entrance read "A Retirement Hotel for the Active Retired."

At first Mrs. Kay did well in her new surroundings. The other residents were mostly widows like herself. A few couples who shared suites were the envy of the single women, even though many of the married folks scarcely seemed to speak to each other in the dining room or on the veranda that faced the ocean boulevard. A few women befriended Mrs. Kay, finding her to be an uncommonly intelligent and worldly woman, which she was. There were many stories to be told about going to college back East, working and living in New York City, traveling with her husband and, of course, about the wonders of children and grandchildren.

A few months after her arrival at the Gregorian, however, a change began to be noticed in Mrs. Kay by her new friends and acquaintances. She would sometimes come down to breakfast sullen and depressed. Deflecting inquiries about her health, she would eat quietly and then leave as soon as the meal was over, withdrawing to her room for most of the day and evening. But even more worrisome were her daily, almost furtive exits in the late afternoon, to return 30 minutes later with a small paper bag that seemed to contain a tall bottle. The strong odor of alcohol that one of the residents noted one day when she came to fetch Mrs. Kay for dinner confirmed the growing suspicion that she had begun drinking—heavily, regularly, and by herself.

And, indeed, she had. Never more than a social drinker, Mrs. Kay, during the long illness of her husband, had happened on the numbing effects of alcohol in her frantic efforts to ease her mind during the long vigils at his bedside. For several months she had sampled from his well-supplied liquor cabinet, steadily working her way from the front to the back. She had, almost symbolically, nearly completed the last bottle of liquor when Mr. Kay died. When she took up residence in the hotel, she had to learn a new skill—finding a liquor store and buying her own liquor. Unfortunately, she mastered the task readily.

CONCEPTUALIZATION AND TREATMENT

The first therapeutic task was to keep Mrs. Kay from dying. Her bizarre behavior in the emergency room of the hospital to which the police officer had taken her suggested an acute brain syndrome, or delirium, which is a reversible malfunction of the brain that can be caused by things such as overmedication, alcohol intoxication, and malnutrition; more details on this are provided later. The examining physician made this diagnosis because of Mrs. Kay's obvious state of alcohol intoxication and because of her age. Older people are particularly susceptible to delirium states. He also made the judgment that her diet might not have been adequate in recent days or weeks, given her disheveled appearance and the tendency for alcohol abuse and malnourishment to go together.

Her son's name and phone number were listed in her wallet; within a few hours he arrived at the hospital and was at his mother's bedside. Blaming himself for his mother's present state, Mr. Kay brooded over his stupidity and callousness at allowing her to leave the safety of his home some months ago. His first impulse was to take her home immediately, but the doctor cautioned him about the danger she was in and the need to restore her to a normal state of brain function through withdrawal from alcohol and a proper diet.

The hospital maintained a social service department, and the following day Mr. Kay and his wife spent an hour with a counselor to discuss the options for his mother. Mr. Kay believed that his mother needed close surveillance and round-the-clock care, which was not available at the retirement hotel. Surely she should move back with his family or enter a nursing home. The counselor, however, on the basis of the history Mr. Kay provided about his mother's recent and distant past, believed Mrs. Kay was capable of far more independent functioning than would be possible in either setting. She urged the son to consider not changing her living arrangement but to try to interest the woman in talking to a therapist on a regular basis while at the same time having a social worker visit her a few times a week to check on how she was doing. Mr. Kay reluctantly agreed to give it a try if his mother would agree to the plan.

Obtaining Mrs. Kay's agreement (in fact, talking about anything at all with her) proved impossible for the next few days. Not yet known to the family was her intent, as she left the hotel that evening with her bottle of scotch, to get as drunk as possible and then walk as far as she could into the nearby surf and drown herself. When she came to her senses several days later to find herself still alive, she experienced the kind of shame and guilt often felt by people who have made an unsuccessful suicide attempt. (This was not revealed until many weeks later, during a treatment session with her therapist.) After a week's time, however, Mrs. Kay was able to discuss things with the counselor and her son and agree to the plan. Its appeal for her, however, was that it avoided having to burden her son and his family again by returning to their home, and it seemed to offer another opportunity to attempt to kill herself at a later date.

Mrs. Kay's return to the Gregorian 2 weeks later was a happy, almost rambunctious event. The manager had planned a surprise welcome, complete with colored bunting and a large sign reading "Welcome back, Helen, we all love you." Mrs. Kay's reaction to this outpouring of affection was mixed. She wanted desperately to believe that she was really wanted and loved, yet she felt unworthy to receive such affection from her hotel friends. On balance, her response was positive because, in her own mind, it meant that even though she had left the hotel a suicidal drinker, she was able to come back for another chance.

Mrs. Kay's therapist was a woman in her late forties, recently graduated from a clinical psychology program that offered specialty training in gerontology. Dr. Gardner had received the usual training of a clinical psychologist and had devoted special study to the physical and psychological problems of older people. The initial session was spent getting acquainted, since the psychologist knew of Mrs. Kay's previous aversion to mental health workers and was accustomed generally to the difficulty many older clients have accepting the idea of talking with a stranger about emotional and personal issues. Her warmth and empathy, however, won Mrs. Kay over, and the woman began in the next session to recount her reasons for the suicide attempt.

As the story unfolded, Mrs. Kay initially liked the retirement hotel because she knew she was no longer "bothering" her son's family and, in a more positive vein, she enjoyed the privacy and increased feeling of independence. The other residents of the hotel, after all, were capable of getting around on their own; no one was blatantly senile, and they all shared some common experiences that could be discussed at meals and at odd hours in rocking chairs on the attractive veranda that looked out onto the oceanfront park. There was something nice about making a reference to the Great Depression without one's listener believing you were referring to the last time someone felt morose and despondent. However, after the initial positive period of a few weeks, her guilt about the death of her husband returned. It was only because he worked so hard all his life that she could now afford to live out her life in these comfortable surroundings; she made no mention of her own contributions to the family's estate. If she had not been so selfish and weak, he would not have been hospitalized and allowed to die, alone among strangers and without the nurturance that a wife should have been there to provide. What good had she really been to him, not only after he became seriously ill but even during the earlier years of their long marriage? What good was she to anybody? Her son's family found her an unwelcome burden, an ordeal to endure because she was a pitiable old woman who had lost her husband. Finally, what kind of person was she that she could not cope with the loss of her beloved husband? Weren't the other widows at the Gregorian managing on their own without the self-blame and hopelessness that tormented her in her waking hours and also during her fitful sleep?

Mrs. Kay had suffered a great loss. Selling her home to move in with her son's family could be expected to engender still further feelings that her life was getting out of her control. Reality, then, was providing some reason to feel helpless and therefore somewhat depressed. But the conclusions Mrs. Kay drew from the facts seemed exaggerated and distorted, suggesting the viability of a cognitive intervention modeled after Beck's work on the treatment of depression (Beck et al., 1979). Of importance also was the fact that Mrs. Kay had been subject to depression all her adult life, and inquiry into these earlier episodes revealed a similar pattern of illogical self-blame and unjustified self-depreciation.

The following transcript of part of one therapy session illustrates the kinds of discussions Dr. Gardner had with her client over a period of several months.

Dr. Gardner: We were talking last week about why your husband died.

Mrs. Kay (eyes cast downward): Yes, I was to blame for it.

Dr. Gardner: I understand you feel that way, Helen, but let's talk about other aspects of his illness some more. You said he'd had an operation 6 months earlier to remove a cancerous lung?

Mrs. Kay (sobbing): Yes. . . . The only reason he got cancer was because of me.

Dr. Gardner: What do you mean?

Mrs. Kay: He smoked a lot till he was almost 60. When we first met in Cambridge, he was smoking two packs a day. Camels, no less. Of course, in those days, the 1920s, no one worried about cancer from cigarettes. Still, I never liked it and told him so.

Dr. Gardner: You did? What was his reaction?

Mrs. Kay: He'd pat me on my fanny and tell me I was cute when I got angry. I guess these days you'd call that pretty sexist. (Almost smiling.)

Dr. Gardner: Yes, I would myself. But then, that was then. Tell me, was it your fault that he had begun smoking in the first place?

Mrs. Kay: Well, not really. . . . Well, I guess not, you see, he'd already been smoking for several years before we met.

Dr. Gardner: Okay, so you were not responsible for his taking up the habit.

Mrs. Kay: I don't see how I could have been. But certainly I could have made him stop.

Dr. Gardner: Tell me.

Mrs. Kay: What do you mean?

Dr. Gardner: Can you tell me how you could have made him stop? How did you fail him in those early parts of your relationship?

Mrs. Kay: Well, I didn't mean to say I failed him or anything. I just . . . well. . . . (Flustered.)

Dr. Gardner: Oh, sorry. I must have misunderstood. I thought I heard you say or at least imply that you were responsible for his smoking.

Mrs. Kay: I guess I did. I guess I have felt that way for a long time.

Dr. Gardner: Is it possible that *he* might have been the responsible one? Or is it possible that he was just addicted to the nicotine?

Mrs. Kay: Is that true? Do people get addicted?

Dr. Gardner: From what I have read, definitely. He might have been able to stop, but only with a lot of effort and pain.

Mrs. Kay: Yes, he tried many times. But it didn't work, somehow. He seemed able to do most anything he set out to do, but that smoking was something he never could handle. Or at least the price seemed too high to pay. You know, he'd be unable to sit still those first few days after stopping, his work went to hell, I mean bad, and he became almost like another person. Mr. Hyde, I used to call him, when he was trying to stop. The children, too, they called him that, and it did break the tension a little.

Dr. Gardner: So he tried, but he didn't make it.

Mrs. Kay: No. But he was a good man.

Dr. Gardner: Of course. I agree a person can be good and still fail at things.

Mrs. Kay: Now, doctor, are you making a point about *me*?

Dr. Gardner (smiling): Well, now that you mention it, I guess I am. But I'm saying something else, Helen, I'm. . . .

Mrs. Kay: I know, my dear. You're telling me that I'm not to blame for everything that's not right with my life, with my dear ones. But I've always been that way. My daddy always told me to look out for others. Jesus did that, you know.

Dr. Gardner: Yes, it's a nice thing to strive for. But it doesn't mean you have to succeed every time.

Mrs. Kay: No, I suppose not. But listen, we were talking about his death. He didn't want to leave our home. (Crying again now.) He wanted to stay, with me at his side. I *know* it.

Dr. Gardner: Helen, how do you know that? He hadn't talked to you for weeks.

Mrs. Kay: Yes, poor man. (Crying loudly now.) He didn't know where he was. He didn't even know me.

Dr. Gardner: Helen, even if he did, do you really think he wanted you to be with him all the time?

Mrs. Kay: Well, now that you ask, we did have some discussions when he was thinking clearly, about his going into a nursing home when it became too much for me, and. . . . (Falls silent.)

Dr. Gardner: And what?

Mrs. Kay (composing herself): . . . and he made me promise that when he didn't know me any more, I would do what the doctors said. And he knew they'd say he should go into a hospital, or something.

Dr. Gardner: Helen, he told you not to sacrifice yourself totally for him.

Mrs. Kay: Yes, dear man. (Crying loudly now.) He was too good to me.

Dr. Gardner: Tell me, Helen, how do you feel about what he said?

Mrs. Kay: What do you mean?

Dr. Gardner: I mean, well . . . did any of the other women at your hotel go through anything like this? You know, taking care of a sick husband at home, and having to let him go after a while.

Mrs. Kay: Yes, there's Mrs. Hancock, a lovely woman. Her husband had gotten senile like my Harold, and she just couldn't take it. She put him in a nursing home, and he seemed okay there. But she had a hard time finding a good one.

Dr. Gardner: Yes, I know, there are some crummy ones around. But good ones, too, and necessary when people need the kind of total care that your husband needed. But besides, it was his cancer, wasn't it? And it was the hospital that you had him admitted to, wasn't it?

Mrs. Kay: Yes, the doctor insisted on it. He said the only way to make him comfortable was to have him in the hospital. The drugs he needed were too powerful and dangerous for me to give to him.

Dr. Gardner: So, it doesn't seem a bad decision.

Mrs. Kay: But then he died the following day, doctor! (Almost shrieking now.)

Dr. Gardner: Oh, my dear Helen, don't you think he'd have died the following day in your house? What could have happened in the hospital to make him die sooner?

Mrs. Kay: Maybe it was just moving him.

Dr. Gardner (conceding to herself that this was a good point): Yes, maybe, but you can't be sure, and besides, didn't the doctor say his death was inevitable, and that the morphine he planned to begin administering would probably have dulled the pain only a little, that his whole body . . .

Mrs. Kay: Oh, please don't say that. (Crying.)

Dr. Gardner (remaining silent for a minute): Helen, I know this is hard to talk about, but you need to face it squarely. You need to look at what happened more objectively. It doesn't seem that anything more could have been done for your husband. You had a wonderful life together, and taking care of him at home gave you time to talk about things with him. But at the end he was gravely ill, and he might have been made more comfortable in the hospital if it wasn't his time to die soon after he got there.

Mrs. Kay: Yes, I can see that now. I see it. Do you really believe what you're saying?

Dr. Gardner: Helen, I'll not lie to you. You're not a perfect individual—who is?—but you were wonderful to your husband, and you did everything, no, you did *more* than could have been expected. You didn't kill him, Helen. (Smiling.) You don't have *that* much power!

Mrs. Kay (smiling): You're quite the joker, doctor. Yes, I'm going to think about that for a while.

People do not change their minds so easily, and Dr. Gardner was under no illusion of having convinced her client to stop blaming herself for her husband's death. But this discussion helped Mrs. Kay begin to consider other ways to construe what happened. Repeated examination over several sessions of her role in the course of her husband's illness did gradually lead Mrs. Kay to admit to herself that there were some things "even she" could not do, and that she could not reasonably blame herself for her husband's demise.

Because the heavy drinking seemed to be due to her depression, no specific treatment was undertaken for this aspect of her problem. Nevertheless, Mrs. Kay was provided with some factual information on how a temporary delirium state could be produced in an older person by excessive alcohol consumption. The psychologist also warned her about drug interactions.

There was a total of 30 therapy sessions. Dr. Gardner had assumed at the outset that she would have to have a number of conjoint sessions with the son and his wife as well. She changed her mind when Mrs. Kay showed progress in reconstruing her responsibility for her husband's death and began to view some negative events as caused by factors beyond her control. With Mrs. Kay's permission, the therapist telephoned the son after therapy had been going on for 1 month to assure him that things were proceeding well and to confirm the suitability of Mrs. Kay remaining in her hotel. The occasional visits by a social worker became less frequent. After 6 months, Mrs. Kay was reasonably comfortable and taking a more active interest than before in the many social functions available to older people in the surrounding community. She had also stopped drinking.

DISCUSSION

Until recently, older people have been neglected by mental health professionals. Even today, few training programs exist that pay adequate attention to the particular physical and psychological problems faced by people as they age. But interest has been growing, perhaps in recognition of the fact that the proportion of people 65 and older is growing steadily; estimated at 10% in 1970, it will rise as high as 15% by 2010, as compared to only 4% in 1900. Better health care, such as the widespread use of antibiotics, plays a central role in this change. As the numbers of senior citizens increase, so will their need and demand for adequate social services.

Old people face many reality problems: medical care that is expensive and often poorly suited to their needs; economic privation; vulnerability to crime; deteriorating health; and loss of friends and loved ones. They seem to have more than their share of woes, and they cope very well as a group. But they also have their full share of psychological problems, particularly depression, which is estimated to affect 25% of people over the age of 65 as compared to about 10% of younger individuals. Most of the depressive episodes among older people are recurrences from their earlier years, as was the case with Mrs. Kay, but some show up for the first time in old age (Gurland, 1976).

Life problems alone would not explain Mrs. Kay's depression; after all, most older people suffer losses *without* becoming profoundly depressed. The case material reveals a long tendency on her part to blame herself for negative events in her life and the lives of others close to her. She also insisted that she excel without help from others. In terms of Beck's theory of depression, the schema she was operating in was one of self-deprecation and self-blame (Beck, 1967). This cognitive structure led her to construe as her fault unfortunate events such as her husband's chronic cigarette smoking, his contracting lung cancer, and his dying in the hospital after her agreement to cease taking care of him at home. The therapy undertaken by the psychologist was aimed at uncovering these unspoken beliefs, examining them openly, considering their validity, and offering other, presumably more realistic, ways of regarding certain happenings in her life. This is a very intellectual therapy, relying on the ability and willingness of clients to understand the basic framework and accept it as applying to their own particular circumstances. Dr. Gardner no doubt saw Mrs. Kay as a promising candidate, considering her keen intelligence and solid educational background. One of the unanswered questions in Beck's approach is whether it applies to people whose abilities and general attitudes toward life do not so readily accommodate a highly intellectual approach.

People at risk for suicide are those who are physically ill, feel hopeless, are isolated from others or have lost loved ones, are in dire financial circumstances, and are depressed. Because these factors are found in abundance among older people, it should come as no surprise that suicide rates are higher for people over 65 than for younger individuals. Some estimate that suicide is three times more frequent in older people (Pfeiffer, 1977). The rate is especially high for white males, increasing steadily into the eighties. Butler and Lewis (1977) suggest that white males are particularly susceptible to suicide because they suffer an especially great loss in status, having held the greatest power and influence in societies like ours. What about women like Mrs. Kay? Suicide rates increase for white females until the age of 60 but then decrease thereafter; rates for nonwhite men and women in the Unites States fluctuate throughout the life span, with no clear patterns as they become old.

One statistic is particularly noteworthy. The ratio of unsuccessful to successful suicides is seven to one for people under 65, but two to one for those who are older. When older people decide to commit suicide, they are more likely to succeed, perhaps because of a greater resolve, perhaps because their bodies are more vulnerable to sleeping pills or falls. Older people also can "give up" and passively kill themselves more readily than younger individuals because life-threatening illnesses are more prevalent among them. Suicide among older adults may be the result of a rational and philosophical decision to stop living, such as when an elderly man decides that the intractable pain of his terminal illness is not worth the effort or the financial drain on his or his children's resources.

Intervention is similar to what is practiced with younger individuals: counseling to help the person consider nonlethal alternatives to desperate situations. Suicidologists hold that life itself is sacred; they are also mindful of the fact that many potential suicides are grateful afterward that they have another chance at life. Even in older people suicidal crises pass, as happened with Mrs. Kay, who did take advantage of a second chance. Cognitive therapy seemed to alleviate the depression viewed as the underlying cause of her attempted suicide.

The most obvious thing about an older person is his or her age. Physiological aging is an inexorable process, affecting all who make it through 60 or 70 years of existence. To be sure, certain cosmetic and medical measures can mitigate somewhat the biological effects of growing old, and there is many a 70-year-old in better physical condition than a 50-

year-old. But gravity is one's worst enemy. Things begin to sag and, in some measure, it is the way older people react to these and more serious physical changes that affect how psychologically sound they are in their later years. The heavy emphasis on youth in our culture does little to reassure most of us that life is worth living beyond one's thirties; the burden may rest especially heavily on women, who are devalued more than men as they grow old. The feminist movement of the 1960s and beyond has helped reduce the stigma of a woman's growing old but, like other things cultural, changes are slow in coming.

In contrast with psychological problems at the beginning of the life span, the problems of older people do not appear as such in *DSM-III*. Notice is taken here and there in the psychiatric nomenclature of the course of particular disorders, but the psychiatric profession has yet to confront aging itself as a major variable in mental and emotional disorders. The sole exception fits the prevalent stereotype that when an old person is unhappy or depressed or paranoid, it is somehow due to physical malfunctions. *DSM-III* does have a separate section on brain dysfunctions, and many of them are linked to diseases found among older people.

Only 5% of older adults have organic brain diseases. They fall into two broad categories: delirium or acute brain symdrome, and senile dementia, also called chronic brain syndrome. Delirium, a problem noted in Mrs. Kay when she was found under the pier by the policeman, is described by *DSM-III* as a "clouded state of consciousness" and is marked by hallucinations, problems focusing attention, and distortions of reality that are so florid that sometimes a diagnosis of schizophrenia is mistakenly made. These states are usually reversible if the underlying cause is temporary, self-limiting, or adequately treated. Brain tissue may malfunction because of a metabolic disturbance without being destroyed. Although it can happen at any age, delirium is especially frequent among older people, whose body chemistry is sensitive to drug effects, overdoses, and malnutrition. It is important for those who care for older people to understand delirium; if not treated, many such states can worsen, brain cells can be destroyed, and the person may actually die. The (unspoken) belief that old people do not get better may sometimes lead professionals to misdiagnose and regard a temporary delirium as the first sign of a progressive and irreversible brain disease.

Just such a disease, or group of diseases, does exist; it is referred to as senile dementia, or chronic brain syndrome. Behaviorally it is marked by a steady and gradual deterioration of intellectual abilities over several years. Memory problems are common, and abstract thinking suffers. Unlike delirium, there is actual destruction of brain cells from such causes as stroke and especially a disease similar to Alzheimer's, in which there is an atrophy or wasting away of cortical cells. Death usually follows within 2 to 4 years of onset. In addition to his cancer, Mr. Kay had suffered from senile dementia.

Brain disease is not a trivial problem for older people, but it accounts for only a tiny minority of the problems they have. Attention must therefore be focused on their psychological difficulties. One set of problems arises from decisions about caring for the person with senile dementia. In the last few years of her husband's life Mrs. Kay was faced with the challenge of nursing him at home. She persisted long after many caretakers would have given up and institutionalized the patient. But the cost is great, and Mrs. Kay did not profit from advice and counsel that is becoming more widely available from mental health workers with training in gerontology. For example, she did not have a nurse come regularly to her home, even though she could have easily afforded it. She gave herself no time off, and her own inordinately high standards for herself continued to take their toll after her husband died. She blamed herself so severely for his death that she almost committed suicide.

Unfortunately, her concern about nursing homes was well founded; even in the better ones patients receive the kind of care that fosters unnecessary dependency and even muscular and mental deterioration. Geared to maximum levels of custodial care, most nursing homes take a conservative approach. If a person needs a walker to get around alone, better to wheel the patient around in a wheelchair because it is faster and poses less risk of injury; if a person spills food but does manage to eat, better to feed that person because it is more efficient and keeps the place neater. Even with the best intentions, this kind of care does not benefit all residents. But worse still are the abuses that have come to light in recent years, ranging from major physical neglect and abuse to excessive billing and gross dishonesty.

Older adults have not been the beneficiaries of political and professional decisions to deinstitutionalize, that is, if at all possible, to maintain in community settings people who are psychologically disabled. Older people are overrepresented in state mental hospitals. When they are discharged, they often find their way to nursing homes, whose populations have doubled over the past 20 years as the numbers of people in mental hospitals have declined. It has been estimated that 80% of nursing home residents have mental health problems (Pfeiffer, 1977), but staff seldom are properly trained to deal with them. Furthermore, most nursing home residents do not require the level of custodial care provided in those settings (Kistin and Morris, 1972). However, for deinstitutionalization to do any good, adequate community-based services must be provided. Zarit (1980), a psychologist specializing in clinical problems of older adults, proposes principles that can foster the development of effective noninstitutional services to the elderly. First, there must be comprehensive community-based services such as the availability of individual and family therapy, telephone hotlines, regular and routine phone checks to see if any help is needed or desired, Meals-on-Wheels, and home visits by professionals to assess directly how things are progressing. The needs of the older person's family must also be considered; someone caring day and night for a bedridden individual can be expected to have mixed feelings and not just the unending patience and concern that we unreasonably expect of them. In addition, intervention should be the minimum necessary; sometimes less is better, especially with an older person, who may perceive an inability to do things easily done before as good reason to become overly dependent on others. Real needs must, of course, be attended to but, argues Zarit, one of those needs is to be an autonomous, responsible human being who is not gratuitously infantalized by helpers.

Mrs. Kay was lucky in many ways. Her son's family cared about her and remained willing to have her live with them. She had her physical health and was therefore less dependent on others for taking care of basic needs such as dressing herself, eating, shopping, and so forth. She also had money, unlike most older people, up to 33% of whom are believed to live below the poverty level and with little prospect of improvement (Schulz, 1976). As a woman, she entered her senior years with a sharp and active mind and a set of interests developed during her own professional career as a journalist. This made her interesting to be around and probably contributed to her popularity in her retirement hotel; the welcome she received when she was discharged from the hospital played no small role in her recovery.

Pessimism has been the rule in caring for the aged. Because they have relatively little time to live—relative, that is, to the mental health professionals whose responsibility it is to look after them—their psychological problems have received less emphasis than those of younger adults. And yet older people suffer from the entire range of psychological disorders—paranoia, anxiety and depression, hypochondriasis, insomnia, psychosis, and sexual dysfunction. The last set of problems may be due as much to ignorance as to anything else. Recent evidence confirms that older people can have satisfying sexual lives, the major difference being that things take longer to happen and, when they do happen, there is less urgency (Masters and Johnson, 1966). For example, a man in his seventies can usually have erections and climaxes, but the ejaculate is smaller in volume and comes forth under less pressure than when he was younger. A woman's vaginal walls lubricate less when she is older; widely available jellies can ameliorate this problem, and orgasms are still possible after she has ceased ovulating, that is, when she is postmenopausal.

Older people also have a set of problems that are more or less unique. People in their eighties have usually outlived their friends and spouses, and new social contacts are often not as easy to acquire as was the case with Mrs. Kay. As mentioned, physical losses can also be a heavy burden, especially when the society at large is geared to people whose reflexes are sharper and whose sensorimotor capacities are speedier and more acute. But evidence is accumulating that psychological interventions can make a positive impact on older people. What is needed now is a strong social commitment to study the ways people change as they age and to develop appropriate methods to help them adapt and continue growing. Failure to change our thinking and actions about the elderly will prove disadvantageous not only to them but to the older adults of tomorrow—*us*.

REFERENCES

Adams, W. A. The Negro patient in psychiatric treatment. *American Journal of Orthopsychiatry*, 1950, *20*, 305–310.

Akhtar, S., Wig, N. N., Varma, V. K., Pershad, D., & Verma, S. K. A phenomenological analysis of symptoms in obsessive-compulsive neurosis. *British Journal of Psychiatry*, 1975, *127*, 342–348.

Akiskal, H. S., & Puzantian, V. R. Psychotic forms of depression and mania. *Psychiatric Clinics of North America*, 1979, *2*, 419–439.

Alexander, F. *Psychosomatic medicine*. New York: Norton, 1950.

Allen, C. *A textbook of psychosexual disorders*. New York: Oxford University Press, 1969.

American Psychiatric Association. *Diagnostic and statistical manual of mental disorders* (DSM-I). Washington, D. C.: American Psychiatric Association, 1952.

American Psychiatric Association. *Diagnostic and statistical manual of mental disorders: Second edition* (DSM-II). Washington, D. C.: American Psychiatric Association, 1968.

American Psychiatric Association. *Diagnostic and statistical manual of mental disorders: Third edition* (DSM-III). Washington, D. C.: American Psychiatric Association, 1980.

Angst, J. *Zur Ätiologie und Nosologie endogener depressiver Psychosen*. Berlin: Springer Verlag, 1966.

Angst, J., Baastrup, P., Grof, P., Hippius, H., Poldinger, W., & Weis, P. The course of monopolar depression and bipolar psychoses. *Psychiatrica, Neurologica et Neurochirurgia*, 1973, *76*, 489–500.

Axline, V. *Play therapy*. Boston: Houghton Mifflin, 1947.

Baastrup, P. D., & Schou, M. Lithium as a prophylactic agent against recurrent depressions and manic-depressive psychosis. *Archives of General Psychiatry*, 1967, *16*, 162–172.

Ban, T. A., & Lehmann, H. E. Nicotinic acid in the treatment of schizophrenia. *Canadian Mental Health Association, collaborative study—Progress Report I*. Toronto: CMHA, 1970.

Bandura, A. Self-efficacy: Toward a unifying theory of behavioral change. *Psychological Review*, 1977, *84*, 191–215.

Bandura, A. *Social learning theory*. Englewood Cliffs, N. J.: Prentice-Hall, 1977.

Barkley, R. A., & Cunningham, C. E. The effects of methylphenidate on the mother-child interactions of hyperactive children. *Archives of General Psychiatry*, 1979, *36*, 201–208.

Baron, M., Gershon, E. S., Rudy, V., Jonas, W. Z., & Buchsbaum, M. Lithium carbonate response in depression. *Archives of General Psychiatry*, 1975, *32*, 1107–1111.

Barrett, C. L., Hampe, E., & Miller, L. Research on psychotherapy with children. In S. L. Garfield & A. E. Bergin (Eds.), *Handbook of psychotherapy and behavior change: An empirical analysis* (2nd ed.). New York: Wiley, 1978.

Bartak, L., Rutter, M., & Cox, A. A comparative study of infantile autism and specific developmental language disorders. I. The children. *British Journal of Psychiatry*, 1975, *126*, 127–145.

Battle, E. S., & Lacey, B. A context for hyperactivity, over time. *Child Development*, 1972, *43*, 757–773.

Beck, A. T. *Depression: Causes and treatment*. Philadelphia: University of Pennsylvania Press, 1967.

Beck, A. T., Rush, A. J., Shaw, & Emery, G. *Cognitive therapy of depression*. New York: Guilford Press, 1979.

Bennet, I. *Delinquent and neurotic children*. London: Tavistock Publications, 1960.

Benson, H. *The relaxation response*. New York: William Morrow, 1975.

Bettleheim, B. *The empty fortress*. New York: The Free Press, 1967.

Bettleheim, B. Bringing up children. *Ladies Home Journal*, 1973, *90*, 28.

Bleuler, E. *Dementia praecox or the group of schizophrenias*. New York: International Universities Press, 1950 (originally published 1911).

Bratfos, O., & Haug, J. L. The course of manic-depressive psychosis: A follow-up investigation of 215 patients. *Acta Psychiatrica Scandinavica*, 1968, *44*, 89–112.

Brodie, H., & Leff, M. Bipolar depression: A comparative study of patient characteristics. *American Journal of Psychiatry*, 1971, *127*, 1086–1090.

Brown, G. W., Birley, J. L. T., & Wing, J. K. Influence of family life on the course of schizophrenic disorders: A replication. *British Journal of Psychiatry*, 1972, *121*, 241–258.

Brown, G. W., & Harris, T. *Social origins of depression: A study of psychiatric disorder in women*. New York: Free Press, 1978.

Buchwald, A. M. Depressive mood and estimates of reinforcement frequency. *Journal of Abnormal Psychology*, 1977, *86*, 443–446.

Bunney, W. E., Goodwin, F. K., & Murphy, D. L. The "switch process" in manic-depressive illness. *Archives of General Psychiatry*, 1972, *27*, 312–317.

Bunney, W. E., Murphy, D. L., Goodwin, F. K., & Borge, G. F. The switch process from depression to mania: Relationship to drugs which alter brain amines. *Lancet*, 1970, *1*, 1022–1027.

Butler, R. N., & Lewis, M. *Aging and mental health* (2nd ed.). St. Louis: Mosby, 1977.

Cade, J. F. J. Lithium salts in the treatment of psychotic excitement. *Medical Journal of Australia*, 1949, *36*, 349–352.

Cadoret, R. J. Psychopathology in adopted-away offspring of biologic parents with antisocial behavior. *Archives of General Psychiatry*, 1978, *35*, 176–184.

Caffey, E. M., Galbrecht, C. R., & Klett, C. J. Brief hospitalization and aftercare in the treatment of schizophrenia. *Archives of General Psychiatry*, 1971, *24*, 81–86.

Cameron, N. The paranoid pseudo-community revisited. *American Journal of Sociology*, 1959, *65*, 52–58.

Cantwell, D. P. Genetic studies of hyperactive children. In R. Fieve, D. Rosenthal, & H. Brill (Eds.), *Genetic research in psychiatry*. Baltimore: Johns Hopkins University Press, 1975.

Cantwell, D. P., Baker, L., & Rutter, M. Family factors. In M. Rutter & E. Schopler (Eds.), *Autism: A reappraisal of concepts and treatment*. New York: Plenum, 1978.

Carr, A. T. Compulsive neurosis: A review of the literature. *Psychological Bulletin*, 1974, *81*, 311–318.

Casper, R. C., Eckert, H. A., Halmi, S. C., Goldberg, S. C., & Davis, J. M. Bulimia. *Archives of General Psychiatry*, 1980, *37*, 1030–1035.

Churchill, D. W. Psychotic children and behavior modification. *American Journal of Psychiatry*, 1969, *125*, 1585–1590.

Clayton, P. J., Pitts, F. M., & Winokur, G. Affective disorder. IV. Mania. *Comprehensive Psychiatry*, 1965, *6*, 313–322.

Cleckley, H. E. *The mask of sanity*. St. Louis: Mosby, 1976.

Colby, K. M. *Artificial paranoia: A computer simulation of paranoid processes*. New York: Pergamon, 1975.

Colby, K. M. Apraisal of four psychological theories of paranoid phenomena. *Journal of Abnormal Psychology*, 1977, *86*, 54–59.

Cole, J. O. Phenothiazine treatment in acute schizophrenia. *Archives of General Psychiatry*, 1964, *10*, 246–261.

Cole, J. O., & Davis, J. M. Antipsychotic drugs. In L. Bellak & L. Loeb (Eds.), *The schizophrenic syndrome*. New York: Grune and Stratton, 1969.

Conners, C. K., Taylor, E., Meo, G., Kurtz, M., & Fournier, M. Magnesium pemoline and dextroamphetamine: A controlled study in children with minimal brain dysfunction. *Psychopharmacologia*, 1972, *26*, 331–336.

Cooper, J. E., Kendell, R. E., Gurland, B. J., Sharpe, L., Copeland, J. R. M., & Simon, R. *Psychiatric diagnosis in New York and London: A comparative study of mental hospital admissions*. New York: Oxford University Press, 1972.

Costello, C. G. Dissimilarities between conditioned avoidance responses and phobias. *Psychological Review*, 1970, *77*, 250–254.

Cowan, P. A., Hoddinott, G. A., & Wright, B. A. Compliance and resistance in the conditioning of autistic children: An exploratory study. *Child Development*, 1965, *36*, 913–923.

Cox, A., Rutter, M., Newman, S. & Bartak, L. A comparative study of autism and specific developmental language disorders. II. Parental characteristics. *British Journal of Psychiatry*, 1975, *126*, 145–159.

Coyne, J. C. Depression and the response of others. *Journal of Abnormal Psychology*, 1976, *85*, 186–193.

Crowe, R. R. An adoption study of antisocial personality. *Archives of General Psychiatry*, 1974, *31*, 785–791.

Davis, J. M. Overview: Maintenance therapy in psychiatry: II. Affective disorders. *American Journal of Psychiatry*, 1976, *133*, 1–13.

Davison, G. C. Elimination of a sadistic fantasy by a client-controlled counter-conditioning technique. *Journal of Abnormal Psychology*, 1968, *73*, 84–90.

Davison, G. C., & Neale, J. M. *Abnormal psychology: An experimental clinical approach.* (3rd Edition) New York: Wiley, 1982.

D'Elia, G., Lorentzson, S., Raotma, H., & Widepalm, K. Comparison of unilateral dominant and non-dominant ECT on verbal and non-verbal memory. *Acta Psychiatrica Scandinavica*, 1976, *53*, 85–94.

Delora, J. S., and Warren, C. A. *Understanding sexual interaction.* Boston: Houghton Mifflin, 1977.

DeMyer, M. K., Pontius, W., Norton, J. A., Barton, S., Allen, J., & Steele, R. Parental practices and innate activity in normal, autistic and brain-damaged infants. *Journal of Autism and Childhood Schizophrenia*, 1972, *2*, 49–66.

Denhoff, E. The natural history of children with minimal brain dysfunction. *Annals of the New York Academy of Sciences*, 1973, *205*, 188–205.

Deniker, P. Introduction of neuroleptic chemotherapy into psychiatry. In F. J. Ayd and B. Blackwell (Eds.), *Discoveries in biological psychiatry.* Philadelphia: Lippincott, 1970.

Depue, R. A., & Monroe, S. M. The unipolar-bipolar distinction in the depressive disorders. *Psychological Bulletin*, 1978, *85*, 1001–1029.

Dohrenwend, B. P., & Dohrenwend, B. S. Social and cultural influences on psychopathology. In M. R. Rosenzweig and L. W. Porter (Eds.), *Annual Review of Psychology.* Palo Alto, Calif.: Annual Reviews, 1974.

Egan, G. *The skilled helper.* Monterey, Calif.: Brooks/Cole, 1975.

Eisenberg, L., & Kanner, L. Early infantile autism. *American Journal of Orthopsychiatry*, 1956, *26*, 556–566.

Ellis, A. *Reason and emotion in psychotherapy.* New York: Lyle Stuart, 1962.

English, H. B. Three cases of the "conditioned fear response." *Journal of Abnormal and Social Psychology*, 1929, *34*, 221–225.

Epstein, A. W. Relationship of fetishism and transvestism to brain and particularly to temporal lobe dysfunction. *Journal of Nervous and Mental Disease*, 1961, *133*, 247–253.

Epstein, S. The stability of behavior: I. On predicting most of the people much of the time. *Journal of Personality and Social Psychology*, 1979, *37*, 1097–1126.

Feingold, B. F. *Introduction to clinical allergy.* Springfield, Ill.: Charles C Thomas, 1973.

Fenichel, O. *The psychoanalytic theory of neuroses.* New York: Norton, 1945.

Ferster, C. B. Positive reinforcement and behavior deficits in autistic children. *Child Development*, 1961, *32*, 437–456.

Fink, M. Myths of "shock therapy." *American Journal of Psychiatry*, 1977, *134*, 991–996.

Fischer, M. Genetic and environmental factors in schizophrenia: A study of schizophrenic twins and their families. *Acta Psychiatrica Scandinavica*, Suppl. 238, 1973.

Folstein, S., & Rutter, M. A twin study of individuals with infantile autism. In M. Rutter & E. Schopler (Eds.), *Autism: A reappraisal of concepts and treatment.* New York: Plenum, 1978.

Fontana, A. F. Familial etiology of schizophrenia: Is a scientific methodology possible? *Psychological Bulletin*, 1966, *66*, 214–227.

Freud, A. *The psychoanalytic treatment of children: Lectures and essays.* London: Imago, 1946.

Freud, S. Mourning and melancholia. In *Sigmund Freud, Collected Papers, Volume IV* (translated by Alix and James Strachey). London: The Hogarth Press, 1925 (first published in *Zietschrift*, 1917).

Freud, S. Notes upon a case of obsessional neurosis. In *Sigmund Freud, Collected Papers, Volume III* (translated by Alix and James Strachey). London: The Hogarth Press, 1925 (originally published in *Jahrbuch für psychoanalytische und psychopathologische Forschungen*, 1909).

Freud, S. Psycho-analytic notes upon an autobiographical account of a case of paranoia (dementia paranoides). In *Sigmund Freud, Collected Papers, Volume III* (translated by Alix and James Strachey). London: The Hogarth Press, 1925 (first published in *Jahrbuch für psychoanalytische und psychopathologische Forschungen*, 1911).

Freud, S. Fetishism. *International Journal of Psychoanalysis*, 1928, *9*, 161–166.

Friedberg, J. Shock treatment, brain damage, and memory loss: A neurological perspective. *American Journal of Psychiatry*, 1977, *134*, 1010–1014.

Garcia, J., McGowan, B. K., & Green, K. F. Biological constraints on conditioning. In A. H. Black & W. F. Prokasy (Eds.), *Classical conditioning, II: Current research and theory.* New York: Appleton-Century-Crofts, 1972.

Gardner, L. H. The therapeutic relationship under varying conditions of race. *Psychotherapy: Theory, Research, and Practice*, 1971, *8*, 78–87.

Garfinkel, P. E., Moldofsky, H., & Gardner, D. M. The heterogeneity of anorexia nervosa. *Archives of General Psychiatry*, 1980, *37*, 1036–1040.

Geer, J. H., Davison, G. C., & Gatchel, R. I. Reduction of stress in humans through nonveridical perceived control of aversive stimulation. *Journal of Personality and Social Psychology*, 1970, *16*, 731–738.

Gershon, E. S., Bunney, W. E., Jr., Leckman, J. F., Van Eerdewegh, M., & DeBauche, B. A. The inheritance of affective disorders: A review of data and of hypotheses. *Behavior Genetics*, 1976, *6*, 227–259.

Gittelman-Klein, R., Klein, D. F., Abikoff, H., Katz, S., Gloisten, A. C., & Kates, W. Relative efficiency of methylphenidate and behavior modification in hyperkinetic children: An interim report. *Journal of Abnormal Child Psychology*, 1976, *4*, 362–379.

Goldfried, M. R., Decenteceo, E. T., & Weinberg, L. Systematic rational restructuring as a self-control technique. *Behavior Therapy*, 1974, *5*, 247–254.

Goodwin, D. W., Guze, S. B., & Robins, E. Follow-up studies in obsessional neurosis. *Archives of General Psychiatry*, 1969, *20*, 182–187.

Gottesman, I. I., & Shields, J. *Schizophrenia and genetics: A twin study vantage point*. New York: Academic Press, 1972.

Gottesman, I. I., & Shields, J. A critical review of recent adoption, twin and family studies of schizophrenia: Behavioral genetics perspectives. *Schizophrenia Bulletin*, 1976, *2*, 360–398.

Goyette, C. H., & Conners, C. K. *Food additives and hyperactivity*. Paper presented at the 85th annual convention of the American Psychological Association, 1977.

Grace, W. J., & Graham, D. T. Relationship of specific attitudes and emotions to certain bodily diseases. *Psychosomatic Medicine*, 1952, *14*, 243–251.

Greenspan, K., Schildkraut, J. J., Gordon, E. K., Baer, L., Aronoff, M., & Durell, J. Catecholamine metabolism in affective disorders: III. MHPG and other catecholamine metabolites in patients treated with lithium carbonate. *Journal of Psychiatric Research*, 1970, *1*, 171–183.

Gross, M. B., & Wilson, W. C. *Minimal brain dysfunction*. New York: Brunner/Mazel, 1974.

Group for the Advancement of Psychiatry, Committee on Therapy. *Shock therapy: Report 1*. Topeka, Kans.: GAP, 1947.

Gurland, B. J. The comparative frequency of depression in various adult age groups. *Journal of Gerontology*, 1976, *31*, 283–292.

Hall, K. S., Dunner, D. L., Zeller, G. & Fieve, R. R. Bipolar illness: A prospective study of life events. *Comprehensive Psychiatry*, 1977, *18*, 497–502.

Hallam, R. S. Agoraphobia: A critical review of the concept. *British Journal of Psychiatry*, 1978, *133*, 314–319.

Harburg, E., Erfurt, J. C., Hauenstein, L. S., Chape, C., Schull, W. J., & Schork, M. A. Socioecological stress, suppressed hostility, skin color, and black-white male blood pressure: Detroit. *Psychosomatic Medicine*, 1973, *35*, 276–296.

Hare, R. D. Electrodermal and cardiovascular correlates of sociopathy. In R. D. Hare and D. Schalling (Eds.) *Psychopathic behavior: Approaches to research*. New York: Wiley, 1978.

Hare, R. D. Psychopathy and crime. In L. Otten (Ed.), *Colloquium on the correlates of crime and the determinants of criminal behavior*. McLeen Va.: The Mitre Corp., 1978.

Harris, B. Whatever happened to Little Albert? *American Psychologist*, 1979, *34*, 151–160.

Hawley, C., & Buckley, R. Food dyes and the hyperkinetic child. *Academic Therapy*, 1974, *10*, 27–32.

Hermelin, B., & O'Connor, N. Measures of occipital alpha rhythm in normal, subnormal, and autistic children. *British Journal of Psychiatry*, 1968, *114*, 603–610.

Heston, L. L. Psychiatric disorders in foster home reared children of schizophrenic mothers. *British Journal of Psychiatry*, 1966, *112*, 819–825.

Hewett, F. M. Teaching speech to an autistic child through operant conditioning. *American Journal of Orthopsychiatry*, 1965, *33*, 927–936.

Hodapp, V., Weyer, G., & Becker, J. Situational stereotypy in essential hypertension patients. *Journal of Psychosomatic Research*, 1975, *19*, 113–121.

Hodgson, R., & Rachman, S. The modification of compulsive behavior. In H. J. Eysenck (Ed.), *Case studies in behavior therapy*. London: Routledge and Kegan Paul, 1976.

Hogarty, G. E., Goldberg, S. C., Schooler, N. R., & the Collaborative Study Group. Drug and sociotherapy in the aftercare of schizophrenic patients: III. Adjustment of nonrelapsed patients. *Archives of General Psychiatry*, 1974, *31*, 609–618.

Hokanson, J. E., & Burgess, M. The effects of three types of aggression on vascular processes. *Journal of Abnormal and Social Psychology*, 1962, *65*, 446–449.

Hollister, L. E., Overall, J. E., Kimbell, I., & Pokorny, A. Specific indications for different classes of phenothiazines. *Archives of General Psychiatry*, 1974, *30*, 94-99.

Horney, K. *Neurosis and human growth*. New York: Norton, 1950.

Hoy, E., Weiss, G., Minde, K., & Cohen, N. The hyperactive child of adolescence: Cognitive, emotional and social functioning. *Journal of Abnormal Child Psychology*, 1978, *6*, 311-325.

Huessy, H. R., Metoyer, M., & Townsend, M. 8- to 10-year follow-up of 84 children treated for behavioral disorder in rural Vermont. *Acta Paedopsychiatrica*, 1974, *40*, 230-235.

Hutt, C., Hutt, S. J., Lee, D., & Ounsted, C. Arousal and childhood autism. *Nature*, 1964, *204*, 908-909.

Ingram, I. M. Obsessional illness in mental hospital patients. *Journal of Mental Science*, 1961, *107*, 382-402.

Jackson, A. M. Psychotherapy: Factors associated with the race of the therapist. *Psychotherapy: Theory, Research, and Practice*, 1973, *10*, 273-277.

Jackson, D. D. A critique of the literature on the genetics of schizophrenia. In D. D. Jackson (Ed.), *The etiology of schizophrenia*. New York: Basic Books, 1960.

Jacobson, E. *Progressive relaxation*. Chicago: University of Chicago Press, 1938.

Kanner, L. Autistic disturbances of affective contact. *Nervous Child*, 1943, *2* 217-250.

Kanner, L. Follow-up of eleven autistic children originally reported in 1943. In L. Kanner (Ed.), *Childhood psychosis: Initial studies and new insights*. Washington, D. C.: Winston/Wiley, 1973.

Kanner, L., & Eisenberg, L. Notes on the follow-up studies of autistic children. In P. Hoch & J. Zubin (Eds.), *Psychopathology of childhood*. New York: Grune and Stratton, 1955.

Kantorovich, N. V. An attempt at associative-reflex therapy in alcoholism. *Psychological Abstracts*, 1930, *4*, 493.

Kardiner, A., & Ovesey, L. *The mark of oppression*. New York: Norton, 1951.

Kaplan, H. S. *The new sex therapy: Active treatment of sexual dysfunctions*. New York: Brunner/Mazel, 1974.

Kaplan, H. S. *Disorders of sexual desire and other new concepts and techniques in sex therapy*. New York: Brunner/Mazel, 1979.

Karlsson, J. L. *The biologic basis of schizophrenia.* Springfield, Ill.: Charles C Thomas, 1966.

Karpman, B. *The sexual offender and his offenses.* New York: Julian Press, 1954.

Kasl, S. V., & Cobb, S. Blood pressure changes in men undergoing job loss: A preliminary report. *Psychosomatic Medicine*, 1970, *6*, 95–106.

Kennedy, J. A. Problems posed in the analysis of Negro patients. *Psychiatry*, 1952, *15*, 313–327.

Kennedy, W. A. School phobia: Rapid treatment of 50 cases. *Journal of Abnormal Psychology*, 1965, *70*, 285–289.

Kety, S. S. From rationalization to reason. *American Journal of Psychiatry*, 1974, *131*, 957–963.

Kistin, H., & Morris, R. Alternatives to institutional care for the elderly and disabled. *Gerontologist*, 1972, *12*, 139–142.

Klein, M. *The psychoanalysis of children.* London: Hogarth Press, 1932.

Kohn, M. L. Social class and schizophrenia: A critical review. In D. Rosenthal & S. S. Kety (Eds.), *The transmission of schizophrenia.* Oxford: Pergamon, 1968.

Kolvin, I. Psychosis in childhood—a comparative study. In M. Rutter (Ed.), *Infantile autism: Concepts, characteristics and treatment.* London: Churchill-Livingstone, 1971.

Kraepelin, E. *Dementia praecox and paraphrenia* (R. M. Barclay, trans.). Huntington, N. Y.: Krieger, 1971 (originally published, 1919).

Kringlen, E. Natural history of obsessional neurosis. *Seminars in Psychiatry*, 1970, *2*, 403–419.

Lane, E. A., & Albee, G. W. Early childhood intellectual differences between schizophrenic adults and their siblings. *Journal of Abnormal and Social Psychology*, 1964, *68*, 193–195.

Lane, E. A. & Albee, G. W. Childhood intellectual differences between schizophrenic adults and their siblings. *American Journal of Orthopsychiatry*, 1965, *35*, 747–753.

Lazarus, A. A., & Davison, G. C. Clinical innovation in research and practice. In A. E. Bergin & S. L. Garfield (Eds.), *Handbook of psychotherapy and behavior change: An empirical analysis.* New York: Wiley, 1971.

Lazarus, A. A., Davison, G. C., & Polefka, D. Classical and operant factors in the treatment of a school phobia. *Journal of Abnormal Psychology*, 1965, *70*, 225–229.

Levenson, R. W., Sher, K. J., Grossman, L. M., Newman, J., & Newlin, D. B. Alcohol and stress response dampening: Pharmacological effects, expectancy, and tension reduction. *Journal of Abnormal Psychology*, 1980, *89*, 528–538.

Lewinsohn, P. M. A behavioral approach to depression. In R. J. Friedman & M. M. Katz (Eds.), *The psychology of depression: Contemporary theory and research*. Washington, D. C.: Winston–Wiley, 1974.

Lewinsohn, P. M., & Libet, J. Pleasant events, activity schedules, and depression. *Journal of Abnormal Psychology*, 1972, *79*, 291–295.

Lidz, T. *The origin and treatment of schizophrenic disorders*. New York: Basic Books, 1973.

Lidz, T., Cornelison, A., Fleck, S., & Terry, D. The intrafamilial environment of schizophrenic patients: II. Marital schism and marital skew. *American Journal of Psychiatry*, 1957, *114*, 241–248.

Liem, J. H. Effects of verbal communications of parents and children: A comparison of normal and schizophrenic families. *Journal of Consulting and Clinical Psychology*, 1974, *42*, 438–450.

Lion, J. R. Outpatient treatment of psychopaths. In W. H. Reid (Ed.), *The psychopath: A comprehensive study of antisocial disorders and behaviors*. New York: Brunner/Mazel, 1978.

Liss, J. L., Alpers, D., & Woodruff, R. A. The irritable colon syndrome and psychiatric illness. *Diseases of the Nervous System*, 1973, *34*, 151–157.

Locke, H. J., & Wallace, K. M. Short marital adjustment and prediction tests: Their reliability and validity. *Marriage and Family Living*, 1959, *21*, 251–255.

Lockyer, L., & Rutter, M. A five-to-fifteen-year follow-up of infantile psychosis. *British Journal of Psychiatry*, 1969, *115*, 865–882.

Lotter, V. Epidemiology of autistic conditions in young children. I. Prevalence. *Social Psychiatry*, 1966, *1*, 124–137.

Lotter, V. Factors related to outcome in autistic children. *Journal of Autism and Childhood Schizophrenia*, 1974, *4*, 263–277.

Lotter, V. Follow-up studies. In M. Rutter & E. Schopler (Eds.), *Autism: A reappraisal of concepts and treatment*. New York: Plenum, 1978.

Lovaas, O. I., Koegel, R., Simmons, J. O., & Long, J. S. Some generalization and follow-up measures on autistic children in behavior therapy. *Journal of Applied Behavior Analysis*, 1973, *6*, 131–166.

Lykken, D. T. A study of anxiety in the sociopathic personality. *Journal of Abnormal and Social Psychology*, 1957, *55*, 6–10.

MacCullouch, M. J., Williams, C., & Birtles, C. J. Successful application of aversion therapy to an adolescent exhibitionist. In C. Fischer & H. L. Gochros (Eds.), *Handbook of behavior therapy with sexual problems*. New York: Pergamon Press, 1977.

Mahler, M. On early infantile psychosis. The symbiotic and autistic syndromes. *Journal of the American Academy of Psychiatry*, 1965, *4*, 554–568.

Mandler, G. Anxiety. In D. L. Sills (Ed.), *International encyclopedia of the social sciences*. New York: Macmillan, 1966.

Mann, A. U. Psychiatric morbidity and hostility in hypertension. *Psychological Medicine*, 1977, *7*, 653–659.

Marks, I. M. New approaches to the treatment of obsessive-compulsive disorders. *Journal of Nervous and Mental Disease*, 1973, *156*, 420–426.

Marks, I. M., Hodgson, R., & Rachman, S. Treatment of chronic obsessive-compulsive neurosis by in-vivo exposure. *British Journal of Psychiatry*, 1975, *127*, 349–364.

Marks, I., & Lader, M. Anxiety states (anxiety neurosis): A review. *Journal of Nervous and Mental Disease*, 1973, *156*, 3–17.

Marlatt, G. A., Demming, B., & Reid, J. B. Loss of control drinking in alcoholics: An experimental analogue. *Journal of Abnormal Psychology*, 1973, *81*, 233–241.

Marlatt, G. A., & Gordon, J. R. *Determinants of relapse: Implications for the maintenance of behavior change*. Paper presented at the Tenth International Conference on Behavior Modification, Banff, Alberta, Canada, March 1978.

Masters, W. H., & Johnson, V. E. *Human sexual response*. Boston: Little, Brown, 1966.

Masters, W. H., & Johnson, V. E. *Human sexual inadequacy*. Boston: Little, Brown, 1970.

May, P. R. A., Tuma, A. H., Yale, C., Potepan, P., & Dixon, W. J. Schizophrenia—A follow-up study of results of treatment: II. Hospital stay over two to five years. *Archives of General Psychiatry*, 1976, *33*, 481–486.

May, P. R. A., Van Putten, T., Yale, C., Potepan, P., Jenden, D. J., Fairchild, M. D., Goldstein, M. J., & Dixon, W. J. Predicting individual responses to drug treatment in schizophrenia: A test dose model. *Journal of Nervous and Mental Disease*, 1976, *162*, 177–183.

McAdoo, W. G., & DeMyer, M. K. Personality characteristics of parents. In M. Rutter & E. Schopler (Eds.), *Autism: A reappraisal of concepts and treatment*. New York: Plenum, 1978.

McCord, W., & McCord, J. *The psychopath: An essay on the criminal mind*. New York: Van Nostrand Reinhold, 1964.

McGrath, S. D. Nicotinamide treatment: An addendum. *Schizophrenia Bulletin*, 1974, *1* (10), 5.

Meehl, P. E. *Manual for use with checklist of schizotypic signs*. Unpublished manuscript, University of Minnesota Medical School, Minneapolis, 1964.

Mendelson, J. H., Johnson, N., & Stewart, M. A. Hyperactive children as teenagers? A follow-up study. *Journal of Nervous and Mental Disease*, 1971, *153*, 273–279.

Mendlewicz, J. X-linkage of bipolar illness and the question of schizoaffective illness. In R. H. Belmaker & H. M. van Praag (Eds.), *Mania: An evolving concept*. Jamaica, N.Y.: Spectrum Publications, 1980.

Mendlewicz, J., & Fleiss, J. L. Linkage studies with x-chromosome markers in bipolar (manic-depressive) and unipolar (depressive) illnesses. *Biological Psychiatry*, 1974, *9*, 261–294.

Miller, N. E. Studies of fear as an acquirable drive: I. Fear as motivation and fear-reduction as reinforcement in the learning of new responses. *Journal of Experimental Psychology*, 1948, *38*, 89–101.

Miller, R. G., Palkes, H. S., & Stewart, M. A. Hyperactive children in suburban elementary schools. *Child Psychiatry and Human Development*, 1973, *4*, 121–127.

Mischel, W. *Personality and assessment*. New York: Wiley, 1968.

Mishler, E. G., & Waxler, N. E. *Interaction in families: An experimental study of family processes and schizophrenia*. New York: Wiley, 1968.

Mitchell-Heggs, N., Kelly, D., & Richardson, A. Stereotactic limbic leucotomy—A follow-up at 16 months. *British Journal of Psychiatry*, 1976, *128*, 226–240.

Mohr, J. W., Turner, R. E., & Jerry, M. B. *Pedophilia and exhibitionism*. Toronto: University of Toronto Press, 1964.

Morris, J. B., & Beck, A. T. The efficacy of antidepressant drugs. *Archives of General Psychiatry*, 1974, *30*, 667–674.

Morrison, J. R., & Stewart, M. A. A family study of the hyperactive child syndrome. *Biological Psychiatry*, 1971, *3*, 189–195.

Morrison, J. R., & Stewart, M. A. The psychiatric status of the legal families of adopted hyperactive children. *Archives of General Psychiatry*, 1973, *28*, 888–891.

Mowrer, O. H. On the dual nature of learning—A reinterpretation of "conditioning" and "problem-solving." *Harvard Educational Review*, 1947, *17*, 102–148.

Mowrer, O. H., & Viek, P. An experimental analogue of fear from a sense of helplessness. *Journal of Abnormal and Social Psychology*, 1948, *43*, 193–200.

Nathan, P. E., Titler, N. A., Lowenstein, L. W., Solomon, P., & Rossi, A. M. Behavioral analysis of chronic alcoholism. *Archives of General Psychiatry*, 1970, *22*, 419–430.

Noyes, R., Jr., Clancy, J., Hoenk, P. R., & Slymen, D. J. The prognosis of anxiety neurosis. *Archives of General Psychiatry*, 1980, *37*, 173–178.

Öhman, A., Erixon, G., & Löfberg, I. Phobias and preparedness: Phobic versus neutral pictures as conditioned stimuli for human autonomic responses. *Journal of Abnormal Psychology*, 1975, *84*, 41–45.

O'Leary, K. D. Pills or skills for hyperactive children? *Journal of Applied Behavior Analysis*, 1980, *13*, 191–204.

O'Leary, S. G., & Pelham, W. E. Behavior therapy and withdrawal of stimulant medication in hyperactive children. *Pediatrics*, 1978, *61*, 211–217.

Pasamanick, B., Rogers, M., & Lilienfeld, M. A. Pregnancy experience and the development of behavior disorder in children. *American Journal of Psychiatry*, 1956, *112*, 613–617.

Perris, C. A. A study of bipolar (manic-depressive) and unipolar recurrent depressive psychoses. *Acta Psychiatrica Scandinavica*, Suppl. 194, 1966.

Pfeiffer, E. Psychopathology and social pathology. In J. E. Birren & K. W. Schaie (Eds.), *Handbook of psychology and aging*. New York: Van Nostrand Reinhold, 1977.

Post, R. M., Kotin, J., Goodwin, F. K., & Gordon, E. K. Psychomotor activity and cerebrospinal fluid metabolites in affective illness. *American Journal of Psychiatry*, 1973, *129*, 67–72.

Quitkin, F., Rifkin, A., & Klein, D. F. Prophylaxis of affective disorders. *Archives of General Psychiatry*, 1976, *33*, 337–341.

Rachman, S. Sexual fetishism: An experimental analogue. *Psychological Record*, 1966, *16*, 293–296.

Rachman, S. The modification of obsessions: A new formulation. *Behavior Research and Therapy*, 1976, *14*, 437–443.

Reitz, W. E., & Keil, W. E. Behavioral treatment of an exhibitionist. In J. Fischer & H. L. Gochros (Eds.), *Handbook of behavior therapy with sexual problems*. New York: Pergamon Press, 1977.

Ricks, D. M. *The beginning of vocal communication in infants and autistic children*. Unpublished dissertation, University of London, 1972.

Rimland, B. *Infantile autism*. New York: Appleton-Century-Crofts, 1964.

Robins, L. N. *Deviant children grown up*. Baltimore: Williams and Wilkins, 1966.

Rosenhan, D. L. On being sane in insane places. *Science*, 1973, *179*, 250–258.

Rosenthal, D. *Genetic theory and abnormal behavior*. New York: McGraw-Hill, 1970.

Ross, A. O., & Nelson, R. Behavior therapy. In H. S. Quay & J. S. Werry, (Eds.), *Psychopathological disorders of childhood*. New York: Wiley, 1978.

Ross, D. M., & Ross, S. A. *Hyperactivity: Research, theory and action*. New York: Wiley, 1976.

Royal College of Psychiatrists. Memorandum on the use of electroconvulsive therapy. *British Journal of Psychiatry*, 1977, *131*, 261–272.

Russell, G. Bulimia nervosa: An ominous variant of anorexia nervosa. *Psychological Medicine*, 1979, *9*, 429–448.

Rutter, M. Prognosis: Psychotic children in adolescence and early adult life. In J. K. Wing (Ed.), *Childhood autism: Clinical, educational, and social aspects*. New York: Pergamon Press, 1966.

Rutter, M. Psychotic disorders in early childhood. In A. J. Cooper (Ed.), Recent developments in schizophrenia. *British Journal of Psychiatry*, Special Publication, *1*, 1967.

Rutter, M. The development of infantile autism. *Psychological Medicine*, 1974, *4*, 147–163.

Rutter, M., & Lockyer, L. A five-to-fifteen-year follow-up of infantile psychosis: I. Description of sample. *British Journal of Psychiatry*, 1967, *113*, 1169–1182.

Samelson, F. J. B. Watson's Little Albert, Cyril Burt's twins, and the need for a critical science. *American Psychologist*, 1980, *35*, 619–625.

Satterfield, J. H., Cantwell, D. P., Lesser, L. I., & Podosin, R. L. Psychophysiological studies of the hyperactive child. *American Journal of Psychiatry*, 1972, *128*, 1418–1424.

Schachter, S., & Latané, B. Crime, cognition and the autonomic nervous system. In D. Levine (Ed.), *Nebraska symposium on motivation* (Vol. 12). Lincoln: University of Nebraska Press, 1964.

Schain, R. J., & Reynard, C. L. Effects of a central stimulant drug (methylphenidate) in children with hyperactive behavior. *Pediatrics*, 1975, *55*, 709–716.

Schildkraut, J. J. The catecholamine hypothesis of affective disorders. *American Journal of Psychiatry*, 1965, *122*, 509–522.

Schlagenhauf, G. K., Tupin, J. P., & White, R. B. The use of lithium carbonate in the treatment of manic psychosis. *American Journal of Psychiatry*, 1966, *123*, 201–207.

Schneider, K. *Clinical psychopathology*. New York: Grune and Stratton, 1959.

Schou, M. Lithium in psychiatry—a review. In D. H. Effron (Ed.), *Psychopharmacology: A review of progress, 1957–1967*. PHS Pub. No. 1836. Washington, D. C., 1968.

Schou, M., Juel-Nielsen, N., Strömgren, E., & Voldby, H. The treatment of manic psychoses by the administration of lithium salts. *Journal of Neurology, Neurosurgery, and Psychiatry*, 1954, *17*, 250–260.

Schulsinger, F. Psychopathy: Heredity and environment. *International Journal of Mental Health*, 1972, *1*, 190–206.

Schulz, J. H. Income distribution and the aging. In R. H. Binstock and E. Shanas (Eds.), *Handbook of aging and the social sciences*. New York: Van Nostrand Reinhold, 1976.

Schwab, J. J., Fennell, E. B., & Warheit, G. J. The epidemiology of psychosomatic disorders. *Psychosomatics*, 1974, *15*, 88–93.

Seligman, M. E. P. Phobias and preparedness. *Behavior Therapy*, 1971, *2*, 307–320.

Semans, J. H. Premature ejaculation: A new approach. *Southern Medical Journal*, 1956, *49*, 353–357.

Shapiro, D., and Surwit, R. S. Biofeedback. In O. F. Pomerleau and J. P. Brady (Eds.), *Behavioral medicine: Theory and practice*. Baltimore: Williams and Wilkins, 1979.

Shevitz, S. A. Psychosurgery: Some current observations. *American Journal of Psychiatry*, 1976, *133*, 266–270.

Siegel, R. A. Probability of punishment and suppression of behavior in psychopathic and nonpsychopathic offenders. *Journal of Abnormal Psychology*, 1978, *87*, 514–522.

Singer, M., & Wynne, L. C. Differentiating characteristics of the parents of childhood schizophrenics, childhood neurotics, and young adult schizophrenics. *American Journal of Psychiatry*, 1963, *120*, 234–243.

Sobell, M. B., & Sobell, L. C. Second-year treatment outcome of alcoholics treated by individualized behavior therapy: Results. *Behavior Research and Therapy*, 1976, *14*, 195–215.

Solyom, L., Beck, P., Solyom, C., & Hugel, R. Some etiological factors in phobic neurosis. *Canadian Psychiatric Association Journal*, 1974, *19*, 69–78.

Snyder, S. H. *Madness and the brain*. New York: McGraw-Hill, 1974.

Sprague, R. L., Cohen, M., & Werry, J. S. *Normative data on the Conners Teacher Rating Scale and abbreviated scale*. Technical Report, Children's Research Center, University of Illinois, Urbana, 1974.

Squire, L. R., & Slater, P. C. Bilateral and unilateral ECT: Effects on verbal and nonverbal memory. *American Journal of Psychiatry*, 1978, *135*, 1316–1320.

Sroufe, L. A. Drug treatment of children with behavior problems. In F. Horowitz (Ed.), *Review of child development research*. Chicago: University of Chicago Press, 1975.

St. Clair, H. R. Psychiatric interview experience with Negroes. *American Journal of Psychiatry*, 1951, *108*, 113–119.

Stern, R. S., & Cobb, J. P. Phenomenology of obsessive-compulsive neurosis. *British Journal of Psychiatry*, 1978, *132*, 233–239.

Stewart, M. A., Pitts, F. N., Craig, A. G., & Dieruf, W. The hyperactive child syndrome. *American Journal of Orthopsychiatry*, 1966, *36*, 861–867.

Stone, L. J., & Hokanson, J. E. Arousal reduction via self-punitive behavior. *Journal of Personality and Social Psychology*, 1969, *12*, 72–79.

Strauss, J. S., & Carpenter, W. T. The prognosis of schizophrenia. In L. Bellak (Ed.), *Disorders of the schizophrenic syndrome*. New York: Basic Books, 1979.

Suedfeld, P., & Landon, P. B. Approaches to treatment. In R. D. Hare & D. Schalling (Eds.), *Psychopathic behavior: Approaches to research*. New York: Wiley, 1978.

Tan, E., Marks, I. M., & Marset, P. Bimedial leucotomy in obsessive-compulsive neurosis: A controlled serial inquiry. *British Journal of Psychiatry*, 1971, *118*, 155–164.

Templer, D. I. The obsessive-compulsive neurosis: Review of research findings. *Comprehensive Psychiatry*, 1972, *13*, 375–383.

Tennant, C., & Bebbington, P. The social causation of depression: A critique of the work of Brown and his colleagues. *Psychological Medicine*, 1978, *8*, 565–575.

Tollison, D. C., & Adams, H. E. *Sexual disorders*. New York: Gardner Press, 1979.

Tramontana, J., & Stimbert, V. Some techniques of behavior modification with an autistic child. *Psychological Reports*, 1970, *27*, 498.

Treffert, D. A., McAndrew, J. B., & Dreifuerst, P. An inpatient treatment program and outcome for 57 autistic and schizophrenic children. *Journal of Autism and Childhood Schizophrenia*, 1973, *3*, 138–153.

Turner, R. J., & Wagonfeld, M. O. Occupational mobility and schizophrenia: An assessment of the social causation and social selection hypotheses. *American Sociological Review*, 1967, *32*, 104–113.

Valenstein, E. *Brain control*. New York: Wiley, 1973.

Vaughn, C. E., & Leff, J. P. The influence of family and social factors on the course of psychiatric illness: A comparison of schizophrenic and depressed neurotic patients. *British Journal of Psychiatry*, 1976, *129*, 125–137.

Waring, M., & Ricks, D. Family patterns of children who became adult schizophrenics. *Journal of Nervous and Mental Disease*, 1965, *140*, 351–365.

Watson, J. B., & Rayner, R. Conditioned emotional reactions. *Journal of Experimental Psychology*, 1920, *3*, 1–14.

Watt, N. F. Patterns of childhood social development in adult schizophrenics. *Archives of General Psychiatry*, 1978, *35*, 160–170.

Watt, N. F., & Lubensky, A. Childhood roots of schizophrenia. *Journal of Consulting and Clinical Psychology*, 1976, *44*, 363–375.

Weiss, G., Hechtman, L., Perlman, T., Hopkins, J., & Wener, A. Hyperactives as young adults. *Archives of General Psychiatry*, 1979, *36*, 675–681.

Weiss, G., Minde, K., Werry, J. S., Douglas, V., & Nemeth, E. Studies on the hyperactive child. VIII: Five-year follow-up. *Archives of General Psychiatry*, 1971, *24*, 409–414.

Weissman, M. M., Klerman, G. L., Paykel, E. S., Prusoff, A., & Hanson, B. Treatment effects on the social adjustment of depressed patients. *Archives of General Psychiatry*, 1974, *30*, 771–778.

Weissman, M. M., & Paykel, E. S. *The depressed woman: A study of social relationships*. Chicago: University of Chicago Press, 1974.

Welner, A. W., Welner, Z., & Leonard, M. A. Bipolar manic-depressive disorder: A reassessment of course and outcome. *Comprehensive Psychiatry*, 1977, *18*, 327–332.

Werry, J. S., Weiss, G., & Douglas, V. Studies on the hyperactive child. I. Some preliminary findings. *Canadian Psychiatric Association Journal,* 1964, *9*, 120–130.

Wheeler, E. O., White, P. D., Ried, E. W., & Cohen, M. E. Neurocirculatory asthenia (anxiety neurosis, effort syndrome, neuroasthenia). *Journal of the American Medical Association*, 1950, *142*, 878–889.

Wickramsekara, I. The application of learning theory to the treatment of a case of exhibitionism. In J. Fischer & H. Gochros (Eds.), *Handbook of behavior therapy with sexual problems*. New York: Pergamon Press, 1977.

Wilner, G. Varying psychological sequelae of lead ingestion in children. *Public Health Reports*, 1970, *85*, 19–24.

Wilson, G. T., & O'Leary, K. D. *Principles of behavior therapy*. Englewood Cliffs, N. J.: Prentice-Hall, 1980.

Winokur, G., & Clayton, P. Family history studies: I. Two types of affective disorders separated according to genetic and clinical factors. In J. Wortis (Ed.), *Recent advances in biological psychiatry* (Vol. 9). New York: Plenum Press, 1967.

Winokur, G., Clayton, P., & Reich, T. *Manic-depressive illness*. St. Louis: Mosby, 1969.

Witzig, J. S. The group treatment of male exhibitionists. *American Journal of Psychiatry*, 1968, *125*, 75–81.

Woodruff, R., & Pitts, F. M. Monozygotic twins with obsessional illness. *American Journal of Psychiatry*, 1964, *120*, 1075–1080.

World Health Organization. *Schizophrenia: A multinational study*. Geneva: WHO, 1975.

Yalom, I. D., & Lieberman, M. A. A study of encounter group casualties. *Archives of General Psychiatry*, 1971, *25*, 16–30.

Yaryura-Tobias, J., & Neziroglu, F. The action of chlorimipramine in obsessive-compulsive neurosis: A pilot study. *Current Therapeutic Research*, 1975, *17*, 111–116.

Yaryura-Tobias, J., Neziroglu, F., & Bergman, L. Chlorimipramine for obsessive-compulsive neurosis: An organic approach. *Current Therapeutic Research*, 1976, *20*, 541–548.

Zarit, S. H. *Aging and mental disorders: Psychological approaches to assessment and treatment*. New York: The Free Press, 1980.

Zerbin-Rüdin, E. Genetic research and the theory of schizophrenia. *International Journal of Mental Health*, 1972, *1*, 42–62.